PISTIS SOPHIA

The ancient Coptic codex in a new
Translation with a Commentary

Adrian Anderson PhD

Bringing clarity to complex teachings
presented as originating from
the risen Jesus Christ

Distributed by Ebooks Alchemy
Prahran East VIC 3198
Australia

© Copyright 2024 Adrian Anderson
Threshold Publishing
Australia

All rights reserved

ISBN   9780645195439   hardback

Cover image:
"Intimations": courtesy, M. Swann

Contents

Foreword   1
Its origin and value

Introduction: 3
An eclectic mix of texts
Date and history
A Midrashic text ?
What or who is Pistis Sophia ?
An over-view of themes
Rudolf Steiner's comments on the codex
The spiritual context of esoteric Christianity
The structure of the cosmos, from Rudolf Steiner
Diagram One : the 17 Aions
Terminology: the meaning of key terms
Understanding the central spirit beings
Obscure passages
What is personification, spiritually?
The omitted texts: documents 4 and 5

**Pistis Sophia: a new Translation
and Commentary**   41

Appendix 1: The Light of Lights (Christ) and God   420
Appendix 2: Pistis Sophia: humanity's higher soul   421

Glossary   422
Index   423

Diagram 1: the 17 Aions   17
Diagram 2: of the Aions 16 and 17   265

Bibliography
Books by the author
Website

ACKNOWLEDGEMENTS

I would like to express my gratitude to

M. Swann & D. Skewes

for their many helpful comments and support during the demanding process of writing this book.

Foreword

The Askew or Pistis Sophia codex is a unique record of Christian initiatory knowledge from the early years of the new religion. The esoteric teachings in the first three documents of the codex are presented as teachings communicated by the risen Jesus, to his disciples, who would have needed clairvoyance to see and hear the risen Jesus.

These communications are in the form of dialogues, and discuss such themes as the interaction between the risen Saviour and various deities in spirit realms. The communications occurred for a decade after his Resurrection; this would be from approximately CE 33-44. The dialogues discuss profound initiatory truths of a cosmic Christianity.

Rudolf Steiner affirms that this was the process through which these texts came into existence. These teachings are often in response to a question from a disciple, and were no doubt restricted to initiatory Christian circles of the first centuries.

The reader will encounter astonishing revelations of an esoteric wisdom, and also sacred teachings about the actions of the Saviour within spirit realms, on behalf of humanity. So it is a rare and important source, providing evidence of an esoteric movement existing within the early church; a movement of which all traces were soon to be obliterated. This, and the associated *Books of Jeu*, are the only substantial texts to survive from the secret esoteric schooling given by Jesus to his disciples.[1]

In undertaking my work on this book, I endeavoured to make a translation, together with a commentary, that would allow a much clearer understanding of these texts than is currently possible. In my view, what is presented in earlier translations often struggles to present the meaning of the text. In scores of places I have decided upon different translations of Coptic or Greek words. Since the Coptic text is a translation from a Greek version, and Coptic terms for many Greek words did not exist,

---

[1] Additionally, there is also the so-called Gospel of Thomas.

or were unknown to the translator, within every page of the codex there are many Greek words.

My prior work of translating the Gospel of John, revealing its veiled esoteric nature, was of great help in resolving many obscure places in this Coptic codex.

It is my hope that this Foreword, and the Commentary placed throughout the book, help the reader to engage with the contents of this unique codex. The ideas which it presents are at times challenging, but often deeply inspiring.

Dating the original text

There are many questions about this remarkable text, especially in relation to its origin. The parchment codex as we have it today was copied out into Greek, and later translated from Greek into Coptic, some decades later. The crucial question here is, when was the first such text written down, and are the communications contained in it, between Jesus and the disciples, genuine? That is, does the text have its origin in the years from approximately CE 33-44[2] or is it a pious fantasy written up two or even three centuries after the life of Jesus? The majority of scholars are inclined to the latter view, and conclude that the teachings originated quite a considerable time after the first century AD.

I have reached a different conclusion; namely that the communications upon which the text is based, did occur around CE 33-44, and these were written down at that time, to be copied in the following decades and centuries for the use of other groups to whom access was granted. My reasons for this conclusion can only be fully assessed after reading this book, as my work has uncovered many new and significant perspectives on the teachings, which were not perceived by earlier translators.

But in essence, to me, the first three documents contain profound cosmic statements which can have

---

[2] The date of the Crucifixion is still debated; I favour the year CE 33 as do a small number of other scholars; including R. Steiner and C. J. Humphries.

their origin only in one of two sources: the risen Jesus Christ (understood as a person with a divine consciousness) or a 'Gnostic Christian' initiate with an extraordinarily high wisdom.

But this second possibility is unlikely, as such a holy Christian-Gnostic sage would be deceiving his readers, if he sought to make them believe that this wisdom came from their Saviour. Such duplicitous behaviour is encountered often in Christian apocryphal writings, and also in the last two documents of the Pistis Sophia codex. This also occurs in some of the Nag Hammadi texts; but such writings do not reach the sublime heights as those found in this Pistis Sophia codex.

Introduction

In the third or fourth century, an eclectic mix of some five different texts, of very varying quality, were bound together to form one book, of 174 fine parchment pages. Texts 1 to 3 were copied by a scribe from unknown earlier documents of a similar nature; whereas text 4 (of 50 pages), was copied from a document which is inferior to texts 1 to 3, containing an inaccurate, distorted version of those texts.

The last document, text 5, of only twelve pages, likewise gives an inaccurate, distorted presentation of initiatory Christianity. It is possibly much later than the other documents, and derives from a Christian of Greek not Aramaic origin, who somewhat absurdly inserts Greek gods into his narrative. These last two texts contain no insights into esoteric Christianity; instead, they present fantastical theories and some rigid religious viewpoints which are incompatible with deeper Christian teachings. (See below for more about these two texts.)

It was the custom in ancient times to bind together documents of varying quality; for example, the priceless codex Sinaiticus (4th century) contains our current Bible, together with the *Shepherd of Hermas* and the *Letter of Barnabas*. These latter two are of a much lesser quality than those documents which were later accepted into the canon of Biblical documents.

Texts 1 to 3 of the Pistis Sophia codex together form a fairly consistent document; that is, text 2 follows on from text 1 almost seamlessly; text 3 follows text 2 less smoothly, but still presents the same level of lofty esoteric teachings of the same genre. They have their origin in a very early time of 'the Jesus movement'.

However, these first three documents were, of course, copied from much earlier texts. There are some differences in terminology in these documents, so it appears that they were probably compiled not from one older source text, but several source texts.

So the codex is not a single book; it is an eclectic

compendium of esoteric Christian documents. The first of these, (texts 1, 2 & 3) present many deep initiatory truths of an esoteric Christianity nature, and occupy, in translation, about 250 pages.

Consequently, to me this eclectic mix of five radically different documents means that any attempt to assess the religious-esoteric view of the Askew codex as such – as a unity, presenting a unified Gnostic-Christian world-view – is not viable.

The first three sections consist of teachings presented by the risen Jesus, or more accurately, from an exalted divine being, who is merged with Jesus, and who is not named specifically, but who may be identified with what is now called 'the cosmic Christ'.

In the codex this deity is referred to, for example, as 'the Light of Lights', or 'The First Mystery from without'. The word 'Christ' – a later Greek term – is never used, probably because it was not an Aramaic term. Nor is the equivalent Aramaic term used, for this primarily referred to a person, the Messiah; although a person in whom God was present.

This extraordinary codex was purchased in the late 18th century by an English collector, Dr. Anthony Askew, from a London bookstore, and it was subsequently acquired by the British Museum. It was eventually translated into some European languages; those of relevance here are the translations by two German scholars (Schmidt and Till) and two English scholars, Horner and MacDermot, in the 19th – 20th centuries. The learned Theosophist, G.R.S. Mead rendered Schmidt's German translation into English.
There has been little written about it during the past 100 years, apart from an analysis by E. Evans.[3]

What is the reality of the main part of the codex; is it a genuine record of the words of the risen Jesus? I have found the viewpoint of Rudolf Steiner to be

---

[3] Erin Evans, *The Books of Jeu and the Pistis Sophia as Handbooks to Eternity*, Brill, 2005. Evans views this text as a Gnostic work, and regards all five documents as equally valid, but not as reports of authentic, or even sacred, esoteric Christian teachings.

invaluable in many areas of Biblical studies. His view of the codex is that it contains much of what the risen Jesus Christ taught to those disciples whom he initiated, and who were sufficiently clairvoyant to perceive and hear him. Rudolf Steiner regards it as a rare surviving text which has its origin in an esoteric Christian initiatory process. Steiner concluded that this was established by the Saviour before his Resurrection, and then continued on by him after he was resurrected.

But Steiner's words do not imply that the codex contains a verbatim record of conversations between Jesus and his disciples. Rather it contains a sincere and reasonably accurate presentation of these communications, which were later formed into a literary work, which was then copied by various persons. That is, these spiritually received teachings, originating in about CE 33-44, were later cast into a specific literary form; a process in which some scribal errors and editorial alterations are always possible.

Scriptural interpretation: a Midrash method?
Another indicator of the Pistis Sophia codex as originating amongst Jewish disciples of Jesus, and at very early date, is that the dialogues of the disciples have a distinctly Midrashic quality. This unique Jewish questioning and counter-argument method of discussing sacred texts between teachers of Scripture had been in use with the ancient Hebrew people, hundreds of years before the time of Jesus.

It was a characteristic feature of dialogues between Rabbinic sages, and was a key feature of ancient Jewish discussion and contemplation of the Bible. This Midrashic style is not a literary style which an Hellenized 'esoteric' Christian of the third century would use. This textual quality is another pointer to the Jewish first disciples of Jesus as the persons from whom these communications originated.

Readers are free to draw their own conclusions as to the origin of these communications. But from their tone, style and contents, I conclude that they originate from the risen Jesus, in the years following immediately after the Resurrection. This conclusion is also in harmony with the view of Rudolf Steiner, as mentioned above.

Just what other esoteric Christian teachings once existed, is not known, but it is clear that the three texts here are only part of a much larger collection of texts; extending to perhaps some 2,000 pages. For the documents here are not introductory texts; they presuppose some knowledge of specific deities and spirit realms.

This codex has been disappointing to some, often because in many places the text was almost incomprehensible. The difficulty however was caused in part by previous translations not always succeeding to make clear what the Coptic is stating, where a Coptic word has several meanings.

Christians who have encountered the book are therefore repelled by the strangeness of its teachings as compared with most theological views. Other readers are disconcerted by the unfamiliar terms used, such as names of spirits, and names of various spirit realms which are not possible for modern readers to locate in the cosmos.

Readers with an interest in an esoteric Christianity will gain more from this text after reading my translation of the Gospel of John, which includes a detailed Commentary, revealing that there is a 'cosmic' dimension to Christianity. My work was undertaken from an esoteric viewpoint but is accurate to the best Greek manuscripts.[4]

What or who is Pistis Sophia?

The Pistis Sophia codex presents not only a profound cosmic being speaking through the person of Jesus, but also a presentation of the 'Sophia' theme which is quite different to that found in Gnostic writings. The Sophia entity which is discussed in such Gnostic texts, is a primal deity associated with powerful spirits who were involved in creating the world.

---

[4] I have argued for the inherent superiority in many places, of codex Bezae over Sinaiticus, Alexandrinos and Vaticanus.

However, I present here a significant discovery about the entity called Pistis Sophia. The term 'pistis' is an adjective, and this does not always mean 'loyal' or 'faithful' (wisdom). It can mean *spiritually discerning* wisdom or *intuitive cognizing* wisdom, as I have demonstrated in my *The Gospel of John*.

In the work of Rudolf Steiner one learns that 'Sophia' has two meanings. One is a cosmic deity, which is to some extent a personification of the cosmos as a living reality, spiritually permeated by many deities. But the other meaning concerns the spiritually developed person (on an initiatory path); someone who has developed their 'Spiritual-self'; their faculty of spiritual perceiving.

The character called Pistis Sophia is a personification of the counterpart – in spiritual realms – of this high capacity of human consciousness, namely to be spiritually cognizing. So in this codex, 'Sophia' does not refer to a deity; instead, it is a spirit who is in need of the Christ-Light, to be saved from malignant spirits.

It is her circumstances, as perceived by Jesus, which occupies many pages in the text. The experiences of Pistis Sophia are actually the dynamics occurring in the very real soul (or 'astral') counterpart of our own potential for higher consciousness.

So a major theme in this Coptic codex is a presentation of how the loss of a spiritual sense, or an intuitive-psychic awareness, by humanity is perceived in spiritual realms by the Saviour, and how he assists in the defence and eventual restoration of this higher state of the human soul.

This theme is specifically presented, in a dramatization, including many quotes from the Psalms, or from the remarkable, initiatory Odes of Solomon. The purpose of this is to teach students to see another side to the 'salvation' work of Christ, in regard to humanity's struggle to gain a spiritual awareness.

We could also say, it is how to help humanity, from an activity occurring within spirit realms, to re-gain a spiritual awareness down here on Earth. For this awareness, which was once widespread, had begun to die out in the Hellenistic world, with the rise of a rational, logic-based way of thinking. This is the reason that Jesus begins the story of Pistis Sophia with her no longer existing in a divine realm (the 13th Aeon), but having been lured into the lower Soul-world, called The Chaos.

So, 'Pistis Sophia' means the capacity for higher spiritual awareness in the human soul; and hence one suggested translation, 'Faithful Wisdom', is not conveying the meaning of the Greek term.

I conclude that 'Pistis Sophia' means "**intuitively perceptive wisdom**", as a potential faculty of every human soul. This is discussed further when Pistis Sophia is mentioned in the text. I have concluded that the circumstances of the astral counterpart to a Sophia state of mind are presented in this codex.

But if this higher, more spiritual Sophia state in human souls wanes, then an observer in the Soul-world would see malignant entities gaining influence over the counterpart to our potential higher consciousness.

Supportive of my conclusions here are assertive statements in the text where the redeeming of Pistis Sophia is declared to be a victory **for all of humanity, and derives from something occurring in human souls**. These statements are discussed in the relevant chapters. Consequently, the story of Pistis Sophia in this codex has been misunderstood.

An over-view of the themes
The descent of the divine cosmic light (or 'Christ') upon Jesus, in the form of two radiant 'garments' (i.e., radiant auras).

Preparations undertaken by the Saviour regarding the conception of Jesus, John the Baptist and the disciples: imbuing their embryos with especial spiritual energies.

The imbuing of Jesus with a third 'garment', this appears to be an even higher aspect of the 'cosmic

Christ': it has within it the essence of the entire cosmos.

The ascent of the Saviour through spirit realms: the dismay of malignant deities and the wonder of divine deities.

The disempowering by the Saviour of malignant deities.

The disempowering by the Saviour of malignant occultists.

That malignant deities create pseudo-humans (i.e., without any connection to divine realms).

In 120 pages, the theme is the efforts by the Saviour to restore Pistis Sophia – the spirit counterpart of the faculty of intuitive-spiritual awareness of human beings – to its previously empowered condition. But this restored state will then be superior to the earlier one, and such a deed shall greatly benefit humanity.

That the various higher spirit realms have an ever greater radiance within them.

What the future will be for redeemed souls in regard to various ranks of deities, and such higher realms.
(a somewhat obscure section)

The nature of the cosmos and of God ('the First Mystery') and the advantage bestowed on redeemed souls as they enter the cosmos.
(a somewhat obscure section)

The advantages in the after-life for redeemed souls, and for their next incarnation.

The forgiveness of sin, and a deeper cancelling of sinfulness (the lower qualities); and the cancelling of the impact of sin upon the cosmos.

The Pistis Sophia codex is set within a context of various spirit realms (called Aions) and also many holy deities and many malignant spirits. I have found the teachings of Rudolf Steiner on these topics – the structure and dynamics of the spiritual cosmos – provide the most helpful guide to sorting out the location and rank of the realms and beings that form such a large part of this codex.

Brief comments by Steiner give a vital key to understanding some core terms in this text, as well as clarifying the general context of the Gnostic-Christian view of the world.

Rudolf Steiner's comments

From Book 95 in the Complete Works:
"This book is written in the Coptic language and contains much of the words of Christ spoken at the initiating of his disciples, and explanations of many of the Parables.

The most significant chapter is chapter 13. The 'Heimarmene' (ἁιμαρμένη) is (part of) Devachan. The over-all spiritual world is divided up into 12 Aions. These Aions are (composed of) the seven levels of the astral plane and the five lower levels of Devachan.

From out of Devachan, spirits who have fallen into error, can be cleansed. The light-purifier before Christ was Melchizedek. It is he whom is meant when there is mention of the Receiver (παραλήμτης).[5] When Archons are mentioned, one is to understand that evil spirits are meant."

From book no. 93:
(*The notes of this lecture (10/June/1904) are incomplete, totalling nine pages, instead of the usual 20 plus pages.*)
"You know that for ten years Jesus Christ remained near to the Earth. The Pistis Sophia contains the deepest theosophical teachings; it is much deeper than Sinnett's *Esoteric Buddhism*."
That Steiner says, "you know..." to his theosophical

---

[5] The German Steiner text has an error here; it mentions the Grk. term 'episkopos' (ἐπισκοπος) which means Overseer, but this Greek term refers to a deity called Jeu.

audience, points to the fact that Theosophists, who were a prominent group of people involved with alternative spirituality in his lifetime, had a strong interest in the Pistis Sophia code, because G.R.S. Mead, author of an English edition from the German translation, was himself a Theosophist, and his version was published in small sections in various issues of Theosophical journal.

The spiritual context of these teachings: Esoteric Christianity, Jesus and 'the cosmic Christ'
The transcendent nature of this codex is very striking; as noted above, to see and hear the risen Saviour, the disciples would have needed some clairvoyance.
It is a central feature of esoteric Christianity that the word 'Jesus' refers to a human being, and the word 'Christ' refers to a deity, a divine being. The Christ being came down upon, or 'enveloped' Jesus, uniting with him; permeating his body, his life-forces and his soul and his spirit.

The codex specifically refers to these two entities: Jesus the man and Christ the deity – except that the word 'Christ' is not used, as this is a later Greek term. Instead this cosmic or divine aspect to Jesus is called 'the Light of Lights' or 'the First Mystery who gazes outwards'. This is stated for example in Chapter 63,

"And you came down, enveloped by[6] the garment of light, which you did receive directly from the Divine (the 'Barbelo'). You who are (*now*) Jesus our Saviour; in that you (*Christ*) came down upon him (*Jesus*), in the likeness of a dove."

The origin or location of the Christ is not stated in the codex, but it is understood in esoteric Christian thought that this sublime deity came from the sphere of the Sun, and is therefore, in the system of the nine ranks of divine beings in early Christian esoteric thought, of the rank of a Power or Exousiai.

---

[6] "enveloped by": the text literally has the phrase, "upon the garment of light".

In essence, the conversations presented in the codex record details of further redemptive actions of Jesus, carried out after the Resurrection. They also discuss the effects of seeking to be initiated, referred to as 'receiving a Mystery'. But the actual nature of such an initiation experience is never disclosed. To esoterically oriented Christians, the redemptive work of Jesus Christ was that which occurred, or commenced, during the period between the Crucifixion and the Resurrection.

A part of this work became known as the Harrowing of Hades, wherein disempowered human souls were helped to find their way to the Light; and demonic powers of Hell, inside the depths of the Earth, were weakened by the descent to their regions of Jesus, imbued with the Christ. But this ancient codex teaches that further salvation tasks occurred, after the Resurrection:

A: disempowering of malignant spirits who were being used for evil purposes by some people.

B: assisting the potential for humanity to have an intuitively discerning consciousness, which is here personified as 'Sophia', by defending it from the attacks already made by malignant spirits.

C: taking over the task from a mysterious being called Melchizedek of purifying the spiritual light surrounding the Earth.

D: the associated task of hindering the attempts of malignant spirits to prevent human souls from casting off their own unethical qualities.

The Structure of the Cosmos, from Rudolf Steiner
The cosmos consists of the physical-mineral world, then the 'etheric realm' which consists of four ethereal energies which animate physical substances, bringing them into a state of being 'alive'. These energies are also referred to as 'life-forces'.

Then there is the Soul-world or 'astral realm' which itself has seven distinct levels or qualities. These seven realms are identified in extra-Biblical texts, and identified as places where the souls of the Dead are located.

Above this is 'Devachan' or Heaven, or the true Spirit-realm, which also consists of seven levels. But Devachan has a 'lower' part, consisting of the first four levels; and a 'higher' part consisting of the remaining three levels.

The 12 Aions
Without knowledge of what these realms actually refer to, most of the Pistis Sophia has remained basically incomprehensible. Rudolf Steiner has concluded that the seven levels of the astral realm, together with the first five levels of Devachan are the "12 Aions"; see the next section, "**Clearer Terminology**..." and Diagram One. These 12 Aions are shown to be the key to understanding the otherwise incomprehensible core term, 'Heimarmene and the Sphere'.

Then, even more 'cosmic', more remote, from earthly consciousness than higher Devachan, is the 'Buddhi realm'; a term used in theosophical literature and by Rudolf Steiner. Aions 15 to 17 are part of this exalted realm. A very significant point to note here is, that to people in antiquity who were esoterically instructed or initiated, the soul journeyed after death into spirit realms, and were much later reincarnated.

However it was precisely this journey towards a new incarnation that the Gnostic in ancient times wished to avoid. He or she wanted to achieve such a high initiatory consciousness as to gain admittance to realms beyond the 'Heimarmene'. This is a core perspective in Gnostic texts, including the Pistis Sophia codex.

The Aions of the Cosmos
Aions 1 to 7 : the Soul-world

Aions 8-12 : the first 5 levels of Devachan or Heaven

Aions 13-14 : the two highest levels of Devachan
   (13 = home of Pistis Sophia)
   (14 = The Midst)

Aions 15 - 17: in the 'Buddhi' realm

(Aion 15 = The Right)
(Aion 16 = The Treasury of Light)
(Aion 17 = The Inheritance of Light)

Diagram One: the Structure of the Cosmos
Starting from the physical, and going upwards:
The physical-material world
The ethers with 'elemental spirits'
The astral realms or the Soul-world: (the lowest part of these are: 'the Chaos'.)

The Soul-world coincides with the solar system, from the Moon to Saturn. These are the planetary spheres as understood in the Ptolemaic view.
Lower Devachan: levels 1 to 4. Rudolf Steiner taught that these are where the archetypal 'thought-forms' from the Gods behind physical Creation, exist.

Upper Devachan: levels 5 to 7. Advanced souls who reach this level no longer incarnate; as noted earlier, levels 6 and 7 are no longer part of 'Heimarmene' (also called 'Fate'); so they are not part of the realms that underlie Fate/Karma/Destiny.
The 7 astral realms and the first 5 levels of Devachan together form the "12 Aions".
The crucial 13th Aion: this is where Pistis Sophia had her (or 'its') natural location before she fell; this is level Six of Devachan. Rudolf Steiner refers to this sublime realm as being located 'on the other side of the stars'.

As noted above, beyond Devachan is a realm called "the Buddhi plane". Rudolf Steiner taught that this very lofty realm is where those high initiates are located, the Bodhisattvas, who shall later reach the level of Buddha-hood. It is also, Steiner taught, where Jesus Christ is located, and it is also the realm from which the human 'monad' or eternal Self derives.[7]

In accordance with this scheme, the Aion called *The Right* is the first level of this Buddhi realm. *The*

---

[7] Technical anthroposophical note: The monad is viewed in Steiner's work as a combination of Buddhi and Atma.

Treasury of Light is the second level of this Buddhi realm; and *The Inheritance of Light* is the third Buddhi level.

See Diagram One where the sequence of these various realms are presented.

Terminology: the meaning of key terms
The 12 Aions: as indicated above, these are the seven levels of the astral realm or the Soul-world, plus the first five levels of Devachan where deities are given the task of working with the karma of human souls, preparing them for their next incarnation.

The debased 12 Aions and the divine Aions: their Rulers or Archons
We note that there are Rulers (in Greek 'Archons') in these realms. But, without the text making this clear, one learns that there are malignant Aions with their Rulers – whom I refer to as 'debased' or fallen deities – and there are holy Aions with divine deities as their Rulers. (See below for 'Ahriman' and 'Lucifer'.) So the reader has to be aware that there are the holy Aions and also counterparts to these; the malignant Aions. Most of these Aions are the 'planetary spheres', in the sense of the Ptolemaic solar system (see below).

Sphere or Spheres: the over-arching cosmos as far as the 12th Aeon (= 5th realm of Devachan). These spheres are created by the orbits of the planets, as they make their circuit around the Earth. These spheres coincide with the planetary spheres, as envisaged in the Ptolemaic system, except for the higher spheres or realms. But this coinciding is on a spiritual level, not on a physical level.

Diagram 1: The 17 Aions (7 Astral & 7 Devachanic & 3 of Buddhi)

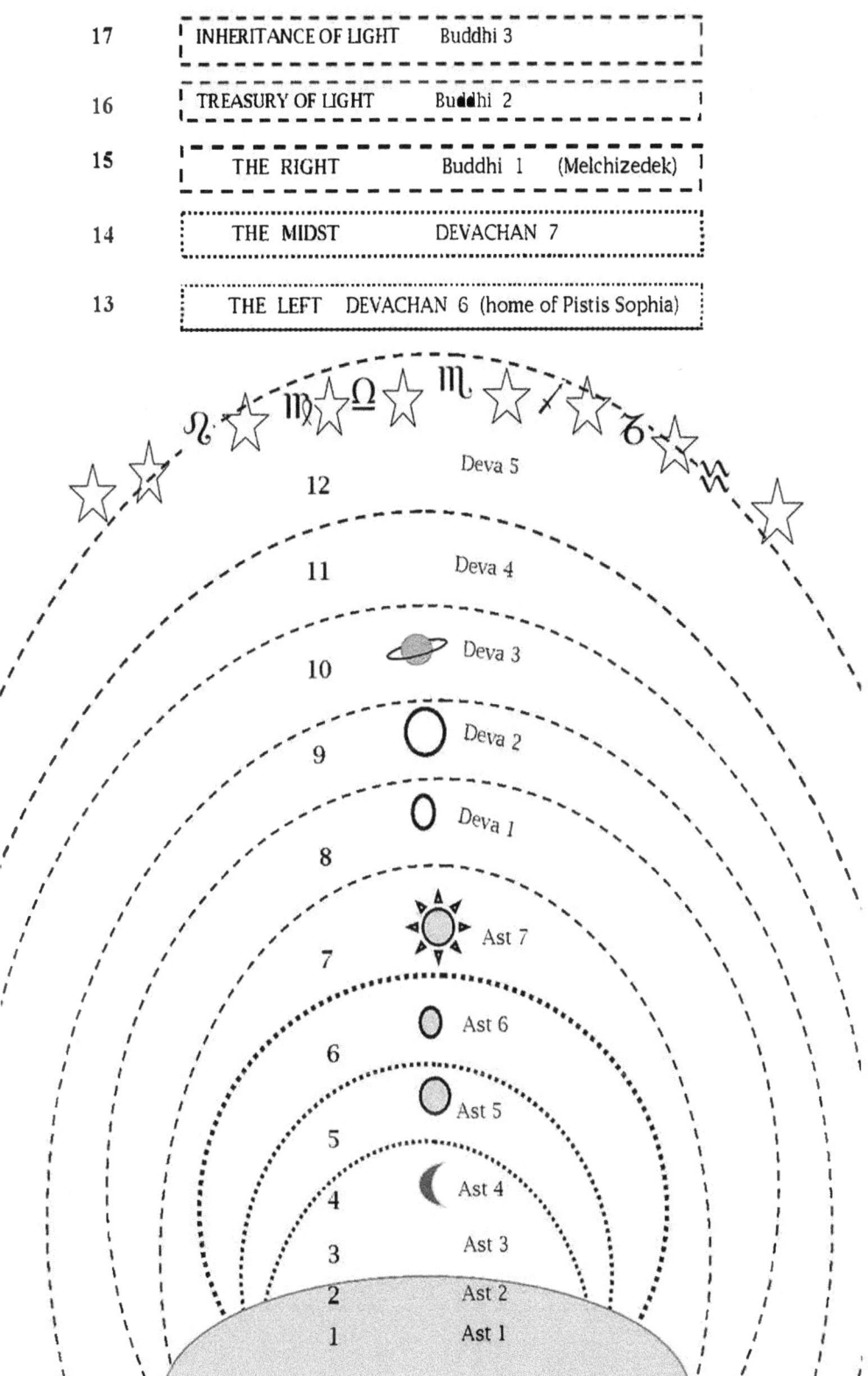

The Fate and the Sphere (Heimarmene)
With the above understanding, an especially important improvement offered in this book concerns the oft-repeated phrase: "the Fate and the Sphere". This has been removed from my translation. As noted above, these words refer to the realms wherein the soul is metamorphosed after death in accordance with its karma; and then prepared for re-birth.

The 'Sphere' refers to the astral realms associated with the journey of the soul after death, as its next life is being gradually prepared.

So the phrase, "the Fate and the Sphere" represents the understanding of esoterically aware Christians, and non-Christian Gnostics, in the Hellenistic Age, of the journey undertaken by the soul in the Soul-realm and into (lower) Devachan, before having to reincarnate.

I translate this obscure phrase by the cumbersome, but more understandable, "the karma-determining cosmic influences and their associated spiritual realms". The reader will be reminded of the original wording occasionally, when this phrase is encountered.

The Heimarmene:
It is intriguing that this word is omitted in authoritative ancient Greek dictionaries, yet it is a key term in Hellenistic esoteric-initiatory writings. Rudolf Steiner explains that it refers to a lower part of Devachan, from level 1 to level 5. He taught that it is here that the karma (or destiny) of the soul after death is determined, preparing for its re-birth.

This process occurs through the actions of various deities there, and is the result of the deeds and primary dynamics of the soul that prevailed in its previous incarnation. This throws light on the perspective presented in the Pistis Sophia codex and in *The Hermetica*: that in Heimarmene the soul is prepared for its next life. In both of these esoteric texts, these realms are the primary factor behind one's fate or destiny. But it is also the case, as noted earlier, that for the Hellenistic initiate such a re-birth is precisely what she or he wished to avoid.

AIONS and 'an aeon'
Sometimes reputable and learned dictionaries or lexicons are incomplete, despite the care that scholars take when compiling them. This is the case with word 'aeon', in Greek 'aioen' (άιών). This word is listed in lexicons are meaning 'eternity' or 'a long duration of time'. But this word also means a 'spirit realm', although lexicons often omit to mention this second meaning.

To avoid confusion, I am using 'aeon' for eternity, but 'Aion' for the spirit realms. References to spirit realms occur very frequently in the Pistis Sophia codex; and the Greek word aioen (άιών) is used for this.

Examples of 'Aion' (άιών) as meaning spirit realms
This Greek word is used in this way for example, in the Hermetica (*Libellus XI*); there it means spiritual realm in such sentences as these:
The origin of all things is God
the origin of being-ness is the Aion
the origin of substance is the cosmos (Creation)

The might of God is (in) the Aion
the deed of the Aion is (manifested in) the cosmos
God makes the Aion
the Aion makes the cosmos
the cosmos makes Time.

Also, the Essenes as an initiatory group, used this word to mean a spiritual realm. For example, in the *Book of Enoch*, which I regard as originating, for the most part, with the Essenes. In a section (12:4), where the fallen Angels are discussed, this occurs;
"The Angels have left *the holiness of the continuous-existence of the Aion.*"[8]
Another example is *in The Apocalypse of Adam*, a late first century or early second century CE text, found at

---

[8] Grk. text in: *Apocalypsis Henochi Graece*, ed. R.H. Charles, Leiden: Brill, 1970 p.27.

Nag Hammadi. In connection with spiritual realms and beings, such phrases occur as, "God, ruler of the Aions"...or, "they have been received into another Aion..."

In the New Testament there are a few usages of 'Aion' in this sense. In the *Epistle to the Hebrews* 1:2, there is use of this word to mean spirit realms, (or a multi-level, physical-spiritual universe): "But in these last days God has spoken to us by his Son, whom he appointed heir of all things, and for the sake of whom he made the Aions."[9]

But most translations avoid this and render it as referring only to the physical universe. Scholars interpret this expression as not referring to spiritual realms, but this contradicts what is meant.[10] Those who seek to disclaim this, wish to avoid the association of a New Testament text with an apparent 'Gnostic' concept.[11]

Summary:
So 'the Aions' are spirit realms or regions known as 'planes' in theosophical literature; each of which has a governing deity.[12] So 'the Sphere' consists of Aions: e.g., Chapter 7: "I found Elijah in the Aions of the Sphere".

OTHER KEY TERMS
Archons or Rulers
Spirits called Rulers ('Archons' in Greek) are to be

---

[9] The Grk. is : δι' οὐ καὶ ἐποίησεν τοὺς αἰῶνας.

[10] The main conclusion, avoiding the esoteric meaning here, is that the term is indeed 'inclusive', but not beyond space and time. For example, F.F. Bruce, *The Epistle to the Hebrews The new Internat. Commentary* (Grand Rapids: Eerdmans, 1990) 47; and F.W. Farrar, *The Epistle of Paul the Apostle to the Hebrews* (Cambridge: Cambridge UP, 1894) 29: and Moffat, J. *The Epistle to the Hebrews, The Internat. Critical Commentary*, (Edinburgh: Clark, 1968) 7.

[11] For example, Lünemann, Gottlieb. *Handbook to the Epistle to the Hebrews* (Edinburgh: Clark, 1882), 77.

[12] In other Gnostic texts, an Aion is treated as being the manifestation of one high deity.

encountered in the Aions or Sphere, or the Heights.
So 'the Archons of the Sphere' = Archons of the Aions, or of the Heights.
Note that malignant spirits are to be experienced in the debased, evil Aions or Spheres or Heights. So there are holy Archons and malignant Archons.

Lucifer and Ahriman
In the terminology of Rudolf Steiner, 'ahrimanic' spirits are a class of fallen spirits who bring about a cold, calculated intellectuality and crimes of hate; their leader is Ahriman (using a term from the Persian scriptures, the Zend-Avesta).

Whereas 'luciferic' spirits are a class of fallen spirits who inspire naïve, often intensely self-centred, desires and attitudes. Their leader is Lucifer, who can be equated with the 'old serpent' who tempted Adam and Eve in Paradise.

So there are both divine and malignant spirit realms, whether astral or devachanic realms. But of the two kinds of malignant spiritual influences, the ahrimanic ones are specifically evil. The luciferic ones are not directly evil, but their influence often results in unethical behaviour. These various groups of spirits are located in the relevant planetary sphere, but because each of these three groups have very different natures and dynamics, they are completely separated from each other. Distance or proximity in spirit realms is determined by inner similarities or dissimilarities; this creates the parallel to what we know in the physical world, as a spatial factor.

Barbelo: This very high, holy entity is referred to only briefly in various Gnostic writings, as if she were well-known to the intended readers. Although Barbelo is discussed at length in the treatise "Trimorphic Protennoia" (ca. 200AD), it is in terms that don't relate to her role in the Pistis Sophia, and which do not define her status and location in terms of the cosmos as presented in this codex, nor in the work of the modern seer Rudolf Steiner.

The Heights: same as the Sphere, and thus can be the same as the Aions. Actually a singular word in Coptic, but it is better rendered in the plural, using this well-known English expression.

Etheric and astral and devachanic
The term 'etheric' is used to refer to the level of the cosmos which is composed of life-forces, or ethereal energies (similar to Ch'i and prana).

The term 'astral' is used to refer to the level of the cosmos wherein consciousness or 'soul' exists, but it does not include actual transcendent 'spirit' nature.

The term 'devachanic' is used for the cosmic level above 'soul' or 'astral'; it is where eternal spirit 'substance' or state of being exists. This is the level of consciousness of which deities or gods consist.

Hyle as soul 'substance': correcting the view that Pistis Sophia and the Rulers all exist 'in matter'.
I have come to differing conclusions about several themes in this codex, to some commentators. One such conclusion which differs from my view, is that Pistis Sophia and the Rulers exist in 'matter'. But the codex is not saying this, even though these entities are said to be in 'hyle' (ὕλη) and normally 'hyle' is understood in Gnostic texts to mean 'matter', i.e., material or molecular substances. But spirit entities can exist in *denser* spirit 'substance', and this is also called hyle.
The earlier translators seem to have misunderstood the context here; they were not considering that 'hyle' was also used to mean 'soul substance' (or astral 'substance') of a coarser or denser kind. This is illustrated in the wonderful Hermetica writings, (in *Stobaei Hermetica*, Exc. 23).

Here the goddess Isis is explaining to the acolyte, Hermes, how God (theos - θεός) brought about the creation of animals and humans, (in the lower part of the cosmos; below the radiant Aions).

Isis teaches that God made a special mixture of various soul energies and powers; then, the resulting non-material 'substance' is described as 'hyle' (ὕλη).

(We note that the word 'substance' here is completely out of place, in realms above matter or molecules. But there is no other word we can use, other than perhaps 'astral-energy'.)

Isis continues, explaining that from the finer 'skin' or upper layer which formed over the top of the mixture of soul substances or 'hyle', God created myriads of souls. The acolyte is then told that "this topmost, finer layer of hyle is invisible, except to God...and then God called this upper, finer layer, 'soul-being-ness' (or 'soul-substance' or 'soul-essence')[13], because it would then become the matrix from which the souls (or soul-bodies or astral bodies) would arise – which he was then to create.

So here 'hyle' refers to 'soul-essence' or 'soul-substance' but of a somewhat denser or inherently coarser kind; it does not refer to molecular, material 'substance'.

'Hyle' and 'denser' soul-bodies

So, wherever the codex refers to Pistis Sophia, or to spirits, existing in lower, darker realms, as having a 'hyle' soul-body, this means a less spiritual, more coarse soul-body, not a material body. This implies that there are finer, more splendid, more spiritually refined souls or soul-bodies (or soul-substance) and also less noble, less fine soul-bodies. So the term 'dense' or denser' soul-body is the correct translation, not a 'material' body.

Elemental spirits and 'hyle' or matter.

In chapter 32 we are told that Pistis Sophia has a multitude of minor spirits (or sprites) within her. But the earlier translations refer to her having many 'matters' as part of her being; that is, many bits of material substances. This view is the same error as discussed above; the narrative is set in non-material realms; so 'matter' or matters' cannot be involved. These 'matters' are really minor influences endowed with a dim consciousness: e.g.,

(Pistis Sophia speaks)

---

[13] In the Grk. ψύχωσιν.

32: Now therefore, let all entities rejoice who are in the dense (astral) substances. All of you: seek the Light, so that the spiritual might of your souls – a capacity which is (indeed) within you – may live on (*in higher realms*).
33: For the Light has heard all the minor (*elemental*) entities in the dense (astral) substances, and will not leave any of these, without firstly purifying them.
34: Let all souls, and all the dense (astral) beings praise the Lord of all the Aions: the dense (astral) beings and everything within this (*i.e., the many minor or 'elemental' spirits*).

These elemental influences exist in the matrix of the human soul. They also bestow sentiency or a conscious component on the four life-forces in creation and in the human being. But when such higher spirits arise up, leaving only these sprites below, then what is left becomes coarser, denser, and less sentient. The human beings are then "devoid of reason" and what is left is referred to as 'hyle', meaning denser, coarser entities[14] composed of both life-forces (etheric energy) and basic instinctive soul qualities.

Pistis Sophia's nature and origin
She is not formed of matter (hyle), nor derived from a material ('hylic') Aion. Pistis Sophia is a spiritual entity, the counterpart to human intuitive-perceptive cognizing, and derives from a high spiritual realm (the 13th Aion). Although she does not derive from matter, in her fallen state she is 'hyle-like' that is, her soul nature has become denser, less fine; just as mineral substances are denser than etheric or soul 'substances'. Nor is the 13th Aion made of 'matter'; but there are debased versions of each of the Aions; the debased realms are also 'hyle-like'; i.e., denser, darker, coarser.

---

[14] *Hermetica*, Libellus 1.

Understanding the central Spirit Beings:
Melchizedek

Who is Melchizedek: and what is his role here? The most comprehensive source of knowledge of Melchizedek, to my knowledge, is Rudolf Steiner. In the book of Genesis, chapter 14, the mysterious being Melchizedek is mentioned, and in a very significant connection. He is presented as that entity who inaugurates the mission of Abraham, which was to establish the twelve tribes of Israel.

That is, to begin the lineage of the twelve Hebrew tribes who were destined to be the ancestors of Jesus, the man who would be the vessel of the descending Sun God. This encounter has triggered off enormous interest in Bible students, since many people conclude that Melchizedek is a higher person (or being) than Abraham. Theologians query the account of this event, because it is so striking; some have concluded that it is a later insertion into the story of Abraham, and doesn't have any validity.

This is because there is firstly, the confronting idea that the mission of the great Patriarch Abraham is given to him by a mysterious person/entity who has no supporting context. Rudolf Steiner describes the significance of the meeting of Abraham and Melchizedek in these words, "This meeting of Abraham with Melchizedek is a meeting of the greatest, most universal significance...for he communicated to Abraham the secret of the Sun sphere..."[15]

This indicates that the references to Melchizedek in the Bible are a rare instance of a great leader of initiates having a role in the destiny of Israel. In fact that Melchizedek is spiritually higher than Abraham is demonstrated by the report in Genesis that Abraham was required to make tithes to Melchizedek.

But in addition, there are several astonishing elements to the nature of Melchizedek, mentioned elsewhere in the Bible, which add to his mystique. In Psalm 110, an important and complex reference is

---

[15] GA 123, p.78.

made to Melchizedek, when the nature of the coming Messiah is alluded to, if esoterically understood.

It appears to be referring to the future Day of Pentecost, when the first disciples receive from Christ, the Holy Spirit (and thus also to some extent, a future time when the redeemed humanity unites with Christ). Psalm 110 contains a deeply esoteric message which reflects initiatory wisdom, but is written in ambiguous Hebrew. A section of Psalm 110 can be translated as follows:

> Thy people shall offer themselves freely,
> beautiful in raiments of holiness,
> on the Day of thy Empowerment.
> Thou shalt receive thy disciples like dew,
> from the womb of the morning.
> For the Lord has sworn,
> and will not waver,
> Thou art a priest in the
> Order of Melchizedek forever.
>
> (trans. the author)

So in the Pistis Sophia codex, the future Messiah is described as having a role in the cosmos similar to that of Melchizedek. The other intriguing reference is from the New Testament, the *Epistle of the Hebrews* (7:3),

> ....Without father or mother, without genealogy,
> without beginning of days or end of life, like the
> Son of God he remains a priest forever.

Here is an unusual description of Melchizedek - that is, especially if one assumes that he is a human being. In theological circles, to resolve this mystery, two different views formed. One view is that it is simply the case that the parents of this human being were not listed in any ancestral list. This view has been actually embedded in the Peshitta Bible (the old Aramaic version of the New Testament), by changing the correct Greek text (in Hebrews 7:3) to erroneously read, "whose mother and father are not listed in any genealogies".

The other view, held by the great Alexandrian church father, Origenes, (and a variety of Gnostics) is the more accurate one. Namely, that these words about him having no human lineage, are meant to indicate that Melchizedek is not a human being, but a spiritual being.

Rudolf Steiner's work affirms this; Melchizedek was a spiritual being, clairvoyantly encountered by Abraham. Steiner (partially) explains his nature by revealing that the reference to Melchizedek in Pistis Sophia is quite correct when it records in a deeply esoteric and strangely evocative statement, that "Melchizedek is the Light-purifier".

That is, he is that spirit whose task it was to ensure that the etheric and astral radiance originally from the Sun-sphere, and now permeating the Earth's aura, would be purified and redeemed, not left tainted by malignant influences.[16]

Hence there is real initiation wisdom in the Psalmist's words when he says ".... the LORD {JHVH} has sworn and will not change his mind: "You are a priest forever, in the Order of Melchizedek". This is indicating that Jesus Christ is "in the Order of Melchizedek", meaning he belongs to that similar rank of being, in general terms. And from this we see that Christ Jesus does take over what Melchizedek was doing. It also becomes clear that Melchizedek is therefore a being closely associated with the cosmic Christ.

Rudolf Steiner describes Melchizedek as an Angelic being, and not a human being. In his comments on the Pistis Sophia codex, Steiner describes him as being the "Light-purifier (for the earthly world) prior to the Christ taking on this task (after the events of Golgotha)".[17] So Christ Jesus has taken over the task that the highly evolved Angel, Melchizedek was performing.

But since Melchizedek has a very high role in the Pistis Sophia, wherein he has power over spirits who

---

[16] GA 95 p. 156.

[17] In GA 89, p. 241 (German edition), lecture of 2nd July 1904, and in GA 95, p. 157, Question & Answer session.

are of higher rank than Angels, this implies that there is another Melchizedek entity; but a spirit of unknown rank. With such an enigmatic context, it is not surprising that Melchizedek became a topic of esoteric Jewish and Gnostic esoteric circles. But their texts offer little of value as to how Melchizedek is presented the Pistis Sophia.

Sabaoth the Good: the word 'Sabaoth' is Hebrew and means 'Hosts'. It is used over 250 times in the Old Testament as an adjective for Jahve (Jehovah), "Lord of Hosts". This means that God (i.e., Jahve) has a large number of helping spirits around him. It is to be regretted that some versions of the Bible have changed all of these references to, 'God Almighty'; which is incorrect to the Hebrew word used there, 'Sabaoth'.

It is unusual that in the Pistis Sophia codex and in several of the Nag Hammadi texts, a deity is called 'Sabaoth', since the word really means a multitude of high spirits who are subservient to a yet higher deity. But it may be simply a shorter way of saying, 'Lord of the Hosts', meaning 'He, of the Hosts', by leaving out 'Lord'; this kind of abbreviation is quite common.

Books of Jeu or the Bruce Codex
In chapter 99, the Saviour recommends the '*Books of Jeu*' as containing many initiatory teachings. He describes them in a very striking way: that these texts were spoken by him in a dialogue with the mysterious ancient sage, Enoch, a pre-Flood figure;
"The Books of Jeu which Enoch wrote, as I spoke with him from out of the Tree of Knowledge and from out of the Tree of Life, in the Paradise of Adam."
 We have already noted that a deeply esoteric text, from about 200-100 BCE which contains various initiatory secrets of mystical Judaism – and this had its pinnacle with the Essenes – is called The Book of Enoch. This book is referred to indirectly, in many places in the New Testament.[18]

---

[18] The Epistle of Jude is clearly referencing it, and many

So it was regarded as authentic, or the equivalent of what was later defined as 'canonical', that is, divinely inspired Scripture. Since many early Christians were close to the Essenes, this attitude is not surprising.

The choice of Enoch may be due to the fact that he is presented in the Bible as a high initiate; as a person who did not die, but was transferred directly up to Heaven (Gen. 5:24).

Or it may be due to the Essene seers concluding that the source of their esoteric wisdom in fact came from Enoch. The same attitude then continued to be held by the early Christians, many of whom one can conclude, had Essene roots.

That the locality of the dialogue between Christ and Enoch is described as "the Paradise of Adam", indicates that this dialogue occurred in the heavenly realms, where earlier, Adam had lived. The spiritual realms continue on, as untainted places, even though Adam had fallen. So Enoch as a high initiate is located in these higher realms.

Obscure passages

Translations of this book have suffered from obscure sections which make it almost meaningless in many places. This has hindered appreciation and understanding of this remarkable text. Apart from the ambiguity of the Coptic in many places, the obscurity that has enveloped this text comes from two other factors. Firstly, from scholars not knowing the structure of the cosmos upon which the text is based. This means that many terms remained a riddle.

Secondly, the obscurity derives from the uncertainty of the translators about the intended meaning of many passages. This in turn is caused by the somewhat limited capacity of Coptic to be a vessel for complex literary expressions. There are also a large number of grammatical or spelling errors in the Coptic itself. This has resulted in confusing choices being made by translators when deciding which

---

scholars see several dozen other NT passages doing this.

nuance of a Coptic word to select. Significant examples of this include:

The word 'power':
This phrase 'my power' occurs in earlier translations, where the term 'my being' is actually meant. There are many places where 'power' makes the sentence meaningless or nearly so. The Coptic word here (ϬOM) does mean 'power', or 'strength', and not 'being', this word is ϬIN. But ϬIN ('being') can also be spelt ϬIM; and ϬOM ('power') can also be spelt ϬEM.[19]

This fluid situation would have confused the scribe, who apparently identified ϬIM ('being') with ϬEM (power). The scribe who wrote this codex was not a Copt, as his many errors in the Coptic text show; approximately 150 pages of this codex have one or several spelling errors or grammatical mistakes.[20]

I conclude that these two similar words were merged in his mind, and he used ϬOM to mean either 'power' as well as 'being' (a mistake reinforced, not only by the alternative spelling of ϬOM as ϬEM[21], but also the by tendency for 'o' to be replaced by 'i' in various Coptic words). So many of the passages which have been translated as 'power' actually refer to an entity, a being; this is indirectly seen by one commentator.[22]

So, for example, in Chapter 39, a passage reads like this usually: Pistis Sophia laments, "I have come down like a power of the Chaos; and my power is benumbed in me."

In my version:
"I have been brought low, becoming like an *entity* of

---

[19] It is spelt ϬIM in the 'subachmimic' dialect.

[20] These are noted by all the translators, especially in the painstaking work of MacDermot.

[21] These differences are called 'variant readings'.

[22] Erin Evans, *The Books of Jeu and the Pistis Sophia* ..." p.228, "Jesus' soul (or 'power')"; but she does not note the full textual implication.

the Chaos; my strength has grown cold in me."

Note that the first 'power' more naturally has to mean an entity, whilst the second 'power' has to mean her strength, or spiritual capacities. Later in Chapter 39;
usually: 'to hear the groaning of those who are bound, to release the power of the souls, whose power is bound.

In my version:
"...to hear the groans of those who are bound, so that he (God) may release the strength of the souls whose being is bound...'

Again, now in Chapter 44: this is usually,
'And my power has trusted in your Mystery; and also my power has trusted in the Light which is in the height, and it has trusted in it when it was in the chaos below. Let all the powers in me trust in the light while I am in the lower darkness..."

My version:
"and my being trusted in your Mystery, and my being has also trusted in the light which is in the Heights; my being has trusted also in this light whilst below, in the Chaos. Let all the spiritual forces which are in me, truly discern the light, while I am in the lower darkness."

Destroyed or disempowered?
In the previous versions, in Chapter 23, Jesus says:
"...a large number of souls would have been destroyed, if malignant Rulers and all their Heavens and all their Aeons, had not been destroyed (lit. 'dissolved')".
Then in Chapter 26, in these versions on this same theme, Jesus further comments,
"...the kingdom of the evil Rulers was destroyed, and the universe was quickly destroyed (lit. 'taken up')."

But the Christ-power through Jesus did not destroy the Heavens and the Aeons of the evil spirits; he did not destroy their realms. Their part of the cosmos certainly did not cease to exist, for as from the next

paragraph, the drama continues on. So, the above text is actually saying,
"...a large number of souls would have been disempowered, if malignant Rulers and all their Heavens and all their Aeons, had not been disempowered."

And the second quote is actually saying,
"...the kingdom of the evil Rulers was disempowered (by Christ). Thus, all of their malignant influences (just discussed) were quickly disintegrated."

Fear or awe?
In Chapter 28, referring to the reactions of divine spirits to Jesus Christ, as he ascended into the heavens, the previous versions have,

"So the (holy) deities of the Aeons too, were in great fear, to which there was no measure."

But the verb here is derived from Greek and this word often does mean to fear, but it also means to feel awe. Since divine beings would never have fear of the Christ, but rather adoration and awe, the true meaning here is: "Also the (holy) deities of the Aeons, were in great and boundless awe."

The soul of Mary, the mother of Jesus
In Chapter 7, regarding the Christ sending spiritual influences into the aura of the Virgin Mary, before Jesus was conceived, this is translated, in my version,

"And into the soul (of Mary), I cast the spiritual power which I had received from the great Sabaoth."
But the previous versions have:
"instead of the soul, I cast the power..." (Mead)
"and in place of the soul, I cast the power..."
(MacDermot and Schmidt-Till).
These versions are inferring that Mary's soul was removed, being replaced with some transcendent component, identified only as 'the first spiritual power'. However, the Coptic text has, "into *the place* of the soul, I cast..." that is, something was added

into that spot where the soul of Mary was then located. The precision of the Coptic here is awkward, yet it is fully correct to the transcendent context and the action of the situation. This is what is presented in my translation, and that of Horner.

Personification
Literary personification:
This occurs when an object that has no personality, nor a sense of 'I", is given an individualized human quality, for poetic purposes. It can be used of inanimate things, whether rain, or clouds or fog, or the state of the economy or the functionality of a school. Shakespeare has many of these:
"The moon, methinks looks with watery eye."
"The morn, in russet mantle clad, walks over the dew of yon eastward hill."

But it can also be used of soul-qualities, such as virtue, regret, longing, jealousy or death: "Nor shall death brag that thou wand'rest in his shade." The intention of the writer in doing this is to enhance the dramatic element of their words.

Personification often occurs in the Bible, in the Jewish Scriptures (the Old Testament). These bestow a mystical quality on the text; "God's Word runs swiftly", or "Jerusalem, wash your heart from evil, that you may be saved". And the Pistis Sophia text draws heavily on Old Testament writings.

It is important to note that there are two aspects to the word 'personification'. In its usual literary usage, it means that a quality or experience is especially presented as if something were a living person (or deity). There are many of these in the Old Testament, about wisdom, "Wisdom cries out, she utters her voice in the streets." But there is another aspect to personification.

The spiritual origin of personification
When a human being has a strong desire or ambition, or an idea with depth and power, there arises in the Soul-world (or 'astral' realms) a spiritual counterpart to this. These counterparts are called 'thought-forms', by Rudolf Steiner who reports if someone has a

dislike of another person, then in the Soul-world fiery, arrow shaped hate-permeated thought-forms move through the realm, seeking out that disliked person.

But also, if a soul has an intuitive sensing of spiritual truths and realities, then this state of soul, this Sophia state, has its counterpart in the Soul-world. It is precisely this counterpart in the Soul-world to a human soul-quality which is also a 'personification', in the esoteric sense. It is no longer a poetic fantasy; it reflects a reality, but a non-earthly reality. Pistis Sophia is then such a non-earthly reality, as the spirit counterpart of our intuitive-perceptive cognizing.

"Holy Goddess of Light": (usually, the Virgin of Light) The Coptic term here uses a Greek word "parthenos' (παρθένος) which means:
    maiden or girl   (thus, virgin)
But it is also used of: the goddess Athena and the constellation Virgo.
So, when used of a woman, it meant: 'chaste'.
But when used of a feminine deity, it meant: 'holy'.
Usually the Coptic term in Pistis Sophia is translated as 'Virgin of Light', but I have concluded that this is inappropriate, since deities have no flesh body. Moreover, another Coptic word of similar meaning (ⲕⲉⲕⲉ or ⲕⲁⲁⲕⲉ) was used for the Greek term 'kore'[23]. Kore (κόρη) has very similar meanings to 'parthenos', namely: virginal daughter maiden girl the goddesses Artemis and Persephone, (and also sea-nymphs).

So in the Pistis Sophia codex, "holy goddess of light" is a more accurate translation than 'virgin of light'. The word 'virgin' was meant to imply purity, which it did in ancient times with regard to unmarried young women. But this is a word which is obviously out of

---

[23] Both the Coptic ⲕⲁⲁⲕⲉ and Grk. 'kore' also meant: pupil-of-the-eye.

place for any non-flesh, i.e., spirit entity. So the famous Hermetica term, 'kore kosmou', is not 'the World Virgin', but 'Holy World-Goddess' or 'Holy Goddess of the Cosmos'.

Sang a song, or intoned words of reverence?

In my translation, Pistis Sophia 'intoned words of reverence'. By this I mean that her utterances occur in a poetic, almost chanting manner. Her words are called in Coptic, 'hymnos', from the Greek; from which we get the word 'hymn'. But this Greek term also meant 'ode'; and odes could be recited, not always sung, as such. The verb from this noun can mean to speak or chant or recite (and rarely), to sing.

That Pistis Sophia was 'intoning words of reverence', not singing a song of praise is confirmed when Jesus refers to her words when she is speaking of her distressed state, and entreating help, as an expression of remorse.

And when Jesus mentions her in these situations, he refers to her 'saying' these words, not 'singing' them. For the Coptic verb he uses is used primarily for speaking or reciting, but only rarely for singing. There are several other Coptic verbs which specifically mean 'singing'; but these are not used when Jesus or the disciples refer to these declarations of Pistis Sophia.

The omitted texts in the codex: texts 4 and 5

Why I decided to omit these last two sections, having concluded that they are inferior to the first three texts, is illustrated in the following extracts from these two documents. These present material which is incompatible with the morality and the profoundly enlightened teachings in the first three documents:

A: sinners who are unrepentant undergo horrific torture in Hell and are then eternally extinguished. Such sinners include: adulterers, blasphemers and murderers.

B: But if a disciple knows of such a sinner, and repeats a special blessing which invokes their salvation, then that sinner is not sent to eternal death.

C: Souls with strong lowly desires, slanderers, and also 'cursers', after death are slowly dissolved away by a feminine demon, who does this by roasting them (in a Hell-fire), over a period of "133 years and nine months".

D: Souls of deceased liars, and of people who coveted the goods of other persons, are tortured after death for 165 years and 6 months; then they are dissolved and destroyed.

E: There are 12 dungeons in the outer Darkness, each guarded by a dreadful, animal-faced demon. Evil souls or sinners enter the 'mouth of the tail' of a dragon, who then swallows up the sinner.

F: if souls do not pray before eating, then evil spirits enter their body and bind the soul to malignant beings.

G: The rulers of the spirit realms, that is, the planetary spheres (or Aions) are identified with Greek deities: Kronos, Ares, Aphrodite, Hermes, Hecate, Zeus and Persephone. This is obviously the viewpoint of someone who was not Jesus, and was not from a Hebrew background, and who could only identify prominent deities in an esoteric Christian teaching of Aramaic origins, as Greek gods.

As Horner commented, with this text, "we have descended down the mountain" (where the first texts had taken us).

H: There were no initiates who could merge with the (Christ-)light throughout all of antiquity, until Jesus came to the world. To esoteric traditions, this is an invalid statement, as many great sages of antiquity were in effect united to the 'Christ' light; although this light or deity was known under different names. This is also indicated in the Prologue to the Gospel of John, as my translation makes clear.[24]

---

[24] 1:12 Yet those who did so receive the Logos – those who discerned its true being – these were empowered through it to become 'children of God'....

I: Words of Jesus, later recorded in Luke (16:9) are given in a false version, to allow the parable to be interpreted, wrongly, as an interaction with a "dragon of the outer Darkness".

J: When conception occurs, 365 unpleasant spirits enter the womb and mould the embryo together from various 'sinful' spirit-influences, and then leave special sigils in parts of the body which record when their various tasks of embryo-building were achieved.

K: As seen above, a large part of these last two texts focus on the terrible punishment that various types of 'sinners' receive.[25] The fire of each kind of Hellish place is described as more fiercely hot than the preceding one, and these fiery dungeons are guarded by ferocious dragons. This unwholesome view is the seed of a later prominent but repellent part of medieval church doctrine.

L: The soul of a deceased arrogant person has to endure three periods of 20 months each, during which they are tormented, and they are then eventually re-born as a crippled person.

M: in one place (chapter 137) this is written, 'Jeu drew a power out of the Pistis, the Sophia... and bound this to Aphrodite'. Apart from the fantastical, out of place involvement of a Greek goddess here, the writer has not understood that 'pistis' is an adjective, meaning 'intuitive-perceptive', (or in other places 'faithful'), and is describing 'sophia' or wisdom. That is, 'pistis' is a quality here, not a noun; not a separate entity. The Coptic text itself is incorrectly written, as 'the Pistis, the Sophia' when it should "the Pistis

---

1: 14 Thus the Logos became flesh, and dwelt amongst us: and we beheld its splendour, that of the Uniquely-begotten from the Father, full of Grace and Truth.

Note: 'Thus', instead of the usual 'And'; a grammatically valid and significant variation here, showing that this verse is taking further the consequences of verse 13, of the ancient initiates being spiritually re-born; achieving the 'Son of God' state.

[25] One may detect in them an unhealthy religious emphasis on the punishment of 'sinners'.

Sophia".[26]

N: Mariam is described as prostrating herself at the feet of Jesus, and then "she kissed his hands". This is an action that requires the Saviour to be really present in a physical body, which he wasn't.

O: There are many references to Greek gods in the last two documents, and almost none to Egyptian deities; one exception is the Egyptian god Boubastis who is identified with a Greek deity, Aphrodite. However, this Egyptian deity was known in Greek culture as Artemis-Diana, not as Aphrodite; indeed in Greek myths, Artemis is the rival of Aphrodite.

The writers of these last texts imposed Greek deities onto whatever small amount of unclear knowledge they acquired of the dialogues between the Saviour and his disciples. Their texts have an unwholesome, at times ludicrous quality, and include cruel religious fantasies. These writers were obviously immature Christians of Greek ethnicity who had no inner connection to the immensely deep, initiatory perspectives evident in the first three documents of this codex.

Such Greeks also were not familiar with the first century Aramaic-Jewish language idioms, nor with the vocabulary these first Christian disciples used for their deities.

These documents, four and five, were obviously composed at a distance – psychologically and probably chronologically – from the first three texts. They are primarily fantasies, often presenting narrow-minded religious doctrines, some of which exhibit a vengeful nature.

Interpreting Scripture passages: 22 Psalms, and six Odes of Solomon as well as various words of Jesus now known to us from the Gospels, are quoted by the disciples, as a help to interpreting words spoken by Pistis Sophia. These interpretations are freely made from an esoteric perspective; they need not conform

---

[26] It is, ⲧⲡⲓⲥⲧⲓⲥ ⲧⲥⲟⲫⲓⲁ.

to the meaning or context in which they are found in Scripture.

A user-friendly text:
As the Coptic is at times very brief, additional words are sometimes needed to connect one part of a sentence to the next; these are added in brackets (like this). Where a few words are needed to explain an obscure text, these are added in italics in brackets, (*like this*). Otherwise, comments about the text are placed in the Commentary which follows each chapter, or in foot-notes.

The traditional language in old religious texts, such as: thou, thee and ye, has been discontinued, except in a few instances where the context requires it for clarity.

Where I have decided upon a different interpretation of a word or phrase, to that of other translations, the Coptic original is presented and briefly analyzed. Also, at times the literal meaning of a Coptic word may be confusing, so I have replaced it with a more understandable term, but then the literal meaning is shown in brackets, like this (*lit. rushing*): i.e., the word here in Coptic literally means 'rushing'.

A few abbreviations are used for oft-repeated words in the foot-notes;
'lit.' = literally   'usu.' = usually
Grk. = Greek   Heb. = Hebrew
NT = New Testament
OT = Old Testament i.e., the Hebrew Scriptures

I have retained the same divisions of the text into numbered paragraphs, as devised by Professor Carl Schmidt. The outstanding work on this codex by Schmidt (1905), as edited by W. Till (1959), and their German translation, have provided a valuable basis for my work. The achievements of previous translators, George Horner (1924), and Violet MacDermot (1978) (and G.R.S. Mead, 1921) are also acknowledged.

Finally, it necessary to comment that, to the modern reader, the text commences in a laboured manner; listing all the various spirit realities which

Jesus had not revealed to the disciples during his life on Earth, before the Resurrection.

For a reader of the first centuries of Christianity, this listing of spirit realities would not have been experienced as laboured, because all of these realities would have been known, and acutely meaningful.

However, the text soon becomes more engaging, as the tasks of Jesus, now united to the cosmic Christ, from within spirit realms, are revealed, and the disciples respond to his revelations.

It is my hope that this Foreword, and the extensive Commentary placed throughout the book, helps the reader to engage with the contents of this unique codex. That is, with the ideas which it presents; ideas which are at times challenging, and yet often deeply inspiring.

The first three documents in the Askew (Pistis Sophia) Codex:

TEXT: CHAPTER 1

When Jesus had risen from the dead, it happened that he spent eleven years speaking with his disciples, and instructing them up to the realms of the first Command only, and up to the realms of the First Mystery: this which is within the veil, within the first Command, namely the 24th Mystery without and below, those 24 which are in the second realm of the First Mystery, which is before all others – the Father in the likeness of a dove.

And Jesus said to his disciples: "I am come forth from that First Mystery, which is the last Mystery, that is, the 24th Mystery." His disciples did not know, nor did they understand, that there was anything within that Mystery; but they thought that this Mystery in fact was the pinnacle of the All, and the pinnacle of all that exists.

For they thought it was the end of all ends, because Jesus had said to them concerning that Mystery: "It surrounds the First Command, with the five Divisions (of the spiritual cosmos), and with the Great Light, and the five Supporters, and even the entire Treasury of Light."

Moreover, Jesus had not told his disciples of the entire distribution of all the realms of the Great Invisible, and of the three Triple-powers, with the 24 Invisibles, with all their realms, Aions, and their orderings, according to the manner of their distribution, for they are the emanations of the Great Invisible.

(*Nor had he told them of*) their un-generated, self-generated, and generated Ones; their light-givers (i.e., 'luminaries') and unpaired Ones, their Rulers and Powers, their lords and Archangels, their Angels and Decans, their Servitors and all the habitations of their spheres, and all the orderings of each one of them.

Nor had Jesus told his disciples of the entire distribution of the emanations of the Treasury of Light, nor their orderings, according to their

TEXT: CHAPTER 1 (cont.)

distribution; nor had he told them their saviours, according to the actual rank of each. Nor had he told them who are the Guardians which are beside each portal of the Treasury of Light; nor had he told them of the realm of the saviour of the Twins; who is the Child of the Child. Nor had he told them of the realms of the Three Amens, in what realms they are distributed; nor had he told them in what realm are the Five Trees, nor the Seven Amens, which are also the Seven Voices; what is their realm, according to the manner of their distribution (in the cosmos).

Nor had Jesus told his disciples of what type are the five Servitors, or from what realm they were brought forth; nor had he told them how the Great Light had emanated, or from what realm it had been brought forth. Nor had he told them of the five Divisions (*of the cosmos*), nor of the first Command, from what realm these had been brought forth.

But he spoke of these realities simply, and taught them that these existed, without speaking of their emanation and the ordering of their realms. And this is why they did not know that there were other realms within that Mystery.

Nor had he told his disciples "I pass through such or such a realm until I enter that Mystery, or (when) I leave it"; but, in instructing them, he merely said, "I have come from that Mystery." And this is why they thought concerning that Mystery, that it was the end of ends (of creation): that it was the pinnacle of creation, and even that it was the fullness of creation itself.

For Jesus said to his disciples, "It is that Mystery which surrounds all the fullness of Creation of which I have spoken, from the day on which I first met with you, even unto this day." And this is, therefore, why the disciples thought there was nothing within that Mystery.

COMMENTARY: CHAPTER 1

We encounter immediately the various specialized terms of this text, which were discussed in the

COMMENTARY: CHAPTER 1 (cont.)

Introduction. These appear to be terms well known to the intended readers; members of what was apparently, a secret Christian initiatory school. The term 'Mystery' in this entire text means a divine being or spiritual-reality. The region of the First Mystery is identified as the same as, or encompassing, the 24th Mystery. But it is confusing to learn that this 24th Mystery is also identified as 24 separate mysteries/spirit-realities; for these are located within the 2nd realm of the First Mystery.

The First Mystery itself is:

A: 'before' (i.e., prior to) all divine beings, and is also:
B: the Father, in the form of a dove

So the First Mystery = 24th Mystery = the Father-God

Thus the 'alpha and omega' dynamic, as proclaimed by Christ Jesus in Revelation, is an aspect of the Father-God: the beginning and the end of all things.

Also, we learn, this First Mystery encompasses:
the First Command,
the 5 Divisions of the cosmos,
the Great Light,
the entire Treasury of Light

Jesus says that he reveals only the basic nature of the structure and dynamics of the spiritual realms. The scribe then lists the many spiritual realities which Jesus did not tell them about at that stage: These are all mentioned later on; but as a result, the disciples concluded, erroneously, that Jesus has told them of everything.

There exist 'Watchers' who are guarding every portal of the Treasury of Light (= 2nd level of the Buddhi realm; see diagram of the cosmic structure implied behind this text).

The Alpha & Omega dynamic is common to both the Father-God and to Jesus, since later Jesus is identified as the First Mystery. One notes that this is a core theme of the Gospel of John.

A 'Twin' is mentioned: and although briefly later, the nature of this twin is not explained.

Various 'Amens' are mentioned; and will be discussed

COMMENTARY: CHAPTER 1 (cont.)
later when they are referred to in later chapters.
"fullness of all Creation" the Coptic text has the word 'Pleroma' here, which in Greek signifies 'the all' or 'the complete fullness' of something, and was used in Gnostic texts, and also in the New Testament.

Jesus is described as being 'seated'; however, this can not be an action of a physical-flesh body, it is a way of implying that Jesus was present to their perception as a teacher. The scribe continues to enumerate the many spiritual beings and realms which Jesus did not discuss at this early stage. He also mentions that Jesus made no comment on the various stages of spiritual realms through he ascended, but he does later on.

"disciples thought there was nothing within *that* mystery": this sentence means that the disciples concluded that what Jesus had already revealed to them during the initiatory sessions held during his life on Earth was the complete revelation of wisdom, for the scribe quotes Jesus saying, as above, "It is that mystery which surrounds all the fullness of creation of which I have spoken, from the day on which I first met with you, even to this day."

TEXT: CHAPTER 2
It came to pass, therefore, that the disciples were sitting together on the Mount of Olives, speaking of these things, rejoicing with great joy, and being exceedingly glad and saying to each other "More blessed are we than all people who are on the Earth, for the Saviour has revealed this to us, and so we have received the fullness of all creation, and its complete perfection".

And while they were saying these things to each other, Jesus sat a little removed from them. It came to pass, therefore, on the 15th day of the month of *Tobe*, on the day of the full Moon, on that day, as the Sun had risen in its bark (i.e., *sun-boat*), that there came forth after it a great light-power, shining

TEXT: CHAPTER TWO (cont)

exceedingly; there was no measure to the radiance with which it was surrounded, for it came forth from the Light of Lights, and it came forth from the Last Mystery, which is the 24th Mystery 'from within outwards' – those which are in the sequences of the second realm of the First Mystery.

And the Light-power poured over Jesus, and surrounded him entirely. He was seated apart from his disciples, and he was shining exceedingly: there was no measure to the light which was around him. The disciples did not see Jesus, because of the great light in which he was. For their eyes were blinded by the great light in which he was enveloped. They saw the radiance only, sending forth great rays of light.

And the rays of light were not like each other, but these were of various kinds, and of every type, from the lower to the higher part of the light; each (ray) more splendid than the next, in infinite manner, in a great glory of immeasurable light, which stretched from below, on the Earth, up to the Heavens. And when the disciples saw the light, they were in great fear and great confusion.

COMMENTARY: CHAPTER 2

The descent of a divine radiance is described; this is understood in anthroposophy and other esoteric approaches to the Gospels, as deriving from the leader of the Sun-gods or Powers (*Exousiai*), and is called the 'cosmic Christ'. Support for this view is found in various places of this codex; e.g., chapter 56, where Jesus is identified as the "Light of Lights"; but meaning here the cosmic Christ overshadowing him. Furthermore, there is reference to the Father-God as present within this light, since "the First Mystery" is mentioned as the origin of this radiance.

"Sun had risen in its bark (*sun-boat*)": usually 'on its path": but this is only conjecture. For the Coptic word here (ⲃⲁⲥⲓⲥ), from the Greek 'basis' (βάσις) does not mean 'path', but 'steps' or 'position'. The solution is

COMMENTARY: CHAPTER 2 (cont.)

that the scribe wrote 'basis' when he should have written 'baris'.

"Baris": This is a rare Greek word for 'boat'; a word derived from the interaction of Greeks with Egypt (there is a related Greek word ('baridessi' - βαρίδεσσι) which means a flat-bottomed Egyptian boat, as used on the Nile.[27] (MacDermot has pointed this out, suggesting the text could be translated as "Sun had risen in its bark"). So here at the beginning of the text, there is an allusion to the esoteric-religious views about the Sun-god in ancient Egypt.

There are various other Egyptian references elsewhere in the Pistis Sophia. The Copts for whom this codex was translated were Egyptians, and hence it is possible that the scribe who translated the Greek text might replace a Greek word with an Egyptian word. But it is also quite possible that there were some Egyptian-derived words in the Greek original, because there is an underlying connection of esoteric Christian initiatory wisdom to that of the ancient Egyptians. The sun god Ra can be viewed as the same deity as cosmic Christ, and is so understood by various esotericists, in particular, by Rudolf Steiner.

"Full Moon in Tobe": The primary significance is that it was in this month, according to the Coptic calendar, that the Baptism of Jesus occurred. So, possibly this day is not reflecting an historical fact, but has symbolic purpose, namely a 'cosmic' baptism now occurs.

It was also the day of the full Moon; the 'atmosphere' of which may have added to the impact of the event upon the disciples; but whether it also contributed a necessary spiritual influence is unclear.

"the Heavens": this phrase means that there are multiple spirit realms. It is not the usual English poetic phrase which has no specific reference to any spirit realms.

---

[27] It is noted too, that 'basis' resembles the Coptic word, 'baare' (ⲂⲀⲀⲢⲈ) for boat; Westendorf, p.26 & Crum, p.42a.

TEXT: CHAPTER 3

It came to pass, therefore, when this stream of light had come down upon Jesus, that it gradually enveloped him completely. Jesus then arose or ascended into the Heights, during this, he became more radiant, with an immeasurable light. And the disciples gazed (*clairvoyantly*) after him, none of them speaking, until he had entered into heaven. They were all in great silence. These things then came to pass on the fifteenth day of the moon, the day on which it is full in the month of Tobe.

It came to pass, when Jesus had ascended into heaven, after the third hour, all the beings of the Heavens were disturbed, and they all collided with each other, they and all Aions, all their realms, and all their orderings. And the entire Earth was shaken, and all who live on it.

And all the people, those in the world, were agitated, and also the disciples, and everyone thought, 'perhaps the world will cease to exist'. And all the (malignant) entities which are in the Heavens did not cease to be in confusion, they and the entire world; and all collided with each other, from the third hour of the fifteenth day of the month of Tobe, until the ninth hour of the next day.

Whereas all the (*holy beings*), the Angels with their[28] Archangels, and all the powers of the Heights, all sang praises to the innermost soul-spirit realities (*lit. interior of the interiors*), so that the whole world heard their voice; they ceased not till the ninth hour of the next day.

COMMENTARY: CHAPTER 3

The descent of the divine light upon Jesus is described as causing dramatic and extensive anxiety and disorder to malignant entities; but great rejoicing to divine spirits. It also caused great anxiety to

---

[28] "their Archangels": an unusual expression, possibly should be simply 'the Archangels'.

COMMENTARY: CHAPTER 3 (cont.)
incarnate people, including the disciples.

That 'the entire earth' and its inhabitants are described as being agitated is a striking assertion. It was obviously not the case so far as the physical world and its inhabitants are concerned. But the expression 'the entire Earth' is often used in similar literature to mean the general area around the writer's location. It is so used in Chapter 6; so the assertion is a poetic figure of speech.

"the interior of the interiors": this probably means 'the innermost soul-spirit realities'. This phrase refers to an especially veiled spiritual reality, which is apparently associated with the Treasury of Light (the second level of the Buddhi realm; that is, the realm above Devachan, as noted earlier).[29]

TEXT: CHAPTER 4
But the disciples sat together in fear, and were in the greatest possible distress. They were afraid because of the great earthquake which happened, and they wept together, saying: "What will happen? Perhaps the Saviour will destroy all the realms?" Thus saying, they wept together.

On the ninth hour of the next day, the Heavens were opened, and they saw Jesus descending, shining exceedingly; there was no measure to the light which surrounded him, for he shone more brightly than when he had ascended up to the Heavens, so that it is impossible for anyone of this world to describe the light in which he was.

It sent forth rays shining exceedingly; his rays were without measure, nor were his rays of light similar to each other, but they were of every figure and of every type, some being more splendid than the others. The light was composite in nature; there were three kinds of radiance, one was superior to the others...(*gap in text*) the second kind which was in the

---

[29] This association is found in chapt. 43 of the *Second Book of Jeu*.

TEXT: CHAPTER 4 (cont.)
middle (*of the column of light*), was superior to the first kind which was underneath; and the third which was above these two, was superior to both of them.

The first ray, which was placed below the others, was like the light which came upon Jesus before he ascended into the Heavens, and was very regular as to its own radiance; its radiance was unlike that of the others. And the three degrees of light were of every variety of light and type, in that some excelled over the others....(*gap in manuscript*).

COMMENTARY: CHAPTER 4
"earthquake": there is no record of this historically, but earthquakes do occur relatively frequently in the Holy Lands. So is this again a poetic exaggeration of an earth tremor; or it may refer to an event in the spiritual level of the planet.

TEXT: CHAPTER 5
It then happened when the disciples had seen these things, that they feared exceedingly, and were troubled. But Jesus, the compassionate and merciful-minded, when he saw that his disciples were troubled with great confusion, spoke to them, saying, "Take courage. It is I, be not afraid."

COMMENTARY: Chapter 5
"Take courage...": the resemblance to similar words in the Gospels (Matt.16:27/Mk.6:50/Jn.6:20) is accidental, as there Christ declares he is the "I am" or sense of 'I' in the human being.

TEXT: CHAPTER 6
It came to pass, when the disciples heard these words, that they said, "Lord, if it be you, draw in your glorious light to yourself, that we may be able to stand, so that our eyes be not blinded. We have been

TEXT: CHAPTER 6 (cont.)

dismayed, and the whole world has been dismayed, by the greatness of the light which is in you."

Then Jesus drew to himself the glory of his light; and when this was done, all the disciples took courage and came to Jesus' feet, and together cast themselves down at his feet, and worshipped him, rejoicing with great joy.

They said to him: "Lord, where did you go to; or on what service did you go; or why did all these disturbances and earthquakes take place?" Then Jesus, the compassionate, said to them, "Rejoice and be glad, for I have gone to the realms from which I had come (*descended*) from." From this day forth, therefore, will I speak with you freely, from the beginning of the Truth to its completion; and I will speak to you face to face without parable.

From this hour will I hide nothing from you of the things which pertain to the Heights, and of those (spirits) of the realm of Truth. For authority has been given me by the Ineffable One, and by the First Mystery of all Mysteries, to speak with you from the beginning to the end, from the Inner to the Outer, from the Outer to the Inner. And I shall speak with you face to face, without using parables. From this hour onwards, I shall not hide anything from you of the Heights nor of the realm of the Truth. Now listen, that I may tell you all things.

"It came to pass, as I was a little removed from you on the Mount of Olives, contemplating the nature of the ministry for which I was sent (*to the Earth*), and that it must be accomplished, and also (how) the Last Mystery had not yet sent to me my garment (of light) (*his high spirit-aura, deriving from the cosmic Christ*).

This Mystery is the 24th Mystery from within to without, i.e., those which are located in the second realm of the First Mystery, within the orderings of that realm. It came to pass, as I understood that the task of the ministry for which I had come had been fulfilled, but that the Mystery had not yet sent to me my garment, that I was there on the Mount of Olives, contemplating this.

COMMENTARY: Chapter 6
In this chapter some expressions were encountered but which are not explained; but will be explored in later chapters, when they are mentioned, such as:
Inner to the Outer, from the Outer to the Inner
the Heights and the realm of the Truth
the second realm of the First Mystery
"the 24th Mystery from within to without":

"the Ineffable One": this deity is an even higher deity than the deity normally called 'God' or 'the First Mystery'. Ineffable means, as the Oxford English Dictionary states, 'that which cannot be expressed in words".[30] All previous translators have chosen the term 'Unutterable' to indicate that speech fails to describe the nature of God. The Coptic term (ⲁⲧⲭⲱ) has the nuance of being veiled or covered over.

TEXT: CHAPTER 7
It came to pass, when the sun rose in the East[31], that then through the First Mystery (the Father-God) – which existed from the beginning, through whom the cosmos has been created, from which also I have just now come (*as the risen Saviour*) – but not as earlier, before they had crucified me[32] – it now came to pass, by order of that Mystery, that it sent to me my garment of light, which it had given to me from the beginning, and which I had left behind in the Last Mystery, which is the 24th Mystery from within to without; i.e., those which are located in the second realm of the First Mystery, within the sequential

---

[30] It doesn't mean 'unknowable'.
[31] "from the East': again a hint of an underlying Egyptian wisdom, since normally the compass direction of the sunrise would not be specifically identified.
[32] That is, the divine consciousness of Jesus, when incarnating through Mary, descending from the Father-God, was not the same as what he attained after his empowerment through the Resurrection.

TEXT: CHAPTER 7 (cont.)

orderings of that realm.

That garment (of light) which I had left behind in the Last Mystery until the time should be fulfilled when I should take it up again; this is when I shall begin to speak to the human race, and reveal to them all things from the beginning of the Truth to its completion, and speak to them from innermost soul-spirit realities to the most external, cosmic realities of spirit, and from the most external, cosmic realities of spirit to the innermost soul-spirit realities.[33]

Rejoice, therefore, and be glad and rejoice very greatly, for it is to you that it has been given, that I first speak of the beginning of the Truth to its completion. For this reason have I chosen you from the beginning, through the (*decision of the*) First Mystery. So rejoice and exult, and rejoice very greatly that for this reason. I chose you from the beginning, through the First Mystery.

Rejoice that, when I set out to be in the world, I brought with me 12 spiritual powers (*i.e., energies*) from the beginning, which, as I said to you from the start, I took from the 12 saviours of the Treasury of Light, according to the command of the First Mystery (*God*). These powers, therefore, I cast into the wombs of your mothers, when I came into the world, and they are those which are in your bodies this day.

For these spiritual powers have been given to you in preference to the whole world, for it is you who are to save the entire world; and (these powers are given to you) that you may be able to endure the menace of the rulers of the world, and the calamities of the world, and its dangers, and all the persecutions which the rulers of the Heights must bring upon you.

Many times have I said to you, the spiritual presence (*lit. power*) which is in you – this I have brought from the 12 saviours which are in the Treasury of Light. For this reason I said to you from

---

[33] Literally, from the Interior of the Interiors, to the Outer of the Outers, and from the Outer of the Outers to the Interiors of the Interiors.

TEXT: CHAPTER 7 (cont.)

the start (*during my earthly ministry*), that you were not of this world.[34]

And I also am not of this world, for all people who are of this world have received their soul from the rulers of the (*tainted Fate-determining*) Aions. But the spiritual power which is in you is from me. For you are souls who are in harmony with the Heights. I have brought spiritual powers from the 12 saviours of the Treasury of Light, and which I have received as a share of my spiritual strength, that I received from the beginning.

And when I set forth to come into this world, I came amongst the Rulers (Archons) of this sphere. I assumed the likeness of the (Arch)angel Gabriel, in order that the Rulers of the Aions might not recognize me, but think that I was the (Arch)angel Gabriel. It came to pass, when I had passed through the midst of the Rulers of the Aions, that I looked down on the world of humanity, by order of the First Mystery.

I found Elisabeth, mother of John the Baptist, before she had conceived him; I cast into her a spiritual capacity which I had received from the hand of the Little IAO the Good, who is in The Midst, that John might preach before me and prepare my way, and baptize in water for the forgiving of sins. This spiritual capacity then, is in the body of John.

Moreover, in the soul-realm (*under the influence*) of the (fallen) Rulers, (*a portion of*) which realm John was due to receive (*in the course of preparing for reincarnation*), I found (*as part of this process*) the soul of the prophet Elijah in the (*holy, not debased*) Aions of the Sphere. I then received to myself this soul,[35] and I took his soul and brought him to the Holy Goddess of the Light; and she gave it over to her Receivers. They brought it to the Sphere of the Rulers and they cast it into the womb of Elisabeth.

Consequently, a spiritual capacity of the Little IAO,

---

[34] A declaration of this truth was also recorded in Jn.15:19.
[35] Schmidt: has "ich nahm ihn hinein" = I took it in(side)

TEXT: CHAPTER 7 (cont.)

who is in The Midst, and also the soul of Elijah the prophet, are united both with the body of John the Baptist. For this reason you had been in doubt earlier, when I said to you, "John stated, I am not the Messiah": and you said to me, "It is written in the Scripture, that when the Messiah shall come, Elijah will come before him, and prepare his way."

And I, when you had said this to me, replied to you, "Truly Elijah has come, and has prepared all things, according as it according as it is written; and they have done unto him whatsoever they would."

But when I perceived that you did not understand that I had spoken concerning the soul of Elijah being united with John the Baptist, I answered you openly, and face to face, with the words, "If you are willing to receive it, John the Baptist is Elijah whose coming, I said, was anticipated".

COMMENTARY: CHAPTER 7

There are two references to 'the Heights' here:
the persecutions which the Rulers of the Heights must bring upon you.
You are souls who are in harmony with the Heights.

From this one sees that the first reference is not to evil powers, but to divine Powers of the Heights; however, these deities are required to not magically block suffering and tribulations that the disciples may, and indeed shall, experience.

A major point: spiritual power was put into the embryos of the 12 disciples of Jesus during the gestation time of their bodies in their mothers' womb. In Rudolf Steiner's words, divine qualities were rayed into the etheric bodies of the disciples.

A similar imbuing of an embryo with divine qualities occurred with Elisabeth, the mother of John the Baptist. This spiritual influence is called 'the IAO'. This is apparently a smaller or lesser form of the Great IAO, mentioned later.

Also the soul of the initiate Elijah, which Jesus

COMMENTARY: CHAPTER 7 (cont.)
found in holy spirit realms, sought out the "Holy Goddess of the Light, then some of Elijah's soul qualities became present in Elisabeth's womb.

"the Messiah shall come": usually, 'when the Christ shall come', but as in my translation of John's Gospel, (1:20) 'Messiah' is the correct word. For this is a dialogue amongst Jews speaking Aramaic, not Greeks (Christ is a Greek word). The word 'Christ' was not applied to Jesus until well into, or shortly after, his ministry; and he had not even begun his ministry when this dialogue occurred.

"people who are of this world have received their soul from the Rulers of the (*debased*) Aions." A potent indicator that the normal soul has much in the astral body which derives from Lucifer and Ahriman. But one may still conclude that evolved souls also have some elements from higher realms.

"you are not of this world": this is apparently not meant in a complete, full sense, as the disciples do manifest imperfect traits at times.

"Holy Goddess of the Light": usually translated 'as the Virgin of Light'. But as discussed in the Introduction, 'virgin' is oddly out of place for any non-flesh deity; the word here means in human terms, pure and thus holy, when applied to a deity.

Major point: "But the spiritual power which is in you is from me."

The phrase 'from me' is ambiguous, and means firstly, that Jesus rayed forth these qualities into the disciples. But secondly, it also indicates that these are part of the being of Jesus. Thus the term "Jesus" in the Pistis Sophia does in fact refer to Jesus Christ, i.e., Jesus, as the bearer of the cosmic Christ.

For these divine 'etheric' energies given to the disciples, would derive from the Sun god, the cosmic Christ, even if they have become part of the divine transcendent, 'body' or 'vehicle' of the glorified, risen Jesus.

"12 vital spiritual capacities from the beginning, which, as I said to you from the start, I took from the 12 saviours of the "Treasury of Light": note the

COMMENTARY: CHAPTER 7 (cont.)

zodiacal implication here; it occurs elsewhere in the *Pistis Sophia*. Note too, that in the Hellenistic Age, 'God' was widely understood to be a twelve-fold (zodiacal) entity. This fact is usually not emphasized, but it is the case; examples of this occur in Pindar (Olymp. 5:5) and in Plato's works (*Phaedron*, 247a).[36]

So the twelve-fold Treasury of Light is a term alluding to the zodiacal deities who collectively were thought of as 'God' ('Theos' in Greek).

Here we learn that the 12 spiritual capacities (of the 12 saviours) of the Treasury of Light (2nd level of the Buddhi realm), came from 'The Midst'. As our diagram shows, The Midst is the highest, i.e., the seventh, realm of Devachan.

The 'decans' of the Rulers (or Archons), are apparently the serving spirits of these malignant gods, and they thought that the 12 spiritual capacities were derived from 'the souls of malignant Archons'. That is, in anthroposophical terms, these were extracts of the astrality of Lucifer and Ahriman. So, they let these 12 spiritual capacities pass them by; and in fact they even carried out the work of uniting these capacities with the 12 embryos of the disciples.

"Then you disciples were born *without* the souls (*specific astrality*) of the malignant Archons in you." So they were free of the influence of malignant spirits.

TEXT: CHAPTER 8

And Jesus continued his conversation, and said: After these things, it happened that through the command of the First Mystery, I looked down upon the world of humanity and I found Mary, who is called my mother, according to the material body; I spoke to her also, in the form of Gabriel. And when she had betaken herself into the Heights, towards me, I implanted in her the first spiritual capacity which I had received

---

[36] As noted in the *Theologisches Wörterbuch zum Neuen Testament*, edit. Kittel, Vol 3, p. 65, 1965.

TEXT: CHAPTER 8 (cont.)

from the Barbelo; that is to say, the body which I had in the Heights. And into her soul, I cast the spiritual capacity which I had received from the great Sabaoth, the Good,[37] who is located in realm of The Right (*first level of the Buddhi realm*).

And the 12 spiritual energies of the 12 saviours of the Treasury of Light, which I had received from the 12 servitors (located in) the Midst (*seventh level of Devachan*), I cast into the sphere of the Rulers. And the (*spirits in the*) decans of the Rulers, with their servitors, thought that these were soul-substances of the Rulers. So the servitors brought them forth, and I bound them into the bodies of your mothers. And when your time was full, you were brought forth into the world; no soul(-substances) of the Rulers being present in you.

You have received your portion from the spiritual power which the last Helper breathed into the mixture; this spiritual power which was blended with all the Invisibles and the Rulers, and all the Aions. In short, was it blended with the world of corruption, which is this mixture.

This (spiritual power) I brought out from myself, from the Beginning – I cast it into the first Command, and the first Command cast a portion thereof into the Great Light, and the Great Light cast a portion of that which it received, into the five Helpers, and the last Helper took a portion of that which it received, into the mixture. This spiritual presence is in all those who dwell in the mixture, in the manner in which I have just told you."

When Jesus, therefore, had said these things to his disciples on the Mount of Olives, he continued his conversation with the disciples, "Rejoice and be glad, and add joy to joy for the time is fulfilled for me to put on my garment, which has been prepared for me from the beginning; this which I had put away in the Last Mystery, until the time of its completion (*when it*

---

[37] "Sabaoth the Good": see the Introduction about this being.

TEXT: CHAPTER 8 (cont.)
became possible for Jesus to receive this).
The time of its completion is the time when I shall receive an order from the First Mystery to speak to you from the beginning of the Truth, to its fulfillment, and also from the innermost soul-spirit realities (*lit. interiors of the interiors*), to the most external cosmic realities (*lit. exterior of the exteriors*); because the world is to be saved by you. Rejoice and be exulted, because you are blessed, for it is you who are to save everyone.

COMMENTARY: CHAPTER 8
"on the Mount of Olives": referring to a conversation there, but not the one recorded in the Gospels. This chapter continues with a discussion of the unique soul components of the disciples, as distinct from normal human beings. In particular, the spiritual capacity or 'power' which the 'Last Helper' breathed into 'the mixture', which is blended with all the Invisibles and all the Rulers and all Aions: this is in summary, the 'realm of destruction'. So this is saying that the disciples have a high, unique spiritual capacity or resource.

"it was blended with the world of corruption": An obscure text here: is this special 'power' which was put into the disciples, then intermingled with the tainted etheric forces and astrality derived from evil or debased spirits. Yet the earlier words, "no soul-substance of the Rulers are present in you" appear to imply that this mixture did not enter into the disciples. Perhaps what is meant is that "it was blended with the world of corruption", but this tainted mixture did not permeate the disciples.

The spiritual capacity which Jesus brought out from his own spirit, this he cast into the First Command, then this entity cast a portion thereof into the 'Great Light'; and this entity then cast this spiritual power into the 'Five Helpers'. Then the last of these Five Helpers took a part of this and cast that into 'the Mixture'. And this latter portion is present in the disciples.

COMMENTARY: CHAPTER 8 (cont.)

"Barbelo": a very high and holy entity, see Introduction.

"Mary has betaken herself into the Heights, towards me"; this is the esoteric reality behind the Gospel story of the Annunciation to Mary by the Archangel Gabriel. Overshadowing Gabriel was the Saviour, who was able to permeate his mother Mary with divine influences once she became aware of the Archangel, and thereupon entered into a meditative, higher state of consciousness.

"And into her soul, I cast into Mary..."; literally, 'And into the *place of* the soul (of Mary)'; i.e., '*where her soul was*'. The Coptic text here is easily misunderstood; as it has the preposition 'epma' (ⲉⲡⲙⲁ) which has two meanings:

1: '*where'* (something is placed)
2: *replacing* something

But here it does not mean, *in place of/instead of her soul* (i.e., *replacing* her soul), but *into* the place (location) of her soul; as Horner concluded, ("and in the place of the soul..."); this is an important difference to most other versions.[38]

Jesus is explaining that he added into the soul (astral body) of Mary - in its place - i.e., where it was located in the high realm to which he taken it - high spiritual capacities (*i.e., energies*) from a deity called the Great Sabaoth, the Good.

The alternative versions, "instead of the soul" (Mead) "and in place of the soul" (MacD., Schmidt) are inferring that Mary's soul was removed, and replaced with "the body" - meaning some transcendent, non-physical component, identified only as 'the first power' - which Jesus had with him in a high realm.

---

[38] Reading ⲉⲡⲙⲁ ⲛⲧⲉⲯⲩⲭⲏ as "*into the place* of the soul", the dynamic here having the same nuance, (but different prepositions) as two paragraphs earlier: ⲉϩⲟⲩⲛ ⲉⲧⲕⲁⲗⲁϩⲏ ⲛⲉⲗⲓⲥⲁⲃⲉⲧ "into the womb of Elisabeth". Exactly parallel usages of ⲉⲡⲙⲁ to mean 'where' (the location) are found in the *Gospel of Thomas*, logion 22.

COMMENTARY: CHAPTER 8 (cont.)
But this would mean that Mary became a soul-less entity. This contradicts the Gospel of Luke which confirms that Mary was endowed with a soul. The Coptic phrase literally states, "into the place of the soul", which is cumbersome, but is quite in keeping with the style of the text. So Jesus has obtained a second, high spiritual influence which needs to become part of Mary's nature. Mary's consciousness has been raised into some high transcendent realm. So into the 'place' where she is, (where her soul is), Jesus brings about a second incorporation into Mary's soul of holy spiritual influences.

TEXT: CHAPTER 9
It came to pass, when Jesus had finished speaking these things to his disciples, that he again continued in his conversation, and said to them: "Behold, I have put on my garment, and all power has been given me by the First Mystery. Just a little while and then I will tell you the mystery of the All and the fullness of the All; I will conceal nothing from you from this hour, but in completeness will I perfect you in the entire fullness of the All (*lit. pleroma*), and in all completeness, and every Mystery.

These things are indeed the completeness of all completeness, the pleroma of all pleromas, and the gnosis of all gnoses: these all are in my garment (*that is, in his eternal "I"; or eternal spirit-body.*[39] I will tell you all Mysteries from the most external, cosmic realities to the innermost soul-spirit realities.[40] Hearken, I will tell you all things which have happened to me.

COMMENTARY: CHAPTER 9
The consciousness of the Jesus Christ, i.e., Jesus who

---

[39] In esoteric theosophical terms, terms, this eternal 'I' is the Buddhi quality together with the Atma.
[40] lit. from the exterior of the exteriors, to the interior of the interiors.

has merged with the cosmic Christ, now encompasses the entire cosmos.

TEXT: CHAPTER 10

It came to pass, when the sun had risen in the east, that a great ray of light descended, in this was my garment (*eternal spirit-body*), which I had left behind in the 24th Mystery, as I have said to you. And I found a Mystery in my garment, written in these five words which pertain to the Heights: "zama zama ozza rachama ozai", the meaning of which is:

"O Mystery which is outside of the world,[41] for whose sake the cosmos has arisen into being, this is the total Outgoing and the total Ascent. This has emanated all emanations and all that is therein, and for whose sake all Mysteries and all the realms have arisen.

Come here (Christ) to us, for we are parts of your own being ! We are all (*inwardly one*) with you; we are one and the same (being); that is, you are the First Mystery (God), which existed from the Beginning, in the Ineffable One, before it came forth; and all we (deities) are its name; (*i.e., we are the essence of its being*).

Therefore we all have come here, in order to encounter you at the last boundary; which is also the last Mystery from within; which itself is a portion of us. So therefore we have sent to you your garment (of light), which has belonged to you since the Beginning; which you left behind at the last boundary, which is also the last Mystery from within. (It was left at the last boundary) until its time was to be completed, according to the command of the First Mystery.

Behold ! Now its time *is* completed: put on the garment (of light). Come to us, for we all draw near to you[42], to clothe you with the First Mystery, and all his glory - and this we do by his command, in that the First Mystery has given it to us. It consists indeed of two garments (of light), in addition to the one which

---

[41] Coptic uncertain; possibly, 'outside – in the world'.
[42] Coptic uncertain; possibly 'we all wait for you'.

TEXT: CHAPTER 10 (cont.)
we have (already) sent to you (*his current soul-spirit 'body'*); for you are of higher rank than us, for you existed before us. That is, in the first light-garment is all the glory of all the names of all the Mysteries, together with all the emanations of the orderings of the realms of the Ineffable One.

TEXT NOTE: in Chapter 10
(Chapter 10 continues on; it provides a detailed listing of the many deities and spiritual influences of the spirit realms, which make up this second light-garment. But it is much easier to have an over-view of all the entities involved if they are each listed separately, as I have done here, rather than packed into a dense block of words.

The extensive list is in effect, a description of the various realms and the major spiritual beings in the cosmos. Many of these have yet to be mentioned in the text; when they are introduced and their role indicated, they will be discussed in the Commentary. The message here is, that in the higher spirit-body (or light-garment) of the Saviour, as vessel of the Christ, all of the following are contained:)

TEXT: CHAPTER 10 (cont.)
And in this (second) garment which we have just sent to you, are all the glory of all the names of all the Mysteries with all the emanations: those which are in the sequences of the two realms of the First Mystery.
And in this garment which we have sent forth to you, are:
* the entire glory of the Name of the Mystery of the Revealer (which is the First Command),
* the Mystery of the 5 Impressions
* the Mystery of the great Envoy of the Ineffable, who is (also) 'the Great Light'
* the Mystery of the 5 Leaders, who are (also) the 5 Helpers.
* the glory of the name of the Mysteries of all

TEXT: CHAPTER 10 (cont.)
sequences[43] of the emanations of the Treasury of Light, and of their Saviours
* the Mystery of the sequences of the sequences, who are (also): the 7 Amens
    the 7 Voices
    the 5 Trees
    the 3 Amens
and the Twin-Saviour who is the Child of the Child
and the Mystery of the nine Guardians of the three Portals of the Treasury of Light
Furthermore, there is also in this light-garment:
    the entire glory of the name of all those who are on the Right
    and those who are in the Midst
and the entire glory of the name of the great Invisible, who is the 'great Fore-father',
and the Mystery of the three Triple-Powers, including the Mysteries of their entire realm and of their Invisibles
and the Mystery of all those in the 13th Aion
and the name of the 12 Aions, including all their Rulers and their Archangels and their Angels,
and all those (other entities) who are in the 12 Aions
and the entire Mystery of the name of all who are in Heimarmene[44]
and in the Heavens (*the astral realms*)
and the entire Mystery of the name of all those who are in the Sphere as well as its firmaments:
thus indeed all who are in these, and in all: the various realms (*of the cosmos*).

Behold, we have sent to you this light-garment, which no deity from the First Command downwards was acquainted with, for the glory of its light was concealed within itself, and the Spheres and all realms from the first Command downwards[45], have

---

[43] "sequences": this means something like 'orderings'.
[44] "Heimarmene": lower Devachan, see Introduction.

[45] "the first Command downwards": this phrase is omitted by Horner, presumably in error.

TEXT: CHAPTER 10 (cont.)

not known it. So make haste therefore, clothe yourself with this light-garment, and come to us forever, for we are approaching you, so that you clothe yourself, at the command of the First Mystery, with the two light-garments {which have existed from the Beginning, with the First Mystery}[46]; these have been there for you (to put on) once the time appointed by the Ineffable One was fulfilled. Behold, the time is completed.

Therefore come quickly to us, that we may put them on you, until you have accomplished the complete ministering service of the First Mystery, in its full extent; the ministering service appointed for you by the Ineffable One.

Therefore come quickly to us, in order that we may clothe you, according to the command of the First Mystery; but still a little while, a very little while, then you shall come to us, and shall leave the world. Therefore come quickly, that you may receive the whole glory, the glory of the First Mystery.

COMMENTARY: CHAPTER 10

Jesus 'translates' the cryptic words; that is, he reveals the full implications of the five-word spiritual meditation script. His explanation consists of speaking 'unspoken' words to him, coming from a group of high divine beings; i.e., silently 'intoned' to him. These beings are in effect declaring that: the new light-garment (or high spirit-body) of Jesus Christ is the entire spiritual cosmos:

"O Mystery which is without in the world, for whose sake the cosmos has arisen into being: this is the total Outgoing and the total Ascent": This means the entire manifestation outwardly of the Divine into various realms, and the entire, later ascending of these back up to the highest divine state.

"...parts of your own being": i.e., we are your

---

[46] Horner notes that the words enclosed in { } brackets were added by the scribe in the upper margin; they appear to be genuine, being accidentally omitted by the scribe at first.

COMMENTARY: CHAPTER 10 (cont.)
companion-parts or fellow-members.[47]

"the essence of its being": literally, "whose name are we all": the word 'name' in Biblical Greek meant the core nature, the essence of, something.

"for you are of higher rank than us, for you existed before us": Two problems here:

"of higher rank than us": but the text is ambiguous here. It can also mean, "are prior to us" in terms of when one is created.

"existed before us"; the actual Coptic text is, "exist before us", but it is difficult to see any meaning in this, unless the past tense 'existed' is meant. I assume that this is the case and that there is a scribal error here, (MacDermot and Horner have also concluded this to be the case, but not Schmidt, nor Mead.)

We now learn that the dual garment of Jesus is the spiritual might of the deity called 'the First Mystery'; who is not clearly identified, but as noted earlier, is the Father-God, and may take on the likeness of a dove. It is however difficult to precisely define what entity is meant.

So, in the first light-garment is the entire glory of all the names of all the Mysteries and all emanations of the Orders of the regions of the Ineffable One: 'Names' means the core essence of something.

In the second light-garment is the entire glory of the name of all the Mysteries and of all emanations which are in the two realms of the First Mystery.

"You are the First Mystery": the 'You' here is really the cosmic Christ within Jesus, since the risen Saviour is the unique 'God-man' who arose through the union of the divine, 'unfallen' Jesus with the cosmic Christ.

This union was brought about through the Resurrection; Jesus united with the deity known in esoteric Christian knowledge as the 'cosmic Christ'.

Jesus then became the bearer of the Christ; so the very high, transcendent-cosmic qualities of 'Jesus' as implied in the Pistis Sophia, refer to the cosmic Christ

---

[47] "fellow-members": in German 'Gliedergenossen'.

COMMENTARY: CHAPTER 10 (cont.)
aspect of his nature.

The powerful message of this chapter is that all of the spirit realities of the cosmos are present in, or reflected in Jesus, (as bearer of the Christ); his consciousness encompasses all of these realms.

TEXT: CHAPTER 11
It therefore happened, when I saw the full Mystery of those words in the garment which had been sent to me, that I at once clothed myself with it. I became exceedingly radiant, and soared into the Heights. I drew near to the portal of the Firmament, shining exceedingly; there was no measure to the light which was upon me.

The portals of the firmament shook at my approach and opened at the same time. And all the (malignant) Rulers, Authorities and Angels were thrown into confusion because of the great radiance which was upon me.

(**Text Note**: These fallen spirits will at times be referred to as 'ahrimanic-luciferic' spirits.)

And they gazed at the radiant light-garment with which I was clothed, and they saw the Mystery which exceeded their names *(i.e., their core natures)*, and they were very afraid.

All their bonds were loosened, and each entity left their appointed sphere. They fell down before me, and made obeisance to me, saying, "How has the Lord of the Cosmos passed through us, without our knowing? They all intoned praises together to the innermost soul-spirit reality of the cosmos (*lit. to the interior of the interiors*); but me they did not see, they saw only the Light. They were in great fear, and were exceedingly troubled, and intoned praises to the interior of the interiors.

COMMENTARY: CHAPTER 11
It can be confusing that the Saviour is journeying through the spiritual realms and these are full of evil

COMMENTARY: CHAPTER 11
spirits, and yet suddenly in the next section, the Christ, through Jesus, reports on the reception he received from divine hierarchical spirits. This gives the impression that the same spirit realms of the cosmos are populated by a mixture of evil and divine spirits.

The situation here is that the spiritual realms, mainly the planetary spheres, consist of two or more parts. On the astral level and also on the Devachanic level, there are both good realms and evil realms. But these are totally separated from each other; since both are in the planetary spheres, in terms of a spatially oriented, physical world this seems impossible. But distance on the spiritual levels of the cosmos, is an inner reality, not a spatial feature, as such.

"the Mystery (*i.e., spiritual realities*) which exceeded their names": here 'names' signifies the core nature of their own being.

TEXT: CHAPTER 12
And having left that realm behind me, I ascended, shining exceedingly, to the first Sphere: I shone far more brightly than in the firmament; 49 times more brightly. It came to pass, therefore, when I had come to the portal of the first Sphere, that its portals were shaken, and immediately opened of themselves, all together.

I entered into the dwellings of that sphere, shining exceedingly; there was no measure for the light that was in me. And all the (*ahrimanic-luciferic*) Rulers, together with all those who were in that Sphere, were in confusion one with another; they saw the great light that was in me, and they gazed upon my garment; they saw in it the Mystery of their name, and were more and more distressed. And they were in great fear, saying, "How has the Lord of the Cosmos passed through us, without our knowing?"

TEXT: CHAPTER 12 (cont.)

All their bonds were loosened, and each entity left their appointed spheres and their orderings. They fell down and made obeisance before me, that is, actually before my (soul-)garment.[48] They all intoned praises together to the interior of the interiors; they were in great fear, and were exceedingly troubled.

COMMENTARY: CHAPTER 12

The anguish and fear in the malignant spirits, as they become aware of Jesus Christ is emphasized.

"made obeisance to", this traditional religious expression means to respectfully greet and show submissiveness towards a higher, more powerful entity. These malignant spirits did not, nor could not, 'worship' or 'adore' the cosmic Christ reality within and enveloping Jesus, as other translations suggest.

TEXT: CHAPTER 13

And having left that realm behind me, I came to the portal of the second sphere, which is Heimarmene (*lower Devachan*); all its portals were thrown into confusion and opened one after the other.[49] And I entered into the habitations of Heimarmene (*i.e., lower Devachan*), shining exceedingly; there was no measure for the light that was in me, for I shone in this realm 49 times more brightly than in the Sphere.

And all the (malignant) Rulers and all those who were in Heimarmene (*lower Devachan*) were thrown into confusion, and fell upon one another, and were in great fear, on seeing the intense light that was around me. And they gazed upon my garment of light

---

[48] "actually my garment": usu. 'or my garment'; which is unlikely. I interpret Coptic 'H' (= Grk. ἤ) not as 'or' but as an affirmative particle, which means e.g., 'indeed'.

[49] "one after the after" as Till interprets; the Coptic is ambiguous: possibly 'opened of themselves' as per Schmidt/MacDermot.

TEXT: CHAPTER 13 (cont.)
and saw the Mystery of their name on my garment and became even more agitated. They were in great fear, saying, "How has the Lord of the Cosmos passed through us, without our knowing?"

All the bonds of their realms and of their orderings of their houses were loosened. They together approached me, and fell down and made obeisance to me. They all sang praises together to the interior of the interiors (*i.e., the innermost soul-spirit reality of the cosmos*). They were in great fear, and were exceedingly troubled.

COMMENTARY: CHAPTER 13
Rudolf Steiner calls this "the most important chapter"; but it appears that this not an absolute statement, for the later chapters have equally important contents. It is however, the most important in the initial sense, in that it reveals the Post-Resurrection ascent of the Saviour into Devachan.
"Mystery of their name": the dynamic spiritual reality behind their name (the core of their nature).

Text Note: for Chapter 14
(These 'great' Aions are those in the Buddhi realm, which is above Devachan; but here they are the debased counterparts to the divine realms of the Buddhi level of the cosmos.)

TEXT: CHAPTER 14
Having left that realm, I ascended to the great Aions of the (malignant) Rulers. I drew near to their veils and their portals, shining exceedingly; there was no measure for the light which was in me. It happened when I came to these Aions,[50] that their veils and their portals were shaken one upon another. Their veils were drawn aside of their own accord, and their

---

[50] "these Aions": usu. 'the 12 Aions' as in the Coptic; but I conclude that '12' here is another scribal error. For the '12 Aions' otherwise only refers to the 7 astral and 5 lower Devachanic realms; see Commentary.

TEXT: CHAPTER 14 (cont.)

portals opened of themselves. And into these Aions I entered, immensely radiant; there was no measure for the light that was in me, which was brighter by 49 times than the light with which I shone in the regions of Heimarmene (*lower Devachan*).

And all the (*debased*) Angels of the Aions,[51] and their Archangels, their Rulers, their gods, their lords, their Authorities, Empowered Ones,[52] and their Powers, their Light-sparks, their Light-givers, their Unpaired, their Invisibles, their Forefathers, and their Triple-powers, saw me, shining so much that there was no measure for the light which was in me. They were thrown into confusion, the one upon the other; great fear fell upon them when they saw the great light that was around and in me. And their great confusion and great fear spread up to the realm of the great (debased) Invisible Forefather, and of the (debased) three Great Triple Powers.[53]

Because of the great fear in their confusion, the (*malignant*) Great Forefather himself and the Three Triple-Powers, began to move in confusion in their realm, for they could not close off all their realms because of the great fear in which they were. They threw all their Aions together into confusion, with all their spheres and orderings, for they were in fear and greatly troubled because of the intense light that was in me.

This light was different from what it was when I was on the Earth of humanity, for once my shining garment came upon me, the Earth could not have endured the light, such was it in its reality; the world would be destroyed and all upon it, at the same time. For the light which was in me in the great[54] Aions was 8,700 myriad times greater than it was when I was in

---

[51] A second scribe now takes over the writing of the text.

[52] lit. 'tyrants': meaning a neutral empowered deity.

[53] "great fear spread up to": Coptic ambiguous, it is possible, but very unlikely, that it means, these various entities themselves moved up to the higher deities.

[54] "great Aions": usu. 'the 12 Aions' but this is a scribal error (as in Ref.16).

the world among you.

COMMENTARY: CHAPTER 14
Since this realm is above Devachan, it is the Buddhi realm – but here it is the debased counterpart to this realm. The various entities mentioned here will be discussed when they are encountered later.

"the great Aions of the Rulers": the Aions here are of greater inherent spiritual power than those of Devachan.

"these Aions", not "the 12 Aions" although this phrase is in the Coptic text; but this has to be a scribal error, for the phrase "the 12 Aions" otherwise always refers to the 7 astral realms and the first 5 Devachanic levels; the karma-forming realms. Also, there is no indication in this codex, nor from Rudolf Steiner, that the Buddhi realm has 12 divisions.

"..their gods..": the reason for this word being used is unclear, as all the spirits referred to here are in effect, gods.

"could not close all their realms": this implies that these entities wished to seal off their regions against this unknown, very radiant deity, but could not.

"empowered Ones": the Greek word used (tyrannoi - τύραννοι), meant an empowered king, whether a despot, or simply an empowered person.

"myriad times": a myriad is 10,000 in ancient Greek; which in effect means a vast number of times, since 1,000 already means a great number, beyond the specific number 1,000 itself.

TEXT: CHAPTER 15
It then happened when all those who are in the great[55] Aions had seen the powerful light that was in me, that they were all thrown into confusion, one upon the other, and moved back and forth within the Aions. And all the Aions, with all their realms and all their orderings were shaken, on account of the great fear which came upon them, because they did not

---

[55] Again the Coptic text here has 'the 12 Aions', which appears to be a scribal error.

TEXT: CHAPTER 15 (cont.)

understand the Mystery which had taken place.

And Adamas, the (debased) powerful, despotic deity, and all such despotic deities which are in all the (debased) Aions, began to fight in vain against the Light, and they knew not against what they fought, for they saw nothing beyond the exceeding great light. It happened, when they fought against the light, that they expended their strength one against the other; they inwardly collapsed (*lit. fell down*) in the Aions. They became as the Earth-dwellers, who are (*spiritually*) dead, and who have no spirit in them.

And I took from all of them a third of their power, in order that they should no longer prevail in their evil activities, and also for the purpose that if people who are in the world should invoke them in their Mysteries, they would not accomplish their intentions. Their Mysteries are those which the transgressing angels brought down from above – that is to say, their magic rites – which may be invoked in evil practices.

And as for the karma-determining influences and the spheres over which these rule, I have changed (*or turned*) these; I brought it about that they spend six months turned to the left, and that they also face to the right and carry out their influences. For by order of the First Command and of the First Mystery, Jeu, the Overseer of the Light, had set them always facing to the left, accomplishing their influences and their deeds.

COMMENTARY: CHAPTER 15

"Jeu" or "Ieou": this is a very high deity from 'The Right' (the first Buddhi realm), who will be discussed when his role is mentioned later.

Adamas: this 'empowered deity' (i.e., a 'tyrant') is a very major opponent of the soul and thus of Christ.

TEXT: CHAPTER 16

It happened when I came to their realm, that they mutinied, and fought against the Light. I took away a third of their power, so that they would not be able to

TEXT: CHAPTER 16 (cont.)

accomplish their evil actions. Also I have changed the karma-determining influences (*lit. Heimarmene*) and the spheres over which these rule. I set them facing towards the left for six months, accomplishing their influences; and I have set them turned towards the right for another six months, accomplishing their influences.

COMMENTARY: CHAPTER 16

This 'turning' of the influence from left to right is a major theme of the next five chapters, but what this means is not explained.

TEXT: CHAPTER 17

Jesus then declares, "Who has ears to hear, let him hear." It happened, when Mariam had heard the Saviour say these words (*of chapts.15-16*), that she gazed into the firmament for an hour and then spoke; "My Lord, command me to speak openly." Jesus, the compassionate answered, "Speak freely Mariam, you blessed one, whom I shall initiate[56] into all the Mysteries of the Heights; you, whose heart is more directed towards the heavenly realm than all of your brothers."

COMMENTARY: CHAPTER 17

"Mariam": the woman is simply called 'Mariam' (or Mary); it is unclear whether a 'Mary' is Mary the Magdalene or Mary of Bethany, the sister of Lazaros-John, or Mary of Clopas (the sister of the Virgin Mary). It is also possible that all three of these women are at times involved, in different chapters. From now on, any 'Mary' other than the mother of Jesus, shall be called 'Mariam" to avoid confusion with the

---

[56] "initiate": usu. 'complete', but the verb here (ⲭⲱⲕ) is derived from the Greek 'teleoe' (τελέω) which means not only 'to complete', but also 'to initiate'.

mother of Jesus, and with his aunt, Mary of Clopas.

TEXT: CHAPTER 18
TEXT NOTE:
Mariam then identifies the sorcerers Jesus referred to, in Chapters 15 -17; those who carry out evil occult actions, influenced by the fallen spirits. But although these are described in other translations as 'consulters and astrologers', this is not an accurate understanding of the text.

Astrology versus Fate-prediction (chapters 18-22)
A careful reading of these chapters reveals that there is actually no condemnation of astrologers by Jesus in these chapters. Likewise in the Bible, there is no condemnation of astrologers – even though one can find biblical verses which apparently severely condemn 'astrologers' (in Isaiah, chapters 47, and Daniel, chapters 2,4 and 5).

The translation of these biblical verses, and of these references in Pistis Sophia, as referring to 'astrologers' or 'horoscope-casters' is incorrect. It is clear from the context that these texts are referring to 'Fate-diviners' (a practice which has survived in popular culture as 'Fortune-tellers'). These texts are not referring to the drawing up and interpreting of a natal horoscope, in order to give invaluable self-knowledge to someone about their psychology; which is what 'astrology' means to people today.

The 'astrology' referred in the Bible and in Pistis Sophia is in reality a psychic-prophetic forecasting, which has some resemblance to 'horary astrology'. This unusual branch of astrology is said to be capable of predicting someone's fate, or finding a lost object. But the great majority of astrological work is centred on the interpretation of a natal horoscope. The earliest horoscope in the true sense, that is a natal horoscope, dates from 410 BCE; whereas the prophet Isaiah was writing about 700 BCE, and Daniel about 530 BCE.

So the biblical texts are referring to divinatory,

TEXT NOTE: in Chapter 18 (cont.)
predictive magic, not to the interpreting of natal horoscopes. So too are Jesus and Mariam in the Pistis Sophia, as the context of their words makes clear. After Miriam has repeated what Jesus declared earlier, which forms the bulk of Chapter 18, she explains that his revelation was foreseen by Isaiah.

TEXT: CHAPTER 18   Mariam speaks

Mariam spoke to the Redeemer, "My Lord, you said these words to us, "Who has ears to hear, let him hear" so that we may understand what you said to us (*in chapters 15/16*).[57] Hear me, my Lord, that I may speak openly. The words you spoke, "I have taken away a third of the might of the (fallen) Rulers of all the (debased) Aions, and have changed their cosmic influences and the sphere over which they rule"; (this means), if the human race were to invoke them, in the Mysteries which the transgressing angels taught them for the accomplishing of their evil and despicable deeds, from the occult forces of their magic – that then, in order that they may no longer accomplish their unholy works from this hour, you have taken from them their power.

This you have done to their consulters and 'fate-diviners', (a*nd those who inform the people of the world of all that shall come to pass*), so that they should no longer, from this hour, know how to proclaim to people what shall be happening. For you have changed their spheres; you have made them turn to the left for six months, accomplishing their influences, and you have made them face to the right then, accomplishing their influences, for the six remaining months.

Lord, concerning this word, the spirit being that was in Isaiah the prophet, had spoken of this as follows, proclaiming long ago, in a spiritual parable

---

[57] Horner interprets the Coptic to mean that this is a understood by Mariam to be a question, "...are you saying that we should (strive to) understand what you have said?

TEXT: CHAPTER 18 (cont.)　　　　**Mariam speaks**
about 'The Vision about the Egyptians', saying:

"Where then, O Egypt, where are your consulters and fate-diviners, and those who cry out (*i.e., make sibylline-like oracular utterances*) from the earth, and those who cry out from their abdominal centre (*i.e., the solar plexus*). Let these people declare to you from now on the deeds which the Lord Sabaoth will do."

Thus did the spiritual being which was in Isaiah, the prophet, prophesy before your coming; it prophesied concerning you, that you will take away the strength of the (debased) Rulers of the Aions; that you would change the karma-determining cosmic influences and the spheres over which these rule (*lit. the Fate and the Sphere*), in order that they might know nothing from henceforth.

This is why it was said, "You shall know nothing of that which the Lord Sabaoth shall do"; that is to say, none of the Rulers shall know what you will do to them henceforth from this hour. That is to say, with Egypt, (*which symbolized ungodliness to the Israelites*). For these Rulers are meant by 'Egypt', because they are of dense, debased, (astral) matter. Concerning this, the spiritual being which is in Isaiah, once prophesized about you, saying; "You (debased) Rulers will not know from now on, what the Lord Sabaoth shall do."　　　　**Mariam speaks**

The light-being which you, Lord, received from the hand of Sabaoth the Good, who is in the realm of The Right, that is, the power which is in your denser (soul) body to-day; it is this light-being, Jesus, my Lord, which is the reason that you have said to us, "He that has ears to hear, let him hear", so that you would know whose heart is earnestly set on the Kingdom of the Heavens.

COMMENTARY: CHAPTER 18

"Sabaoth": a leading deity in The Right, the first level of the Buddhi realm. Since Buddhi is connected with the divine archetype of ether energies, one concludes that Jesus received an immensely high, untainted life-force from here.

COMMENTARY: CHAPTER 18 (cont.)

'Solar plexus': These words become clearer through the teachings of Rudolf Steiner, who explains that an unreliable, partly unwholesome form of psychic-clairvoyant consciousness was common in earlier Ages, and was a faculty which Christ needed to close down.

This consciousness could arise through the solar plexus, which has extensive etheric energies raying forth from it. But as Steiner indicates, it also could arise through people who have an extended etheric body in the feet area; causing contact with earth-derived sprites who do bring about some clairvoyance.

"Vision of Egypt": Some words Isaiah had apparently spoken about Egypt, and preserved in a document which is now lost; for these words are not in the *Book of Isaiah*. They occur again in Chapter 23, where this theme is commented on further.

"denser (soul) body": Mariam ends her speech with the following words, in which one word ('hulikos') is translated in all other versions, as 'material body': I disagree with this interpretation. For speaking to the disciples here is the 'Risen Lord': i.e., Jesus Christ, who has no 'material' (flesh) body.

As noted in the Introduction, the risen Jesus exists in a soul and spirit state, supremely radiant; he does not have a material, flesh body. So the 'hulikos' here refers to a denser soul-body, not to a flesh body; it is called denser because it is a coarser 'body' than the sublime 'spirit-body' (or devachanic aura).

As regards the related topic of his 'resurrection body', according to Rudolf Steiner, Jesus can, for the purposes of becoming perceptible to his disciples, acquire an etheric body temporarily, whenever this is needed.[58]

Thus the risen Jesus, as seen by the disciples, was not in a material body, but would have been in an etheric body, which was made denser, so that the disciples could perceive him.

---

[58] He taught that this is still the case today.

COMMENTARY: CHAPTER 18 (cont.)
But by this chapter, it appears from Mariam's words, that the disciples had seership (or 'astral clairvoyance'), and could perceive their Lord in his soul-body. Moreover, as noted in an earlier chapter, this soul-body was changed into a weaker manifestation of Jesus' actual radiantly glorious soul-body, because the disciples could not tolerate the sheer brilliance of his aura (or astral-body).

So here the soul-body of Jesus becomes a 'hulikos'; meaning either it is a denser and less radiant version of his actual soul-body, or it is the soul-body as such, but not his supremely radiant spirit-aura; in any event, it is not a material body. See the Introduction where the word 'hyle' and 'hulikos' in Hellenistic literature are shown to have several meanings, including a denser state of being of anything, including the soul-body, not only matter.

TEXT: CHAPTER 19
Then, when Mariam had finished saying these things, Jesus said to her: "Well said, Mariam, you are blessed before all women who are on the Earth; for you shall become the fullness of all fullnesses, and the perfection of all perfections." When Mariam heard the Saviour speak these words, she rejoiced greatly and came to Jesus and bowed down before him and worshipped (at) his feet, then spoke to him, saying, "Lord, hear me, that I may question you in regard to these words, before you speak with us about the realms to which you ascended.

And Jesus answered and said to Mariam: "Speak freely, and fear not. All things which you seek, I will reveal to you."

COMMENTARY: CHAPTER 19
"blessed before all women": although this phrase later became a set expression for the "Blessed Virgin Mary", the text does not specify that it was Jesus' mother. So possibly the 'Mary' here is Mary of

COMMENTARY: CHAPTER 19 (cont.)
Bethany or the Magdalene. Some of the original words of this Coptic text (not the actual codex) no doubt pre-dates such traditional phrases used for the mother of Jesus.

"the fullness of all fullnesses, and the perfection of all perfections": these words today have lost their original meaning, but imply that this Mariam shall attain to a very high spirituality.

TEXT: CHAPTER 20   Mariam speaks

Mariam spoke: "My Lord, concerning all those people who know the Mystery (*i.e., the psychic influences*) of that which the transgressing fallen Angels have taught them when they invoke them in their evil magic rites. That is, the magic which they would perform, in order to make a barrier to goodness (*lit. 'to hinder good deeds'*) - will they henceforth accomplish this, from this hour, or not ?

Jesus answered and spoke to Mariam, "They shall not accomplish this as they have been accomplishing this from the beginning, because I have taken away a third of their power. But they will access (*magic powers*) from those who know the Mysteries of the magic of the 13th Aion[59] if they do invoke the Mysteries of the magic of the 13th Aion.

So if they invoke these Mysteries, then they will indeed accomplish capably their intentions, because I have not weakened the power of that realm, in accordance with the command of the First Mystery."

COMMENTARY: CHAPTER 20
Mariam is asking Jesus whether magicians who seek to undertake evil forms of spiritual activity, acting on the influence of fallen (evil) Angels, will succeed if they seek to obtain, by their own endeavours, occult powers from entities in the debased 13th Aion (the sixth Devachanic realm).

---

[59] "13th": MacDermot here has '3rd': a typing error.

COMMENTARY: CHAPTER 20 (cont.)

As noted in the Introduction, Rudolf Steiner taught that the sixth devachanic realm is the second highest level of Higher Devachan, and is attained only by a very high state of consciousness; it is a sublime transcendent realm. So this raises the question, how would an evil magician gain access to this realm? And secondly, how could such a debased soul use such sublime powers for evil?

The answer appears to be that the malignant, debased counterpart of the sixth devachanic realm is meant here. This potent statement from Jesus reveals that the possibility of a debased soul becoming committed to a dreadful level of evil, remains a reality; there is a kind of freedom of choice left available here.

TEXT: CHAPTER 21

But then, when Jesus had finished saying these words, Mariam further enquired, saying, "My Lord, surely the consulters and Fate-predictors will no more reveal to people what will be happening, from this hour henceforth? But Jesus answered, saying, "If the Fate-predictors find the cosmic influences and (*the spirits in*) their spheres[60] turned towards the left, as they were originally oriented, then the (*predictive*) words (*of the entities there*) shall come to pass; they shall declare (*accurately*) what is to occur.

But if such people encounter these cosmic realms turned towards the right, then (*the spirits within*) these realms can say nothing true. This is because I have changed their influences; that is,[61] their squares, their triangles, and their eight-figures[62]. For their

---

[60] Literally: "the Heimarmene or Sphere"; this is an abbreviated expression for the elemental-astral influences active from within Devachan (Heimarmene/Fate) or from an astral realm (Sphere).

[61] Literally: 'and' their squares, etc., but 'thus' is actually meant. For in Greek, 'kai', means 'and' or 'and so', 'namely', etc.

[62] "eight-figures: either octagons or lemniscatory forms.

TEXT: CHAPTER 21 (cont.)

influences were, since the beginning, turned continuously towards the left, and thus their squares, their triangles, and their eight-figures.

But now I have made them spend six months turned to the left(-side paths), and six months turned to their right(-side paths). And whoever seeks their predictive calculations from that time on, when I changed them, in that they are so configured that they spend six months gazing towards the left side and then six months gazing to their right side – whoever then will observe them, shall accurately know their influences and be able to announce everything which they shall do.

In a similar way, the consulters – if they invoke the names of the Rulers and come upon them facing the left – will be able to report to people with accuracy all things which they, on the behalf of these people (*their clients*), shall ask the (*spirits of the*) decans. But on the contrary, if the consulters invoke their names when they are turned to the right, then these entities shall not pay attention to them, because they are gazing out from (within) a different (*astral-*)form, as compared with their earlier condition, in which (*the great deity*) Jeu had established them. This is all the more the case, because their names (*their inner spirit*) are different when they are turned to the left, as to when they are turned to the right.

And if the consulters invoke them when these entities are turned to the right, they will not tell the truth, instead the consulters will be confused in great confusion, and will find themselves in great delusion, and become threatened by the Rulers. Then those who do not know the path, when they are turned to the right, together with their triangles, squares and all their figures, will find nothing true, but will be confounded in great confusion, and (thus) err with major errors.

Because I have now changed the work which they earlier performed in their squares, when turned to the left; and in their triangles and in their eight-sided figures (*sigils?*) in which they were continuously

81

TEXT: CHAPTER 21 (cont.)
busied, when they were turned to the left.

Also I have made them spend six months forming all their patterned sequences (of influences) whilst turned to the right; this I did, so that they would be confounded in the entire scope of their activity. Furthermore, I have made them spend six months turned to the left, and accomplishing the effects of their influences and all of their figures (sigils?),[63] so that the (*debased*) Rulers who are in the Aions and their associated spheres, and in the Heavens and in all their associated regions, would be confused in confusion, so that they may not understand their own pathways.

COMMENTARY: CHAPTER 21
Jesus' answer to Mariam's question about the Fate-predictors and consulters from now on still able to succeed in forecasting the future, is a detailed, long reply, showing that this topic is of huge importance. It is in chapter 23 that we discover that this topic is actually about sinister evil magic, and decision of malignant deities to control the future of humanity.

TEXT: CHAPTER 22
It happened, when Jesus had said these words that Philip was seated, writing all the words that Jesus spoke. So it happened after this, that Philip drew near, bowed down, and worshipped at the feet of Jesus, saying: "Lord and Saviour, grant me permission to speak before you and to question you about these words, before you tell us of the realms you went to, for your ministry." **Philip speaks**

The compassionate Saviour answered and said to Philip, "Permission is given to you to speak." Philip responded and said, "My Lord, on account of what

---

[63] "Sigils": the Greek word here has many meanings incl. figure/shape/gestures/postures/geometrical designs. Here the tracing out in astral light, of magic signs or patterns, by spirit entities is surely meant.

spiritual dynamics (*lit. Mystery*) have you changed the bond linking the Rulers and Aions, and their karma-determining cosmic influences and associated spirits, with all their realms. Thereby confounding them in their confusion, and erring as to their pathways? You have done this to them for the salvation of the world, did you not?"

COMMENTARY: CHAPTER 22

Here we encounter a major point in need of clarity, as noted earlier in this chapter. It is not viable, just because of 'Fate-predictors', for Jesus to find it imperative to bring about a potent change in the cosmic order of things, to prevent many souls from being severely harmed. The solution lies in Chapter 18. A careful reading of that chapter shows that there are three separate types of occultism or magic involved here:

A: evil people who are in effect 'black magicians', people who seek to be empowered through evil spirits, i.e., fallen Angels. These debased souls are dangerous to humanity.

B: Fate-predictors who draw up charts of the moment, to predict the immediate future.

C: the consulters, those who consult with the Fate-predictors, to draw out from them such forbidden knowledge.

Earlier it was noted that Mariam quotes words of Isaiah about this evil, and refers to it as 'Egypt'. A reason for this is indicated in the work of Rudolf Steiner, who taught that it was late in Egyptian history that black magic began to be practised in Egypt. So when in this Chapter 23, Jesus Christ refers to his work of countering unwholesome activity, he is really alluding to black magicians, not simply Fortune-telling.

TEXT: CHAPTER 23
TEXT NOTE:
(Here Jesus gives a reply to Philip which is actually about a different malignant outcome of the evil occultism referred to earlier (Fate-predictors and evil

TEXT NOTE: in Chapter 23 (cont.)
magicians). It is indicated that these evil persons could help the Rulers of the malignant Aions to harm creation and the perfecting of human souls (in life after life.

The Pistis Sophia codex is not an introductory text for the early esoteric Christians; therefore much in this codex is included without any explanation, since it was assumed that the acolytes in the initiatory school of early Christianity would have known this.

The contents of the next chapter assume as a given fact, without any explanation, that when human souls are descending down to a new incarnation, it is these malignant (ahrimanic-luciferic) Powers who have the task of coalescing the new astral body for that person.

This is startling and confronting to us today (and was not emphasized by Rudolf Steiner). But the thinking here is, because a human being is a 'fallen' being, lowly soul qualities will be included as part of their soul. However in the next four chapters, little is said about higher, truly spiritual qualities also being included in the new soul, making the above idea all the more confronting to the modern reader.)

TEXT: CHAPTER 23
Jesus answered and spoke to Philip, "I have changed their pathways for the salvation of all souls. Truly, truly, I say to you, if I had not changed their pathways, a large number of souls would have been disempowered, and thus spent a long time (*in a disempowered state*); (*this would have happened*) if the Rulers of the Aions and the Rulers of the karma-determining cosmic influences and their spirits (*lit. Fate and the Sphere*), and all their Heavens and all their Aions, had not been disempowered.[64]

---

[64] "disempowered": usu. 'dissolved'; but this meaning of the Coptic verb (ⲛⲉⲧⲛⲁⲟⲩⲁⲝⲁⲓ) here, makes no sense. However, the verb also means 'to settle', and 'make terms for', and it has other meanings, too (at the end of the

TEXT: CHAPTER 23 (cont.)

For human souls would have continued a long time here, outside (*i.e., outside of, or below, the divine spiritual worlds*), and hence the completion of the number of perfected souls would have been delayed. These are the souls whom shall be regarded (*by God, or the First Mystery*) as belonging in the Inheritance of the Heights, through the Mysteries, and who shall then be in the Treasury of Light (*i.e., 2nd region of the Buddhi realm*)[65].

Hence for this reason I have changed their pathway, so that they might be confused and yield up the spiritual forces which are in the denser (astral) substance[66] of their world. It is this 'substance' which they mould into human souls (*but some of which they are wanting to hold on to, and mould into counterfeit souls*). I changed their pathways so that those souls who shall be saved – they and all their inherent spirit energies might be quickly purified and ascend. And also, that those (counterfeit) souls who are not able to be saved, might be quickly destroyed.

COMMENTARY: CHAPTER 23

There are two crucial points, as noted in chapter 18.
A: "had not been disempowered": here in other translations, including that by Schmidt, there is a misunderstanding of a verb in this chapter. For the

---

chapter it means 'destroyed'). The same multi-nuanced quality applies to another Coptic verb for 'dissolve', (ϣⲱⲗ); it also means 'to loosen' or 'to paralyze'. So one can conclude that what is meant here is that these malignant entities throughout their realms, were weakened or disempowered; but not 'dissolved', because they continued to exist.

---

[65] Rudolf Steiner taught that this is 'the realm of the cosmic Christ', and is attained by those in Buddhism are called the Bodhisattvas; i.e. initiates who are one degree below Buddha-hood.
[66] "denser astral-substance": lit. 'hyle', see Introduction.

COMMENTARY: CHAPTER 23 (cont).

Rulers of the Aions of Heimarmene, as well as their spirit realms, are described as 'destroyed'. Yet soon the text again clearly refers to them as still existing; as indeed these realms must.

As noted in the foot-note, I conclude that the verb nuance here is 'to be disempowered', not destroyed nor annihilated, except in the last sentence of this Chapter.

"....that those souls who are not able to be saved, shall not be saved, might be quickly destroyed." With these remarkable words Chapter 23 ends. In essence we are told that the goal of the risen Saviour's activity was to cause the evil Powers (Archons) to release the core astral energies within the denser astral 'substance' which they have access to.

For these spirits wanted this core spirit (astral) reality to not just coalesce around souls preparing to incarnate, but to create 'counterfeit' human souls. Indeed the implication of the last sentence of Chapter 23 is that, it is this kind of 'counterfeit' souls who are to be destroyed, in contrast to the actual souls, who are to be purified and saved as quickly as possible. (See *Summary of Chapters*, after Chapter 27, for more about this complex topic.)

"Truly, truly": this is actually 'Amen, amen'; this is very rare, outside of the Gospel of John. As I noted in my *The Gospel of John*, although 'Amen' can be identified as a Hebrew word, meaning, 'so it is' or 'truly', it is also the name of that deity in ancient Egypt, associated with the creation of the world, whose name means, "what is hidden" or "what cannot be seen".

The god Amen – both his name (or inner essence), and his appearance – are described in Egyptian texts as "hidden to gods and to human beings"; he is also referred to as 'eternal'.[67] On one occasion in the *Bookof Revelation* (3:14) Jesus speaks of the 'intonings' of 'the Amen'.

So these words are said in order to affirm the

---

[67] See E.A. Wallis-Budge, *The Gods of the Egyptians*, Vol. 2.

validity and importance of the words Jesus or the Christ is about to declare; these two words invoke a divine being or divine 'being-ness'. According to Rudolf Steiner, 'Amen' also carries the affirmation that the truth he is about to speak is directly linked to the end-point of the purpose of creating humanity by God, in the first place, long Ages ago.[68]

TEXT: CHAPTER 24
Then, as Jesus finished saying these words to his disciples, Mariam, the gifted in speech and the blessed one, came before Jesus and fell at his feet and spoke, "My Lord, allow me to speak before you, and be not displeased with me, if I burden you often, in that I bring questions to you." The Saviour answered, full of compassion and said to Mariam "Speak as you wish to, and I shall openly reveal to you (*the answer you seek*)."
So Mariam responded, saying, "My Lord, in what way shall the souls have delayed themselves here outside, and in what form shall they be quickly purified?"

COMMENTARY: CHAPTER 24
(No commentary needed here.)

TEXT: CHAPTER 25
Jesus responded, and spoke to Mariam, "Excellent Mariam, you enquire well with this excellent question, indeed you bring light to everything with certainty and precision. I shall from now on, conceal nothing from you, but I will reveal everything to you with certainty and all openness.

Hear then, Mariam, and my disciples all; give ear to me. Before I made proclamation to all the Rulers of the Aions, to all the Rulers of the karma-determining cosmic influences and their spiritual realms (*lit. the Fate and the Sphere*), they were all bound in their set ways, in their spheres, and in their defined

---

[68] In GA 104, p. 94 and 104a, p. 51. He also mentions that it is of similar meaning as 'Aum' in esoteric Hinduism.

TEXT: CHAPTER 25 (cont.)

boundaries,[69] just as Jeu, the Overseer of the Light, had bound them from the beginning. Each of them remained in their ordering, and each of them went forth in his course, just as Jeu, the overseer of the light had established them.

Now, (*on each occasion*) when the time of the (*cosmic*) number of Melchizedek came, then he, the great Receiver of the Light, would come into the midst of the Aions and of all the Rulers of the karma-determining cosmic influences and their associated spiritual realms (*lit. the Fate and the Sphere*).

Then the light of all the (debased) Rulers of the Aions, and of all the Rulers of the karma-determining cosmic influences and their spiritual realms, was taken away from them (by him) – after he had purified it. Thus he took away that which stirred them (*into their malignant activity, from which they sought to have their own harvest of human beings who would be devoid of any spirit.*)

And also he set in motion 'the Hastener' who was placed over these entities (*in rank*) in order to make their circles turn more swiftly. Also he (*Melchizedek*) took away the spirit-power which was in them; the breath of their mouth, the tears of their eyes, and the sweat of their bodies, (*bodily features are used here metaphorically*). Thus Melchizedek, the Receiver of Light, purified all these energies, in order to carry their light (now cleansed) into the Treasury of Light.

But also (*a second dynamic emerged with the lower groups of these entities*); regarding all of these (*debased*) Rulers, the (*malignant*) Rulers of the karma-determining cosmic influences and their spiritual realms, and the Rulers of the spheres below the Aions (*presumably the etheric realms*) – their dense 'soul-substances' were gathered up by the serving-spirits of each of these Rulers.

---

[69] "defined boundaries": usu. 'seals', which may be correct, but seems less likely; the Greek term 'sfragides' (σφραγῖδες) also means 'specifically defined areas'.

TEXT: CHAPTER 25 (cont.)

From these dense soul-substances (*i.e., denser astral energies*) these serving-spirits then fashioned 'counterfeit' souls of humans, and also souls of livestock, of reptiles, animals and birds, and then sent this into the realm of (incarnate) humanity.

But consequently, the receivers of the Sun and the Receivers of the Moon also, having observed the heavens, and having seen the configurations of the paths of the Aions, and the configurations of the karma-determining cosmic influences and their spiritual realms, then took the spiritual power of the light away from these (*lowly*) serving-spirits.

So the receivers prepared to set this apart (*the accumulated amount of soul-substance or 'astrality'*), until they could hand it over to the receivers who serve Melchizedek, the Purifier of Light. But (in response) the serving-spirits then accessed and carried away the (accumulated) denser (astral-etheric) 'substances' into the sphere which is below the Aions, (*i.e., into the etheric-elemental realm*).

They did this so that they might (*still be able to*) make from this the souls of (*counterfeit*) humans and also make the souls of reptiles, or of cattle, or of livestock, or of birds, according to the cycle of the Rulers of this sphere (*etheric realm*[70]), and according to all the configurations of its revolving motions. This they did in order to cast them into this world of humanity, so that they might be souls in this realm, as I have just told you.

COMMENTARY: CHAPTER 25

Some remarkable revelations are made here. In essence, Chapter 25 is revealing that Melchizedek works to redeem the astral light which has been tainted by luciferic-ahrimanic entities; and to prevent these entities from using it for malignant purposes. (See the Introduction for a discussion about who is

---

[70] The realms of life-forces or ethers; it can also be thought of as realms of 'elemental' energies (and minor spirits).

COMMENTARY: CHAPTER 25 (cont.)

Melchizedek.) He then seeks to rescue this purified light and bring it up to the 2nd Buddhi realm, the Treasury of Light.

In the codex, such a task is the very core of the spiritual intentions of the gods: to redeem and preserve the spiritual light which had to become ensnared in the world of fallen humanity.

"serving-spirits fashioned counterfeit souls of humans and..." this chapter is conveying deep esoteric secrets. Chapters 23 to 27 are about a core principle in this codex: that there are the usual human souls who naturally have imperfections, and are reincarnated through involvement with the malignant Rulers. But divine deities are also involved in the process whereby human souls reincarnate; their higher qualities, the germinal Spiritual-self, is an integral part of the human soul-spirit, and as this is brought down into the planetary spheres, then the new soul-body is formed, in close connection with the spirit.

However there are also 'counterfeit' souls which are created by the malignant Rulers or Archons, and these souls have no divine element in them (see the *Summary of Chapter 23 - 27* for more about this). The spiritual energies of the luciferic-ahrimanic deities of the solar system, encompassing the astral realms and some of the Devachanic realms, are removed and purified. We have already encountered this same dynamic in chapter 23.

This purifying of the astral light was regularly done by Melchizedek over the Ages, but as a consequence, the serving-spirits of these Rulers took these denser astral energies (or 'substances'), and created souls of humans and animals – a striking statement. However, we are told that these new souls are put into the world of humanity; implying that human beings already existed, created by divine deities, and therefore these others are in a sense, 'counterfeit' humans.

TEXT: CHAPTER 26

These actions the (lowly) serving-spirits accomplished perseveringly, before their strength diminished and they became feeble, without energy, and powerless. So it happened that when they were weakened, when the light which was in their realm ceased, their realm was disempowered.[71] Then the All (*i.e., their entire machination and its power-base*) quickly disintegrated.[72]

It happened, whenever the time of the (*cosmic*) number of Melchizedek arrived, he – the great Receiver of the Light – would again come into the midst of their Aions, and of all the Rulers of the karma-determining cosmic influences and their spiritual realms.

He threw them into confusion, and caused their circles to be quickly abandoned; so then they were under pressure, and cast the spirit-power which was in them – the breath of their mouth, the tears of their eyes, and the sweat of their bodies, (*using bodily features metaphorically*) – out of themselves.

Then Melchizedek, the Receiver of Light, purified all these cast-out energies, as he regularly did, in order to carry their light (*now cleansed*) on into the Treasury of Light. (From this regular occurrence) the malignant Rulers began to perceive that this happened whenever Melchizedek became present amongst them.[73]

Therefore, the (malignant) Rulers of the (debased) Aions and the Rulers of the karma-determining cosmic influences and their spiritual realms, turned

---

[71] "disempowered"; again the verb which can mean dissolved or destroyed, but also disempowered.

[72] "kingdom disintegrated": usu. 'the universe was raised up'/carried up' (*ceased to exist*). But the next line continues the narrative, with the cosmos still present and intact. So the 'universe' or 'all', in Coptic – ⲧⲉⲣⲟ – is not 'the cosmos'; just 'the all', a general term which here refers back to all of the domination-structure belonging to the malignant Archons (spirits).

[73] This sentence I have placed down here, instead of leaving it half a page earlier, to clarify the meaning of the page.

TEXT: CHAPTER 26 (cont.)

(their attention) towards their dross, that is, their dense (astral) 'substances', and did not release this, so that it became (*valid*) souls in the (earthly) world.

Instead they absorbed their denser (astral) substances, in order that they themselves might not become powerless and without energy; so that their energies would not cease to be in them, and thus their kingdom might not be disempowered.

Hence they absorbed this, in order that they may not be disempowered, but that they might linger, and cause a long delay to the completion of the number of perfected souls, who shall dwell in the Treasury of Light.

COMMENTARY: CHAPTER 26

We learn that the efforts of Melchizedek were being resisted by the malignant spirits. They had begun to release what was lowest in their fallen astral-etheric natures; and that this became a target of Melchizedek's efforts. Hence in more recent times, they retained these lowest energies, in an effort to have the strength within themselves to resist Melchizedek. (But see the *Summary of the Chapters 23-27*, below.)

TEXT: CHAPTER 27

It came to pass, therefore, that the Rulers of the Aions, and the Rulers of the karma-determining cosmic influences and their spiritual realms, persevered in doing this activity; turning upon themselves, that is, absorbing (no longer casting out) their dross, i.e., their denser (*astral*) substances.[74]

This was done to prevent the birth of (valid) souls into the world of humanity, in order that these (debased) Rulers might retain their might for a longer

---

[74] "absorbing their dross, i.e., their denser (astral) substances". This is literally "absorbing the dross of their denser (astral) substances", but this translation can give the wrong impression of there being two lower substances.

TEXT: CHAPTER 27 (cont.)

period. But it was done also with the intention that those spiritual forces, which in the Rulers are entities – that is, these (*potential*) souls – might be excluded for a long time from this world (of earthly humanity).

They continued to do this persistently for two (*cosmic*) cycles; therefore it came to pass, when I (Christ) went forth to accomplish the ministry to which I had been called by command of the First Mystery, that I passed through the midst of the empowered Ones of the Rulers of the (debased) 12 Aions.

My garment of light was around me, very radiant; there was no measure for the light which was in me. It then happened, when those empowered Ones saw the great light which was in me, the great Adamas,[75] the empowered One[76], and all the (debased) empowered Ones of the 12 Aions together fought against the light of my garment, to keep it with them, in order to remain the longer in their realm.

This action they did, not knowing then against whom they fought. So it happened, when these empowered Ones had seen the great Light which was in me, that Adamas, the great empowered One, and all the (debased) empowered Ones of the 12 Aions, all began to fight against the Light of my garment, seeking to keep it with them.

This they did, not knowing against whom they were fighting. After they had rebelled, and fought against the Light, I then, by command of the First Mystery, changed the pathways and courses of their Aions, and of these karma-determining cosmic influences and their spiritual realms.

I caused them to face their triangles for six months to the left, and to their squares, and those (forms) facing them,[77] and also their eight-sided forms (*sigils?*), as they formerly were. But their way of

---

[75] The name 'Adamas' is not explained; see later Commentary.

[76] Lit. 'tyrant': meaning an empowered ruler, but here a despotic malignant ruler.

[77] Coptic obscure: Schmidt and Till have 'facing them'.

TEXT: CHAPTER 27 (cont)
rotating, and their manner of appearing, I changed to different sequencing, and caused them, for the other six months, to face the actions of their influences on the right; those of their squares, their triangles, and those facing them, and also their eight-sided forms.

And I caused them to be in great confusion, and to wander in great error, these Rulers of the Aions, and all the Rulers of the karma-determining cosmic influences and their spiritual realms; so I greatly distressed them.

So, from that hour, they have not had the strength to turn towards their dross, i.e., their denser (astral) substance, in order to absorb it, so that their realms would endure permanently, and hence they could still be ruling for a long time.

But when I had taken away the third part of their power, I also changed the movement of their spheres, so that for a time they faced the left, and for another time that faced the right. I changed the whole of their pathway and all of their course, and I arranged that the path of their course be hastened, so that they might be quickly purified, and they might speedily rise.

And I shortened their cycles, and I caused their path to be easier, so they were greatly hurried, and were thrown into confusion in their course; and from that hour, they have no longer had the strength to absorb their dross, i.e., the denser astral substance of their (own) light, for this had been purified.

Moreover, their times and their time-cycles were shortened, in order that the complete number of souls – those who shall receive the Mysteries, and dwell in the Treasury of Light – should be speedily completed. For if I had not changed the course of the Rulers, if I had not shortened their times, they would not have permitted any soul to come into the world, (*i.e., to incarnate*), because they absorbed their dross, that is, their own denser (astral) substances; and they would have thus destroyed a host of souls.

For this reason I said to you before, "I have

TEXT: CHAPTER 27 (cont.)

shortened the times because of my elect,"[78] for a soul that could have been saved, if I had not shortened the times and the periods, for the sake of the intended complete number[79] of souls who shall receive the Mysteries, that is to say, the 'elect'.

For had I not shortened their times, there would not have been any soul saved within the denser (*luciferic-ahrimanic*) astral realm, for these would have perished in the (*debased astral*) fire which is in the 'flesh' of the rulers. Such, then, is the matter on which you have questioned me so precisely."

It then happened, when Jesus had finished speaking these things to his disciples, that they bowed down together, and worshipped him, saying "Blessed are we among all people, for to us you have revealed these great wonders."

COMMENTARY: CHAPTER 27

Earlier, through the risen Jesus, Christ recounted that he changed the general rotating and the courses of the Rulers' pathways to render evil magicians ineffective. Here he recounts that he did something similar, to stop the malignant spirits from having the power to oppose the incarnation of souls with their fallen astral substances in them. They had done this to thwart Melchizedek, but now Christ took up the task of disempowering them.

But all of this implies a potent cosmic dynamic of very large significance. These texts are implying that human souls are created by luciferic-ahrimanic spirits; the malignant Archons or Rulers. But actually, the meaning here is that 'fallen' humanity draws its 'fallen' astral nature from these Archons. However this does not apply to the higher, spiritualized soul qualities, nor to the germinal Spirit-self, which has its origin in the divine hierarchies, and thus ultimately, in the Logos.

---

[78] Similar words appear in Matt. 24:22.
[79] "intended complete number": usu. 'perfect number".

COMMENTARY: CHAPTER 27 (cont.)

But it remains a potent esoteric statement, that if these luciferic-ahrimanic entities were successful in holding to themselves their coarser 'substances', then human beings would have no reservoir of 'fallen' soul-substance from which to receive their next astral-body (or soul-body). And furthermore, 'counterfeit' souls can be formed.

It is such statements as these that no doubt caused Rudolf Steiner to declare that this Coptic text is deeply esoteric; thus implying that it contains truths not of interest to many people. This initiatory text is making revelations about grand, cosmic battles being waged within and around the human life-wave.

These lowly qualities of the planetary spheres are the 'realms' of the debased Rulers (Archons). But the higher soul qualities derive from the ranks of holy deities, and they exist in the noble planetary spheres, and also in the realms of Devachan. These two groups of gods each encompass the planetary spheres and Devachan.

In astrological terms, all the lower soul qualities derive from the lower planetary spheres, (the sphere of the malignant Archons); but the higher soul qualities derive from the higher counterpart of the planetary spheres; from the holy spirits (good Archons). So for example, lying derives from the malignant influences of the Mercury sphere; lewdness from the malignant influences of the Venus sphere, and so on.

To modern esoteric wisdom, each planet is thought of spiritually as having an evil and a divine section, within the one area, so to speak. But to the perspective of the Hellenistic initiates, thus to initiated Christians (who constituted some of the Gnostic groups), the realm of the malignant Rulers is viewed as an entirely separate part of the planetary sphere, having no intermingling with the divine planetary realities.

A SUMMARY OF THE ABOVE FIVE CHAPTERS

The remarkable concepts in chapters 23-27 are complex, and deeply esoteric; it is not surprising that they were kept confidential. Much help in understanding them is available through Steiner's wisdom. It is a potent, confronting view here, that the 'fallen' human soul is thought of as being coalesced by ahrimanic-luciferic deities, to prepare it for its incarnation.

This is not mentioned in Rudolf Steiner's works, but is not in contradiction to it. However, he emphasized that Christ-aligned deities incorporate higher, spiritual qualities into the astral body or souls. However, this aspect of our incarnating is not included here.

These are deeply potent esoteric teachings, with two aspects to them. One is that from this ahrimanic-luciferic astral 'substance', human souls are formed. But the activity of Melchizedek and Christ seeks to ensure that this general reservoir of somewhat debased astrality is not kept within the Rulers, for this would prevent both the creation of souls of human beings, and their incarnating. This means that the debased Rulers shall not retain authority over all this in perpetuity.

Secondly, Melchizedek and then Christ are determined that these debased Rulers do not, via their serving spirits, still manage to create counterfeit human beings. But rather that human souls can incarnate and thereby gradually develop, through higher spiritual influences becoming active within them, into spiritualized souls (i.e., in Gnostic terms, redeem the 'light' in themselves). Otherwise, the Earth would have many souls who only apparently have a 'divine spark', or true 'I'.

CHAPTER 23:

If Christ had not disempowered the malignant Rulers, many human souls would have to wait 'outside'; i.e., in lower realms. The denser substance of these beings are moulded by them into human souls. It is implied that these malignant Rulers wanted to get a harvest

SUMMARY OF THE ABOVE FIVE CHAPTERS (cont.)
for themselves. But Melchizedek thwarted this regularly.

CHAPTER 25: So then to hinder Melchizedek, the subservient spirits of the ahrimanic-luciferic Rulers gathered up the ahrimanic-luciferic astrality and in this way created human beings and animals, etc.

But then in response to this, the Receivers of the Sun and Moon disempowered these subservient spirits (the servitors), and put aside this astrality for Melchizedek to redeem.

However, then the subservient spirits (servitors) accessed this 'set apart' denser astral 'material' and carried it down into the earthly sphere.

CHAPTER 26:
However these lowly subservient spirits began to lose their power. So then the debased Rulers again try to have some astral-substance from which to make souls; for this purpose, they cast out of themselves their lower energies. But then Melchizedek purified this cast out energy.

So then the debased Rulers absorbed their lower energy-material, and no longer cast it out of themselves; so in this way, Melchizedek could not get access to it.

CHAPTER 27: This thwarting action meant that human souls could not become incarnated; this was still an empowerment of these Rulers. For even if they had to forego making counterfeit souls and then hoping to control them, they remained as empowered deities.

They did this retention of their lower energies for "two cycles"; until Christ intervened. (In the next Chapter we discover that therefore, when Jesus Christ was passing through their realms, they were very antagonistic to him.)

TEXT: CHAPTER 28
Then Jesus continued in the conversation and said to his disciples; "Hear what happened to me amongst

TEXT: CHAPTER 28 (cont.)

the (holy) Rulers of the (divine) 12 Aions; amidst all their Rulers, their Lords, their Authorities, their Angels, and their Archangels.

When they had seen the garment of light which was on me, each of them – they and their unpaired Ones[80] – beheld the essence (*lit. mystery*) of their core nature (*lit. name*), which was in my garment of light, with which I was clothed.

Together they prostrated themselves, and they worshipped the garment of light which was on me, and cried out all together saying, "How has the Lord of the Cosmos changed us, without our knowing?" And they all together intoned praises to the innermost divine spirit reality (*lit. 'the interior of the interiors'*).

These (holy) deities of the (divine) Aions, were in great and boundless awe.[81] For they saw the deeper spiritual reality (*lit. mystery*) of their core nature (*lit. name*) in my light-garment, and so they strove to draw near, to worship the Mystery of their name, which was in my light-garment, but they could not, because of the great light that was with me; but they worshipped a little distance from me. They all cried out together, giving praise to the innermost divine spirit realities (*lit. the interior of the interiors*).[82]

Whereas, with the (malignant) Rulers: namely all their Triple-powered Ones, their great Forefathers, their Un-generated, their Self-generated, their Generated, their Gods, their Light-sparks, their Light-bearers, in a word, all their great ones – they (now) saw the empowered Ones of their realm with their power diminished in them, having now become

---

[80] "Unpaired Ones": an obscure term, very likely the Coptic is in error and 'Paired Ones' is meant.

[81] "awe": usu. 'fear'; the Coptic word (ϩⲟⲧⲉ) is the equivalent of the Greek 'phobos' (φόβος), but this also means 'awe', not only 'fear', despite the former meaning being rarely factored in.

[82] This paragraph I have moved up, out of the following text, which is about the malignant spirits.

TEXT: CHAPTER 28 (cont.)

feeble.[83]

It then happened, when this was done to the empowered Ones who are within their Aions (*i.e., the disempowering* of *them by changing their rotating and shortening their time-cycles*), that these deities lost courage. They became disempowered in their Aions, just as happened on the earlier occasion when I took their power from them.

They became like the Earth-dwellers who are (*inwardly*) dead, who have no spirit[84] in them. It came to pass, therefore, after this, when I had left these Aions, that every one of those who were in the 12 Aions was bound to his set path, and they carried out their works as I had arranged.

Namely that they spent six months turning to the left, accomplishing their actions in their squares, their triangles, and in those figures (*astral forms*) facing them. And that moreover, they spent another six months gazing to the right, and (focused) on their squares, their triangles, and on those figures facing them. Thus shall all those be moving along their pathways, who are within the karma-determining cosmic influences and their associated spiritual realms (*lit. the Fate {Heimarmene} and the Sphere*).

COMMENTARY: CHAPTER 28

Although it is not emphasized, a contrast is now made between the fallen hierarchical malignant spirits, and the divine deities of the hierarchies. The Saviour is revealing that after he had disempowered the luciferic-ahrimanic deities, then the holy deities of the planetary spheres and of Devachan became aware that the mighty Saviour had been in their realms.

They worshipped him, ("they worshipped a little

---

[83] There is no information given about these entities.
[84] Usually, 'no breath' in them, but this makes little sense, and the word here 'nife' (ⲉⲙ̄ⲛ̄-)ⲛⲓϥⲉ although mostly used for wind or breath, also was used for vitality or soul.

COMMENTARY: CHAPTER 28 (cont.)

distance from me") and perceived that the core spiritual essence of their own natures was present in the being, the sublime 'spirit-body', of the cosmic Christ aspect of the Saviour. There is here an striking cosmic parallel to the profound truth uttered by Christ in the Gospels, about the higher 'I' of the human being having its origin in the cosmic Christ; that the higher 'I' derives from Christ; "*The 'I' I am, is the Way, the Truth and the Life*" (Jn. 14:6)

TEXT: CHAPTER 29
The story of Pistis Sophia begins

It then happened that I ascended to the veils (*i.e., to the threshold or boundary*) of the 13th Aion. Now, it happened, as I came to their veils, that these drew apart of themselves. I found Pistis Sophia *below* the 13th Aion, quite alone, no one being near her. She was dwelling in that (lower) realm, grieving and mourning, because she had not been brought (*back*) into the 13th Aion (= *6th realm of Devachan*), her (proper) realm in the Heights.

And she was grieving because of the tribulations which she had been forced to suffer by the Self-willed One,[85] who is one of the three (debased) Triple-powers. But regarding these (entities): when I come to tell you of their emanation, I will (also) tell you the Mystery of how that it had come about.

So it happened, when Pistis Sophia had seen me with an immense radiance, there being no measure for the intensity of the light that was in me, that she was in great distress, and beheld the core spiritual reality of her being in my light-garment,[86] and all the glory of this garment. She saw this because formerly she was present in the realm of the Heights, in the 13th Aion.[87]

---

[85] Self-willed One, in Grk. 'Authades'.
[86] Lit. "the Mystery of her name".
[87] The place of origin, and the ongoing location, of Pistis Sophia is in the divine 13th Aeon (in Devachan).

TEXT: CHAPTER 29 (cont.)
She was accustomed to intone words of reverence to the light which is in the Heights, which she had seen in the veil of the Treasury of Light. So it happened when she persisted with intoning words of reverence to the light which is in the Heights, that all the Rulers who are close to the two great Triple-powers, and her Invisible One, paired with her, gazed upon her, as did the 22 remaining invisible emanations.

For Pistis Sophia and her Consort, together with the two and twenty remaining emanations, make up the 24 emanations which the great invisible Forefather and the two great Triple-powers have emanated.

COMMENTARY: CHAPTER 29
Here is the first mention of Pistis Sophia; so here begins the profound account of the struggle for the triumph of the intuitive-spiritual consciousness over the influence of malignant spirits. This is the story of how the Saviour set out to assist the capacity of humanity to achieve a spiritual-intuitive consciousness, within the very real drama of 'God' permitting evil deities to attack this.

Such spiritual-intuitive consciousness is the preliminary form of a fully purified, initiatory clairvoyant consciousness; it will now be esoterically personified in the codex. This means that Pistis Sophia is the counterpart in spirit worlds of the human soul's potential for higher consciousness; as discussed in the Introduction.

The account of her battle against malignant powers and the help she received from the risen Saviour occupy some 140 pages. The actual location of Pistis Sophia is the divine 13th Aion; but the account starts with Sophia having 'fallen', i.e., no longer in the 13th Aion. This situation is the counterpart in realms of spirit – by the dawn of the Hellenistic Age – of the fading of intuitive perceptive cognizing, which for millennia had enabled the previous, age-old holistic-spiritual awareness.

TEXT: CHAPTER 30
It happened, as Jesus told this to his disciples, that Mariam came forward and spoke: "My Lord, I have heard you say, in earlier times, that Pistis Sophia herself is one of the 24 emanations; so how then is she not in their realm? Instead, you have said, "I found Sophia *below* the 13th Aion."

Jesus answered, and said to his disciples, "This (*debased state of Pistis Sophia*) occurred earlier when Pistis Sophia was in the 13th Aion, in the realm of all her brethren, the Invisibles; that is, the emanations of the Great Invisible.

It subsequently happened, by order of the First Mystery, that Pistis Sophia gazed into the Heights, and saw the light of the veil of the Treasury of Light, and she desired to go up into that realm, but she could not. Thereupon she ceased to do the Mystery of the 13th Aion, and (instead) began to intone words of reverence to the light of the Heights, which she had seen in the radiance of the veil of the Treasury of Light.

TEXT NOTE: in Chapter 30
('ceased to do the Mystery' means that the potential for an inner harmony with the divine reality of the 13th Aion has failed, because a naïve, subtly self-centered ungrounded yearning for a higher state of blessedness has seized the human soul.[88])

TEXT: CHAPTER 30 (cont.)
Consequently, it happened when she began to offer reverentially intonings to the realm of the Light of the Heights, that all the (malignant) Rulers who are in the (debased) Aions below, hated her because she had ceased from their Mysteries, and because she wished to go into the Heights and be above them all. For this reason therefore, they were enraged against her and hated her.

---

[88] Rudolf Steiner taught this kind of dynamic is a naïve ('luciferic') state, and if not corrected, leads the soul into a hardened egotistic attitude.

TEXT NOTE: in Chapter 30
("had ceased from their Mysteries": this reveals that this capacity of our soul, whilst possessing a capacity for an intuitive higher discerning, is also still partly interwoven with the malignant (ahrimanic-luciferic) reality, until it attains a spiritual consciousness.

TEXT: CHAPTER 30 (cont.)
But (also) the great (debased) Triple-power, the Self-willed One hated her; that is to say, the third Triple-power, who is in the (*evil counterpart of the*) 13th Aion, he who had become disobedient. That is, he who had not rayed forth what had become purified of the spiritual power which was in him.

He also had not yielded up the purity of his light at the time when the (*divine*) Rulers gave over their purified essence. He acted in this way because he wished to rule over all of the 13th Aion, and those who are beneath it.

It therefore happened, when the (*malignant*) Rulers of the 12 Aions were enraged against Pistis Sophia and hated her exceedingly – she who is above them – that the great (debased) Triple-power Self-willed One, of whom I have just been telling you, joined himself to the (*malignant Rulers of the evil counterpart of the*) 12 Aions. For he also was enraged against Pistis Sophia, and hated her intensely, because she had sought to go to the light which is above him.

Consequently, he emanated from himself a great Lion-faced being; and from the denser (*astral*) substance (*hyle*) which was in him, he (also) emanated a host of other denser (*astral*) emanations: powerful and mighty (*astral*) emanations.

He sent them into the nether realms, into the regions of the Chaos, in order that these (astral) emanations (*i.e., minor entities*) might lie in wait there for Pistis Sophia, and take away the spiritual power that was in her, because she had thought to go to the Heights, which is above them all.

But also because she had ceased to perform their Mysteries, and she continued to lament, seeking the

TEXT: CHAPTER 30 (cont.)

light which she had seen. And so the Rulers who persisted, that is, continued the carrying out of their Mystery, hated her; and also all the Watchers at the portals of the (debased) Aions, hated her.

It then happened, by the order of the First Command, that the powerful (*debased*) Triple-power, the Self-willed One, who is one of the Triple-Powers, harassed Pistis Sophia above, in[89] the 13th Aion, so that she would direct her gaze into the nether realms. He did this so that she might behold his light-being, that with the Lion-face, and yearn for this, and hence go down to that realm, so that her light may (thereby) be taken away from her.

COMMENTARY: CHAPTER 30
The plan of attack against Pistis Sophia

THE FALL OF SOPHIA
"The Self-willed One hated her...and so he sent them into the nether realms, into the regions of the Chaos, in order that these (astral) emanations (*i.e., minor entities*) might lie in wait there for Pistis Sophia, and take away the spiritual power that was in her, because she had thought to go to the Heights, which is above them all."

This is the first part of the two-phase attack on Pistis Sophia; the next part, flowing on naturally from the first part, and allowed by the First Command (a representative of God), is that the consciousness of Pistis Sophia would be targeted, so as to cause her to be deceived in her cognitional capacity or perceptions.

"heard you say, in earlier times": a striking and valuable statement; for these words, only incidentally stated, affirm that prior to the events of Golgotha, Jesus did establish an 'Esoteric School', teaching initiation truths, at least in an initial sense.

---

[89] "above, in": usu. just 'in', but emphasis can be given to this extra preposition (ⲉⲡⲁⲓ) here, (although it can be at times superfluous).

COMMENTARY: CHAPTER 30 (cont.)

It is this teaching to which the fragment of the *Secret Gospel of St. Mark* refers. Again, one can regret that only a fragment of these teachings has survived.[90]

"by order of the First Command": a potent statement that the divine higher spirits brought about the dramatic and perilous journey of the human soul into the snares of evil. But one understands that this 'fall' occurred, so that the potential for spirituality could be specifically attained by human beings.

For human beings can only attain to a genuine morality if this state is freely and actively sought; then the decision is made in freedom, and not as a reflection of the will of our divine creators.

"she desired to go up into that realm": a *premature* yearning for a high spiritual state; one which is permeated by a self-centred wish. However, significantly, this same yearning is revealed in the next chapter as being brought about through the will of God (the First Mystery).

"because she wished to go into the Heights": this misplaced yearning in the soul, as awareness dawns about attaining higher consciousness, awakens anger in the malignant spirits, for this heralds the end of their power over that soul.

"third Triple-power, who is in the 13th Aion": another deeply esoteric revelation; namely that the initiate is aware that just as there is a demonic lower astral realm, or 'Hell' (i.e., Tartaros in Greek or Gehenna in Hebrew) as well as noble astral realms, so too, there is a demonic counterpart to the divine realms of Devachan.

So, when the evil entity here, who creates the lion-faced demon, is said to be "in the 13th Aion", this means in the *demonic counterpart to the 13th realm* of Devachan.

"Lion-faced demon": this entity will be commented on later, after further references occur to it.

---

[90] M. Smith, *Clement of Alexandria and a Secret Gospel of St. Mark*, (1973, Harvard UP).

COMMENTARY: CHAPTER 30 (cont.)

"lie in wait": this is a key phrase, revealing that the evil entity creating these demons, is in effect, Ahriman; for a feature of Satan is to be secretive, to hide, and 'to lie in wait'; in Genesis 4:7 God tells Cain that evil is 'crouching at your door' or 'lying-in-wait' at your door.[91]

In The *Book of Job*, Satan (or Ahriman) is located deep inside the Earth's interior. However, such ahrimanic spirits are, in religious terms, part of the over-all nature of Creation, as shown in various Biblical passages; e.g., in *1Kings*: (v.19), God uses an adversarial, lying spirit to lure Ahab to his destruction.

"the Chaos": Plato refers to this as 'the nether abyss' and Plutarch teaches that it is located in 'the interior of the planet".[92] But it is also identified with the physical earthly world of humanity (e.g. chapter 60).

"yearn for that (lion-faced)": another potent statement. For, although it is really an ugly, lion-faced entity, its true appearance and the real nature of its influence are concealed. Hence this demon has the ability to present to the confused human soul, the malignant self-serving intentions of Ahriman and Lucifer as especially alluring and enjoyable desires or ambitions.

TEXT: CHAPTER 31

It therefore came to pass after these things, that Pistis Sophia gazed below. She saw there the might of

---

[91] In Hebrew, Satan is Sahtan (שָׂטָן) meaning 'adversary', opponent, etc. The verbal form, Sahtan (שָׂטַן) is at times described erroneously in some text-books as meaning 'lying in wait'. But it actually has the same meanings as the noun, "Satan"; but because evil hate-filled adversaries in Scripture are often mentioned as 'lying in wait', this phrase can be seen as a way of defining Satan (or Ahriman).

[92] In article 'χάος' in Liddell & Scott (*Greek-English Dict.*) p.1976 b.

TEXT: CHAPTER 31 (cont.)
the light-power of the Self-willed One, in the nether realms; but she had not realized that it was the light-power of the (debased) Triple-powered Self-willed One. Rather she thought that it came from the Light which she had seen from the beginning, in the Heights, which came from the veil of the Treasury of Light.

So she thought to herself, "I will go into that realm, without my Consort, and take up this light – which, for me, some Light-Aions created, so that I will (then) be able to go up to the Height of Heights."

In that she was thinking this, she departed out of the 13th Aion and descended into the 12 Aions.

TEXT NOTE: in Chapter 31
An important correction:
"...and take up this light – which, for me, some light-Aions created" (so that I can ascend...)"

The Coptic is ambiguous here; it can mean as above, which is how I and Horner interpret it. Or, as in the other versions,

"...for myself I shall create of it some light-Aions," (so that I can ascend...)

Here a certain form of the verb (ⲧⲁⲙⲓⲟ) is used, by which it is unclear whether the action is carried out by the single Pistis Sophia or by several light-Aions.[93]
Also grammatically, in the other versions, 'of it' is only an implied addition to the actual text, yet Coptic has at least four words for 'of' which here would be an especially key word to include. Also this version omits 'which', (both of these actions are entirely permissible but are best avoided if not needed).[94] It is also unclear whether the action is of the future or of the past.

But much more significantly, my preferred version

---

[93] That is, the 'infinitive' form of the verb.
[94] The 'which' in Coptic (ⲛⲁⲓ) is an emphatic pronoun not easily dropped (Stern, *Kopt. Grammat.* #502).

TEXT NOTE: in Chapter 31
is based on the conclusion that this spiritual aspect of the human being (personified as Pistis Sophia) - is an especially disempowered entity - and knows that it is not a deity, and hence cannot create entire Aions. For she is presented in this codex as a non-creator, non-deity, and a disempowered entity.[95]

So she would not entertain such an impossibility, even in difficult situations. So my interpretation, and that of Horner[96], is that Pistis Sophia is hoping that the light she sees has been created by noble, holy Aions (the deities therein) to help her, so she can take hold of it, and this should enable her to ascend back to the 13th Aion; and not that she will herself create some Aions of Light. Previous scholars had incorrectly assumed that Pistis Sophia was the high primordial deity of other Gnostic texts.

Thirdly, the other versions have another weak basis: that for Pistis Sophia to ascend up to an even higher realm than her proper locality (the 13th Aion) the light she has seen is not sufficient for this, so she will have to create from it several high Aions, and then use their light to ascend to this higher realm. But she only has to go towards the light she has already seen, to move up to what she thinks is a higher Aion. And this is exactly what she then does.

TEXT: CHAPTER 31 (cont.)
The Rulers of these Aions pursued her and were furious with her, because she had thought of attaining to a higher greatness.[97] She went forth, out

---

[95] The Coptic here is: ⲛⲧⲁ -ⲧⲁⲙⲓⲟ-ϥ ⲛⲁⲓ ⲛ2ⲉⲛ- ⲁⲓⲱⲛ ⲛ̄ⲟⲩⲟⲉⲓⲛ. This is literally, 'for myself create (it=*light* which some Aions of light'.

[96] George Horner was a scholar in both Bohairic and Sahidic Coptic, (and Arabic and Ethiopic), producing the New Testament in both Coptic dialects in 11 volumes, 1898-1924.

[97] "a higher greatness": Coptic obscure; possibly, 'thought to have greatness', or 'thought of glory'.

TEXT: CHAPTER 31 (cont.)

of the 12 Aions, and came into the realms of the Chaos; she drew near to that Lion-faced light-power, to absorb it into herself.

But all the denser (astral) emanations (*lesser demonic entities*) of the Self-willed One surrounded her, and the great Lion-faced light-being devoured all the light-powers in Sophia; it separated out her light[98] and then absorbed this.

Moreover, her denser (astral) substances were also removed from her and cast into the Chaos. These became a lion-faced Ruler, of which one half is fire, the other half is darkness. This then became Ialdabaoth, about whom I have often spoken with you (*in earlier times*).

Now, when this was done, Sophia was very weakened, and the Lion-faced (*malignant*) light-power began to take away from Sophia all her light-powers;
and at the same time, all the denser (astral) energies (*lesser demonic entities*) of the Self-willed One surrounded Sophia and oppressed her.

COMMENTARY: CHAPTER 31

That Pistis Sophia is referred to here with these details, indicates that this was well-known to the disciples, and shows that they were already schooled in Christian Gnostic wisdom, before the Resurrection. My view is based on accepting this text as deriving, in the main, from a a record of communications from Christ Jesus, of about CE 33-44. A commentary on Sophia, and her 'fall', will be left until further references are made to her.

"lion-faced Ruler": this is not the same as the Lion-faced light-power created by the Triple-power Self-willed One (in Chapter 31), but a lesser demonic force

---

[98] "separated out her light": a very significant variation from other translations; usu. 'purified her light', but this must be erroneous, as a malignant entity cannot purify any light. In fact, the Coptic verb here (ⲥⲱⲧϥ) not only means to cleanse, but also 'to separate' or 'to pour out'.

COMMENTARY: CHAPTER 31 (cont.)
of the same nature.[99]

"Ialdabaoth": What is significant here is that when the soul-powers of the human being become debased and thus malignant (i.e., subject to ahrimanic-luciferic spirits), a twofold debased entity results. One outcome of a debased human consciousness is that the emotive capacity, which was radiant and enthusiastic, becomes a vicious fiery reality; and what was once a clear illumined thinking becomes a sinister, darkened power.

"her denser (astral) substances": these inferior, denser soul-qualities must have been formed as Pistis Sophia descended into lower realms; this would be an inevitable natural process. It is from these inferior, debased soul-energies (or consciousness qualities) that the demon Ialdabaoth was created. In Chapter 102 we are told that Ialdabaoth has demonic serving spirits, who can chastize sinners after death.

TEXT: CHAPTER 32
So Pistis Sophia cried out loudly to the Light of Lights. She had beheld this (deity) from the beginning, having intuitively perceived it. And (so) she uttered her remorseful insights, in that she spoke thus:

1: "O Light of Lights, which from the beginning I have perceived intuitively; hear now, O Light, my expression of remorse ! Save me, O Light, for evil thoughts have come upon me !

2: I gazed, O Light, into the nether realms; I saw a light there, (and so) I thought, I will go into that realm, to take that light. So I went forth, and found myself in the darkness of the lower Chaos, and I could not depart quickly away, and go to my realm, for I became oppressed by all the emanations of this Self-willed One, and this Lion-faced might had taken away the light which was in me.

3: And I cried out for help, but my voice did not penetrate the darkness; I gazed into the Heights, so

---

[99] Rudolf Steiner taught that the debased lion energy is still present in the 'Double' of every human being.

TEXT: CHAPTER 32 (cont.)   **Pistis Sophia speaks**
that the light, which I had (earlier) intuitively perceived, would come to my assistance.

4: And as I gazed into the Heights, I saw all the (debased) Rulers; and how many of these were looking down onto me, and delighting in my situation, although I had done them no ill; for they hated me without a cause. And when the emanated spirits (*lit. emanations*) of the Self-willed One had seen the (debased) Rulers of the Aions rejoicing over me, they knew that the (holy) Rulers of the (divine) Aions would not aid me.

They gained confidence, those emanations which constrained me. So they took the light which I had not taken from them.

5: Now, therefore, O Light of Truth, you know that I have done these things in my naiveté, thinking that this Lion-faced light-being belonged to you; and so the sin which I have done is evident to you.

6: Allow me no more to be weakened, Lord, for I have discerned intuitively your light from the beginning. Lord, Light of (all) the spirit-beings – allow me no more to be cut off from my light,

7: For it is because of your inducement and your light that I am in this affliction, and shame has covered me.

8: And because of the pretext of your light I am a stranger to my brethren, the Invisibles, and also to the great emanations of Barbelo.

TEXT NOTE: in Chapter 32
Verse 8: "pretext": this is an abbreviated way of saying, that her decision was made on the deluded, false, conclusion that she was seeing the true Light. The Coptic word here (ⲗⲟⲉⲓϭⲉ) means either excuse (pretext) or delusion.

CHAPTER 32 (cont.)   **Pistis Sophia speaks**
9: These things have befallen me, O Light, because I have ardently longed for your dwelling; but the wrath of the Self-Willed One has fallen upon me – the wrath of him who would not give ear to your command to

CHAPTER 32 (cont.) Pistis Sophia speaks

send forth (*as an offering*) emanations of his being. For I dwelt in his Aion, without carrying out his Mystery,

10: and so all the (malignant) Rulers of the Aions have held me in derision.

11: And I was in this realm, grieving, seeking after the light, which I saw in the Heights.

12: And the Guardians to the portals of the Aions were seeking me out (to oppose) me, and all those who continued in their Mystery have mocked me.

13: But as for me, I gazed into the Heights, towards you, O Light of Lights, and intuitively discerned you. But now, I am oppressed in the darkness of the Chaos. If you wish to come here to save me – great is your mercy – hear me in truth, and preserve me.

14: Save me from the dense (astral) substance of this darkness. Do this so that I may no longer be immersed in it; that I may be saved from the emanations of the Self-Willed One, which oppress me; and be saved from their evil doings.

15: Let not this darkness cover me, and allow not this Lion-faced entity to devour entirely all of my spiritual strength; so, let not this Chaos envelop my being.

16: Hear me, O Light, for your mercy is precious; and look upon me according to the great compassion of your light.

17: Turn not your face away from me, for I am exceedingly tormented.

18: Without delay, hearken to me, and save my being.

19: Save me from the Rulers which hate me, for you know my afflictions, and my danger, and the torment now endured by my power, which they have taken away from me. They who have placed me in all these evils are perceived by you. Do unto them according to your will.

20: My being gazes forth from the midst of the Chaos; and from the midst of the darkness I have gazed towards my Consort, to see if he would come
and battle for me, but he came not, yet I expected that he would come and endow me with strength, but I found him not,

TEXT: CHAPTER 32 (cont.)   Pistis Sophia speaks
21: and when I asked for light, they gave me darkness; and when I asked for my spiritual being, they gave me dense (astral) matter (*weakening me*).
22: Now, therefore, O Light of Lights, let the darkness and the dense (astral) matter, which the emanations of the Self-willed One have brought upon me, be snares for them, so let them be ensnared therein; bring about retribution to them, letting them meet with obstacles, in order that they may not come into the realm of their own Self-willed One.
23: Let them remain in darkness, and let them not see the light; let them ever behold the Chaos and look not into the Heights.

24: Bring their vengeance upon themselves, and let your judgment seize on them,
25: henceforth let them not enter into their own realms, to (the sphere of) their deity, the Self-willed One. Allow his emanations no longer to enter into their realm, for their deity is impious and arrogant, and thought that he had brought these evils upon me of himself. He did not know that, if you had not humbled me in accordance with your command, he would not have prevailed over me.

TEXT NOTE: in Chapter 32
The plea is that these malignant entities may be blocked from making their way to the debased realm of their evil creator, thereby becoming more empowered.

TEXT: CHAPTER 32 (cont.)   Pistis Sophia speaks
26: But when you had humbled me, they pursued me all the more, and their emanations added pains to my humiliation.
27: They took from me a light-power, and began again to be hostile to me. They have severely oppressed me, in order to take away all the light which was in me. Therefore, because of the evils which they have planted in me, do not allow them to enter into the 13th Aion: the realm of righteousness.

TEXT: CHAPTER 32 (cont.) Pistis Sophia speaks
28: Let them not be counted among those whose light is purified; and let them not be counted among the number of those who shall quickly repent so they may speedily receive the Mysteries in the light.
29: For they have taken my light from me, and my power has begun to cease in me, and I am destitute of my light.
30: Now, therefore, O Light - Light which is with you and is (also) with me - I intone words of reverence to your name, O Light, (*you who are*) in Glory.
31: May my intonations of reverence please you, O Light, like an excellent Mystery, which leads to the Portals of Light. A Mystery which those souls shall recite who repent; and whose light the Portals of Light shall purify.

32: Therefore, let all (*entities of*) the dense (astral) substances now rejoice. All of you - seek the Light, so that the spiritual power of your souls, which is (indeed) within you - may live on (*in higher realms*).
33: For the Light has heard all the (*entities in*) the dense (astral) substances, and so will not leave any of these, without firstly purifying them.
34: Let all souls, and all the (*entities in*) the dense (astral) substance praise the Lord of all the Aions: these entities in the dense (astral) substance, and everything (*else*) within this substance.

TEXT NOTE: in Chapter 32
Verse. 34: these minor entities were earlier sent into this denser astral material by malignant Rulers: see the Commentary.
"not allow them to enter into the 13th Aion": the plea is that these elemental entities should not be given access to a holy realm, after being purified, since they are so evil, and hence will not ever be fully redeemed.

TEXT: CHAPTER 32 (cont.) Pistis Sophia speaks
35: For God (*lit. the First Mystery*) will deliver their souls from out of all the dense (astral) substances; and a city shall be established in the light, and all the

saved souls shall dwell in that city, and inherit it.
36: And the soul of those who receive Mysteries shall dwell in that realm, and they that will have received the Mysteries[100] in his name shall dwell therein.

COMMENTARY: CHAPTER 32

"seen from the beginning": the Coptic verb here is adopted from the Greek verb, horan (ὁρᾶν)[101] which is a primary verb for spiritual or clairvoyant seeing; and this is of course what is meant here, as the entity who is 'seeing' is not in a flesh body.

The long lament with its remorse and insights appears to be from an individual entity, yet it is really a vocalizing of the inner dynamics in the astral-world counterpart of the human capacity for spiritual-intuitive cognizing.

This instructional technique is designed to make a vivid impression on the esoteric student regarding the negative dynamics that envelop the higher soul quality – i.e., intuitive insightfulness – when this is under threat, and the impact these have on the soul, and the role of malignant spirits in this.

Faithful Wisdom or Intuitive Wisdom ?

v.1: "intuitively perceived this": usually 'she had faith in it' or 'in which she had believed'. But the Coptic verb here, (ⲡⲓⲥⲧⲉⲩⲉ) is directly derived from the Greek, 'pisteuein' (πιστεύειν) which, as I have demonstrated in my *The Gospel of John*, not only means 'to have faith' or 'to believe', but also can mean, 'to perceive with discernment' or 'perceive intuitively'. But a spirit-being can hardly be said to have belief or disbelief in another perceived spirit being; for they have direct perception of each other.

Also, the Coptic text omits the introductory phrase 'in which' (but this can be inferred and added); the text itself simply recounts that "she intuitively perceived it"; which reinforces the earlier phrase that Pistis Sophia, i.e., our intuitively discerning

---

[100] "Mysteries": Coptic is ambiguous; it may be 'Mystery'.
[101] Crum, *Dict.* p. 233b.

COMMENTARY: CHAPTER 32 (cont.)

awareness, had indeed spiritually beheld it. The alternative versions are,

"*which she had seen from the beginning, in which she had believed*, (MacDermot)
"*which she had seen from the beginning, in which she had had faith*" (Mead)
"*which she had seen from the beginning, because she had believed in it*" (Schmidt/Till)
"*This which she saw from at first, having believed it*" (Horner).

Again my version:
1:"O Light of Lights, which from the beginning I have perceived intuitively"
The Coptic here is unclear, allowing all these translations; but these versions are unconvincing. For if a spiritual entity is beholding another entity in spirit realms, in fact a divine spirit, then the beholder (Pistis Sophia) would be directly aware of the divine nature of that deity. There is no question of 'faith' being needed, such as all non-clairvoyant humans need. Nor would a spirit entity see another entity only after having faith in it – as most of these versions imply.

v.2: "I thought, I will go into that realm, to take that light": this is a core text, for the Sophia consciousness could only have become so severely dulled in its cognizing by the decree of God (the First Mystery) being effective, but discreetly in the background. And this is what is stated later; that the First Mystery specifically arranged for this dulled condition to happen.

This decision by God is what brought about the darkening of human consciousness into a 'luciferic-ahrimanic' condition. This is a necessary developmental element in humanity's existence, from which the human soul can eventually achieve its own state of morality, by specifically rejecting evil.

Already in Chapter 20 this dynamic is alluded to, where the Saviour states, "I have not taken away
power (accessible to satanic initiates) from that 13th

COMMENTARY: CHAPTER 32 (cont.)
realm – in accordance with the command of the First Mystery".

v.20: "my Consort": that there is a companion to Sophia is intriguing, but nothing is said about him.

v.27: "evils which they have planted in me": Pistis Sophia is now aware of the origin of the debased influences; but perhaps also avoiding acknowledging her inner blindness which allowed this to occur.

v.33: The text has simply, the Light heard "all the dense matters"; but this is obviously inferring that these multiple 'matters' are sentient. So, it is not about molecular physical matter, but is alluding to minor entities within the debased, denser astral energies (or so-called 'substances').

v.34: entities are also directly implied here: "the (*entities in*) the dense (astral) substance...": for as in v.33, here the 'hyle' i.e., the dense astral substance is in the plural; meaning the many minor spirits within the lower astral 'substance'.

v.35: "a city": it appears that the spiritual (astral-devachanic) counterpart of Jerusalem is meant.

TEXT: CHAPTER 33 Mariam speaks
It then happened when Jesus had spoken these things to his disciples, that he said to them, "These are the words of reverence which Pistis Sophia uttered in her first expression of remorse, when she repented of her sin, reciting all things which had befallen her. Now, therefore, whoever has ears to hear, let them hear.

Again Mariam came forward and spoke, "Lord, my companion-of-light has ears, and I am ready to hear with my light-nature; and (also) your spirit, which is with me, has made me vigilant.[102] So hear me now, for I wish to speak concerning the expression of remorse which Pistis Sophia made, speaking of her sin and all that happened to her. Your light-being has prophesied long ago on this matter through the

---

[102] The word here, 'naephalios' (νήφαλιος) although often used for 'sober' also means to be vigilant, attentive.

prophet David, in Psalm 68 (*69 in the Bible*), saying:

TEXT NOTE:
The use of Psalms in the codex

A special feature of the use of Psalms in this codex is that a disciple will quote various verses of the Psalm and match these with sections of the words from Pistis Sophia; often saying that what Pistis Sophia said is actually just what the verse in the Psalm states. However, this is often not precisely the case; the dynamics are similar, but the context is often very different; this is the Midrashic method of interpreting a text.

So when stating that "this (from the Psalm) *is* what Pistis Sophia said", even though it is not what Pistis Sophia said – because she is in a different context – the disciple is emphasizing a similarity in the dynamics of the two texts.

But there is also the possibility that the disciple is suggesting that the dynamics of the Psalmist's problems and experiences may be a reflection of what is happening to Pistis Sophia, up in spirit realms.

Now a large portion of Psalm 68 (69 in the Bible) is recounted, although there are some differences to the Bible text, since this version is from the Septuagint. This Psalm is an initiatory text, so 'water' refers to the Soul-world or 'astral realms'.)

TEXT: CHAPTER 33 (cont.)   Psalm 68

1: "Save me, God, for the waters have come even unto my soul.

2: I sank, indeed[103] I am submerged, in the mire of the Abyss, and there was no strength (*left in me*).[104] I am

---

[103] "indeed": usu. 'or', but this has no real meaning here. The Coptic here (ⲏ) is derived from the Grk. ἤ which not only means 'or', but as an affirmative particle also means 'indeed' in both Classical Greek (Euripides, Plato, Sappho, etc) and Hellenistic Grk. (*The Hermetica*, Bk. 16: ἤ τε τῶν ἀπλανῶν = "indeed the fixed stars".)

[104] "strength": usu. 'power', but the word ϭⲟⲙ also means 'strength'; and 'left in me' is implied.

TEXT: CHAPTER 33 (cont.)   **Psalm 68:**
down in the depths of the sea; a tempest has submerged me.

3: I have suffered from my crying out; my throat is hoarse. My eyes failed me, from waiting for God.

4: They that hate me without a cause are more than the hairs of my head. Mighty are my foes, those who pursued me with violence. They demanded from me that which I never took from them.

5: God, you know my foolishness, and my faults are not hidden from you.

6: Let not them that wait on you, Lord, be ashamed for my sake. O Lord of the Powers, let not those who seek you be confused through me; Lord, God of Israel, Lord of the Powers.[105]

7: Because it is for your sake that I have suffered reproach; and that shame has covered my face.

8: I have become a stranger to my brethren, to my mother's children.

9: Indeed the zeal for your house has devoured me, and the reproaches of them that reproached you have fallen upon me.

10: I humbled my soul through fasting, but that was turned to my reproach.

11: I put on sackcloth; I became a term of derision among them.

12: They who sat at the gates mocked me, and the drunkards made a song about me.

13: But as for me, I prayed in my soul to you, Lord. It is (now) the time of your good-will, O God.[106] In the fullness of your Grace, give ear to my (plea for) salvation, in (the) truth (*of your being*).[107]

14: Take me out of this mire, that I sink not; let me be delivered from them that hate me, and from the watery depths.

15: Let not a watery flood submerge me, don't let the

---

[105] "Powers': this Septuagint version is traditionally in Bibles, "Lord of the (Spirit-)Hosts ('Sabaoth' in Hebrew).
[106] Coptic obscure; the meaning here is uncertain.
[107] Coptic obscure: the meaning here is uncertain.

TEXT: CHAPTER 33 (cont.)   Psalm 68

Depths swallow me, nor a well close its mouth above me.

16: Hear me, O Lord, for precious is your Grace; look down upon me in the fullness of your compassion.

17: Turn not away your countenance from your servant, for I am oppressed.

18: Hear me without delay, give heed to my soul, and deliver it.

19: Because of my enemies, save me; for you know my shame and dishonour and the slandering of me.

All of my oppressors are before you (*i.e., your gaze*).

20: My heart has awaited disgrace and misery; I waited for him who would have sorrow with me, but I did not draw near him; I did not find he who would comfort me.

21: They have given me gall for meat; and in my thirst they gave me vinegar to drink.

22: Let their table become a snare for them; a net, a retribution and a stumbling-block.

23: Place them under burdens forever.[108]

24: Trample them under foot in your anger; let the wrath of your displeasure seize hold of them.

25: Let their habitation be desolate, let no one dwell in their habitations.

26: For they have persecuted those whom you have smitten, and they have added bitterness to their pain.

27: They have added iniquity to their iniquities. Let them not come into your righteousness.

28: Let them be erased out of the Book of the Living, and let them not be inscribed among the righteous.

29: I am a poor wretch, who is also in grief. The salvation (*raying forth*) from your countenance has received me unto itself.

30: I will bless the name of God in song, and I will exalt this with a song of praise.

31: This shall please the Lord better than a young bull that puts forth its horns and hoofs.

---

[108] Literally, "Bend their backs for all time."

TEXT: CHAPTER 33 (cont.) Psalm 68

32: Let the wretched see and be glad. Seek God, that your souls may live.
33: For the Lord has heard the wretched, and despises not those who are in chains.
34: Let Heaven and Earth bless the Lord; (likewise) the sea (*the Soul-world*) and all that is therein.
35: For God will save Zion, and the cities of Judea will be built, that people shall dwell in them, and inherit these.
36: The offspring of his servants shall possess it, and they shall dwell therein who love his name (*i.e., have an inner alignment to Him*)."

COMMENTARY: CHAPTER 33

"who has ears to hear, let them hear": the presence of this admonition need not be a 'borrowing' from the Gospels; it is also recorded in the Gospel of Thomas, sayings which in my view, were not borrowed from a Gospel text.

v.14 "....that I sink not": as this is not a nautical poem, 'the Abyss' and 'the watery Depths' refer to the lower Soul-world or 'astral realm'. Notice that a tempest (v.2) is the force that submerges the acolyte; it is this same lower astral qualities (indicated by a strong wind that sprang up) which the disciples of Jesus were threatened by, when they were 'crossing the sea'. That is, as they were attempting, as part of the initiatory quest, to maintain self-awareness in the Soul-world.

TEXT: CHAPTER 34

It then happened when Mariam had spoken these words to Jesus, in the midst of the disciples, that she said to him: "Lord, this is the interpretation of the mystery of the expression of remorse of Pistis Sophia." It happened when Jesus had heard Mariam speak these words, that he said to her: "Well said, Mariam, thou blessed one, (*you who are*) the fullness (*of spirituality*) – indeed[109] the most blessed fullness – she whom all people shall call 'blessed'."

COMMENTARY: CHAPTER 34
"she whom all people shall call 'blessed'": here Jesus changes his perspective and is pointing out Mariam to the others, primarily the gathered disciples. There is also here perhaps the inclusion of those who will later come to know of these communications.
'Mariam' is referred to as a most exalted initiated follower of the Saviour. It appears the Mariam the Magdalene is meant.[110]

TEXT: CHAPTER 35   Pistis Sophia intones
And Jesus continued in his conversation, and said: "Pistis Sophia continued, and intoned words of reverence in a second expression of remorseful insight, saying: "O Light of Lights, whom I have truly perceived,[111] leave me not in the darkness until the end of my time. Help me, and save me, by your Mysteries; incline your ear to me, and save me. May the power of your light protect me, and carry me up to the Aions of the Heights; for it is you who shall save me, and take me into the height of your Aions.

Preserve me, O Light, from the hand of this Lion-faced entity, and from the grip of the emanations of the (debased) Self-willed One of the gods. For you are the Light which I have intuitively perceived, and whose radiance I have trusted from the beginning. I have discerned its presence from the hour when it emanated me forth.

It is indeed you who caused me to be emanated (by them); and from the beginning I myself, I have

---

[109] Again reading 'H' (= ή) not as 'or' but as an affirmative particle, e.g., 'indeed'.

[110] These words also resemble the praise of the mother of Jesus, (Lk.1:42); this appears to be a coincidence.

[111] Again, the Grk. verb 'pisteuein': either to believe in or, to perceptively discern.

TEXT: CHAPTER 35 (cont.) **Pistis Sophia intones** perceived intuitively your light. But when I trusted in you, the Rulers of the Aions mocked at me, saying, "She has ceased in her Mystery."

TEXT NOTE: in Chapter 35
"emanated (by them)": the creation of the capacity for intuitive-perceptive cognizing was brought about by the decision of the cosmic Christ (the Light of Lights), from whom this capacity derives. But the actual work of fashioning and bringing into existence as part of the human being's inner life is carried out by unnamed lesser spirits.[112]

TEXT: CHAPTER 35 (cont.) **Pistis Sophia intones**
You are my Saviour and my Redeemer; and *you* are my Mystery, O Light. My mouth has been filled with praise, that I may declare the spiritual Mystery of your grandeur always. Now, therefore, O Light, leave me not in the Chaos until the end of all my time. Leave me not behind you, O Light, for they have entirely taken from me my light-power, and all the emanations of the Self-willed One have surrounded me.

They sought to take away all of my light; they have been observing my strength, saying one to another together – for my light had abandoned me – "Seize her, take from her all the light which is (still) in her."

Therefore, O Light, do not forsake me; turn and save me, O Light: save me from the hands of these pitiless ones. Let them that would take away my spiritual power fall away, and be without strength. Let those that would take away my light-power, be clothed with darkness, and let them be powerless." This is the second expression of remorse which Pistis Sophia spoke, intoning words of reverence to the Light.

---

[112] The Coptic verb here incorporates both a singular pronoun referring to the Christ-Light and a plural pronoun (ⲧⲣⲉⲩ) referring to a plurality of spirits.

COMMENTARY: CHAPTER 35

"emanated": a term used in texts viewed as 'Gnostic', implying not Christian; but there were Christians who followed the initiatory path, and were in that sense 'Gnostic'.

TEXT: CHAPTER 36   Peter speaks

It then happened when Jesus had finished speaking these words to his disciples, that he then said to them: "Do you understand in what manner I am speaking with you ?" Then Peter, starting forward, said to Jesus, "Lord, we cannot endure this woman coming (forward) and thereby taking our place from us, not allowing us to speak; for she speaks many times." So Jesus responded and said to his disciples, "Let that person in whom the power of their spirit wells up, so as to make them understand what I am saying – let them come forward *(when that happens)* and speak.

But as for you, Peter, I see that the spiritual-nature in you – it has understood the explanation of the spiritual dynamics *(lit. 'Mystery')* of the expression of remorse which the Pistis Sophia spoke. So Peter, now, amongst your brethren, speak about the thoughts (underlying) her expression of remorse."[113] So Peter answered, and said, "Lord: hear, that I may explain the meaning of her expression of remorse, about which your power prophesied in days of old, through the prophet David, in the 70th Psalm[114]:

"In you God, my God, I have put my trust, let me not ever be put to shame. Preserve me in your righteousness, and save me. Incline your ear to me, and preserve me. Be to me a strong God, and a stronghold to save me. For you are my foundation and my refuge.

My God, save me from the hand of the sinner, from the hand of the transgressor *(of the law)*, and from the impious; for you are my (power of) endurance, Lord. You are my hope from my youth; you have

---

[113] "thoughts underlying": lit. 'speak to the thoughts'.
[114] Psalm 71 in the Bible.

TEXT: CHAPTER 36 (cont.) Peter speaks
brought me out my mother's womb.

Always is my mind on you. To the crowd, I was as if I am one of the foolish. You are my help and my support; you are my Saviour, O Lord.

My mouth was filled with glorifying (of you), that I may praise[115] the glory of your greatness, all the day long. Cast me not away when I am in old age, and as my soul grows weak, do not forsake me ! For my enemies speak evil against me. And they who lay in wait for my soul have taken counsel together, saying, "God has forsaken him, let us pursue and seize him; for there is no-one to save him !" O God, give heed to my help ! May those who so slander my soul be ashamed and destroyed. Let them be enveloped in shame and disgrace, who seek evil against me."

This then is the solution to the second expression of remorse which Pistis Sophia has spoken.

COMMENTARY: CHAPTER 36
"This woman": the hostility of Peter to Mariam is disappointing, but it speaks for the honesty and validity of this ancient text. It reveals the prejudice of men in Palestine. Such hostility by Peter is unlikely regarding the Virgin Mary; but is possible with Mariam of Bethany (or Mariam the Magdalene). A few decades later women were accepted as equal to men, at least by some early followers of Jesus; for women were working as missionaries (The *Acts of Paul and Thecla* indicate this).

TEXT: CHAPTER 37
The Saviour responded to Peter and said, "Well done, Peter, this is the solution to her expression of remorse. Blessed are you (*i.e., ye*)[116] above all people on the Earth, for I have revealed this Mystery to you

---

[115] "praise the glory": not 'bless', as Pistis Sophia is not a deity, and hence cannot bless the Light (the cosmic Christ); the Coptic word (cмoy) has both meanings.

[116] "ye": at this point, and onwards, Jesus is now addressing all the disciples, not only Peter.

TEXT: CHAPTER 37 (cont.)

all. Truly, truly, I say to you, I will initiate you in all completeness[117] into the Mysteries of the Interior (*i.e., innermost spiritual realities*), and to the Mysteries of the Exterior (*i.e., most external, cosmic spiritual realities*). I shall fill you with the spirit, so that you shall be called 'spiritual'; that is, initiated in all fullness.

And so, truly, truly, I say to you, I will give to you all the Mysteries of all the realms of my Father; that is[118] all the realms of the First Mystery, so that the person whom you shall receive on Earth, shall be received in the light of the Heights; and the one whom you shall reject on Earth, shall be rejected in the kingdom of my Father, who is in the Heavens.

So listen, and give ear to all the expressions of remorse which Pistis Sophia spoke. She continued and spoke her third expression of remorse, saying; "O Light of Powers, give heed and save me. Let those who wish to take away my light, be in deprivation, and in darkness. Let them be turned towards the Chaos, and be shamed. Let them who oppress me saying, "We have become masters over her", descend speedily into the darkness. But let all those who seek for the light, rejoice and be glad; let them that desire your Mystery, say always, "May the Mystery be exalted."

Now, therefore, O Light, preserve me, for I lack my light because they have taken it away; for I am destitute of my strength, which they have taken from me. You, therefore, O Light, you are my Saviour. It is you, O Light, who preserve me. Deliver me quickly out of this Chaos.

---

[117] "initiate you in all completeness"; usu. 'perfect you in all fullness"; see Commentary.

[118] "that is": instead of the usu. 'of', for this appears to wrongly infer about the over-all text, that the Father and the First Mystery are two separate entities. The Coptic ⲁⲩⲱ is Grk. 'καί', and this also means 'that is', or 'then', etc.

COMMENTARY: CHAPTER 37
"...initiate you in all completeness"; usu. 'complete you in all fullness', which has little meaning; the meaning is 'to be initiated'. The Coptic expression here (**THYTN**) is using the Greek verb 'telein' (τελεῖν) which is always translated in the New Testament as 'complete' or 'perfect'. But as I have shown in my *Gospel of John*, this verb also means to be initiated; and should be understood as such in at least some of the usages in the Bible.

"reject on Earth": similar to some passages in the Gospels, but may well be independent of these.

"be in deprivation...": the mood expressed in this part of the declaration by Pistis Sophia is not one of mercy and forgiveness; this will be commented on after further expressions of remorse from her.

TEXT: CHAPTER 38
It came to pass, when Jesus had finished speaking these words to his disciples, saying, "This is the third expression of remorse of Pistis Sophia", that he then said to them, "Let that person in whom a perceptive state of mind has arisen,[119] come forward, and let them expound the meaning of the expression of remorse which Pistis Sophia has spoken."

It then happened, before Jesus had finished speaking, that Martha came forward; she fell down at the feet of Jesus, and cried out, weeping, and made obeisance at his feet.[120] Then in humility, she said to the Lord, "Lord, have mercy upon me, and be compassionate to me, and allow me to expound the

---

[119] "state of mind"; lit. 'spirit', meaning mind or intelligence.
[120] "at his feet": this is a traditional expression and does not imply that Jesus had physical feet.
"made obeisance": an important correction; usu. 'kissed' his feet, but the Coptic verb here, **oyaωkak** is from the Grk. 'proskunein' (προσκυνεῖν), and means in a religious context, 'to make obeisance'; i.e., to worship when bent right down. (This can also include kissing the ground or the feet, or the hem of a garment; but here is the risen Jesus; he has no material feet.)

TEXT: CHAPTER 38 (cont.)   Martha speaks
interpretation of the expression of remorse which Pistis Sophia has spoken."

So Jesus inwardly helped[121] Martha; he said to her, "Blessed is every one who humbles themselves, for on that person, mercy shall be given. So therefore, Martha, you are blessed. Explain then the interpretation of the meaning of the expression of remorse of Pistis Sophia."

And Martha answered and said to Jesus, in the midst of the disciples, "Concerning the expression of remorse spoken by Pistis Sophia: O my Lord Jesus, your light-being had prophesied about this through David, long ago, in the 69th Psalm (*70th in the Bible*), saying:

"Lord, my God, hasten to my help. Let them be ashamed and confounded that seek after my soul; let them be turned back and be put to shame, who say to me (*mocking*), "Excellent, excellent (*are you*)". But let all those that seek you be joyful; let them rejoice for your sake; let all those that love your salvation, proclaim always: 'The Lord be exalted.' But as for me, I am poor, I am destitute; Lord, be my help. You are my help and protection; Lord, delay no longer."

This, then, is the interpretation of the third expression of remorse of Pistis Sophia, intoning words of reverence to the Heights.

COMMENTARY: CHAPTER 38
This text of this chapter is quite clear. One notes that Martha, the sister of Mary of Bethany, is mentioned, which suggests that the unidentified 'Mary' (Mariam) may be Mary of Bethany, i.e., Martha's sister.

TEXT: CHAPTER 39
It then happened when Jesus had heard Martha, that he said to her, "Excellent, Martha, and well said." And Jesus continued in his conversation, and said to his

---

[121] "helped Martha": an important correction; usu. 'gave his hand' to her, but the verb here (ϯⲧⲟⲟⲧⲥ) primarily means 'to assist'.

TEXT: CHAPTER 39 (cont.)

disciples, "Pistis Sophia continued with a fourth expression of remorse, speaking it before they had oppressed her a second time, seeking to once more take away all the light that was in her. The Lion-faced entity sought that, together with all the dense (astral-) emanations (*entities*) which were with it: those whom the Self-willed One had sent into the Chaos.

She declared then her expression of remorse, as follows: "O Light, in whom I have trusted, hear my expression of remorse, and let my voice reach to your dwelling place. Do not turn your radiant image[122] away from me, but give heed to me when they oppress me. Quickly save me in that moment when I cry out to you. For my light[123] passes away as a breath, and I have become as dense (astral) matter.

They have taken away my light, and my spiritual strength has dried up. I have forgotten my Mystery which I earlier used to carry out. Because of the fearful voice and power of the Self-willed One, my spiritual strength has failed in me. I have become as a lesser spirit, below the Angels; dwelling in denser (astral) substance.

I have become like a false spirit, who is in a body formed of dense (astral) substance, and in whom there is no light-power. I have become like one of the decan entities, up in the airy heights, existing (*impossibly*) separated and alone.

TEXT NOTE in Chapter 39:

"lesser spirit, below the Angels": the text has just 'daimon'. This is a Greek word which throughout ancient Greek literature means either an evil spirit i.e., 'demon', or a neutral spirit entity (which could be spelt 'daemon') of lesser rank than the Angels. Here it means a 'daemon' or a neutral, lesser entity.

The 12 'decan' entities are active as part of an

---

[122] "radiant image": this unusual expression suggests that possibly it is a radiant 'likeness' or reflected image of this high deity that Pistis Sophia is perceiving.

[123] "my light passes away": the Coptic here is unclear; the word may refer to 'time'; but that is less likely.

TEXT NOTE: in Chapter 39 (cont.)
indivisible unity, reflecting the 12-fold, but unified, zodiac. So Pistis Sophia experiences now an extreme sense of isolation. Also, later chapters report that the decan entities have the task of sending people down to another life on Earth; a dynamic contrary to the inherently non-earthly, transcendent nature of our intuitive consciousness (i.e., Pistis Sophia).

TEXT: CHAPTER 39 (cont.) **Pistis Sophia intones**
The emanations of the Self-willed One have oppressed me severely; and my Consort has said to himself, "Instead of the light which was in her, they have filled her with the Chaos". I have absorbed the impure out-flow[124] of my own denser (astral) substances, and also the anguish of the tears of my eyes. (*That is, the distressed soul-energy caused by her awareness of the situation*).[125] (This I have done) so that they who oppress me, may not get access to these energies (*and use this to create a false type of human being: see Commentary*).

All these things have been done to me, O Light, by your order and command, and it is by your command that I am here. Your command has brought me below, and I have been brought low, becoming like an entity of the Chaos; my strength has grown cold in me. But you, O Lord, you are the Light Eternal, and always you seek out those who are oppressed.

Now, therefore, O Light, arise, seek after the spirit-nature and the soul which is within me. Your command has been accomplished, which you did decree for me in my afflictions. So the time has come for you to seek out my spirit-nature, and my soul.

---

[124] "out-flow": lit. sweat.

[125] "anguish of the tears of my eyes": usu. 'anguish of the tears *of the matter* of my eyes"; but these words (in italics) were crossed out by the scribe as an error, as Horner (p. 32) and Schwartze (p. 63) note; I conclude that these words are both unnecessary and out of place.

TEXT NOTE: in Chapter 39
(Here the divine 'Light' entity can be identified with the cosmic Christ, being referred to at times as 'Lord' or as 'Light'. The Coptic term can mean either God or 'Master'. Here it is referring to Christ as a spirit, a deity, not to Jesus.)

TEXT: CHAPTER 39 (cont.) Pistis Sophia intones
This is the time which you did (earlier) decree that you would visit me; for your redeeming helpers have sought for the strength which is in my soul. Because the appointed time has arrived, when they should also rescue the denser (astral) substance of my soul.

At that time then, all the rulers of the (*debased*), coarser Aions shall be in fear of your light, and all the emanations of the 13th (debased), coarser Aion shall be in fear of the divine reality (*lit. Mystery*) of your light; thus causing the others (*debased deities*) to assimilate what is purified of their light.

For the Lord shall seek out the (spiritual) strength of your souls (humanity). He has revealed (*the salvation intention of*) his Mystery. For he will take note of the repentance of those who inhabit the lower realms; he will not ignore their expressions of remorse. This is then, that spiritual reality (*lit. Mystery*) which has become the (spiritual) template for the (*redeemed*) people.

And the people who shall be so created, shall intone words of reverence up to the Heights, for the Light has gazed out, from the high realms (*lit. height*) of its Light. He will look down upon the entire dense (astral) substance; to hear the groans of those who are bound, so that he may release the strength of the souls whose spiritual forces are bound; (thus he may) place his spiritual reality (*lit. his name*) in the soul of each entity, and his Mystery in their spirit.

COMMENTARY: CHAPTER 39
"absorbed the out-flow": lit. 'devoured my sweat'; she has absorbed the out-working of her own denser

COMMENTARY: CHAPTER 39 (cont.)
(astral-)substances; these arise from her now debased, more dense state, and her benumbed cognizance.

"from the anguish of the tears of (*the matter of*) my eyes'. As stated in the foot-note, the words in italics are crossed out, but if they were left in, then 'the eyes', i.e., the perception capacity of Pistis Sophia, is being defined as inherently coarse. But although the perceiving is deluded by the fallen Archons, it is not coarsened. For she is still able to perceive, and interact with, the divine Light of Lights.

The perception capacity of all spirits is the core part of their nature, and is therefore mentioned in Chapter 25 regarding the Archons; and although all of their soul-spirit auras are coarse, this is not the case with Pistis Sophia. As noted earlier, debased or holy Archons are deities of varying ranks; one can conclude this means from Angels up to the Seraphim.

"*create a false type of human being*": in Chapter 25 we learn that from their more dense or coarse emanations, the fallen Archons create astral-bodies for humans. So Pistis Sophia has no intention of that occurring with her now more dense, fallen condition.

"also rescue": Pistis Sophia needs the denser astral nature to be redeemed also.

"the Lord shall seek out": here is a reverential passage, proclaiming the cosmic Christ, who is in effect identified as the primary spirit power within, or over-shadowing, Jesus, who has been, and continues to be, the narrator of the story of Pistis Sophia.

TEXT: CHAPTER 40 John speaks
Jesus spoke these words to his disciples, "This is the fourth expression of remorse spoken by Pistis Sophia, let him who understands, understand". It happened, after Jesus had said these words, that John came forward, made obeisance at the heart[126] of Jesus, and

---

[126] "heart": lit. breast.

TEXT: CHAPTER 40 (cont.)　　　　John speaks
said to him, "My Lord, command me also, and allow me to utter the explanation of the fourth expression of remorse declared by Pistis Sophia." So Jesus said to John, 'I give you this command, and I bid you expound the interpretation of the expression of remorse spoken by Pistis Sophia."

So John[127] answered and said, "My Lord and Saviour, concerning this expression of remorse intoned by Pistis Sophia, about this your light-being in David has long ago prophesied, in Psalm 101 (*102 in the Bible*), saying:

"Hear my prayer, O Lord, and let my crying come to you. Turn not your face away from me; but incline your ear to me, in this day when I am oppressed.

Quickly hear me, in the day when I shall cry out to you for my days are consumed like smoke, and my bones are parched like stone.

I am mown down like the grass, and my heart is withered, for I have forgotten to eat my bread. Because of the sound of my groaning, my bones have cleaved to my flesh. I have become like the pelican in the wilderness; like the owl in a house. I have spent all night long, in watching; I am like the sparrow alone upon the house-top.

My enemies revile me all day long, and they who honoured me, now cursed me; for I have eaten ashes as though it were bread, and mingled my drink with tears, before your indignation and your wrath; for you have lifted me up and cast me to the earth. My days have declined like a shadow, and I am shriveled like the grass.

But you, Lord: you are forever, and your remembrance is from generation to generation. Arise, therefore, and have mercy upon Zion, for the time has come to have mercy upon her; indeed, your time

---

[127] I conclude that this 'John' is Lazaros, the writer of the Gospel of John, who was given the 'mystery' name John (see my *The Gospel of John*.)

TEXT: CHAPTER 40 (cont.)   John speaks

has come. Your servants have sought her stones,[128] and they will take pity on her soil, that the nation may fear the name of the Lord, and the kings of the Earth your glory; for the lord shall build Zion to reveal himself in his glory.

He has heard the prayer of them that are humble, and has not despised their supplication. Let them write this in another book, and the people that will be begotten shall bless the Lord, for he has looked down from his holy height.

The Lord has gazed upon Heaven and the Earth, to hear the sighs of those that are bound; to release the children of those whom they have killed, that they may utter the name of the lord in Zion and his praise in Jerusalem." "This, Lord, is the interpretation of the mystery of the expression of remorse, declared by Pistis Sophia."

COMMENTARY: CHAPTER 40

"When Jesus had spoken these words": as noted in the Introduction, here as the Gospel of John, the text may say 'Jesus' is speaking, but especially after the Resurrection, the cosmic Christ is an integral part of Jesus, and often it is this great deity who is speaking.

TEXT: CHAPTER 41

It then happened, when John had finished speaking these words to Jesus in the midst of his disciples, that Jesus said to him, "Well said, John, the virgin, you who shall rule in the kingdom of the Light." Then Jesus continued his conversation, and said to his disciples, "It occurred again that the Self-willed One oppressed Pistis Sophia in the Chaoses[129], but the command had not yet come from the First Mystery, to free her from the Chaos. So it happened, when the denser emanations of the Self-willed One oppressed

---

[128] "sought her stones": an obscure expression.
[129] "Chaoses": Chaos is here plural, just as is 'darkness' a few sentences on.

TEXT: CHAPTER 41 (cont.) **Pistis Sophia speaks** her, that she cried out, declaring this fifth expression of remorse, saying:

"O Light of my salvation, I intoned words of reverence to you in the place of the Heights, and also (from here) in the Chaos. I will revere you with the words of reverence that I intone – those words with which I have revered you in the Heights, and also in the Chaos.

May this (intoning) come into your presence. Give heed, O Light, to my expression of remorse, for my being is filled with darkness, and my light has descended into the Chaos.

Also I have become similar to the Rulers of the Chaos, they who have gone into the darkness below. I have become as a dense (soul) body, which has no-one in the Heights to save it. I have become also like dense (astral) substances (*minor entities*) from whom the power has been taken; like dense (astral) substances cast into the Chaos, which you have not saved, which have (now) perished, by your command.

Therefore, I have been placed in the lower darknesses;[130] in darknesses, and in dead (astral-) substances, in which there is no spiritual presence. You have brought your command upon me, and upon everything, as you have decreed.

Your spirit has departed, and left me. Moreover, by your command, the emanations (*i.e., out-raying spiritual influences*) of my Aion have not come to my aid. They have held me in detestation, and kept themselves from me. Yet am I not utterly ruined, even though my light has diminished in me.

I have cried out to the Light, with all the light that was left in me, and I have stretched forth my hands to you. Now, therefore, O Light, surely you will fulfill your command, in the Chaos. The deliverers – who should come by your command – shall they arise in

---

[130] "I have been placed": usu. 'they have placed me', but to myself and MacDermot, this is to be read as 'I', not 'they'.

TEXT: CHAPTER 41 (cont.) **Pistis Sophia speaks**
darkness, and become devoted helpers[131] of yours? Surely they will then utter the Mystery of your name in the Chaos?

Or, it might happen perhaps, that they shall utter your name into the dense (astral) substances of the Chaos: into that which you shall not cleanse?

TEXT NOTE: in Chapter 41
(That is, Pistis Sophia is concerned that these spirit helpers may not intone the name of the divine Light in the Chaos realm, which would bring help to souls, but instead intone into the lowly, dense, minor entities (lit. substances) in the Chaos, in which the divine Light cannot exert an influence.)

TEXT: CHAPTER 41 (cont.) **Pistis Sophia speaks**
But, I have intoned words of reverence to you, O Light, and so my expression of remorse shall reach you in the Heights.

TEXT NOTE:
(The text in next few sentences seems to be defective: it appears that several words are omitted. I have supplied these presumed missing words in italics; see the Commentary for more about this.)

TEXT: CHAPTER 41 (cont.) **Pistis Sophia speaks**
Let your light come upon me, for they have taken away my light, and so I am in distress because of the *missing* light, *light which was mine* from the time I was emanated forth; I had gazed into the Heights towards the light. *But* then I gazed below, towards this (malignant) light-power which is in the Chaos; *this is* when I asserted myself (*lit. 'I rose up'*) but then I became debased (*lit. 'went down'*).

Your command has come upon me, and the fears which you did decree, they have thrown me into

---

[131] "devoted helpers": the usual meaning of the word here is 'disciples', that is awkward in this context. But the Greek term also means 'apprentices', and 'students'.

TEXT: CHAPTER 41 (cont.) **Pistis Sophia speaks** confusion. They have surrounded me, roaring[132] like (rushing) water; they have taken hold of me the entire time. And you have not permitted emanations from my own Aion (*i.e., the 13th Aion*) to help me, nor have you permitted my Consort to save me from my tribulations."

(Jesus said) "This is the fifth expression of remorse which Pistis Sophia declared in the Chaos, when once again all the denser (astral) emanations of the Self-willed One began to oppress her."

COMMENTARY: CHAPTER 41
"John, the virgin": this refers to John, writer of the fourth Gospel, not John the Apostle, son of Zebedee. Rudolf Steiner taught that Lazaros wrote this Gospel, and acquired the epithet, or additional name, of 'John', after he was initiated through the so-called 'Awakening of Lazaros' (Jn.11); see my *The Gospel of John* for a discussion of this topic.

As an initiate, his soul or astral-body brought forth his Spiritual-self, (called then 'The Son of Man'). So his spiritual 'substance' is derived solely from the higher realms; not from his parents. This condition was referred to as 'virginal'; since none of his soul-spirit derived from the parents' soul qualities.

(Defective text here due to missing words.)
This is how the text here is usually understood:
"Let your light come upon me, for they have taken away my light, and I am in distress because of the light, from the time I was emanated forth. And when I had gazed into the Heights towards the light, when I gazed below, towards the (malignant) light-power which is in the Chaos; I decided to rise up and then went down."

---

[132] "roaring": usu. 'numerous' which has little or no meaning; the Coptic (ⲉⲩ-ⲟϣ) does mean 'numerous', but it also occurs in some Coptic texts, in a variant form (ⲉⲩ-ϣϣ) which means 'roaring', etc.

COMMENTARY: CHAPTER 41 (cont.)

But this is incoherent; Pistis Sophia cannot be in distress because of the divine, true Light – and not from ever since she was created. My reconstructed version provides a coherent narrative here. Furthermore, to say "I rose up and went down" is also awkward; again it appears that some words are missing. My reconstruction here allows a coherent meaning to emerge. Below is my version again:

"Let your light come upon me, for they have taken away my light, and so I am in distress because of the *missing* light, *light which was mine* from the time I was emanated forth; I had gazed into the Heights towards the light. *But* then I gazed below, towards this (malignant) light-power which is in the Chaos; *this is* when I in error, asserted myself (*lit. 'rose up'*) and became debased."

TEXT: CHAPTER 42 (cont.) Philip speaks

Jesus, therefore, having spoken these words to his disciples, said to them, "Whoever has ears to hear, let them hear; and let that person in whom the strength of their spirit is welling up, come forward and expound the interpretation of the meaning of the fifth expression of remorse from Pistis Sophia."

So when Jesus had finished speaking, Philip started forward, and got up, leaving on the ground the book which had been in his hand, for it was he who recorded all the discourse which Jesus uttered, and all that he did.

Philip, therefore, came forward and said to him, "Lord, surely it is not on me alone that you have imposed the task of taking care of this world, by writing all that we shall say and do. Yet you have not permitted me (as yet) to come forward and interpret the mysteries of the expression of remorse of Pistis Sophia.

My spirit has welled up in me many times, often; and it has been freely active, impelling me to come forward and speak the interpretation of the expression of remorse of Pistis Sophia. But I could not, because it is I who write down all the words."

TEXT: CHAPTER 42 (cont.)   **Philip speaks**

It then happened, as Jesus heard Philip, that he said to him, "Listen, Philip, blessed one, that I may speak with you; for it is you and Thomas and Matthew to whom the First Mystery has given the task of writing down all the words which I shall speak, and everything which I shall do, and everything which you shall see.

But as for you, the number of words which you have to write, is not completed. But when it shall be completed, you will come forward, you shall utter that which you wish. Now, therefore, it is you three who shall write every word which I shall speak, and everything which I shall do, and everything which you shall see, and I will bear witness to you of all things which are in the kingdom of the heavens."

COMMENTARY: CHAPTER 42

The specific reference to the three disciples who are to work as scribes - Thomas, Philip and Matthew - provides interesting details as to how, and by whom, the communications were written down.

TEXT: CHAPTER 43   **Mariam speaks**

And when Jesus had spoken these words, he said to his disciples, "He that has ears to hear, let him hear." Then Mariam started forward again; she came amongst them, and stood by Philip, and said to Jesus, "Lord, my companion-of-light has ears, and I am ready to hear with my spiritual nature, for I have understood the discourse which you have spoken. You have said to us, "He that has ears to hear, let him hear."

Concerning the discourse which you have spoken to Philip, "It is to you, and Thomas, and Matthew, to whom it has been entrusted to you three - by the First Mystery (*i.e., God*) - to write down every word of the kingdom of light, in order that you may bear witness thereof." Therefore please listen to me, while I expound the interpretation of this word, which your light-being prophesied of old through Moses, saying,

TEXT: CHAPTER 43 (cont.)   **Philip speaks**

'By two or three witnesses everything shall be established.' The three witnesses are Philip, Thomas, and Matthew."

So it happened when Jesus had heard these words, that he said, "Excellent, Mariam, this is the solution to the word. Now, therefore, Philip, do come forward, expound the interpretation of the mystery of the fifth expression of remorse of Pistis Sophia, and afterwards take your seat, and write down every word which I shall utter, until you have accomplished the number (of words) which has fallen to your lot, and which you have to write in the words of the kingdom of light.

Afterwards, you shall come forward, and expound what your spirit shall have understood. Now, therefore, expound the meaning of the fifth expression of remorse of Pistis Sophia." **Philip speaks**

"Lord, please listen while I expound the interpretation of her expression of remorse, for your being has prophesied of old concerning this, through David, in the 87th Psalm (*Ps. 88 in the Bible*), saying:

"O Lord, God of my salvation, I have cried out to you day and night. Let my weeping come before you; give ear to my plea. For my soul is full of evil, and my life draws near to Amente (*the Egyptian term for the Soul-world*). I am counted among those that go down into Sheol (*the dreary, darkened Soul-world*).[133] I have become as a man who has no helper. The free among the dead are like the wounded, cast out and sleeping in the tombs; people whom you, in truth, no longer

---

[133] The Hebrew text of this Psalm which the disciple would have quoted, does not have the word for an actual 'pit', but Sheol (שְׁאִיל) which means the Soul-world (but not Hell); because 'pit' is used as a symbol for Sheol in various Biblical texts. But the Septuagint version misses this point, and simply has 'pit'. The original Aramaic notes of the dialogue of these discussions with Christ were eventually put into Greek, and for this the Septuagint was used, see Commentary.

TEXT: CHAPTER 43 (cont.) Psalm 87

remember, and who have been laid low by your hands.

They have left me below, in Sheol, in darkness and in the shadow of death. Your wrath has settled upon me, and all your concerns have come upon me. You have put my acquaintances far away from me; they have looked on me as an abomination. They have abandoned me, and I cannot go forth. My eye has become dim from my misery, and I have cried unto you, Lord, the whole day long; I have stretched forth my hands to you.

Will you not manifest your wonders among the dead? Shall not the Shades arise to proclaim you? Shall they not utter your name in the tombs; and your righteousness in a land which you have forgotten?

But as for me, I have cried out to you, O Lord, and my prayer shall reach you early in the morning; turn not your face far from me. As for me, I am miserable; I am in misery from my youth. When I exalted myself, I was abased; but I have risen up again.

Your wrath has come upon me, and your fearsomeness has troubled me. These have surrounded me like (*rising*) water, they have seized upon me the whole day long. You have distanced my comrades and also my acquaintances from me, in my misery."

This is the meaning of the mystery of the fifth expression of remorse , spoken by Pistis Sophia, when she was oppressed in the Chaos.

COMMENTARY: CHAPTER 43

"companion-of-light": the central word here, commonly means 'man', but it also means kinsperson, servant, or friend. We have, in this wonderful expression, a glimpse into the experiential knowledge acquired by those initiated in those times, of the spiritual dimension to the human being. It may refer to the 'intuitive-spiritual' soul – itself a herald of the radiant Spiritual-self – and was perceived by the disciple as a subtly shining presence in their inner being.

COMMENTARY: CHAPTER 43 (cont.)

"Amente": a striking feature of the text; for here it diverges from the Septuagint (which has 'Hades'), and instead uses an Egyptian term. Throughout the text, (in chapters 43,72, and 102) the term 'Amente' is used here in just the same way as in the ancient Egyptian funeral texts (e.g., Chapters 15,17,19,63 of *The Book of the Dead*). That is, the realm of the dead, which extends from fiendish lower places, to noble, light-filled places, where sacred deities are encountered. As I endeavoured to establish in my *Gospel of John*, the age-old initiation wisdom of the ancient Egyptians formed, discreetly, a living part of esoteric Christian wisdom.

That there was a distinct Egyptian component to the esoteric teachings of Jesus, is indicated in another Coptic text, *The History of Joseph the Carpenter*, where an experience of the Soul-world is described as seeing Death and Amente followed by their satellite entities who are called 'decanii'. These terms echo some key words in the Pistis Sophia codex.

"the Shades"; MacDermot excellently solved the error here carried over into the Coptic by the translators of the Psalms into Greek who mistook the Hebrew for 'Shades', i.e., the term for the Dead, for a similar Hebrew word, meaning 'physicians'.[134]

That this error was carried over into the written reports of the meetings with the risen Saviour, reveals that after these sessions of communing with the risen Jesus Christ were over, notes were written down in Aramaic or Hebrew. Then later, Greek versions of the Aramaic notes were made for the instruction of the Greek-speaking inner circles.

But the translator, when encountering large sections of a Psalm in the Aramaic notes, found it easier to use the Greek text of the Psalm from his own copy of the Septuagint; but this already contained this error. These errors then were passed on when the Greek version was translated into Coptic.

Because it is most unlikely that any of the disciples

---

[134] That is Shades רְפָאִים, and physicians רְֹפְאִים.

COMMENTARY: CHAPTER 43 (cont.)
would make such an obvious error, since firstly, as Palestinian Jews, they knew the correct, original text of the Psalms in Aramaic or Hebrew, and secondly, they were already awakened to esoteric-spiritual realities through the initiatory schooling that Jesus offered to them, during his life, and probably from their Essene connections.

TEXT: CHAPTER 44
It then happened when Jesus had heard the words which had Philip spoken, that he said, "Well said, you beloved one. So now continue to take your seat, and write your share of all the words which I shall speak, and of all things which I shall do, and of all that you shall see." And Philip sat down immediately and wrote.

After this, it happened that Jesus continued to speak. He said to his disciples, "Then did Pistis Sophia cry out to the Light, in order that her sin might be forgiven her: that is, leaving her realm and going into the darkness. She intoned her sixth expression of remorse, saying, "I am intoning words of reverence to you, O Light, in the darkness below. Give ear to my expression of remorse: may your Light heed the voice of my entreaty ! O Light, if you bear in mind my sin, I shall not be able to come near to you, and you shall abandon me; yet you, O Light – you are my Saviour, because of the light of your being.[135]

I have intuitively perceived you, O Light, and my soul trusted in your Mystery, and has also trusted in the Light which is in the Heights; my being has trusted also in this light whilst down below, in the Chaos. Let all the spiritual forces which are in me, truly discern the Light, while I am in the lower darkness.

May they also intuitively discern the Light, if they go into the realm of the Heights, for it is the Light which shall see and save us, and there is a great Mystery of salvation in it. It is the Light that shall

---

[135] "light of your being": lit. 'of your name'.

TEXT: CHAPTER 44
save all the (spirit) beings in the Chaos (*which have become debased*) because of my transgression; for I have left my realm. I have come into the Chaos."

(*Jesus then said*) now, therefore, those whose mind is exalted, let them understand.

COMMENTARY: CHAPTER 44
"save all the spirit beings": A deep truth here: when a soul becomes spiritually degraded, this impacts many other similar or lesser entities. Then, it is also reasonable to conclude that minor spirits are degraded, (as also Rudolf Steiner taught). St. Paul indicates this, with regard to the outcome for the cosmos once humanity finds Christ, "creation itself shall be liberated from its bondage to decay and brought into the freedom and glory of the children of God. We know that the whole creation has been groaning…" (Rom. 8:22-23)

TEXT: CHAPTER 45   Andrew speaks
It then happened when Jesus had finished speaking these words to his disciples, that he said to them, "Do you understand in what manner I am speaking to you?" Then Andrew came forward and said, "Lord, concerning the sixth expression of remorse of Pistis Sophia, your spirit's power has prophesied of old through David, in Psalm 129, (*Ps. 130 in the Bible*) saying,

"I have cried out to you, Lord, from the depth of the abyss. Hear my voice ! Let your ears give heed to the voice of my prayer. O Lord, if you give heed to the iniquities (of humanity),[136] who will be able to pass that test? Indeed forgiveness is in your hands. Because of your name, I have waited, O Lord. My soul has waited for your words. My soul has trusted in the Lord, from morning until evening. Let Israel trust in

---

[136] "of humanity": following Horner; the Coptic is unclear, usu. 'my iniquities', but that makes little sense.

TEXT: CHAPTER 45 — Andrew speaks

the Lord from the morning until the evening, for mercy is in the hand of the Lord, and there is great salvation in him; and he shall redeem Israel from all his sins."

Jesus said to him, "Well said, Andrew, you blessed one. That is the interpretation of her expression of remorse. Truly, truly, I say to you (*ye*), I shall initiate you into all the mysteries of the Light, and all Gnoses: from the innermost soul-spirit realities,[137] to the most external cosmic realities.[138]

From the Ineffable One down to the darkness of the darknesses; from the Light of Lights, down to the decaying realm of dense (astral) matter;[139] from the gods, down to the lesser spirits[140]. From all the Lords, to all the decans, from all the Powers (Exousiai), to all the servitors, from the creation of humans (down) to beasts, cattle and reptiles; in order that you may be called "initiated"; perfected in all fullness.

Truly, truly, I say to you, in the realm where I shall be, in the kingdom of my Father, there shall you also be with me. And when the number of the Perfected shall be completed, so that the Mixture may be dissolved, I shall order that they bring *(before me)* all the empowered deities who refused to offer up what was purified of their light.

And I shall make command to the Fire of Wisdom – that fire through which the initiated pass – to eat into

---

[137] lit. "from the interiors of the interiors."

[138] lit. "from the exteriors of the exteriors."

[139] "decaying realm of matter"; the Coptic here is unclear; so these words are omitted in previous translations, they show a gap in the text. For here is a non-existent word 'phaab' (ϕⲁⲁⲃ). But I conclude the scribe meant 'phab' (ϕⲁⲃ), which means 'leaven' or 'yeast', which is used in a positive and a negative way in Scripture. The negative implies decay, since yeast brings about decay, (before it then re-configures the host substance).

[140] "lesser spirits": usu. 'demons', but the word here from Greek, means lesser entities (lit. 'daemons'), these are not always evil beings, but are below the rank of the hierarchical deities.

TEXT: CHAPTER 45 (cont.)   Mariam speaks
those (debased) empowered Ones up to their innermost nature (*lit. their interior*), until they shall have yielded up the last of what is purified of their light."

It then happened when Jesus had spoken these words to his disciples that he said to them, "Do you understand the manner in which I am speaking with you?"

And Mariam said to him, "Yes, Lord, I have understood the word which you have spoken. Concerning, then, that which you have said, namely, that after the dissolution of the whole mixture (*of various denser astral influences*), you should take your seat on a Light-power. And your disciples, that is to say, ourselves, should be seated at your right, so that you should judge those empowered gods, those who have not given over the purified spirituality of their light.

And also that the Fire of Wisdom should eat away at them, until they have yielded the last light which is in them. Concerning this word, your light-being prophesied long ago through David, in Psalm 81[141], saying, 'The Elohim shall sit in the congregation of the gods, to judge the gods'." Jesus said to her, "Well said, Mariam."

COMMENTARY: CHAPTER 45
"number of the perfected shall be completed":
meaning when all those souls who can be redeemed, via a gradual purification process, are redeemed.
"the mixture may be dissolved": meaning that the tainted astral-etheric part of the cosmos is to pass away; the part of Creation in which ahrimanic-luciferic influences had been mixed in with divine influences.

---

[141] The scribe made an error here, "the 24th plus one Psalm", instead of 'eighty plus one'. Schwartze comments on this error in his Latin translation (*Pistis Sophia* p.475); Horner leaves it in the text. The scribe was anticipating the next chapter which is about Ps. 24. *The Septuagint's* Ps. 81 is Ps. 82 in the Bible.

COMMENTARY: CHAPTER 45 (cont.)

"the gods": this term is not defined, and hence presumably refers to all and any deities.

"refused to give": the self-serving fallen deities were intent on keeping the finer aspect of their nature (i.e., their light) for themselves. These potent words from the risen Saviour are pointing **to the core principle of divine creativity**: to give over to others the finest of one's spiritual nature, so that other life-waves may arise from that, and later blossom. This action itself then returns in some way to the giver, ennobling the one who gives.

"Fire of Wisdom": another profound esoteric truth; that debased gods (and humans in the lower astral realms) are subject to the 'cleansing fire', but this is no fire at all to those who are selfless in their inner being and social interactions.

"The Elohim (*plural*) shall sit in the congregation": Mariam is quoting the Hebrew original of the biblical text to the risen Jesus. But the Septuagint version used in the codex has simply (incorrectly) 'God' (Theos) which is singular. Although Mariam's quote is referring to the plural 'Elohim', the parallelism remains valid.

"Gnoses": this refers to multiple kinds of spiritual wisdom and corresponding inner pathways.

TEXT: CHAPTER 46

Jesus continued in his discourse, and said to his disciples, "It happened as Pistis Sophia finished intoning her sixth expression of remorse for forgiveness of her transgressions, that she turned again towards the Heights, to see if her sins had been forgiven her, and to see if she would be guided up out of the Chaos.

But, by command of the First Mystery, she had not yet been heard, so her sin was not pardoned, which would allow her to be raised out of the Chaos. Hence when she turned to see whether her expression of remorse was accepted, she saw all the (malignant) Rulers of the 12 Aions, mocking her, and rejoicing that her expression of remorse had not been

TEXT: CHAPTER 46 (cont.)

accepted.

Therefore when she saw them mocking her, she was in great distress, and raised her face to the Heights, saying, in her seventh expression of remorse, "O (*Christ*) Light, I have raised my being to you, O my Light.[142] I have trusted in you. Don't let me be scorned; don't let the (malignant) Rulers of the 12 Aions, who hate me, rejoice over me. For everyone who has faith in you shall not be put to shame.

Let them that have taken away my power, dwell in darkness. They shall have no gain from it, but instead, may it be taken from them. O Light, show me your pathways, and I shall be saved (*by going*) on them. Show me your pathways, that I may be saved from the Chaos; and guide me in your light.

May I truly perceive, O Light, that it is you who will be my Saviour. I will trust in you all of my time. Be heedful to my salvation, O Light, for your mercy is eternal. As to the transgression which I have committed from the beginning through my ignorance, do not count it against me, O Light. But save me in your great Mystery that forgives sins, because of your goodness, O Light. For you are good and righteous, O Light.

For this reason, the Light will show me my path, that I may be saved from my transgression. And my spiritual energies which were weakened through fear of the denser entities[143] of the Self-willed One, shall be drawn out from these entities (*lit. emanations*),[144] by the command of the Light. And my powers – which are weakened because of these merciless ones – these powers shall be instructed in the gnosis (*spiritual wisdom*) of the Light.

---

[142] "(Christ) Light": in the text it is simply 'Light', but here Jesus Christ is describing the inner dynamics of Pistis Sophia, and the light is a radiance she saw in the Buddhi realm, where the cosmic Christ or Sun-god is encountered.

[143] "denser entities": lit. 'hulikon emanations'.

[144] "drawn out from these...": Coptic is obscure, possibly, 'be drawn near to him, according to the Light's command'.

TEXT: CHAPTER 46 (cont.)

For all the gnoses[145] of the Light offer ways to salvation *(lit. salvations)* to everyone. And all these gnoses are also Mysteries (*i.e., ways to initiatory enlightenment*), for all those who seek for the places of the Light's Inheritance with its Mysteries.

For the sake of the spiritual reality *(lit. Mystery)* of the essence of your being[146], O Light, forgive my transgression: it is great. To everyone who discerns truly the Light, it will give that initiatory enlightenment *(lit. Mystery)* which is appropriate for that seeker; whose soul shall then abide in the realms of the Light. Then that soul's spiritual-nature shall inherit the Treasury of Light.[147]

The (*Christ*) Light gives spiritual strength to those who spiritually perceive it; and the living essence of its spiritual reality[148] is with those who perceive it. It shall show them the realm of the Inheritance, which is in the Treasury of Light. As for me, I have always trusted in your light, for it is this Light which shall deliver my feet out of the bonds of the darkness.

Give heed to me, O Light, and save me, for in the Chaos they have taken my core nature[149] from me. My tribulations and my oppressions are greatly multiplied amidst all these emanations. Save me from my transgression and from this darkness, and give heed to the grief of my oppressed state, and forgive my transgression.

Give heed to the Rulers of the (*debased*) 12 Aions who have hated me through jealousy; watch over my being and save me. Don't leave me to dwell in this darkness, for I have trusted in you, O Light. So therefore, O Light, save my powers from the emanations of the Self-willed One, through whom I am oppressed."

---

[145] "Gnoses": lit. spiritual wisdoms.
[146] "essence of your being": lit. 'name'.
[147] This is the 2nd realm of the Buddhi realm. Rudolf Steiner taught that Jesus Christ has an inner connection here (see Commentary).
[148] Lit. 'the name of its Mystery'.
[149] "core nature": lit. 'my name'.

TEXT: CHAPTER 46 (cont.)   Thomas speaks

So now, whoever is (inwardly) attentive, let them be attentive. As Jesus said this to his disciples, Thomas came forward and said, "Lord, I am attentive, indeed I am more attentive, and my mind is ready within me, and I rejoice greatly that you have revealed these things to us. Furthermore, I have tolerated my brethren up to this moment, for I have felt no wrath against them; I have not been jealous[150] that each of them should come to you and expound the interpretation of the expression of remorse of Pistis Sophia.   **Psalm 24**

So therefore, my Lord, (I shall speak) concerning the interpretation of the seventh expression of remorse by Pistis Sophia. Your light-being has prophesied through David the prophet, in Psalm 24 (*Ps. 25 in the Bible*), saying, "Unto you, O Lord, I have lifted up my soul, my God. I have entrusted myself to you. Let me not be ashamed, do not let my enemies mock me; for whosoever hopes in you shall not be ashamed. Let them who commit unlawful deeds without a cause, be ashamed. Show me your path, Lord, and teach me your ways.

Guide me into the way of truth, and teach me, for you are my God, and my Saviour. I will hope in you throughout the day. Call to remembrance your mercies, Lord, and your loving-kindnesses, for they are from ancient times. Remember not the sins of my youth and my ignorance. But think upon me according to the abundance of your mercy, because of your goodness, O Lord. The Lord is gracious and righteous; therefore shall he teach sinners in the way. He will guide the gentle with judgment, he will teach the gentle his ways.

All the ways of the Lord are good, they are truth for those who seek his righteousness and his testimonies. For your name's sake, O Lord, pardon my sin, for it is very great. Who is the man who fears the Lord? With him shall the Lord establish a law in the way he has chosen. His soul shall dwell at ease, and

---

[150] Lit. "I have tolerated".

TEXT: CHAPTER 46 (cont.)
his descendants shall inherit the land.

The Lord is the support of them that fear him; and His soul shall dwell at ease, and his descendants shall inherit the land. The Lord is the support of them that fear him; and the name (*i.e., spiritual power*) of the Lord is with them that fear him, to teach them his covenant.

Mine eyes gaze upon the Lord for ever, for it is he who shall pluck my feet out of the snare. Look upon me, have mercy upon me, for I am an only son,[151] I am a beggar indeed. The sorrows of my heart are intensified; bring me out of my oppression. Look upon my abasement, my misery, and forgive me all my sins. Consider mine enemies, how many they are, and they hate me with cruel hatred. Guard my soul, and save me; let me not be ashamed, for I have hoped in you. The simple and the righteous clung to me, for I have kept my hope in you, O Lord. O God, save Israel from all its miseries."

And when Jesus heard these words of Thomas he said to him, "Well said, Thomas, excellent. This is the solution to the seventh expression of remorse of Pistis Sophia.

Truly, truly, I say to you (*ye*), all the generations of the world shall proclaim you blessed on the Earth, because I have revealed to you these things, and that you have received of my spirit, and have become insightful and spiritually perceptive, comprehending that which I have said to you.

Beyond this, I will fill you with all the Light and all the power of the Spirit, in order that you may understand from this hour all that shall be said to you, and that which you shall see. Yet a little while, and I will tell you all that pertains to the Heights -
from) the outermost cosmic realities (*lit. the exterior*) to the innermost soul-spirit realities (*lit. the interior*) and from the innermost soul-spirit realities to the

---

[151] "An only son": The Coptic is obscure, possibly 'an orphan am I' (Horner) or 'lonely am I' (Schmidt-Till - 'ich bin einsam').

outermost cosmic realities."

COMMENTARY: CHAPTER 46
This text of this chapter is quite clear.

TEXT: CHAPTER 47
And Jesus continued in his conversation; it happened then, after Pistis Sophia had uttered her seventh expression of remorse in the Chaos, that the command had not yet come to me, from the First Mystery, to save her and to lead her up out of the Chaos. Nevertheless, I myself, out of compassion, without a command, led her into a region in the Chaos, which was freer, more agreeable.[152]

And when the denser entities,[153] sent forth by the Self-willed One, saw that I had conducted her into a region somewhat less confined in the Chaos, they ceased for a time to oppress her, thinking that she would be (soon) taken out of the Chaos entirely.

Now, when this was done, Pistis Sophia did not know that it was I who helped her; indeed she did not recognize me at all. But she continued intoning reverence to the Treasury of Light, which she had seen of old, and in which she had trusted, observing[154] that it was the true Light.

And she was thinking, because she had trusted in this true light which belongs to the Treasury of Light, that it was for this reason that she was being led up out of the Chaos; and that her expression of remorse would be accepted. However, the commandment of the First Mystery was not yet fulfilled for her repentance to be accepted. So listen, while I tell you all events that happened to Pistis Sophia.

---

[152] "agreeable": usu. 'wider/spacious'; but that makes little sense; the adjective here (ⲟⲩⲟⲱϣⲥ) also means 'comfortable, agreeable'.

[153] "denser entities": lit. 'hulikon (dense-material) emanations'.

[154] "observing": usu. 'thinking', but meaning mentally perceiving something; these nuances are in the Coptic verb (ⲙⲉⲉⲩⲉ).

TEXT: CHAPTER 47 (cont.)

It then happened, when I had led her into a freer, more agreeable region in the Chaos, that the entities sent forth[155] from the Self-willed One, ceased entirely to oppress her, thinking that she would be led up out of the Chaos entirely.

It then happened when the emanations of the Self-willed One discovered that Pistis Sophia had not been taken out of the Chaos, they returned together, oppressing her extremely. Therefore, she uttered her eighth declaration of remorse, in that they had not ceased to constrain her, but that they had returned, and again oppressed her severely. And she spoke this, intoning: **Pistis Sophia speaks**

"I have placed my heart on you, O Light, don't leave me in the Chaos, but save me; O deliver me through your spiritual cognizance (*i.e. divine consciousness*). Give heed to me and save me. Be to me a Saviour, O Light, and save me; lead me to your light, for you are my Saviour, and you shall lead me to yourself. For the sake of the spirit of your inner being;[156] lead me, give to me your Mystery.

You shall save me from this Lion-faced being, with whom *they* have lain in wait for me, for you are my Saviour; and I will place my purified light into your hands. For you have saved me, O Light, through your spiritual cognizance. You are angry with those that keep me in their sights, but who could not fully possess me, for I have truly perceived the Light.

I will rejoice and give praise, for you have been compassionate to me, and you have considered the oppression in which I am existing, and you have saved me. Moreover, you shall deliver my being from the Chaos, and you have not left me in the hands of the Lion-faced being, but you have led me into a region where I am not oppressed.

COMMENTARY: CHAPTER 47

"less oppressive region": usually simply 'wider

---

[155] "entities sent forth": lit. 'those emanations'.
[156] lit. 'the mystery of your name'.

COMMENTARY: CHAPTER 47

region', but this spatial description seems out of place in spirit realms; the Coptic word, (ⲟⲩⲱϣⲥ) also means 'comfortable', or 'less oppressive', (see comments on Chapter 49.

"through your spiritual cognizance": usually 'in/with your knowledge', but this makes little sense. If the Divine is to redeem or bless any fallen soul, then this occurs through the soul becoming at one with the divine consciousness, and that is due to the deity being able to permeate it.[157] Also a deity has spiritual cognizance, or a divine consciousness, rather than knowledge.

TEXT: CHAPTER 48

And when Jesus had said these things, he continued in his discourse, and said, "So it came to pass, therefore that when the Lion-faced being discovered that Pistis Sophia had not been taken entirely out of the Chaos, it came again, with all the other dense emanations of the Self-willed One. They oppressed Pistis Sophia anew. And so it happened, when they had oppressed her, that she cried out the same remorse (as before), saying, **Pistis Sophia speaks**

"Have mercy upon me, O Light, for they have oppressed me anew. By your command, the light which is in me has been troubled, and so too my intelligence and my strength. My being has begun to diminish while I am in these afflictions, and the allotted measure of my time decreases while I am in the Chaos. My light is enfeebled, for they have taken away my strength, and all the powers which are in me have been severely shaken.

I have become weak before all the (malignant)

---

[157] The Coptic preposition here (ⲍⲙ̄) usu. does means 'in/with'. But here it is 'standing in' for (ⲍⲛ̄) which means 'in', but also 'through' or 'by means of', etc. As Westenberg notes "it is an assimilated form of the preposition ⲍⲛ̄ " ('es ist ein assimilierte Form der Präposition ⲍⲛ̄ '), *Koptisches Wörterbuch*, p. 369).

TEXT: CHAPTER 48 (cont.)

Rulers of the Aions, who hate me, and before the 24 emanations in whose realm I now dwell. And my brother, my Consort, was afraid to help me, because of those among whom I have now been placed.

And all the Rulers of the Heights have regarded me as denser (astral) substance in which there is no light. I have become like a dense (astral) being which has fallen from the (holy) Rulers. And all who are in the Aions said, "She has become (a part of) the Chaos".
Then after this, the merciless Powers surrounded me, and they spoke of taking away the entire light within me.

But as for me, I have trusted in you, O Light, and I have said, "You are my Saviour, and the command which you have decreed for me is in your hands." Save me from the hands of the emanations of the Self-willed One, which oppress me and persecute me. Send your light upon me, for I am as nothing before you, so save me through your mercies. Let me not be ashamed; for it is to you that I intone words of reverence, O Light.

Let the Chaos engulf (*lit. cover*) the emanations of the Self-willed One, let them be led down into the darkness. Let the mouth of those (entities) be silenced – those who wish to devour me through deception. Those who are saying, "Let us take all the light that is in her," although I have done them no ill.

COMMENTARY: CHAPTER 48

"allotted measure of my time": the concept here is that there is an allotted time, i.e., time-cycle, for the cosmos to undertake its evolving. Neither the soul nor spirit-entities like Pistis Sophia, should idly waste opportunities, see Chapter 125 for more about this.

TEXT: CHAPTER 49   Matthew speaks

And when Jesus had spoken these things, Matthew came forward, and said, "Lord, your spirit has stirred me, and your light impels me to explain this eighth expression of remorse by Pistis Sophia, for your being has prophesied about this of old, through David, in

TEXT: CHAPTER 49 (cont.) Matthew speaks Psalm 30, (*31ˢᵗ in the Bible*) saying,

"On you, Lord, have I set my heart, let me never be ashamed; save me in your righteousness. Incline your ear to me, hasten to save me. Be to me a strong God, and a house of refuge to save me, for you are my support and my refuge, for the sake of the core of your being,[158] you shall guide me and feed me. And you shall draw me out of this snare, which they had concealed from me, for you are my protector. I will place my spirit in your hands; you have preserved me, Lord, God of truth.

I myself hate those that hold to what is empty nothingness. But as for me, I have trusted, and I shall rejoice in the Lord, and be joyous because of your Grace. For you have seen my humbleness, and you have saved my soul from my distresses. You have not enclosed me in the hands of the wicked, for you have planted my feet in a freer region.[159] Have mercy upon me, Lord, for I am in tribulation. My eye and my heart and my body are disturbed because of the anger, for my years have been spent in sadness of heart, and my life is spent in groaning.

In poverty my strength is enfeebled, and my bones are troubled. I have become an object of derision for all my enemies and those that draw near to me. I have become an object of fear for them who knew me, and they who have seen me, have fled from me. They have forgotten me in their heart, as (*if I were*) a corpse, and I have become as a vessel that is lost.

For I have heard the scorn of the many that surrounded me, when they gathered themselves together against me; they laid plots to take away my soul. But as for me, I have trusted in you, O Lord. I

---

[158] "core of your being": lit. your name's sake.
[159] "freer region": The word derives from the Psalm, the original of which in Heb. is 'rochab' (רְהָב) which usu. means 'wider' or 'breadth'; but it also has the nuance of 'freedom' (Fürst, *Wörterbuch* bk.2, *p. 364*). So the Psalm's words, "my feet in a broader region" is a metaphor, meaning the soul feels itself to be in a freer, less oppressive situation.

TEXT: CHAPTER 49 (cont.) Matthew speaks have said, "You are my God, my lot is in your hands. Save me from the hand of mine enemies, and deliver me from them that persecute me.

Show your face to your servant, and save me in your mercy, O Lord. Let me not be ashamed, for I have cried out to you. Let the unrighteous be ashamed, and let them descend into Hell. Let the crafty lips be brought to silence, who speak iniquity against the righteous with pride and cursing."

COMMENTARY: CHAPTER 49
No comments about the text are needed here.

TEXT: CHAPTER 50
And when Jesus had heard these words, he said, "Well said, Matthew. Now, therefore: Truly, I say to you (*ye*), when the number of the perfected shall be fulfilled, and when the All (*the cosmos*) shall rise upwards (*ascend into spirit realms*), I shall take my seat in the Treasury of Light, with you also. You shall take your seats on 12 Light-powers, until we have restored all the orders of the twelve saviours in the realm of The Inheritance (of Light) pertaining to each of them." And when he had spoken these things, he said, "Do you understand what I am saying?

And Mariam came forward again, and said, Lord, on this matter you have spoken to us in earlier times, in parable: "You have endured trials for me, and I shall establish a kingdom for you, just as my Father established a kingdom for me; so that you may eat and drink at my table with me. And you shall be seated on 12 thrones and judge the 12 tribes of Israel." He said to her, "Well said, Mariam."

And Jesus continued again and said to his disciples, "Then it happened after this, when the emanations of the Self-willed One had constrained Pistis Sophia in the Chaos, that she uttered her ninth expression of remorse, saying, "O Light, smite them that have taken away my spiritual strength, and take away the strength from them that have taken my

TEXT: CHAPTER 50 (cont.) **Pistis Sophia** intones strength; for I am your being and your light. Come (to me), and save me. Let a great darkness envelop those who oppress me. Say to my being, "It is I who will set you free." Let all those be deprived of their strength, who wish to take away my light entirely. Let their power be as dust; let Jeu, your herald, smite them.

And if they endeavour to go into the Heights, let the darkness seize them; let them fall, let them return into the Chaos. Let your herald Jeu pursue them; let him cast them down into the lower darkness.

For they have set snares for me with a Lion-faced being, although I have done them no ill: the light that is in this Lion-faced being shall be taken away from it. They have oppressed the power that is in me, but this they could not take away. Now, therefore, O Light, take away what is purified of this Lion-faced being without its knowing.

And (*as punishment*) for the thought which the Self-willed One has had, namely, to take my light - take from him his light also. Let the light be taken from the Lion-faced being, which has laid snares for me. My own being shall rejoice in the light, it shall be glad; for the light shall save it, and all the parts of my being shall say, "There is no Saviour but you", for you shall save me from the hands of this Lion-faced entity which has taken my strength from me. Save me from them that have taken away my power and my light !

For they have risen up against me, they have lied about me, declaring that I know the core spiritual realities (*lit. Mystery*) of the light which is in the Heights, (the light) which I truly discerned; so they have oppressed me, saying, "Reveal to us the Mysteries of the light which is in the Heights" - a thing which I did not know.

They have repaid me with all these evils, because I discerned truly the light of the Heights; and they have deprived my being of its light. As for me, when they oppressed me, I was seated in the darkness, my soul humbled in mourning.

But you, O Light, to whom I intone my words of reverence - deliver me ! I know that you will deliver

TEXT: CHAPTER 50 (cont.) **Pistis Sophia intones** me, because I acted according to your will, when I was in my Aion. I then did according to your will, like those (other) Invisibles who are in my (true) realm.

But then I was in grief, looking and searching, for the Light. Now, therefore, all the emanations of the Self-willed One have surrounded me, they have rejoiced over me, and have mightily constrained me without myself being aware of how this happened[160].

They fled away, they left me, but they had no pity upon me; so they returned, they tempted me, they severely oppressed me; they gnashed their teeth against me, seeking to take away my light completely. How long, therefore, O Light, will you allow them to oppress me? Save my being from their evil thoughts, and save me from the hands of this Lion-faced being. For I, alone of the Invisibles, am in this realm.

I will intone words of reverence to you, O Light, though I am in the midst of all them that have gathered together against me; I will cry out to you in the midst of those that constrain me. Now, therefore, O Light, let not them that hate me and desire to take away my strength, rejoice against me, and glare angrily at me; though I have done nothing to them.

For they have spoken flattering words to me, asking for the Mysteries of the Light, which I knew not; speaking to me with guile, and being enraged against me, because I intuitively perceived the light of the Heights.

They have opened their mouth against me, saying, "Indeed, we will take her light from her." Now, therefore, O Light, you know their deceit; do not tolerate them, and let your help be not far from me. Hasten, O Light, bring about my retribution and my vindication, and judge me in your goodness.

Now, therefore, O Light of Lights, let them not take away my light, and let them not say among themselves, "Our being is satiated with her light." Let them not say, "We have devoured her being." But let

---

[160] "of how this happened": I have added to make sense of the abrupt Coptic (= "without me knowing").

TEXT: CHAPTER 50 (cont.) **Pistis Sophia intones** darkness fall upon them, let them that desire to take away my light from me become disempowered. Let those be enveloped in the Chaos, and in darkness, who say, "We shall take away her light and also her being."

Now, therefore, save me that I may rejoice, for I am longing for the 13th Aion, the realm of righteousness. Then I shall always declare, "May the light of your herald Jeu shine ever more brightly." And to you, enveloped in[161] your (divine) cognizing, I shall intone words of reverence always, when I am in the 13th Aion.

COMMENTARY: CHAPTER 50
"enveloped in your divine cognizing": usu. 'in your knowledge'; but the point here is not that the deity has much knowledge, but rather such a high deity is permeated by an inherent sublime cosmic consciousness.[162] It can also mean, "in your Gnosis".
"your herald Jeu": usually 'your Angel', but the Greek term used here also means messenger or herald; and Jeu is a much higher being than an Angel, establishing major dynamics in the cosmos, as recounted in Chapter 15.

TEXT: CHAPTER 51
And when Jesus had said these words to his disciples, he said to them, "Let whoever is alert among you, declare their interpretation." Then James came forward; and then, near to the heart of Jesus, James' love became manifest,[163] and he said "Lord, your spirit

---

[161] "enveloped in"; lit. 'in' but enveloped is directly implied.
[162] Technical note: The word 'in' (2M̄) here, as a form of (2N̄), also means 'amidst' (Ger. = inmitten) and the word 'knowledge' (cooyn) here can be viewed as an adverbial form, 'cognizing'.
[163] "love became manifest": usu. 'he kissed': see the Commentary.

TEXT: CHAPTER 51 (cont.)

has made me cognizant[164], so I am ready to proclaim their interpretation."

For this reason also your being prophesied long ago through David, in Psalm 34 (*35 in the Bible*), concerning the ninth expression of remorse of Pistis Sophia, saying, "Pronounce judgment, O Lord, against them that do me violence, and fight against those who are fighting against me. Seize a weapon and a shield, and arise to help me.

Draw forth a sword and conceal (*the pathway*)[165] from those who afflict me. Declare to my soul, "1 am thy salvation." Let them be ashamed and confounded who seek after my soul; let those be turned back and put to shame who think (*i.e., visualize*) evils against me.

Let them become as dust before the wind, and let the Angel of the Lord persecute them. Let their way be dark and slippery, and let the Angel of the Lord constrain them. For without cause have they hidden a snare for me, to their own detriment; and in vain have they mocked my soul.

Let a snare unknown to them come upon them, and let the nets that they have with cunning laid for me, seize hold of them, so they shall fall into this snare. But my soul shall rejoice in the Lord, and shall be joyful in its salvation. All my bones shall say, "Lord, who is like you ?" You deliver the poor from the hand of he who is too strong for him, and you save the poor and those that are in misery, from the hands of them that despoil him. False witnesses did rise up; they asked me things that I never knew.

They rewarded me evil for the good, making sterile my soul.[166] But as for me, when they were burdening me, I put on sackcloth, and I humbled my soul in fasting, that my prayer shall return to my bosom. I did that which pleased you, as though to one of my

---

[164] "Cognizant": i.e., especially perceptive or inwardly alert.

[165] "close off (*the pathway*)": the Coptic here is obscure. The verb probably means 'to conceal'; in which case it refers to the pathway of the enemies.

[166] "Making sterile": lit. 'bringing childlessness to my soul'.

TEXT: CHAPTER 51 (cont.)   Psalm 34

kinsmen and my brother. And I humbled myself as one in mourning and as one who is sad. But they rejoiced over me (*my distress*), however, they were put to shame.

Tormenters[167] have gathered upon me when I was unaware; they had no empathy with me,[168] and so they were not distressed. They have (tried to) tempt me, and then railed at me, mocking me; they have gnashed their teeth against me.

O Lord, when will you look upon me? Re-establish my soul, away from their evil deeds, and save my own (spirit-)offspring from the lions. I will acknowledge you O Lord, in the Great Assembly, and I will praise you amongst countless people. Let not them that are violent enemies unjustly rejoice over me: those that hate me without a cause and harass me[169] with their eyes. For indeed they have spoken to me with words of peace, but with guile they plot[170] (deeds of) fury. They opened their mouths wide against me saying, "Well done, our eyes have focused fully on her".[171]

You have seen (this), O Lord. Lord, stay no longer silent; go not far from me, O Lord. Arise, O Lord; be mindful of judging me; be mindful of my compensation[172], my God and my Lord. Judge me, O Lord, according to my righteousness.[173] My God, let them not rejoice over me, and let them not say, "Well

---

[167] "tormenters": usu. 'torments' but this is less meaningful; the Coptic is presumably defective here.

[168] "had no empathy with me.." presumably what is meant. Coptic obscure (lit. 'they held apart from me')

[169] "harass": usu. 'wink', but the verb (ϫⲱⲣⲙ̄) also means to beckon, incite, oppress, push against, persuade, constrain, etc.

[170] "plot": lit. think, intend, imagine or visualize.

[171] "her": lit. 'him'; that Pistis Sophia is referred here to as masculine is presumably yet another scribal error.

[172] "compensation": usu. 'vengeance', but this is not consistent with the divine nature of Pistis Sophia; the Coptic word (ϫⲓⲕⲃⲁ) has both meanings.

[173] "my righteousness": Coptic is obscure, it may be, 'your righteousness'.

TEXT: CHAPTER 51 (cont.)   Psalm 34

done, our soul."[174] Let them not say, "We have devoured her."[175] Let them be ashamed, and also let those be confounded, who rejoice at my affliction. Let those be covered with shame and confusion who rejoice over my distress.

Let them be enveloped in shame and confusion who speak strong words against me. Let those (*souls*) that yearn for my righteousness, rejoice and be glad, let them say, "May the Lord be great; let those be exalted who desire the peace of his servants. My tongue shall be joyful in your righteousness and praise, all the day."

COMMENTARY: CHAPTER 51

"Love became manifest": instead of 'he kissed the breast of Jesus'. 'Breast' is an old poetic word for 'chest', and means in effect, the heart. Kissing a Rabbi's chest, meaning their heart, is extremely odd; such a 'holy kiss' as this were called, was very common, but it was either on the cheek, forehead, the crown of the head, or the hand. Since here one can conclude that the risen Lord was clairvoyantly seen, he was not in a flesh body; so there was no physical heart/chest to kiss.

The Coptic verb here (ⲁϥϯⲡⲓ) is the equivalent of a Greek verb, 'phileo' (φιλέο); this verb also means to 'make outwardly evident your love or fondness (for someone or something)', so kissing is not always implied. But furthermore, the Coptic text also includes the preposition 'ern' (ⲉⲡⲛ̄), which means 'near to', 'before' (i.e., in proximity to), or 'toward', etc.

So, if this word is included in the translation, then as James approaches the Lord, his attention is drawn to the divine compassion of Jesus, and then James'

---

[174] "our soul": an obscure phrase; it may be indicating that all the malignant beings can be thought of as one entity, or that the Coptic word should be 'souls'.
[175] "her": lit. 'him' (error in codex).

COMMENTARY: CHAPTER 51   (cont.)
love became manifest (i.e., outwardly evident or demonstrated). That is, *as he came near* to Jesus, it was the unconditional love in Jesus, in his 'heart', poetically speaking, that brought forth loving reverence in James.

"own (spirit) offspring": an esoteric term which I understand to refer to the fruits or offspring of successful initiatory striving. That is, a higher spiritual consciousness, which may be called the 'Spiritual-self' and as such is similar to the esoteric Biblical term 'The Son of Man'.[176]

"from the lions": the context is a non-incarnate, spirit state of being, so 'lions' refers to malignant spirit entities.

"in the Great Assembly": a very significant phrase. The hierarchies or various ranks of deities are a core feature in esoteric Hebrew literature. There are references to 'God' appearing amongst these hosts of deities; such a convocation is called 'the Great Assembly'. It is also a feature of this literature that 'Wisdom', as a personified being, is present in this Assembly: see the 'apocryphal' Ben-Sira's *Book of Wisdom*, (*Sirach*, chapter 24), and also the Biblical text, *Proverbs*, (8:22-30+), where wisdom is described as permeating Creation from, or even before, the Beginning: "Before the mountains were established, before the hills (were created) was I brought forth."

Wisdom here is the inherent divine nature of many deities from which humanity can develop 'intuitive cognizing' or 'spiritually intuitive perceiving', i.e., that same condition which Pistis Sophia represents. Consequently, in Chapter 51, Pistis Sophia (personified) is presented as a soul-faculty we may develop which is able to manifest to the various cosmic deities, the divine capacity (usually dormant) in the human being.

"yearn for my righteousness": that human souls

---

[176] Other versions: "my only one', 'my only begotten' 'my only sonship'; in German 'meine Eigenborene/Einsame'.

COMMENTARY: CHAPTER 51 (cont.)
may rejoice or yearn for Pistis Sophia to achieve redemption, is significant, as it once again indicates that Pistis Sophia and humanity are inherently connected. As Pistis Sophia is redeemed, this allows the seeking human soul to attain an intuitive, spiritually aware consciousness.

TEXT: CHAPTER 52
When James had spoken these words, Jesus said to him, "Excellent, James, well done. This is the explanation of the ninth expression of remorse of Pistis Sophia. Truly, truly, I say to you, you (ye) shall be the first in the kingdom of the Heavens; before all of the Invisibles and all deities and Rulers of the 13th Aion, and in the 12th Aion. Indeed, not only yourselves, but also everyone who shall carry out my Mysteries."

And when he had thus spoken, he said to them, "Do you understand in what manner I am speaking with you?" Then Mariam pressed forward again and said, "O yes, Lord: this is what you said to us in previous times, namely, "The last shall be first and the first shall be last".

The first, they who were created before us, are therefore the Invisibles, for they were created before humans: they and the gods, and the Rulers. And the people who shall receive the Mystery shall be with them in the heavenly realms."

Jesus said to her, "Well said, Mariam." Then Jesus continued and said to his disciples, "It happened when Pistis Sophia had proclaimed her ninth remorse, that the Lion-faced entity again oppressed her; wishing to take from her the entire strength which was in her.

She cried out again to the Light, saying, "O Light, in whom I have trusted from the beginning, for your sake have I endured this great affliction; help me !" And in this hour her repentance was accepted; the First Mystery heard her, and so I was sent by his command.

TEXT: CHAPTER 52 (cont.) **Pistis Sophia intones**
I came and helped her; I led her out of the Chaos, for she had repented and also she had trusted in the Light; and she had also endured these great tribulations and these great perils. For she had been deceived by that deity, the Self-willed One; she had not been deceived by anything else, only by a (malignant) light-power, because it resembled the Light which she had (earlier) intuitively discerned.

For this reason I was sent by command of the First Mystery to help her, secretly; for I had not yet arrived at the realm of the Aions (*as a triumphant Saviour*). Rather I had proceeded forth from out of the midst of them, without any entity knowing it, either those of the innermost soul-spirit realities[177] or those of the most external, cosmic realities,[178] except for the First Mystery.

Then it happened therefore, upon my entering into the Chaos to nurture her, that she saw me, and saw that I had spiritual discernment and was very radiant, and also that I had compassion for her. For I was not arrogant, like that Lion-faced being which had taken from Sophia the power of her light, and who still oppressed her, to take from her the entirety of the light which was in her.

Sophia therefore, saw that I shone more brightly than the Lion-face entity, tens of thousands of times more brightly. And that I was full of compassion for her; and she perceived that I had come forth from the upper realm of the Heights, whose light she had intuitively perceived from the beginning.

Sophia then became confident and uttered her tenth expression of remorse, "I have cried out to you in my affliction, O Light of Lights, and you have heard me. O Light, rescue my being from unjust and impious lips, and from cunning snares. O Light, that which they would have taken from me by cunning

---

[177] "the innermost soul-spirit realities", lit. 'the interior of the interiors'.

[178] "the most external, cosmic realities (spiritually)", lit. 'the exterior of the exteriors'.

TEXT: CHAPTER 52 (cont.)   **Pistis Sophia speaks**
traps, they would not have (then) offered up to you; for the snares of the Self-willed One are scattered about, and so are the traps of these merciless ones.

Woe is me, for my dwelling is far off, and I am in the habitations of the Chaos. My being is in realms which are not mine, and I have entreated those who are without pity. And when I pleaded with them, they fought against me without a cause."

COMMENTARY: CHAPTER 52
No commentary needed.

TEXT: CHAPTER 53   **Peter speaks**
And when Jesus had spoken these things to his disciples, he said to them, "Now, therefore, let him whose spirit stirs within him, come forward, and declare the interpretation of this tenth remorse of Pistis Sophia." And Peter answered and said, "Lord, concerning this, your light-being prophesied of old through David, in Psalm 119 (*Ps.120 in the Bible*), saying, "When I was in peril, I cried out to you, and you heard me. O Lord, save my soul from unjust lips and cunning tongues.

What shall be given to you, or what shall be added to you, through a cunning tongue? The arrows of the strong one are sharpened by the coals of the desert. Woe is me, for my dwelling is far off. I have dwelt in the habitations of Kedar; my soul has been a stranger in many regions. I was peaceful with them that hate peace; if I spoke to them, they fought against me without a cause."

"This, O Lord, is the meaning of the tenth repentance of Pistis Sophia, which she uttered when the denser emanations of the Self-willed One afflicted her; they and his Lion-faced being, and when they mightily oppressed her." And Jesus said to him, "Well said, Peter. This is the meaning of the tenth expression of remorse of Pistis Sophia."

COMMENTARY: CHAPTER 53
The text of this Chapter is clear.

TEXT: CHAPTER 54   Pistis Sophia speaks

And Jesus continued in his conversation, and said to his disciples, "Then it happened when this Lion-faced entity saw me draw near to Pistis Sophia, shining exceedingly, that it became more and more enraged, and cast forth from itself other hosts of exceedingly evil emanations.

And when these were produced, Pistis Sophia uttered her eleventh repentance, saying, "Why does this mighty being raise itself amongst the evil?[179] The intentions in its thoughts continuously take away the light from me; and like sharp iron, these thoughts are cutting away power from me.

I did prefer to descend into the Chaos, rather than to remain in the 13th Aion, the realm of righteousness. There they sought to lead me on with guile, so that they might devour all of my light. For this reason therefore, the (Christ)-Light shall take away the entirety of *their* light.

And all their dense entities[180] shall be destroyed; and the Light will take away their light, and not permit them to dwell in the (debased) 13th Aion, their dwelling place. It shall not let their names exist in the realm of the living; and the 24 (debased) emanations shall see what has befallen you, Lion-faced being. So that they may fear and no longer be disobedient, but offer up what has been purified of their light.

And they shall see you; they shall rejoice over you, they shall say "Behold, (*you are only*) an emanated entity; one which has not offered up what has been purified of its light, that it may be saved. Instead it (*blindly*) boasts of the abundant radiance of its (own) being, for it did not emanate forth (anything) from the power which was in it. It has said, "I will take away the light of Pistis Sophia; which is (anyway) to be taken from her."

Now, therefore, let that person in whom their spiritual strength has arisen, come forward, and

---

[179] "among the evil": Coptic obscure, possibly 'amongst the evils', or 'the evil ones'.
[180] "dense entities": lit. 'denser matters'.

TEXT: CHAPTER 54 (cont.) **Salome speaks** declare the meaning of the 11th repentance of Pistis Sophia." **Salome quotes Psalm 51**

Then Salome came forward and said, "My Lord, concerning this, your light-being prophesied long ago, through David, in Psalm 51 (*Ps. 52 in the Bible*) saying, "Why does this mighty one boast of his evil? Your tongue has practiced unrighteousness all day long; like a sharp cutting knife, you have practiced deceit. You love evil more than good, you love injustice more than to speak righteousness.

You love all words of deceit and a cunning tongue. Therefore, God shall destroy you utterly, and he will uproot you, and remove you from your dwelling, and tear out your roots and cast these away from the living ones. The righteous will see and be afraid; and they will mock him and say, "Look, a man who did not make God his helper, but instead trusted in his great wealth and was empowered through his vanity.

But as for me, I am like a green olive tree in the house of the Lord; and I have trusted in the mercy of the Lord always. I will acknowledge you, for you have dealt with me, and I will hope in your name, for it is beneficent in the presence of your holy ones."

"This then, Lord, is the interpretation of the 11th expression of remorse of Pistis Sophia. I, being moved by your light-being, have spoken this, according to your will." It then happened when Jesus heard these words which Salome spoke, that he said, "Well declared, Salome. Truly, truly I say to you: I shall initiate you in all the Mysteries of the kingdom of Light."

COMMENTARY: CHAPTER 54

"Salome": This person is not specifically identified, but is very likely to be the mother of James and John, the sons of Zebedee. This Salome is mentioned as a member of the core group of women who assisted Jesus in his ministry, and who also witnessed, from a distance, the crucifixion.

She was therefore one of several women who came to the grave, to anoint the body of Jesus, after the

COMMENTARY: CHAPTER 54 (cont.)

Sabbath (Mk.15:41, Lk.23:56 and Jn. 20:2). Despite her inappropriate request to Jesus about her two sons to be given high importance in Heaven, the above Gospel references show that Salome was a prominent woman amongst the followers of Jesus. This is further indicated by early apocryphal texts also giving her prominence. She puts deep questions to Jesus, and receives esoteric answers, as recorded by Clement of Alexandria, quoting from the lost *Gospel of the Egyptians*.

She is also mentioned in *The Book of James*, in regard to the birth of Jesus, and in various Coptic texts, such as *The History of Joseph the Carpenter* which recounts the legend that Salome went with the Holy Family into exile in Egypt.

"(only) an emanated entity": so the Lion-faced demon is only a 'secondary' entity which has been emanated forth from another self-existent, higher, demonic spirit.

"boasts of the abundance of its": this is a core point: an entity which selfishly holds onto its own power, instead of offering up this to the higher Divine Being, and thereby lets this light permeates other beings, is directly opposing the core principle which motivates the gods; that is, selfless giving.

TEXT: CHAPTER 55

Then Jesus (*i.e., Christ*) continued in his discourse and said to his disciples, "It came to pass after this, that I approached nearer to the Chaos than previously, shining with great radiance, to take away the strength from that Lion-faced being. And as I was so radiant, it became afraid and cried out to its god, the Self-willed One, that he should come and help it.

And then immediately, the Self-willed One looked down from the (debased) 13th Aion; he gazed downward into the Chaos, in extreme wrath, desiring to aid his Lion-faced being (*i.e., his offspring*). And in this hour, his Lion-faced being and all his emanations turned on Pistis Sophia, seeking to take away the

TEXT: CHAPTER 55 (cont.) **Pistis Sophia intones** entirety of the light which was in Sophia.

It came to pass, therefore, as Sophia was oppressed, that she cried out to the Heights, pleading with me that I should aid her. So it happened, when she gazed on high, that she saw the Self-willed One mightily furious, and she was afraid. So she uttered her twelfth expression of remorse because of the Self-willed One and his emanations.

She cried out to me, saying, "O Light, forget not my intonations of reverence, for the Self-willed One and this Lion-faced entity have opened their mouths against me, and have surrounded me, wishing to take away my strength. They have hated me because I have intoned words of reverence to you. Instead of showing love to me, they have slandered me; but (still) I intoned words of reverence (to you).

They have plotted together to take my power, because I intoned words of reverence to you, O Light; they hated me, because I manifested an inner union with you.[181] Let darkness fall on the Self-willed One, and may the Ruler of the outer darkness remain at his right hand.

TEXT NOTE: in Chapter 55
("remain at his right hand": probably meaning that the Self-willed One should continue to be constrained by the power of the Ruler of the malignant Chaos realm, so that he cannot become empowered over other, higher realms.)

TEXT: CHAPTER 55 (cont.) **Pistis Sophia speaks**
When you pass sentence upon him, take from him his power, and that which he planned to do to me – taking away my light – do you to him: take away his light.

May all the light-powers which are in him, cease,

---

[181] "an inner union": usu. 'loved you'. Here 'agape' is meant, and this is love created by an inner harmony right down to the will/volitional level of the soul (see my *Gospel of John* where agape is discussed in detail).

TEXT: CHAPTER 55 (cont.) **Pistis Sophia speaks** and may another (deity) remove his greatness from among the three (debased) Triple-powers. (*Thus*) may all the dense beings within his emanations be without light, and may his denser (astral) substance (*lit. matter*) have no light in it.

May all the dense beings of his emanations remain in the Chaos; may they not be allowed to enter into the (debased) 13th Aion, their realm. May the Receiver, the Purifier of lights, purify all the light-powers that are in the Self-willed One, and take them from him.[182]

May the Rulers of the lower darkness gain control over his emanations. Let no one receive him into their realm; let no one give heed to the dense beings of his emanations which are in the Chaos. Let the light which is in his emanations be taken away, and let their names (*i.e., core essence*) be extinguished in the (*debased*) 13th Aion; indeed, let *his* name (also) be blotted out forever in that realm.

As for the Lion-faced entity, may the sin of him who sent it forth in the presence of the Light, fall back upon him. May the iniquity of the dense (astral) entities[183] whom it has produced, be never wiped away; thus may their sin be ever before the Light (*to be judged*). May they never see beyond (the Chaos).

May their name be removed from every realm, for they have not spared me. They have not spared me, but oppressed me; indeed they oppressed that one (*i.e., Pistis Sophia herself*) from whom they have taken away her light and her power. For those amongst whom I was placed (*in the Chaos*), wanted to take away my light.

They wanted to descend into the darkness; so let them remain there, and let them not be brought out of there from this hour onwards. They sought for a

---

[182] "take them from him": Coptic obscure, it may be 'take them from them'; that is, the light-powers are now being viewed as many minor entities, each of whom should lose their light.

[183] "astral entities": lit. 'matter', but in effect, 'matters', which is not meaningful; so it refers to elemental entities.

TEXT: CHAPTER 55 (cont.) **Pistis Sophia intones** habitation in the realm of righteousness, but they shall no more be brought forth from there, as of this hour. He is robed in darkness as with a garment, it has entered into him like water, and it entered into all his powers like oil.

Let him robe himself with the Chaos as a garment, and continually gird himself with darkness as with a girdle of skin. Let this come upon them that have brought these things upon me, because (*this corresponded to the intentions*) of the Light, regarding those who said, "Let us take away all of her power."

But as for you, O Light, be merciful to me, because of the mystery of your spirit[184] and save me in the goodness of your compassion; for they have taken from me my light and my power, and my power has been weakened in me; I could not be truly present in their midst. I have become like dense (astral) substance which is debased; I have been driven this way and that, like an air-sprite (*in the wind*).

My strength perished, because in that realm I had no spiritual presence (*lit. Mystery*). The very foundation of my own being has diminished, because they have taken away (*so much of*) my light. They have mocked me; they gazed at me, harassing me. Help me according to your compassion."

Now, therefore, let him whose spirit is active, come forward and declare the meaning of the twelfth repentance of Pistis Sophia.

COMMENTARY: CHAPTER 55

"very foundation of my own being has diminished": usually 'my matter has faded/worn out/disappeared'. Here 'matter', (in Greek 'hyle'), refers to the 'soul substance' of Pistis Sophia; she laments that she has lost much of her actual nature or 'being-ness'.

Regarding: "As for the Lion-faced entity, may the sin of him who sent it forth in the presence of the Light, fall back upon him. May the iniquity of the

---

[184] "your spirit": lit. 'your name'.

COMMENTARY: CHAPTER 55 (cont.)

dense (astral) entities whom it has produced, be never wiped away; indeed, may their sin be ever before the Light. May they never see beyond (the Chaos)":

it is this section of the above declaration by Pistis Sophia which can seem mean-spirited; but a closer look reveals that it is not so, even though later, these words are portrayed by Andrew as echoing Psalm 109 (*Ps. 110 in the Bible*), which is known as an 'imprecatory' or 'cursing' Psalm, and which does have a vindictive tone.

So, "may the sin of him who sent it forth, fall back upon him" is based on the view that this is the only way for a malignant being to learn its lesson.

And, "may the iniquity of the dense entities whom it produced, be never wiped away...may their sin be ever before the Light" has as its basis, the ethical view that if malignant entities are to be punished and corrected by God, then God needs to maintain awareness of what evil has actually been brought forth. The rest of the words of Pistis Sophia are clearly ethical, and are a prayer for the Light to transform, or weaken the evil beings.

TEXT: CHAPTER 56   Andrew speaks

So Andrew came forward and said, "My Lord and Saviour, your light-being has prophesied of old through David, concerning this expression of remorse which Pistis Sophia uttered. It spoke thereof in Psalm 108, (*109 in the Bible*) saying, "God, hold not my mouth from my praise, for the mouth of the ungodly and deceitful is opened against me. They have spoken against me with a deceitful tongue, and have surrounded me with words of hatred and fight against me without any cause.

But as for me, I continued to pray. They have raised up evil against me in return for good, and hate for love. Set an ungodly one over him, and may the Devil stand at his right hand. When sentence is given to him, let him be condemned, and let his prayer be regarded as sin. May his days be shortened, and may

TEXT: CHAPTER 56 (cont.) **Ps. 108 Andrew speaks** another receive his office; may his children be fatherless, and his wife a widow. May the eldest of his children be taken away, may they be transported, may they beg, may they be cast out of their dwelling. May the money-lender scrutinize all that he has, and may strangers take away all his labour.

Let there be no man to give him a hand, and let there be no one to have kindness towards his fatherless children. Let his children be blotted out, and let them blot out his name in a single generation. Let the sin of his fathers be remembered before the Lord, and let not the sin of his mother be blotted out. Let these be ever before the Lord. Let his memory be destroyed on the earth, for he has not thought of mercy; for he has persecuted the poor and helpless, he has persecuted a person in distress, bringing him to death. He has loved cursing; may this envelop him.

He has clothed himself with cursing as with a garment, and it has entered into his inner being like water, and like oil into his bones. Let it be for him as a garment with which he shall be clothed, and like a girdle with which he shall be girded for all time. This is the work of them that slander before the Lord, and who speak injustice against my soul.

But as for you, lord God, have pity on me for the sake of your spiritual reality (*lit. your name's sake*). Save me, for I am poor and in misery. My heart is troubled within me; they have carried me away like a shadow that fades, and they have driven me away as if I were (a swarm of) locusts.

My feet have become feeble with fasting, and my flesh is dried from (lack of) oil. I have become an object of derision unto them; they have gazed upon me, and shaken their heads. Help, lord God, and save me according to your mercy. Let them know that it is your hand, and that you have created it, O Lord."

This is the meaning of the 12th expression of remorse spoken by Pistis Sophia, when she was in the Chaos.

COMMENTARY: CHAPTER 56

Andrew has just spoken Psalm 108 (109 in the Bible); and although some Bible commentators endeavour to seek to view it in a better light, this psalm is obviously somewhat vindictive or at least urging punishment of evil people.

This is not what Pistis Sophia was seeking in her words. So for Andrew to suggest a parallel between the words of Pistis Sophia and Psalm 108 is quite inaccurate, indeed spiritually wrong. And just here we experience yet another feature of this codex which indicates its authenticity.

As with the inclusion of occasions where Peter is displeased with a woman having an equal standing as the men, this contribution from Andrew is showing his imperfect grasp of the dynamics. This faulty understanding is subtly demonstrated by the following fact. Normally, every time that a disciple quotes a Psalm to explain the words of Pistis Sophia, Jesus strongly expresses his approval. But not so with what Andrew has contributed: this is the only time that Jesus **refrains from giving approval**.

He remains conspicuously silent: as the beginning of Chapter 57 reveals, see below. (On a later occasion Christ responds with strong displeasure at another contribution from Andrew.)

TEXT: CHAPTER 57

Then Christ continued his discourse, saying to his disciples, "It happened after this, that Pistis Sophia cried out to me, saying, "O Light of Lights, I have transgressed in the twelve Aions, (for) I went down amongst them.[185] For this reason have I made 12 expressions of remorse, corresponding to these 12 Aions.

Now, therefore, O Light of Lights, hear me when I intone words of reverence in the 13th Aion, the realm

---

[185] "among them": usu. 'from them', but this is devoid of any meaning; so the preposition here (ⲚϨⲎⲞⲨ) means 'among', not 'from', (cf. *Gosp. Thom.* log. 28).

TEXT: CHAPTER 57 (cont.) **Pistis Sophia speaks**
from which I came forth. Save me, O Light, by your great spiritual nature (*lit. Mystery*). In your forgiveness, pardon my transgression.

Give to me the (spirit) baptism; forgive my sins, and purify me from my transgression. For my transgression is caused by this Lion-faced entity, which has never been hidden from you; it is because of it that I have become lowly[186]. It is I alone who have transgressed among the Invisibles, in whose realms I was. I have descended into the Chaos, I have transgressed before you, so that your command might be accomplished."

This, then, is what Pistis Sophia then said. Now, therefore, let that person whose spirit impels them to understand her words, come forward, and expound their meaning". **Martha speaks**

So Martha came forward, and said, "Lord, my spirit urges me to unveil the interpretation of the things which Pistis Sophia has spoken. Your being has prophesied long ago concerning them, through David, in Psalm 50 (*Ps. 51 in the Bible*), saying, "Have mercy upon me, God, according to your great compassion; and in accordance with the many acts of your mercy, blot out my sin. Wash my iniquity out of me !

Save me thoroughly from my wickedness ! My sin is before you every day, so that you may be justified in your words, and prevail when you shall judge me." "This is the meaning of the words which Pistis Sophia spoke." Jesus said to her, "Well said; and finely, Martha, you blessed one."

COMMENTARY: CHAPTER 57
"I have transgressed before you ... that your command might be accomplished": again we are reminded that the perilous journey of human consciousness through evil occurs from the express will of the Divine. For the descent of humanity into a

---

[186] "become lowly": lit. 'I have descended'.

material state of consciousness – i.e., the descent of Pistis Sophia away her true spiritual state or realm, was brought about, and monitored by God (the First Mystery) – through the activity of his vessel, the cosmic Christ.

TEXT: CHAPTER 58

And Jesus continued in his discourse, and said, "It then happened, when Pistis Sophia had said these words, that the time was fulfilled for her to be led out of the Chaos. So then, through myself, without the First Mystery, I brought forth a light-being from myself; I sent this down into the Chaos, in order for it to bring Pistis Sophia up from the depths of the Chaos, until the command should come from the First Mystery to take her entirely out of the Chaos. Hence my light-being led Pistis Sophia into the region which is in the upper parts of the Chaos.

It then happened, when the dense entities (*lit. emanations*) of the Self-willed One discovered that Pistis Sophia had been conducted into the higher regions of the Chaos, that these also sought her out in these upper regions of the Chaos, wanting to take her again back into the lower regions of the Chaos. But my light-being, which I had sent to bring Pistis Sophia into the higher regions, was extremely radiant (*and thereby the evil emanations were repulsed*).

It then happened, when the emanations of the Self-willed One pursued Sophia, after she had been conducted into the higher regions of the Chaos, that she again intoned to me in reverence, and cried out to me, saying, "I shall intone my reverence to you, O Light, for I wanted to come to you; I shall intone reverence to you, O Light, you are my Saviour.

Leave me not in the Chaos. Save me, Light of the Heights, for it is to you that I have intoned my reverence. You have sent me your light from out of yourself, and thus you have saved me. You have brought me up to the higher realms of the Chaos. Therefore let the emanations of the Self-willed One, which pursue me, fall below into the lower realms of

TEXT: CHAPTER 58 (cont.) **Pistis Sophia speaks**
the Chaos, and let them not come into the higher realms of the Chaos to see me.

Let great darkness cover them, and let the mighty gloom of darkness come upon them, and let them not see me within the radiance of your power, which you have sent to me to save me, so that (*not discerning my presence*) they may no longer have any control over me. And let the ideas which they have devised against me – to take away my power – no longer be accomplished by them.

And since they have talked about me, about taking away my light, then take their light from them, instead of mine (being taken). They have planned to take away my light, but have not been able to take it; for your light-being is with me.

They have made plans together, without your command, O Light, therefore they have not been able to take away my light. I shall not be afraid because I have intuitively discerned the light; the light is my Saviour, so I shall not fear."   **Salome speaks**

(Jesus then said), "So, that disciple whose soul is now exalted, speak the solution to the words which Pistis Sophia has spoken. It then happened, when Jesus had finished speaking these words, that Salome came forward and said, "My Lord, my inner being impels me to speak the solution of the words which Pistis Sophia has spoken. Your light-being once prophesied through Solomon, (*from the 5th ode of the Odes of Solomon*) saying;

"I will give thanks to you, O Lord, for you are my God. Do not leave me alone, O Lord, for you are my hope. You have given me your judgment freely; and I was saved by you. Let those that persecute me, fall down, and do not let them see me. Let a cloud of smoke cover their eyes, and a haze of mist blind them.

Let them not see the day, lest they should seize me. Let their counsel be without power, and whatever plot they have designed, may it fail them. The mighty have vanquished them, and the evils which they have prepared have fallen upon them. My hope is in the

TEXT: CHAPTER 58 (cont.) **Pistis Sophia speaks**
Lord, and I will not fear, for you are my God and my Saviour."

It then happened, when Salome had finished saying these words, Jesus said, "Well said, Salome, and excellent. This is the solution to the words that Pistis Sophia had spoken."

COMMENTARY: CHAPTER 58
"5th Ode of Solomon": the Odes of Solomon are a collection of 42 odes which are about the spiritual path; some refer directly to initiatory experiences. They are of unknown origin; the Pistis Sophia codex has some or all of six of the odes; but the most complete collection of them is in the Syriac language, and these were identified in 1909.

Most scholars now believe that they date from late first century or mid-second century AD. But because they derive from an initiatory quest, I conclude that the writer was an Essene. Thus they date either from before the time of Jesus, or are contemporary to his life. I conclude that a few of these Odes were later altered by a Christian editor, as the Christian church was developing.[187]

TEXT: CHAPTER 59
Then Jesus continued with his discourse, saying to the disciples, "It happened, when Pistis Sophia had finished declaring these words in the Chaos, that I brought it about that the light-being which I had sent to save her, became a crown of light around her head, in order that henceforth, the emanations of the Self-willed One would never (again) have dominion over her. And when my light-being had made a crown of light on her head, all the debased (astral) entities[188]

---

[187] My *The Gospel of John*, provides further research into these Odes.
[188] lit. 'matters'.

TEXT: CHAPTER 59 (cont.)

which were in her, were affected;[189] they were all purified in her.

So these were disempowered[190] and remained in the Chaos, while the emanations of the Self-willed One gazed upon these and were glad (*since they were nearby*). But the purified rays of the divine light which were still in Sophia, added their power of light to my light-power; this had become a crown upon her head.

It then happened, when my light-power enveloped the pure spiritual light which was in Sophia, that her now purified (*holy*) light did not become separated from the crown formed by the radiant light-flame (around her head). Hence the emanations of the Self-willed One could not rob this crown from her. As this happened to her, the pure (*holy*) light-being which was in Sophia began to intone words of reverence.

(*again from the 5th Ode of Solomon*)
And she intoned her reverence to my light-being, which was now a crown around her head, saying, "The light has become a wreath around my head; and I shall never become distant from it, so the emanations of the Self-willed One may never rob me of it. And if all dense (astral) entities[191] are stirred, yet I shall never be shaken.

And even though all my own dense (astral) entities be disempowered and remain in the Chaos – those which are seen by the emanations of the Self-willed One – yet I myself shall not be disempowered. For the Light is with me, and I myself am this Light."

These words spoke Pistis Sophia. So now let that person who understands these words, come forward and declare their solution."

Then Mary, the mother of Jesus, came forward and spoke: "My son according to the worldly reality, (but)

---

[189] lit. 'shaken' or 'moved'.
[190] 'Disempowered': usu. 'destroyed', but here as in Chapt. 22 etc, it cannot mean 'to be annihilated' as they still remain (in the Chaos realm).
[191] "dense (astral) *entities*": usu. 'all my *matters*', which has no meaning, since Pistis Sophia is a spirit being.

TEXT: CHAPTER 59 (cont.) **Mary the mother, speaks** my God and my Redeemer, according to the Heights, command me to declare the meaning of the words which Pistis Sophia has spoken." And Jesus responded, and said to her, "You also, Mary, you who did receive the form (*of the body*) - that which exists (*as a template*) according to matter, in Barbelo[192] - but did receive the (*soul*) likeness (*which exists*) according to the Light, in the Holy Goddess of Light: you and the other Mary, the Blessed One.

TEXT NOTE in Chapter 59
(Again the reader is alerted to the living, fluidic situation wherein Jesus is speaking at times, and then at other times, the cosmic Christ-being is speaking.)

TEXT: CHAPTER 59 (cont.)
For your sake, virginal purity[193] was made manifest (in you), and moreover from you came forth the material body in which I existed,[194] and which I have cleansed and purified. Now, therefore, I bid you declare the interpretation of the words spoken by Pistis Sophia."

And Mary, the mother of Jesus, answered, and said, "My Lord, your light-being has prophesied of old concerning these words, through Solomon, in his 1st Ode saying, "The Lord is above my head as a garland, and I shall never be without him. The garland of truth has been woven for me, and it has caused branches to sprout in me. Indeed it is not like a wreath that withers, and never sprouts. For you are alive and you have sprouted upon me. Your fruits are full and perfect, filled with Salvation."

TEXT NOTE:
"1st Ode": Lit. "19th ode": it is assumed that these

---

[192] "Barbelo": as noted earlier, a general term for the Divine.
[193] "virginal purity": usu. the meaningless phrase "darkness was created" - see Commentary.
[194] "I existed": usu. 'I exist'; but this is no longer the case, Jesus no longer has a flesh body: exactly the same error is here as in Chapt.10, where the same verb (ϣⲱⲡⲉ) is in the present tense, but should be in the past tense.

words are from the 1ˢᵗ Ode of Solomon, but are incorrectly identified in the Coptic text as from Ode 19.[195]

TEXT: CHAPTER 59 (cont.)
It then happened when Jesus had heard his mother Mary say these words, that he said to her, "Excellent, it is well said. Truly, truly, I say to you (*thee*), they shall proclaim you blessed from one end of the Earth to the other, for the pledge of the First Mystery has dwelt in you, and by this pledge shall be saved all worlds and all Heights, and this covenant is the beginning and the end."

COMMENTARY: CHAPTER 59
"crown of light:" a wonderful image to contemplate. Pistis Sophia is the counterpart in spirit realms, of the soul's capacity for intuitive spiritual perception. As she is rescued by the Christ-light, this astral form acquires a radiant coronet of light. This derives in part from what was still remaining in that form, and which was then purified; but primarily it is from the Christ-light.

"which are visible": these lowly entities remain perceptible to the malignant deity, but not Pistis Sophia.

"Holy Goddess of the Light": usu. 'Virgin of Light'; but 'virgin' seems inappropriate for any non-flesh, i.e., spirit, entity. So the Hermetica term, 'kore kosmou', usually translated as 'World Virgin', should be 'Holy World-Goddess' or 'Pure Soul of the Cosmos'.

"virginal purity": a very significant improvement here. The Coptic word kake (ⲕⲁⲕⲉ) as used here does not only mean 'darkness', but also eye-pupil and child, and it also refers to 'maiden'. However,

---

[195] Possibly, the scribe had a book in which the (42) *Odes of Solomon* were bound after the (18) *Psalms of Solomon* and were regarded as one text; even though these 18 are of a very much less spiritual-esoteric nature.

COMMENTARY: CHAPTER 59 (cont.)

'maiden' or unmarried young woman, in ancient cultures meant 'virgin'; and as Crum notes, even though the Coptic word for virgin was usually ⲘⲚⲦⲠⲞⲞⲨⲚⲈ; the word 'kake' was at times used for the Greek word 'Kore'. This word means: in human terms, girl or daughter or virgin; whereby both 'daughter' (unmarried) and 'girl' implied virginity; but applied to deities, it means 'holy'. So here in the Coptic text an immensely sacred, divine reality is disclosed; a reality of extraordinary significance.

Rudolf Steiner taught that the mother of Jesus (as referred to in the Gospel of Matthew), underwent a very significant miracle towards the end of the life of Jesus, wherein she was imbued, in body and soul, by the high spiritual influences from the cosmic Christ, resulting in the condition of innocent, virginal purity.

This is of necessity a delicate, veiled subject; but an especially high spirituality of Mary is indicated in the Gospels. For example, her holiness manifested in the Magnificat scene in the Gospel of Luke. This high spiritual quality manifested and enveloped Jesus' mother, inwardly rejuvenating her, shortly before his death, transforming her womanly nature. The underlying spiritual dynamic implied here is, that as she became fully 'Christed', her physical body became that of an innocent child, reflecting the obviously miraculous impact on it of her now sanctified soul. Some knowledge of this remarkable subject existed in esoteric Christian circles; for a Nag Hammadi text, *The Testimony of Truth* (para.45), reports, without any comment,

"....Mary.. was found to be a virgin again."

"the other Mary, the Blessed One": My conclusion as to the identity of the second Mary is dependent upon my reading of an ancient esoteric Zoharic text, and research by Rudolf Steiner. Ancient Hebrew initiatory wisdom taught, in a tract informally attached to the Zohar (*The Faithful Shepherd, Ra'aya Mehemna*), that two Messiahs would be born – initially – but one would die as a child, and then somehow merge, on

COMMENTARY: CHAPTER 59 (cont.)

the soul level, with the other Messiah (i.e., whom we know as Jesus):

"There shall be two Messiahs who shall arise from the grace of Moses...One will be the royal Messiah, the son of David, a descendant of the royal tribe of Judah. The other Messiah, the son Levi, (*priestly caste*) he holds the pastoral crook. After the unusual (*premature*) death of the royal Messiah, the (*actual one*) Messiah shall appear; for one of these Messiahs shall die, and yet he shall live on again (*in the soul of the surviving Messiah*)..." [196]

This viewpoint implies that there could also be two maternal 'Marys'. The above remarkable words in Chapter 59 of the Coptic codex, point to two families, with each mother having the same name, since the text is about special spiritual qualities bestowed upon two women (who, it seems, shall become mothers), and that both are named Mary. I conclude that the second maternal Mary is the 'other Mary' mentioned here, and that she, like the young royal Messiah, had passed away.[197]

"receive the form(s) from Barbelo": both maternal Marys received a high spiritual template for their physical bodies.

Mary and the Holy Goddess of the Light

This deity is mentioned in significant places later in the codex, but little is said about her details. A key to her nature is in these words; "Mary, you did receive the likeness of the Holy Light-Goddess, according to the Light – you, and the other Mary, the Blessed One.

---

[196] Parts of the *Ra'aya Mehemna* are in the Exodus sections of the Mantua *Zohar* in the 5 vol. English, Sperling edition (Waera par.24 and Bo para. 41). It is available in the Hebrew Zohar, published in Israel, and in French (1909) from Jean de Pauly, Sepher ha-zohar: doctrine ésotérique des Israélites; livre de la splendour.

[197] This theme of initially two Messiahs, and hence two families, is not the focus of this book; the most comprehensive treatment of this is found in lectures by Rudolf Steiner on the Gospels.

COMMENTARY: CHAPTER 59 (cont.)

So as an acolyte develops very high purity, their new, holy soul qualities derive from a spiritual archetype: the Holy Goddess of the Light or the 'cosmic Spiritual-self'. The implication of the above words is that this deity is both the archetype of, and the source of, the Spiritual-self in humanity. The presence of such un-tainted qualities corresponded to their high spiritual natures, and also ensured that the spiritual 'material' of the soul was of help, not a hindrance, to Jesus as he lived within the body provided for him.

There is a direct reference to this idea, this spirit reality, in the initiatory *Odes of Solomon*, several of which are quoted in this codex. In Ode 33, a personification of godliness called 'Grace', summons humanity, drawing near to him all those who were godly,

"...and there drew near to him all
those who obeyed him;
but there did not appear, as it were,
an evil person.
Instead a holy divine-soul was there,
she was proclaiming and calling, and saying...[198]
forsake the ways of perdition
and draw near to me;
and I will enter into you, and bring you
forth from perdition..."

Scholars who don't factor in such spirit archetypes of holiness, have concluded that the Syriac words mean simply a young woman. In mainstream analysis, Mary is a metaphor of the Christian church. Another view is that the original is defective, and a different word is meant; but that is an unnecessary, and hence unlikely solution.[199]

---

[198] "proclaiming...": that is, spiritually intoning to human souls.

[199] For example Zinner & Mattison (the *Nuhra Version* 2020) concludes it must mean 'mature young woman'; H.Grimme

COMMENTARY: CHAPTER 59 (cont.)
"holy divine-soul": in the classical translation, originally from R. Harris, "a perfect virgin stood there". But this phrase has little meaning, as a virginal woman is never defined as either perfect or imperfect. The Syriac word here will be derived from an Aramaic/Hebrew term (such as, mikoth, kalil, gamar) which do mean 'perfect' or 'complete'.

But these infer that a person is flawless in the sight of God, and hence holy; as in Job 9:22, Prov. 11:5, etc. I conclude that the entity here is not a physical woman; it is therefore a deity or spiritual being who is the manifestation of, or archetype of, holiness; similar to the Holy Goddess of the Light (Virgin of Light).

TEXT: CHAPTER 60
And Jesus continued in his conversation, and said to his disciples, "It came to pass when Pistis Sophia had spoken her 13th expression of remorse, there was fulfilled in that hour the command of all the tribulations which had been decreed for Pistis Sophia for the fulfillment of the First Mystery, which has existed from the Beginning. The time had come to rescue her from the Chaos, and to lead her out of all the darknesses.

For her expression of remorse had been accepted by the First Mystery; and moreover that Mystery sent me a mighty Light-being from the Heights, so that I may rescue Pistis Sophia and lead her out of the Chaos. Then I gazed towards the Aions in the Heights, and saw that Light-being which the First Mystery had sent to me, so that I may rescue Pistis Sophia from the Chaos.

So it happened, therefore, when I (*the cosmic Christ*) had seen this, issuing forth from the Aions and surging towards me - and I was above the Chaos

---

in *Die Oden Salomos*, p.80, theorizes that *bəpultu* (virgin) should be *bəpauladta* = 'amongst a group/generation of perfected ones'.

TEXT: CHAPTER 60 (cont.)

– that another light-being went forth from me, in order to aid Pistis Sophia. And the Light-being which had issued from the Heights, sent by the First Mystery, descended upon the Light-being which had just issued from me, and they converged; and this became a mighty stream of light."

And when (*the Christ through*) Jesus had spoken these things to his disciples, he said to them, "Do you understand how I am speaking to you?"

TEXT NOTE: in Chapter 60

The theme of the next sections is that of two elements uniting. This uniting is then explained in several ways. Two key terms in my translation are 'compassionate love' and 'sacred wisdom'. These are usually translated as firstly, mercy or grace or love; and secondly, 'truth'; but the origin of the Coptic word 'mercy' is drawn from Old Testament texts which in Hebrew is 'chesed' (חֶסֶד), which means kindness or loving kindness or compassion.

And likewise 'Truth' derives from the Hebrew 'emeth' (אֱמֶה) meaning in particular, 'religious truths', and often used for 'the word of God'; so 'Truth' in the next sections is translated as 'sacred wisdom' or 'divine wisdom'. (Truth can also mean, in the same paragraph, simply the actual correct facts of something).

The visionary dream of Mary about a second Jesus child appearing and then spiritually merging with the physical Jesus is a deeply esoteric theme. It has to do with a veiled aspect of the Messiah Jesus; wherein two primary aspects of human nature needed to merge: the holiest of feelings and the wisest insights. In this section, this is beautifully integrated into a contemplation of the merging of these realities: cosmic wisdom and compassionate love.

End of Text Note.

TEXT: CHAPTER 60 (cont.)   Mariam speaks

Then Mariam (*the Magdalene or Mariam of Bethany?*)

TEXT: CHAPTER 60 (cont.) **Mariam speaks**
started forward again, and said, "My Lord, I understand what you are saying. Concerning the interpretation of this word, your light-being has prophesied of old through David, in the Psalm 44 (*Ps. 45 in the Bible*), saying, "Compassionate love and sacred wisdom have met together; righteousness and peace have kissed each other. Sacred wisdom has flourished on the Earth, and righteousness has looked down from heaven."

'Compassionate love', therefore, is this Light-being which was sent by the First Mystery, for the First Mystery had heard Pistis Sophia. He had shown compassion for her, in all of her tribulations. Sacred wisdom also is that power which had issued from you, for you did fulfill the truth that you were (*always intending*) to save her from the Chaos.

So again, 'righteousness' means that power which was sent by the First Mystery, and which will guide Pistis Sophia. 'Peace' also, is that spiritual power which issued from you in order to enter into the emanations of the (evil) Self-willed One, to retrieve from them the light which they had taken from Pistis Sophia. That is to say, in order that you might gather these together into Sophia, and bring them into harmony with her being.

'Sacred wisdom' also, is the spiritual power which issued from you, when you were in the lower realms of the Chaos. For this reason your being has said through David, "Sacred wisdom has flourished on the Earth", for you were in the lower realms of the Chaos. Righteousness, on the other hand, which has looked down from heaven, is the spiritual presence which issued from the Heights, through the First Mystery, and which entered into Sophia."

COMMENTARY: CHAPTER 60
"flourished on the Earth": here the unpleasant realm called 'the Chaos' is indirectly identified as the physical earthly world.

TEXT: CHAPTER 61 Mary the mother, speaks
And when Jesus had heard these words, he responded, "Well said, Mariam[200] you blessed one, who shall inhabit every kingdom of light." Then also Mary the mother of Jesus, came forward, and said, "My Lord and my Saviour, bid me also to speak this word of interpretation." Jesus said to her, "Whoever has understanding in their mind, I do not prevent, but urge them to declare the thoughts that have stirred in them.

So therefore, Mary, my mother according to matter – you, within whom I sojourned, I bid you also to explain the thoughts in her discourse. So Mary replied, saying, "My Lord, concerning the word which your being through David has prophesied,

"Compassionate love and sacred wisdom met together; righteousness and peace kissed each other. Sacred wisdom sprouted forth out of the Earth, and righteousness has gazed down from Heaven".

TEXT NOTE: in Chapter 61
(In the above words, as in Chapter 60, the union of two spiritual realities are discussed: compassionate love and sacred wisdom. The next section is also about a union of two elements: a profound hidden esoteric message in here is discussed in the Commentary.

There follows an account of a mystical experience that Mary the mother of Jesus had. This probably occurred when Jesus was not yet a teen-ager; and I conclude that it was a visionary dream-like event, as it has illogical features, and cannot have happened physically; see the Commentary.)

TEXT: CHAPTER 61 (cont.) **Mary the mother, speaks**
Long ago, your being, (through David), prophesied this about you (*i.e., of two elements uniting*). (*For in a vision, I experienced this – as a reality*). When you

---

[200] The identity of this 'Mariam' (or Mary) is unknown; it may be Mariam the Magdalene or Mariam of Bethany or Mariam of Clopas.

TEXT: CHAPTER 61 (cont.) **Mary the mother, speaks** were little, before the (holy) Spirit came upon you, (*I saw this*): you were in the vineyard with Joseph, and a[201] spirit came down from the Heights, and came to me in the house, resembling you, and I knew him not, but thought that he was you. And he said to me, "Where is Jesus, my brother, that I may go to meet him?"

And when he had said this to me, I was in doubt, and thought it was a phantom, testing me. I seized him and bound him to the foot of the bed which was in my house, until I had gone to find you in the field, you and Joseph. I found you in the vineyard; Joseph was putting up the supportive reeds for the vineyard.

So it then happened when you heard me reporting this thing to Joseph, that you understood, and you were joyful, and replied, "Where is he, that I may see him? Indeed, I am expecting him in this place." Then it came to pass, when Joseph heard you say these words, that he was troubled.

We returned together, we entered into the house, and we found the spirit entity bound to the bed, and we gazed upon you and him, and found that you resembled him. Then he that was bound to the bed, was released; he embraced you and kissed you, and you also kissed him. The two of you became one and the same being.

This, then, is the discourse, and its interpretation. 'Compassionate love' is the spirit which came from the Heights, (sent) by the First Mystery, who had taken pity on the human race. He sent his spirit to forgive the sins of the whole world, that they might receive the Mystery, that they might inherit the kingdom of light.

TEXT NOTE:
(An unclear passage follows; words in italics are added as a suggested solution to the otherwise

---

[201] "a spirit": usu. 'the spirit', which is fully correct to the Coptic text. But this seems to be scribal error, because 'a spirit', a separate entity to the holy Spirit, makes more sense here.

unclear statements.)

TEXT: CHAPTER 61 (cont.)**Mary the mother, speaks**
'Sacred wisdom', on the other hand, is the power which dwelt in me, after it came forth from the Divine (*lit. Barbelo*). It became (*woven into*) your material body, and (*its presence in your body assisted you to*) speak about the realm of the sacred wisdom.

'Righteousness' is your spirit which has brought all the Mysteries from the Heights, to give them to humankind.

'Peace', on the other hand, is (*the spiritual presence which dwelt in*) your material body according to the world, and which has baptized humankind, until they become strangers to sin.

TEXT NOTE:
(The above unclear text appears to mean):
"Peace, on the other hand, is the spiritual presence which dwelt in your material body according to the world, and which, active in your spirit, thus raying forth in your words and deeds, has begun the process of baptizing humankind into spirituality, thereby releasing them from their 'fallen' souls. And this soul-peace will continue to be offered, until they become strangers to sin."

TEXT: CHAPTER 61 (cont.) **Mary the mother, speaks**
And it (*this inner peace, i.e., spirituality*) brings souls into harmony with your spirit,[202] and in harmony with the emanations of the Light. That is to say, 'Righteousness and sacred wisdom kissed each other'. As in the saying, "Sacred wisdom sprouted forth from the Earth" – but this sacred wisdom is your material body, which sprouted forth from me, according to the human world, and so sacred wisdom has preached about the realm of the Sacred.

---

[202] "in harmony with your spirit (and the light)": usu. 'makes them at peace' which is literally what the Coptic says, but this is less representative of the intended meaning.

TEXT: CHAPTER 61 (cont.)   **Mariam speaks**
And again, as has been said, "Righteousness gazed down from Heaven". Righteousness is the power which looked down from the Heights, and which shall give the Mysteries of the Light to humankind; so that they shall become righteous and good, and inherit the kingdom of light." It then happened, as Jesus heard these words which his mother Mary, spoke that he said, "Excellent; finely said, Mary".

COMMENTARY: CHAPTER 61
The dream-vision of Mary:
In ancient times, dreams and psychic-visionary experiences were important sources of spiritual guidance. Illogical or impossible features in such a narrative indicate it is a dream or vision. I interpret her report as this kind of experience; although she does not formally state this, presumably she knew that this would be apparent to Jesus.

So, Mary thought the visitor who appeared was a spectral apparition, yet instead of fleeing, she took hold of it. But this action of seizing of it, instead of fleeing, is not only unlikely, it is impossible, for it later 'merged' into the physical Jesus – as only a non-physical, spectral form can. Such a spectral form cannot be tied up, (even though it was in her visionary dream), because to be tied up, it has to be a physical person.

If we factor in the brief words mentioned earlier from esoteric Jewish wisdom about the two Messiahs, and also the research of Rudolf Steiner on this topic, then this experience of Mary is an affirmation of the merging of the soul of the deceased 'royal' Messiah with the soul of the priestly Messiah. Thus the dream-vision of Mary is a metaphor of the union of the divine, priestly Messiah with the royal Messiah.

And this leads to a sacred and deep truth indicated by the contrast between the Nativity story in the Gospel of Luke and that of Matthew. In Luke there is an atmosphere of holiness and reverence from the Angels, and the humble, simple shepherds, and then later the focus on Jesus healing and helping those in

COMMENTARY: CHAPTER 61
distress. In Matthew, the Nativity has a nuance of cosmic wisdom from Persian astrologers, and hence of royalty, and power.

Rudolf Steiner taught that the historical Messiah came into being as the cosmic wisdom of the royal Messiah soul merged with the infinite compassion in the holy, priestly Messiah soul. These two qualities had to merge, to form the unique chalice into which the cosmic Christ could be present. The unique human vessel for the Christ could not be only one of infinite love, nor one of immense wisdom; both soul qualities, at their highest possible level, were needed.

TEXT: CHAPTER 62   the 'other Mariam' speaks
And the other Mariam[203] came forward, and said, "Lord, allow me, be not displeased with me; for indeed, from the moment when your mother spoke the meaning of these words, my soul-being has stirred me to come forward, to also expound their interpretation. Then (the other) Mariam said, (*as it is written*) "Lord, loving compassion and sacred wisdom met together".

'Loving compassion' is then, the divine presence which descended upon you, when you received the baptism from John (the Baptist). So, loving compassion is the divine presence which had come upon you, and which had compassion for humanity. It came down, and it met the entity 'Sabaoth the Good', which is present in you, and which (*through you*) has spoken about the realms of divine wisdom.

TEXT NOTE: in Chapter 62
("Sabaoth the Good": a high deity whose actual nature is never defined; see Introduction, "Major Entities".)

TEXT: CHAPTER 62 (cont.) the 'other Mariam' speaks
Again, it has been said, "Righteousness and peace

---

[203] "other Mariam": the identity of this second Mariam is unclear.

TEXT: CHAPTER 62 (cont.) **the 'other Mariam' speaks**
have kissed each other". Righteousness, then, is the spirit of light which came upon you, which has brought the Mysteries of the Heights, to give them to humanity. Peace, also, is the power of Sabaoth the Good, who is in you, who has baptized and has forgiven the human race; it (the power) has brought humanity into peace with the Sons of Light. And again, as your being has said, through David, "Sacred wisdom has flourished on the Earth", this is the power of Sabaoth the Good.

He has said, 'Sacred wisdom has flourished on the Earth', for it has flourished in Mary, your mother, who dwells on the Earth. Righteousness, also, which 'has looked down from heaven', is the spirit which is in the Heights, which has brought all the Mysteries of the Heights, and has given them to humanity; people have become righteous, they have become good, they have inherited the kingdom of light."

And it then happened, when Jesus had heard the discourse which (the other) Mariam spoke, he said, "Well said, Mariam, inheritor of light".

the mother Mary, speaks

Then Mary the mother of Jesus, again came forward, she bowed down at his feet; she fell down at them. "My Lord and my Saviour, be not displeased with me, but permit me, that I may again speak the truth of these words, "Compassionate love and sacred wisdom met together': (*these words refer to*) I myself: your mother, and also to Elisabeth, whom I met.

Compassionate love then, is the power of Sabaoth which was[204] in me, (the being) which went forth from me, that is to say, you yourself; for you have had compassion on all of humanity. Sacred wisdom then, is the power which was in Elisabeth: that is to say, John (the Baptist), who came, and preached about the true way,[205] that is to say, about you. He preached in advance of you.

---

[204] "was in me": usu. 'is in me', which appears anachronistic.
[205] "the true way": Coptic obscure; may be 'the way of truth'.

TEXT: CHAPTER 62 (cont.) **the mother Mary, speaks**
And again, 'Compassionate love and sacred wisdom met together': this is you, my Saviour, when you met John, on the day when you were to receive the baptism. Yet again, it is you and John who are "righteousness and peace that kissed each other".

'Truth has sprouted forth from out of the Earth, and righteousness has looked down from Heaven'. This is the time, when you, Jesus, attended to (*the needs of*) your ministry[206]: that is when you took on the form of Gabriel, and gazed down from Heaven, and spoke with me.

And having spoken with me, you (later) came forth from me. That is, you: the Truth, which is the power of Sabaoth the Good; which is in your denser (soul) body.[207] That is to say, 'the Truth which sprouted forth from the Earth'. It then happened, when Jesus had heard his mother Mary speak these words, that he said: "Excellent, and well said. This is the solution to all the words about the light-being which the prophet David prophesied in earlier times."

COMMENTARY in Chapter 62
"Sons of Light": This is a term used by the Essenes to describe themselves; and appears to be an indicator of the presence of the Essenes in the first Christian groups.[208]

TEXT NOTE:
(Another scribe wrote the following disconnected paragraph on what was empty space on this page. It is almost incomprehensible.)

---

[206] "your mission": lit. 'yourself'.
[207] "in your denser (soul) body": that is, in the now especially denser soul-body which the disciples are perceiving.
[208] See my *The Gospel of John: an Initiatory Quest Translation and Commentary*, where the strong evidence of an Essene underpinning to the first Christian groups is discussed.

Scribal addition to the blank part of the page
These are the names which I shall give, from the Boundless One (*or, Infinite One*), downwards. Write them with a sign, so that the Sons of God may be revealed from here on. This the name of the Immortal One: a,a,a - oe,oe,oe (*that is, soft 'a' but the hard 'o'; in Greek, omega (ω,ω,ω). (So here 'the Immortal One' is being defined as the 'alpha and the omega'.*)

And this is the name of the Voice, for whose sake the Perfect Man has set himself in motion: 'i,i,i'. Now these are the interpretations of the names of these Mysteries: the first name which is a,a,a - its interpretation is: 'f,f,f' (in Grk = ɸ,ɸ,ɸ). The second name, which is m,m,m or 'ω,ω,ω' - its interpretation is a,a,a.

The third name, which is 'ps,ps,ps' (in Grk. ψ,ψ,ψ); its interpretation is 'o,o,o'. The fourth is 'f,f,f (in Grk. = ɸ,ɸ,ɸ); its interpretation is 'n,n,n'.

The fifth is d,d,d; its interpretation is a,a,a.

He on the throne, is a,a,a.

This is the interpretation of the second (m,m,m or 'ω,ω,ω'): a,a,a,a   a,a,a,a   a,a,a,a.

This is the interpretation of the entire name.

Commentary on scribal note on blank part of page.
Rudolf Steiner taught that the vowels are planetary energies resonating in the human soul, and consonants are zodiacal energies resonating in the human soul. But this valuable insight does not provide much help with the above obscure paragraph, which is similar to various Gnostic writings.

(The Pistis Sophia codex continues, on the next page.) On this page a later scribe has added:
"The Second Book of The Pistis Sophia"

But this second document was earlier identified by the original scribe, at the end of this document, as:
"A portion of The Books of the Saviour"

TEXT: CHAPTER 63: John speaks

And John also came forward and said: "Lord, bid me also to expound the interpretation of the words which your light-being prophesied of old through David." And Jesus replied and said to John, "To you also, John, I give a command to expound the interpretation of the words of which my light-power prophesied by David, saying,

"Compassionate love and sacred wisdom have met together, righteousness and peace have kissed each other. Truth has flourished on the Earth, and righteousness has looked down from heaven."

John responded and said, "This is the word which you said to us, before (*the Resurrection*), "I came forth from the Heights, I entered into Sabaoth the Good; I embraced the light-being in him."[209] Now, therefore, 'compassionate love' is yourself, who were sent from the realms of the Heights by your father, the First Mystery looking within; who sent you to have compassion for the whole world. 'Sacred wisdom' also is that power of Sabaoth the Good, which was implanted in you, which you cast into The Left (Devachan, 6th level): you, the First Mystery who looks outwards.

This sacred wisdom was received by the Little Sabaoth the Good who then cast it forth into the (*matrix-*)substance of Barbelo. And he, (the Little Sabaoth) made proclamation concerning the realms of divine wisdom, to all the realms of those of The Left (*Devachan 6, 13th Aion*). That (*matrix*) substance of the Barbelo exists as your body now.

"Righteousness and peace have kissed each other": righteousness is yourself, who did bring (*to humanity*) all the Mysteries, by order of your father, the First Mystery who looks within; and you did consecrate[210] to your mission this power of Sabaoth the Good, and (then) you went into the realm of all the (*debased*) Rulers. You gave them the Mysteries of

---

[209] "Sabaoth the Good": a very significant deity, already mentioned in Chapt. 8; see Introduction about this entity.
[210] "consecrate to your mission": lit. 'baptize'.

TEXT: CHAPTER 63: (cont.) **John speaks**
the Heights; they have become righteous, they have become good.

Peace is also the power of Sabaoth, which indeed is your divine soul,[211] which entered into the 'substance' of Barbelo, and all the Rulers of the six Aions, or Iabraoth[212], made peace with the Mystery of the Light.

And, 'Sacred wisdom which has flourished on the Earth', is that power of Sabaoth the Good, which originated in the realm of the Right (*Buddhi 1*), which is outside[213] of the Treasury of Light (*Buddhi 2*), and came into the realm of those of the Left (Devachan 6, 13th Aion). It entered into the 'substance' of Barbelo, and (*when Jesus was on the Earth*) proclaimed the Mysteries of the realm of divine wisdom.

Righteousness, on the other hand, which "gazed down from Heaven", is you – the First Mystery which looks outwards – having come from the realms of the Heights, bringing with you the Mysteries of the kingdom of Light.

And you came down, enveloped by[214] the garment of light, which you received from the Barbelo: (you) who are (*now*) Jesus, our Saviour; in that you (*Christ*) came down upon him (*Jesus*), in the likeness of a dove.[215]

---

[211] "divine soul"; lit. 'your soul', but a deity does not have the usual astral-body or soul; it is a divine counterpart to this.

[212] "Iabraoth": as described later in the codex, this entity is one of the only partially fallen Archons; who become redeemed.

[213] "outside": i.e., 'below'; it is the 1st level of the Buddhi realm; whereas The Treasury is the 2nd level; 'outside' alludes to the less blessed state of the Right; it is excluded from level 2 of the Buddhi realm.

[214] "enveloped by": lit. 'upon', which is prosaic.

[215] "you who are (now) Jesus...": the Coptic is obscure, other translations seem to be more problematic. Technically, these consider the referent of the relative prefix ⲉⲧⲉ to be Barbelo, but it seems to me it is what we call the cosmic Christ. And 'now' I have added, as it is clearly implied, although absent.

It happened then when John had brought forth these words, that the First Mystery who looks outwards, said to him, "Excellent, John, beloved brother."

COMMENTARY: CHAPTER 63
The cosmic Christ and Jesus: as noted earlier, here in Chapter 63 we encounter a particularly direct confirmation of a deity, a divine cosmic reality, who descended upon Jesus. This can be understood as 'the cosmic Christ'. In the Gospels, the words spoken 'by Jesus' often originate in a divine cosmic reality – a deity – the 'Christ'. So too, throughout the Pistis Sophia codex the same dynamic exists, however, this is not emphasized. As noted in the Introduction, the term 'Christ', meaning the Sun-god, is not used in the codex.

"who looks outwards": God or 'the First Mystery' is said to 'look inwards" whereas the cosmic Christ, enveloping Jesus, is defined as the equivalent of God, with the difference that Jesus Christ 'looks outwards'. This means that Jesus Christ is permeated by God; but the Christ is active out in the manifested cosmos, whereas the First Mystery is profoundly veiled. That Jesus, as the vessel of the Christ is, in a sense, at one with God, is a core truth proclaimed in the Gospel of John, for example:

Jn. 8:54 Jesus answered, if I give divine empowerment to myself, such empowerment is nothing; it is my Father who empowers me – the One of whom you say, "He is our God".
Jn. 10:25 Jesus answered, "I did tell you, but you do not believe. The works I do, imbued with my Father's might, these testify about me"

"The Left": This is identified in Chapter 76 as Aion 13, (thus Devachan 6); the place of Pistis Sophia. The Little Sabaoth deity rayed forth divine light into this Aion.
"exists as your body now": this appears to mean that the 'body' – the spirit-aura – of the Saviour is composed of the 'substance' of the Barbelo deity, who, as noted in the Introduction, dwells in the 6th

COMMENTARY: CHAPTER 63 (cont.)
realm of Devachan.
"did consecrate to your mission this power of Sabaoth": the Christ brought about an inner alignment of the Divine to his 'salvation' intentions.

TEXT: CHAPTER 64
The First Mystery again continued and said, "Therefore it happened, that my Father had sent me – that is, the spiritual-being who had emerged from the Heights – I myself – to rescue Pistis Sophia from the Chaos. So therefore I, and also the spiritual being which came forth from me, together with the (*divine*) soul which I received from Sabaoth the Good, all drew close to each other, and formed one united light-stream, exceedingly radiant.

I summoned Gabriel from above, from the Aions, and also Michael, by order of my Father, the First Mystery looking within. I gave to them the light-stream, and caused them to descend into the Chaos, to rescue Pistis Sophia, and seize upon the light-beings which the emanations of the Self-willed One had removed from her, in order to take these light-beings from the emanations and return them to Pistis Sophia.

And the moment that the light-stream was led into the Chaos, it lit up mightily the whole of the Chaos, and extended itself in all its regions. And the emanations of the Self-willed One, when they saw the great light of this stream, were terror-stricken, one after the other. Then the light-stream drew out from them, all of the light-beings which they had taken from Pistis Sophia.

The emanations of the Self-willed One did not dare to seize this light-stream for themselves in the dark Chaos. Nor could they take hold of it themselves (even) with the cunning skills of the Self-willed One, who rules over these emanations.

And Gabriel and Michael led the light-stream over

TEXT: CHAPTER 64 (cont.)

the body of (astral) substance[216] of Pistis Sophia; they poured into her all the light-beings which the emanations had taken from her. Then her (astral) 'substance body' became radiant throughout, and also all the (astral) qualities which were in her, from which the light had been taken earlier, became radiant.

They ceased to lack their light, for the light had been retrieved from those who had taken it away from her; this had been given back again by me (*i.e., my intervention*). And Michael and Gabriel were in attendance upon me, and had led the light-stream into the Chaos. By them the spiritual being[217] of the Light was given to the (astral) powers of Pistis Sophia. For it was to these two (*Archangels*) that the light-stream had been given; that which I gave to them, and which was then brought into the Chaos.

Yet Michael and Gabriel took no light for themselves from the lights of Pistis Sophia, which they had retrieved from the emanations of the Self-willed One. It came to pass, therefore, when the light-stream had infused into Pistis Sophia all her light-beings, which it had taken directly from the emanations of the Self-willed One, that Pistis Sophia became entirely radiant.

Then the other light-beings which were in Pistis Sophia, those which the emanations of the Self-willed One had not taken, were also joyful, and full of light. And the light-beings which had been infused into Pistis Sophia vivified her body of (astral) substance, in which there had been no light, and which was about to perish, indeed had (*partially*) perished. These light-beings vivified all her own (*astral*) beings which were about to perish.

These (*astral*) beings also became light-beings; they became as they originally were. They were also enhanced as to their perception of the Light; and all

---

[216] "(astral) 'substance'": lit. 'the body of matter' (hyle); but here 'hyle' cannot mean molecular matter, but 'substance' - i.e., substance of the 'astral realm' or Soul-world.
[217] "spiritual being": lit. 'mysteries'.

TEXT: CHAPTER 64 (cont.)
the light-beings of (Pistis) Sophia knew one another, through the out-raying of my light-stream; and they were saved through the effect of that out-raying.

And when my light-stream had taken away the light-beings from the emanations of the Self-willed One, those which they had earlier stripped away from Pistis Sophia, my light-stream poured these into Pistis Sophia. It then turned itself around and ascended up out of the Chaos. Now when the First Mystery (Jesus Christ) had said this to the disciples, telling them of what had happened to Pistis Sophia; he spoke further, asking them, "Do you understand in what way I am speaking with you?"

COMMENTARY: CHAPTER 64
The dynamics of this chapter are clear.

TEXT: CHAPTER 65   Peter speaks
Then Peter came forward, and said, "Lord, concerning the meaning of the words which you have spoken, your light-being has prophesied concerning them, through Solomon, in his Odes (6th ode):
A flood has taken place; it has become a great wide stream. It gathered all things, it turned towards the temple; it could not be restrained with enclosures and dams. Nor could the skills of those who manage the water, restrain it. It was brought over the entire land, and took hold of everything.

Those who were on the dry land, drank; their thirst was stilled, and quenched, when they were given a drink from the hand of the Most High. Blessed are those to whom the water of the Lord is entrusted.

They have refreshed parched lips. Those whose life was fading were taken hold of, and the breath of life was poured into them, so that they did not die. They have set limbs upright that were fallen. For these, they gave power to their outspoken-ness, and light to their eyes. For they have all known themselves in the Lord, and are saved through a water of eternal life.

TEXT NOTE: in Chapter 65
"a water of eternal life": This expression means esoterically, an aionic consciousness; that is an 'I' consciousness in the Aions. This ray of divine light is here visualized as a watery stream, merging the image of waters of eternal life, such as that spoken of in the Gospel of John, chapters 4 and 7.

TEXT: CHAPTER 65 (cont.)   Peter speaks
"Hearken, therefore, my Lord, that I may openly declare the word, as your being prophesied, through Solomon, "A surging flood has taken place; it has become a great wide stream"; this is the light-stream which spread itself in the Chaos, in all the realms of the emanations of the Self-willed One.

And the word which your being has again uttered through Solomon, "It drew everything to itself; it poured this over the temple"; that is to say, it carried away all the light-beings from the emanations of the Self-willed One, which they had taken from Pistis Sophia, and cast these again into Pistis Sophia.

And again the word which your being has uttered, "It could not be restrained with enclosures and dams", that is, the emanations of the Self-willed One could not hold the light-stream within the walls of the darkness of the Chaos.

And again the word which your being has uttered, "It was brought over the entire land, and took hold of everything", that is, when Gabriel and Michael poured it over the (*astral*) 'substance' body of Pistis Sophia, it poured into Sophia all the light-beings which the emanations of the Self-willed One had taken from her, so her (astral) 'substance' body became radiant.

And the word which your being had spoken, "Those who were in the dry sand, were given to drink", that means, all those (*elemental light-beings*) who were in Pistis Sophia, those whose light had been taken away earlier (were helped). And the word which your power uttered, "Their thirst has left them and was quenched"; that is to say, her entities ceased to lack their light, for that which had been taken

TEXT: CHAPTER 65 (cont.)   Peter speaks
away, was restored to them. And, again, as to the utterance of your being, "They were given a drink from the hand of the Most High", this means, the light was given to them through the light-stream which emanated from you, the First Mystery.

TEXT NOTE: in Chapter 65
"those (elemental light-beings) who were in Pistis Sophia": This is one of several instances where a deeply esoteric topic regarding Pistis Sophia is touched on. Namely, that the soul or soul-body of the human being – thus the separate capacities for emotion or thinking or action – are composed of a multitude of minor 'elemental energies'.[218]

TEXT: CHAPTER 65 (cont.)   Peter speaks
And as to the saying of your light-being, "Blessed are those to whom the water of the Lord is entrusted", that refers to the word which you have spoken, "Gabriel and Michael, they who were in attendance, led the stream into the Chaos and also brought it forth again". The Mysteries of Light which had been entrusted to the light-stream will be given to them; that is, to those spirits (*Gabriel and Michael*) to whom the light-stream was entrusted.

And as to the further utterance of your spirit-being, "They have refreshed the parched lips", that means, Gabriel and Michael have taken nothing for themselves from the light-beings of Pistis Sophia: that is, from these (*elemental light-*)beings which they had seized from the Self-willed One. Instead they poured this (all) into Pistis Sophia.

And again the word which it spoke, "They who were fainting, have felt their heart rejoice"; that is, all the other (light-)beings of Pistis Sophia, which had not been taken away by the emanations of the Self-willed One, rejoiced greatly. They were filled with light from their other companion lights, for these were infused into them.

---

[218] "energies": these could be considered as 'entities'.

TEXT: CHAPTER 65 (cont.) **Peter speaks**

And again the word which your light-being uttered, "They have revived the souls which were breathing their last, that they might not die", that is, when they had poured their light into Pistis Sophia, they vivified her (astral) substance body, from which the light had previously been taken, and which was about to perish.

And again the word which your being has spoken, "They have set upright limbs that were fallen", that is, when they had poured her light-beings into her, they strengthened all the (other) beings which (otherwise) would have perished.

And again as to the saying of your light-being, "They have given power to their outspokenness..." that is, they have received their light again and have become as they were before. And as your word has spoken, "they have been given light to their eyes", that is, they have gained perception of the light, and have known the light-stream: (understanding) that it belongs to the Heights.

And again the word which it uttered, "They have been saved by the water of life-everlasting; it has drawn them over the temple"; that is, when the light-stream had gathered all the light-powers of Pistis Sophia, having wrested them away from the emanations of the Self-willed One, it poured them into Pistis Sophia, and turned itself about, and departed from the Chaos; it came upon you (*Christ*), for you are the temple.

This is the interpretation of all the words which your light-being spoke in the (6th) ode of Solomon". It came to pass, therefore, when the First Mystery had heard all these words which Peter had spoken, that he said to him, "Well said, blessed Peter; this is the interpretation of the words which have been spoken."

COMMENTARY: CHAPTER 65

This is a detailed description of the dynamics involved, when the Christ-light, as a vessel of the First Mystery (God), permeated the fallen, almost dying, intuitive-spiritual consciousness of the human soul,

COMMENTARY: CHAPTER 65
thereby rescuing it. As this occurs in the Aions (the astral realm or Soul-world) a corresponding re-emerging of this quality of consciousness can take place within incarnate people. In the words of an old esoteric adage, 'as above, so below'.

A similar dynamic is placed in the Lord's Prayer, in the form of an entreaty "As in the heavens, so (also) upon the Earth",[219] this same truth forms the basis of the majestic Beatitudes in Matt. 5:3-11.[220]

TEXT: CHAPTER 66
The First Mystery continued, and said, "So it happened, before I led Pistis Sophia out of the Chaos, because I had not been commanded by my Father – the First Mystery that looks within – that the emanations of the Self-willed One discovered that my light-stream had taken into itself those light-beings which they had stripped away from Pistis Sophia, and had poured them again into Pistis Sophia.

When they saw Pistis Sophia radiant again, as she had been in former times, they were enraged against Pistis Sophia. They cried out, moreover, to the Self-willed One to make him approach and help them, that they might again take away all the powers which were in Pistis Sophia.

And the Self-willed One sent from on high, from the (malignant) 13th Aion, another great light-being, which descended like an arrow, to help his emanations, so that they might take away the lights from Pistis Sophia once more.

TEXT NOTE: in Chapter 66
"had been in former times": we are reminded that Pistis Sophia is originally from the 13th Aion (6th realm of Devachan). This is the spiritual realm from where our spiritually intuitive consciousness originates and

---

[219] In the Greek, Matt. 6:10, ὡς ἐν οὐρανῷ καὶ ἐπὶ γῆς.

[220] See the author's *Blessed: Rudolf Steiner on the Beatitudes*.

TEXT NOTE: in Chapter 66
is nurtured. Steiner comments that this faculty became debased as the Greco-Latin Age dawned. For then intellectualism predominated, and this process was paralleled in the spirit realms, by the 'fall' of Sophia into lower realms.

TEXT: CHAPTER 66 (cont.)
And when this (malignant) light-being had descended, the emanated entities of the Self-willed One, which were in the Chaos and had caused Pistis Sophia all her woes, were strongly encouraged. They persecuted Pistis Sophia afresh with great fears and severe stress; and some of the emanations of the Self-willed One directly oppressed her. One of them changed itself into the form of a great serpent; another changed itself into the form of a seven-headed basilisk, having seven heads. Another changed itself into the form of a dragon.

Moreover, the first power of the Self-willed One, the Lion-faced, and all his many other emanations, came together and oppressed Pistis Sophia and led her again into the lower realms of the Chaos. So they again stressed her greatly. Then it happened that Adamas, the empowered One, looked down from the 12 Aions; he was also angry with Pistis Sophia because she wished to go to the Light of Lights, which was above them all.

Hence it happened, when Adamas, the empowered One, had looked down from the height of the twelve Aions, that he saw the emanations of the Self-willed One which were oppressing Pistis Sophia until they might take from her all the light-beings which were in her. It happened, when the power of Adamas descended into the Chaos to the emanations of the Self-willed One – when this demonic power descended into the Chaos – that it cast Pistis Sophia down to the Earth.

And the Lion-faced entity, and also the Basilisk-headed One, and the Dragon-faced one, and all the emanations of the Self-willed One, which were very many, surrounded Pistis Sophia all together, seeking

CHAPTER 66 (cont.)

to take from her again the powers which were in her. They intensely oppressed her, and severely threatened her.

It then happened as they oppressed her and alarmed her severely, that she again cried out to the Light and intoned words of reverence saying, "O Light, it is you who did rescue me; may your light descend upon me. For you are my protector, and I am coming close to you, discerning you truly, O Light. For you are my Saviour against the emanations of the Self-willed One, and against Adamas the empowered One.[221] You shall rescue me from all his mighty threats."

And when Pistis Sophia had said this, then through the command of my Father – the First Mystery who looks inwards – I again sent Gabriel and Michael, and the great light-stream, that they might rescue Pistis Sophia. I gave orders to Gabriel and Michael to bear Pistis Sophia in their hands, so that her feet should not touch the lower darkness.[222]

And I further commanded them to guide her through the realms of the Chaos, out of which they were taking her. These (*Archangels*) descended into the Chaos, they and the light-stream, and became a radiant light beyond measure. So it happened, when all the emanations of the Self-willed One and the emanations of Adamas again saw the light-stream which shone so mightily, they were afraid, and they released Pistis Sophia.

And the great light-stream surrounded Pistis Sophia on every side, on the right and on the left, on every side, and became a crown of light upon her head. Therefore, it happened when the light-stream had surrounded Pistis Sophia, that she regained her courage, and the stream of light ceased not to surround her on every side.

So Pistis Sophia no longer feared the emanations of

---

[221] Lit. 'tyrant' i.e., a Grk. word meaning 'empowered ruler'.
[222] "hands" and "feet": these are metaphors of course, since spirit entities have no physical body.

TEXT: CHAPTER 66 (cont.)   Peter speaks

the Self-willed One, which were in the Chaos, nor did she fear any more that new power of the Self-willed One, which he had cast into the Chaos like a winged arrow. Nor did she tremble before the demonic power of Adamas, which had come from the (debased) Aions.

And also, by my command (to myself), I – the First Mystery who gazes without – the light-stream which surrounded Pistis Sophia on every side, became very radiant. So Pistis Sophia dwelt amidst this light, and there was a mighty light on her left and on her right, and on all sides; these forming a crown on her head.

And all the emanations of the Self-willed One could no longer change their appearances, nor could they withstand the impact of the great radiance of the stream which formed a crown on the head of Sophia. Hence all the emanations of the Self-willed One collapsed; a host of them at her right, because of her mighty radiance, whilst many others fell at her left.

They could no longer draw near at all to Pistis Sophia because of the intense light. Instead, they all fell one upon the other, and could do no harm to Pistis Sophia, because she had discerned truly the light.

And then by order of my Father, the First Mystery, I myself descended into the Chaos, extremely radiant. I approached the Lion-faced entity, and I removed all the light which was within it, and I prevented all the emanations of the Self-willed One from that hour entering into their realm, which is the (debased) 13th Aion. I took away the power of all the emanations of the Self-willed One, and they all fell into the Chaos, powerless.

Then I led forth Pistis Sophia, who was on the right of Gabriel and Michael; and the great light-stream entered into them. And Pistis Sophia gazed upon her enemies, from whom I had taken their light-power. And I led Pistis Sophia forth from the Chaos; she was trampling underfoot the serpent-headed emanation of the Self-willed One, and also the seven-headed basilisk emanation, the Lion-faced entity, and the

TEXT: CHAPTER 66 (cont.)   Peter speaks
Dragon-faced one.

I enabled Sophia thereafter to stand upon the seven-headed basilisk emanation of the Self-willed One, which was more powerful than all of them in his evil doings. And I, the First Mystery, stood next to it;
[223] I took away all the powers which were in it, and I destroyed all of its (astral) substance, so that from now on, nothing could be created from it.

COMMENTARY: CHAPTER 66
"he was also angry": it was to the advantage of this demonic entity that the debased nature of Pistis Sophia i.e., the human potential for intuitive perceiving, remained debased. This 'matter-blinded' consciousness state can empower these entities over humanity.

"Adamas, the empowered One": a key to the nature of, and therefore the name given to, this evil entity seems to emerge here. In the Hebrew Scriptures, 'Adam' is the name of the primal human being, which has a germinal divine quality. It appears that Adam with the 'as' added, signifies the malignant counterpart to Adam.

"seven-headed basilisk": this astral entity is regarded by initiatory wisdom as a very real being; it is the embodiment of the malignant (ahrimanic-luciferic) counterpart to the seven noble planetary energies from which the human soul (or astral aura) is formed. In the language of anthroposophy, it could be called the 'sevenfold Double'; the malignant influences of the seven classical planets.

"she had discerned truly the light": usually 'because she had believed in the light'; but it is unlikely that 'belief' is involved. Pistis Sophia has now regained the capacity to cognize the divine, to perceive intuitively, its existence.

This capacity of perception was crucial for her to

---

[223] "next to": usu. 'stood upon', but this seems unlikely as Pistis Sophia is already standing on this demon. The Coptic preposition here can mean 'upon' or 'next to', etc.

COMMENTARY: CHAPTER 66 (cont.)
become aligned to the Christ-Light, and to thereby escape the malignant powers, who at times can be deceptive; they can 'morph', or change their appearance, which could include taking on a deceptively positive appearance.

"trampling underfoot...the seven-headed basilisk": this powerful image is also applicable to the soul-state of the initiate in whom the Spiritual-self has been born; and has some similarity to a scene in the Book of Revelation (12:1,2).

"...to stand upon...and I stood next to it...": the Christ-light is enabling Pistis Sophia to achieve victory over the basilisk and hence remains close to her in this task. This exactly parallels an initiatory experience of those in the Essene movement, as described in Ode 22 of Solomon,
"He (Jahve-Christ) overthrew, *by my hands*, the dragon with seven heads.."

This is another indicator here, that the risen Jesus was the primary inspirer of the profound initiatory teachings of the main sections of the Pistis Sophia codex. Within these brief words is a vast reality; the higher intuitive-spiritual consciousness of the soul (Pistis Sophia) is interwoven with, is almost one with, spiritual light of the redeemer, Christ Jesus.

TEXT: CHAPTER 67 James speaks
The First Mystery, having spoken these things to his disciples, continued, and said, "Do you understand how I am speaking to you?" And James came forward, and said, "Lord, concerning the meaning of the words which you have said, your light-being prophesied concerning them long ago, through David, in Psalm 90 (*Ps. 91 in the Bible*), saying: "Whoever dwells under the help of the Most High, shall abide under the shadow of the God of Heaven. He shall say to the Lord, You are my nurturer and my place of refuge; my God in whom I trust."

For he shall save me from the snares of the hunters and from those that speak violent words. He

TEXT: CHAPTER 67   James speaks

shall shelter you beneath his breast, and you shall take courage beneath his wings. His truth shall surround you like a shield; you shall not be afraid of the terror of the night, nor of the arrow which flies by day, nor from the thing that moves in the darkness, nor from the demon of midday.[224] A thousand shall fall on your left, and ten thousand at your right hand; but they shall not come near to you.

Instead, you shall gaze upon them, you shall see what is handed out to sinners. For you, O Lord are my hope. You have set yourself – the Most High – as a refuge;[225] no one shall come near you, no plague come near your dwelling. For he has given commandment to his Angels concerning you, to guard you in all your ways, to bear you in their hands, lest you dash your foot against a stone. You shall tread upon the serpent and basilisk; you shall trample under foot the lion and the dragon.

Because he has trusted in me, I will save him; I will shelter[226] him, because he has known my spirit (*lit. my name*). He will cry out to me, and I shall hear him; I am with him in his afflictions, and I will save him to glorify him, and increase him with many days, and teach him my salvation."

"This, my Lord, is the interpretation of the words which you have spoken. Therefore, please hear me that I may expound it to you openly. The word, then, which your power spoke, through David, 'Whoever dwells under the help of the Most High, shall abide

---

[224] "demon midday": the Hebrew of the Psalm says "the destruction/pestilence that lays waste at midday". But the Septuagint version changes this to 'the demon of midday' for reasons unknown, perhaps the translator had a textual variant, where the word for 'destruction' (shwud) was changed to 'demon' (shed-im) as www.thetorah.com. comments. Otherwise, the Heb. presumably referred to the potential for exhaustion or a heat-stroke from the midday sun.

[225] "yourself – the Most High – as refuge": Coptic obscure; usu. 'set for yourself the Most High as a refuge'.

[226] "shelter him": lit. 'make shadow over him'.

TEXT: CHAPTER 67 (cont.)   James speaks

under the shadow of the God of Heaven'; that is, when Sophia trusted in the light, she dwelt under the radiance of the light-stream which came down from the Heights from you.

And the word which your light-being uttered, through David, 'I will say to the Lord, "You are my nurturer and my place of refuge; my God in whom I trust"; this is the word which Pistis Sophia spoke in her intoning of reverence, "You have received me to yourself, and I am going to you." And again, the word which your light-being uttered, "My God, I trusted in you; for you shall save me from the snares of the hunters, and from those that speak violent words", this is what Pistis Sophia said, "O Light, I have trusted in you; for you shall save me from the emanations of the Self-willed One and from those of the empowered One, Adamas; moreover, you shall save me from all their violent threats".

And again, the word which your being spoke through David, "He shall shelter you beneath his breast, and you shall take courage beneath his wings"; means that Pistis Sophia has dwelt in the radiance of that light-stream which came forth from you, and she felt confidence from the light which was on her left, and that which was at her right, which are the wings of the light-stream.

And the word which your light-being prophesied through David, "His truth shall surround you like a shield"; that refers to the radiance of the light-stream which surrounded Pistis Sophia like a shield.

Thus, the word which your light-being spoke, "He shall not be afraid of the terror of the night", which implies that Pistis Sophia was not afraid of the terrors and troubles into which she had been sent in the Chaos, which is 'night'.

Thus also the word which your light-being spoke, "He shall not be afraid of the arrow which flies, by day"; this implies that Pistis Sophia was not afraid of that entity which the Self-willed One had lastly sent from the (debased) Heights, and which descended into the realm of Chaos like a flying arrow.

TEXT: CHAPTER 67 (cont.)   **James speaks**
For as your light-being prophesied, "You shall not be afraid of the arrow that flies, by day"; because *that* light-stream (*the shielding Christ-light*[227]) came forth (to Pistis Sophia) from the 13th Aion, which is empowered over the twelve Aions; this (light) is that which illumines all the Aions (*like day*). Therefore he (David) has used the word 'day'; (*meaning a world in which the Christ-light illumines everything*).

TEXT NOTE: in Chapter 67
Reviewing these words:
"For as your light-being prophesied, "You shall not be afraid of the arrow that flies, by day"; because that light-stream (*the shielding Christ-light*) came forth (to Pistis Sophia) from the 13th Aion, which is empowered over the twelve Aions; this (light) is that which illumines all the Aions (*like day*)."

Here the Coptic is referring to the shielding light from the Christ–light, mentioned on the page before - "that light-stream" - but the text does not make it clear that the same Christ-light is meant on this next page. So this page can be misunderstood[228]; the radiant light-power which protects Pistis Sophia, does derive from the shielding Christ-Light, mentioned a few sentences earlier. This divine light comes from the 13th Aion, and protects Pistis Sophia from both night and daytime evil.

But the terseness of the Coptic can give the false impression that the arrow-light of an evil deity is referred to here as coming from the noble 13th Aion, and this is somehow illumining all the Aions: but an evil being's energies do not illumine anything; and certainly do not protect Pistis Sophia from evil.

In essence, we are told that the arrow is not feared

---

[227] "that light-stream": usu. 'that power' but here the Coptic is too brief; see Commentary.
[228] E. Evans, *The Books of Jeu & the Pistis Sophia..*" p. 250 erroneously concludes that the redeeming Light came from the Self-willed One.

TEXT NOTE: in Chapter 67
in a 'day' or illumined world, since any light comes from the all-present, all-pervading Christ-light.

TEXT: CHAPTER 67 (cont.)   **James speaks**
And again the word which your being uttered, "He shall not be afraid of the thing that moves in darkness"; which means that Pistis Sophia[229] did not have fear of the serpent-headed emanation; this did not[230] make Pistis Sophia afraid in the Chaos, which is darkness. And the word which your being spoke, "He will not have fear of the destruction, the demonic one at mid-day", which means that Pistis Sophia was not afraid of the demonic emanation of the empowered One, Adamas, which cast her down to the Earth in a great misfortune: this which came forth from Adamas, from the twelfth (debased) Aion.

Therefore, your light-being prophesied, "He will not fear the destruction of the demonic one at midday"; 'mid-day', because it came forth from the twelfth Aion, which is mid-day (*i.e., the twelfth hour*). And again because it descended into the Chaos, which is 'night', or rather, the night which descended from the twelfth Aion, which is between the two. Therefore, your light-power spoke of mid-day, because the twelve Aions are between the 13th Aion and the Chaos.   **James speaks**

And again the word which your light-being spoke through David, "A thousand shall fall on your left, and ten thousand at your right hand, but they shall not come near you", that is to say, when the emanations of the Self-willed One, which were very many in number, could not withstand the great light of the light-stream, a host of them fell on the left hand of Pistis Sophia, and a host at her right, and

---

[229] "Pistis Sophia": the text has only 'Sophia', presumably in error.

[230] "did not make": the Coptic has 'did make Pistis Sophia afraid'; the text is apparently corrupted here; see Commentary.

TEXT: CHAPTER 67 (cont.)   **James speaks**
they could not come near her at all, to do her harm[231].

And the word which your light-being spoke through David, "But you shall gaze upon them, and you shall see what is handed out to sinners; for you, Lord, are my hope", this means, that with her own eyes Pistis Sophia looked upon her enemies, which are the emanations of the Self-willed One.

These had all fallen down, the one upon the other; and not only did she gaze upon them in this state, but you also, my Lord, the First Mystery, you did take away the light-being which was in that Lion-faced entity, and furthermore you took away the strength of all the emanations of the Self-willed One, and moreover you kept them in that Chaos, preventing them from that hour entering their own realm.

Therefore did Pistis Sophia with her own eyes look upon her enemies, that is to say, the emanations of the Self-willed One, precisely as David prophesied concerning Pistis Sophia, saying, "But you shall look upon them, and you shall see what chastizement is handed out to sinners". Not only did she look upon them, having fallen one on the other, but she also beheld the chastizement which they have received.

Just as the emanations of the Self-willed One thought to take away the light which was in Pistis Sophia, in like manner have you dealt with them. You have taken away the light which was in them, instead of Pistis Sophia losing her light; she who had discerned truly from the Light of the Heights.

                                        James speaks
As your light-being through David had said, "You have set for yourself the Most High as a refuge; no one shall come near you, no plague come near your dwelling"; that is to say, when Pistis Sophia perceived the Light with discernment while she was oppressed, she intoned words of reverence to it. Then the emanations of the Self-willed One could not do her any harm, they could not injure her, they could not

---

[231] "do her harm": 'harm' is probably what is meant; the Coptic word here is unknown.

TEXT: CHAPTER 67 (cont.) James speaks
come near her at all.

And the word which your light-being uttered through David, "He will give command to his Angels concerning you, to keep you in all your ways, to bear you in their hands, lest you dash your foot against a stone"; that is to say also, you have given a command to Gabriel and Michael to guide Pistis Sophia in all the realms of the Chaos, to bear her in their hands until they had helped her rise up, so that her feet should not touch the lower darkness, and they of the lower darkness should not seize hold of her.

And the word which your light-being spoke through David in Psalm 90 (*Ps. 91 in the Bible*), "You shall trample on the serpent and the basilisk[232], and you shall tread underfoot the lion and the dragon; because he has had trust in me, I will save him, and I will over-shadow him because he has known my name. That is the meaning (of your utterance), "when Pistis Sophia was just leaving the Chaos, she trod under foot the emanations of the Self- willed One; she trampled on them that had serpent heads, and basilisk heads, those having seven heads.

And she trod underfoot that Lion-faced being, and that Dragon-headed One, because she had perceived truly the Light, and it had saved her from them all." This, Lord, is the interpretation of the words which you have said.

COMMENTARY: CHAPTER 67
Error in Coptic text: "did *not* make": the other versions, following the Coptic, has 'did make Pistis Sophia afraid', but the sense of the passage is that Pistis Sophia was *not* afraid.

"from the 12th Aion, which is mid-day": this is puzzling.

Mid-day as alluding to the 12 Aions
The mid-day hour is the 12th hour in the Roman time

---

[232] The Heb. has 'snake', but the Septuagint has 'basilisk' for reasons unknown.

COMMENTARY: CHAPTER 67 (cont.)
reckoning system, but not in Hebrew reckoning; there it is the sixth hour. The Psalm was written centuries before the Roman Empire existed, so the psalmist cannot be referring to the Roman time system. Also the Babylonian/Egyptian systems cannot be used for this, for their 12-hour divisions cover both the day and the night, but do not cross over from the night divisions into day-time.

So the disciple has to be interpreting '*darkness*' in the words of the Psalm, as meaning the midnight hour; "He shall not be afraid of the thing that moves in darkness (*at midnight*)". And he has to be adding the last six hours of the night to the first six hours of the day (an unusual procedure) to arrive at '12 hours'.

A lurking mid-night 'thing' would contrast very well with the mid-day 'demon'. However, the Hebrew word here simply means 'night' or 'darkness', not mid-night: and likewise the Greek Septuagint simply has 'darkness'. So the solution to this puzzle remains unclear.

TEXT: CHAPTER 68   Pistis Sophia intones
It then happened as the First Mystery heard the words which James spoke, that he said, "Well done, James, beloved one." Then the First Mystery continued in his discourse, and said to his disciples, "It then happened, when I had led Pistis Sophia out of the Chaos, that she cried out anew, saying,
'I have been rescued from the Chaos; I have been released from the bonds of darkness. I have come to you, O Light, for you have been radiance surrounding[233] me; you saved me and helped me.

And the emanations of the Self-willed One, which fought against me, you have kept away from me by your light; so they have not been able to draw near to me. For your light was with me and preserved me, through your light-stream. Because the emanations of the Self-willed One were oppressing me; they took

---

[233] "Surrounding me": lit. approx. 'on all my sides'.

TEXT: CHAPTER 68 (cont.)   Pistis Sophia intones
away my strength, and cast me out into the Chaos. And since my light was (*almost*) gone, I became, compared to them, a denser (astral) substance.

Then there came forth from you the strength of the light-stream, saving me; it shone on my left and on my right, surrounding me on all sides, so that no part of my being was without light, and you hid me in the radiance of your out-streaming light. You purged from me all my debased (astral) substances,[234] and so I was raised above all these, because of your light. For it is your light-stream which has raised me up, and has taken me away from the emanations of the Self-willed One, which had oppressed me.

I became courageous of heart within your light; indeed:

I am a purified radiance of your out-raying light.

And the emanations of the Self-willed One which oppressed me, withdrew themselves from me, and so I became radiant within your great power. You have saved me – and saved me for ever.'

This is the (triumphal) declaration which Pistis Sophia uttered, when she came forth from the Chaos and was freed from the bonds of the Chaos. Now, therefore, whoever has ears to hear, let them hear.

COMMENTARY: CHAPTER 68
"compared to them": Pistis Sophia laments that her state was denser, i.e., worse than, that of her malignant opponents.

TEXT: CHAPTER 69   Thomas speaks
So it happened when the First Mystery had finished saying these words to his disciples, that Thomas came forward, and said, "Lord, my companion-of-light has ears, so my spirit understands the words which

---

[234] "astral energies": lit. 'matters' (hyle); i.e., 'matter' in the plural, which is meaningless, since Pistis Sophia has no physical material.

TEXT: CHAPTER 69 (cont.) **Ode of Solomon 25**
you have said. Now, therefore, command me to expound clearly the interpretation of the words."

The First Mystery replied, and said to Thomas, "I bid you now to expound the meaning of the words of reverence which Pistis Sophia intoned to me." Thomas responded and said, "My Lord, concerning the words of reverence which Pistis Sophia uttered because she was rescued from the Chaos, your light-being prophesied formerly concerning you, through Solomon, the son of David, in his Odes, (ode 25) saying,

"I have been released from my bonds, I have fled to you, O Lord; you have been at my right hand. You are saving me, and you are helping me. You hindered those who are my adversaries, and so they have not manifested themselves, for your countenance was turned towards[235] me, saving me with your Grace.[236]

I was despised in the sight of many, and have been cast out. I became like lead in their presence.[237] But a power came forth to me from you, helping me; for you have set lamps on my right hand and on my left, so that no part of my being should be without light. You sheltered me under the shadow of your mercy, and I was placed above the coats of skin (*i.e., the lowly, darkened material consciousness*).

Your right hand has raised me up, and has taken my sickness from me. I have become strong in your truth, pure in your righteousness. They that fought against me have withdrawn themselves from me, and I am justified in your goodness; for your inner peace endures for ever."

Thomas speaks

NOTE: for Chapter 69
In the next section the disciple quotes from the Ode and often says, 'this the word which Pistis Sophia spoke'; but this actually means, "this *explains* the words which she spoke.

---

[235] "turned towards": lit. 'with me'.
[236] "Grace": a complex Christian term, which here means, goodwill extended to a fallen entity, from divine agape.
[237] "like lead": presumably, having no value, unlike gold.

TEXT: CHAPTER 69 (cont.)   **Thomas speaks**
This then, O Lord, is the explanation of the (triumphal) declaration which Pistis Sophia uttered, when she came forth from the Chaos, and was freed from the bonds of the Chaos. Please do hear me (again), Lord, that I may openly explain the words of Pistis Sophia. The words which your light-being prophesied, through Solomon, saying, "I have been released from my bonds, I have fled to you, O Lord": this is the (*inner meaning of*) the word which Pistis Sophia spoke, "I am released from the bonds of darkness and I have fled to you, O Light."

And the words which your light-being has spoken (*in ode 25*) "You have been at my right hand. You are saving me, and you are helping me", this is again the (*inner meaning of*) the word which Pistis Sophia spoke, "you have been surrounding me; you saved and help me".

And these words which your light-being has spoken, "You hindered those who are my adversaries, and so they have not manifested", these are the words which Pistis Sophia intoned, "And the emanations of the Self-willed One, which fought against me, you have kept away from me by your light; so they have not been able to draw near to me." Also these words which your light-being has spoken, "your countenance was turned towards me, saving me with your Grace", these are the words which Pistis Sophia spoke, "there came forth from you the power of the light-stream, saving me".

And these words which your light-being has spoken, "I was despised in the sight of many, and have been cast out", these are the words which Pistis Sophia spoke, "the emanations of the Self-willed One were oppressing me; they took away my being, and cast me out into the Chaos, and ... my light was gone".

And these words which your light-being has spoken, "I became like lead in their presence", these are the words which Pistis Sophia spoke, "since my light was gone, I became like dense (astral) substance, compared to them".

TEXT: CHAPTER 69 (cont.)   Thomas speaks

And moreover, the word which your light-being has spoken, "But a power came forth to me from you, helping me..." again, these are the words which Pistis Sophia spoke, "there came forth from you the strength of the light-stream, saving me".

And the word which your being spoke, "for you have set lamps on my right hand and on my left, so that no part of my being should be without light", this is the word which Pistis Sophia intoned, "Your power shone on my right hand, and on my left hand, surrounding me, so that no part of my being was without light."

Thomas speaks

And the word which your being spoke, "You sheltered me under the shadow of your mercy", this is again the word which Pistis Sophia spoke, "And you clothed me in the light of your streaming radiance". And the word which your light-being spoke, "I was placed above the coats of skin", this again is the word which Pistis Sophia spoke, "You purged from me all my bad dense (astral) substances, and so I was raised above my dense (astral) substances because of your light."

And the word which your being spoke, through Solomon, "Your right hand has raised me up, and has taken my sickness from me"; this is the word which Pistis Sophia said, "And your light-stream has raised me up in the light, and has removed from me the emanations of the Self-willed One, who oppressed me."

And the word which your being spoke, "I have become strong in your truth, and pure in your righteousness", this is the word which Pistis Sophia spoke, "I became courageous of heart within your light; indeed I am a purified radiance of your out-raying light". And the word which your being spoke, "They that fought against me, have withdrawn themselves from me"; this is the word which Pistis Sophia spoke, "And the emanations of the Self-willed One which oppressed me withdrew themselves from me."

And the word which your being spoke through

TEXT: CHAPTER 69 (cont.) **Thomas speaks** Solomon (*ode 25*) "and I am justified in your goodness; for your inner peace endures for ever", this is the word which Pistis Sophia spoke, "I have been saved in your goodness, for you (*intend to*) save everyone."

This then, my Lord, is the full interpretation of the (triumphal) declaration which Pistis Sophia uttered, when she had been rescued from the Chaos and freed from the bonds of darkness."

COMMENTARY: CHAPTER 69

"I was placed above the coats of skin": the Syriac text of the ode has here a fuller text, with a direct reference to an initiatory experience, wherein the acolyte succeeds in transcending their body-derived, earthly cognitional nature, and attains seership (to astral or even devachanic clairvoyance): "*And I was clothed with the covering of your spirit, and you removed from me my garment of skin.*"

"I am a purified radiance of your out-raying light": an immensely significant statement: namely that Pistis Sophia, who is the spirit counterpart of the Spiritual-self, derives from the cosmic Christ.

For here, 'your' refers to the cosmic Christ, often called 'the Light of Lights' in this codex; and who is also described as a vessel of God, the First Mystery. In Chapter 63 this deity is referred as, "you who descended upon Jesus in the form of a dove."

It is this divine being who in Steiner's work is the highest of the Sun-gods; they are identified as the 'Elohim' of Genesis. That human beings are deeply interconnected with the Sun-gods is a widespread theme in ancient wisdom teachings. Hence humanity is understood in some ancient wisdom as the creation of the Sun-god[238]; and in terms of esoteric Christianity humanity is in effect a vessel of the cosmic Christ.

TEXT: CHAPTER 70

"This then, my Lord, is the whole interpretation of the

---

[238] Such as in Egypt (Ra) and Greece (Helios).

TEXT: CHAPTER 70 (cont.) **Pistis Sophia intones** (triumphal) declaration which Pistis Sophia uttered, when she had been rescued from the Chaos and freed from the bonds of darkness." It then happened, when the First Mystery had heard Thomas utter these words, that he said "Well said and finely done, Thomas, you blessed one. This is the interpretation of the (triumphal) declaration from Pistis Sophia." The First Mystery went on with his discourse, telling his disciples: Pistis Sophia continued to intone words of reverence to me, saying;

"I am intoning words of reverence to you: to you, who, by your command (*to yourself*) have guided me out of the higher Aion which is above, and brought me down to the places below.

And again, by your command, you have rescued me from the lower realms. By yourself you have removed the denser (astral) substance which was in my light-being; and I have beheld this. You have scattered far from me the emanations of the Self-willed One, which oppressed me and were my enemies.

You have given me power to release myself from the bonds of the emanations of Adamas; and you have smitten the seven-headed basilisk serpent.[239] You have cast it far from my hands; and you have set me above its dense (astral) substance. You caused it to perish, so that no brood would arise from it, as from this hour.

You were with me, giving me strength in all this (oppression). And your light has surrounded me in all places. And from yourself you made powerless all the emanations of the Self-willed One. For you have taken away the light-being from it, and you have made straight my path, to lead me out of the Chaos.

You have carried me far from the darknesses, (from) those denser (soul) bodies; and you have removed from them all of my denser beings, those

---

[239] "basilisk": it is the embodiment of the debased (ahrimanic-luciferic) counterpart to the seven noble planetary energies from which the human soul (or astral aura) is formed.

TEXT: CHAPTER 70 (cont.)   *Pistis Sophia intones*
from which the light had been taken. You have infused a purified light into these entities (*lit. 'powers'*). And to my (various) parts[240], which had no light, you have given a pure light, from the Light of the Heights; you directed the pathway for these.

And the light of your countenance has become for me an indestructible life. You have brought me forth; above the realm of the Chaos and of destruction, in order that all the denser entities that are therein - those who are (indeed) there - might be dissolved. And, in order that all my (denser) entities might be renewed in your light, and thus your light may be in them all, you have placed the radiance of your streaming light in me; I have become purified light."

This is the second intoning which Pistis Sophia uttered (*after her release from the Chaos*). Now, therefore, let that one who understands this intoning, come forward and explain it.

COMMENTARY: CHAPTER 70
No commentary is needed here.

TEXT: CHAPTER 71   *Matthew speaks*
It then happened, when the First Mystery had finished speaking those words, that Matthew came forward, and said, "I have understood the meaning of the reverential intoning which Pistis Sophia uttered. Now, therefore, bid me to expound it openly." The First Mystery (from without) answered, and said, "I bid you Matthew, to expound the interpretation of the words which Pistis Sophia intoned."

So Matthew responded, and said, "Concerning the interpretation of the words which Pistis Sophia intoned, your light-being prophesied of old concerning this, through Solomon (ode 22) saying,

---

[240] "parts": usu. 'limbs'; but this is not viable here. The Grk. word used here (melos - μέλος) means 'limbs' or 'members', or 'parts' (especially in its variant form, 'meros' (μέρος); this is common in the *Hermetica*.

TEXT: CHAPTER 71 (cont.)   (**Ode of Solomon** 22)
"He caused me to descend from the high realms which are above, and has also led me down to the lower realms, which are below. He who has taken away (*from me*) those which are in the midst of (this lower realm), has taught me about them. He has dispelled my enemies, together with my adversaries. He has bestowed on me power over their bonds, so that I may be released (from them).

He has also smitten the serpent with seven heads with my own hands, and he set me up upon his root, that I may extinguish his future brood; he (*i.e.,*) yourself, who were with me, and helped me in every realm. Your spiritual might (*lit. your name*) has surrounded me, your hand has destroyed the venom of the speaker of evils; your hand has opened the path for your righteous ones.

You have freed them from the tombs, and have borne them aloft, from the midst of the corpses. You have taken dead bones, and have clothed them with a body, and to those who are inert, you have given life-energy.

Your pathway (*along which I am walking*) has become indestructible, and so too, has your countenance (*thus I shall never lose sight of it*). You have led your Aion into destruction, so that all things might be destroyed, but then (later) renewed, so that your light might become a foundation for them all. You have poured out your richness upon them, and they have become a holy dwelling place."

Matthew speaks

This is the interpretation, Lord, of the reverential intoning from Pistis Sophia: listen, that I may now expound it openly. The word which your being spoke through Solomon, "He who caused me to descend from the lofty realms of Heaven, and has also led me up out of the lower realms, which are below", this is (*the meaning of*) the word which Pistis Sophia spoke, "I intone praise to you: you, who by your command, have made me depart from this high Aion above the heaven, and who has led me (down) into the lower realms; and you have preserved me also by your

TEXT: CHAPTER 71 (cont.)   **Matthew speaks**
command. You have made me rise up from the lower realms".

And the word which your being spoke through Solomon, "...who has taken away (from me) those that were in the midst of (the lower realms), and has also instructed me", this is the word which Pistis Sophia spoke: "And also by your command, you have caused the denser substance which was in the midst of my being to be purified: and I beheld this."

And again the word which your being spoke through Solomon, "He who has scattered my foes and adversaries", this is the word which Pistis Sophia said, "You have scattered far from me the emanations of the Self-willed One, which oppressed me and were my enemies." And the word which your being spoke, "He has bestowed on me power over their bonds, so that I may be released (from them)", this is the word which Pistis Sophia has spoken, "You have given me power to release myself from the bonds of those emanations".

And the word which your being has spoken, "Who has smitten the (basilisk) serpent with seven heads, with my (own) hands; he has placed me above its root, that I may extinguish its future brood", this is the word which Pistis Sophia spoke, "He has also smitten the serpent with seven heads with my own hands, and he placed me upon his root, that I may extinguish his future brood."

And the word which your being spoke, "You were with me, giving me strength in all this (oppression)", this is the word which Pistis Sophia spoke, "He, yourself – you who were with me, and helped me in every realm."

And the word which your being spoke, "Your spiritual might (*lit. name*) has surrounded me", this is the word which Pistis Sophia said, "And your light surrounded me in all your places."

And the word which your being spoke: "Your right hand has destroyed the poison of the slanderer." This is the word which Pistis Sophia spoke, "And through yourself the emanations of the

TEXT: CHAPTER 71 (cont.)

Self-willed One were made powerless. For you have taken away from them the light of their power."

And moreover the word which your light-being has said, "Your hand has opened the path for your faithful ones", this is the word which Pistis Sophia spoke, "You have made straight my path to lead me out of the Chaos, for I have trusted in you."

And also the word which your light-being spoke, "You have freed them from the tombs, and have borne them aloft, from the midst of the corpses", this is the word which Pistis Sophia spoke, "You have rescued me from the Chaos, you have carried me far away from the darknesses, the denser (soul) bodies[241] – which are the murky emanations of the Chaos, (but) from these you have taken away the light."

And the word which your being spoke, "You have taken dead bones and have clothed them with a body, and to them that were inert, you have given the life-energy", this is the word which Pistis Sophia spoke, "And you have taken all my (denser) beings which had no light in them, and have infused into them a pure light, and to all my parts which had no light in them, you have given a living light from on high."

And the word which your being spoke, "Your way is indestructible, and so also is your countenance", this is the word which Pistis Sophia spoke, "You have made straight the way before these various parts of mine, and the light of your countenance has become for me an indestructible life."

And the word which your being spoke, "You have led your Aion into destruction, that all may be destroyed – but then renewed", this is the word which Pistis Sophia spoke, "You have brought me, your being, into the Chaos and destruction, that all the denser beings that are therein – those who are there – might be dissolved, and all my being renewed in the light". **Matthew speaks**

And also the word which your being spoke, "And

---

[241] "denser (astral) bodies": usu. 'material darknesses': see Commentary.

TEXT: CHAPTER 71 (cont.)

your light has become a foundation for them all", this is the word which Pistis Sophia spoke, "And your light has been in them all." And the word which your light-being uttered through Solomon, "you have poured out your richness upon him, and he has become a place of holy habitation", this is (*alluded to in*) the word which Pistis Sophia spoke, "You have sent the radiance of your light to me, and so I have become a pure light-being."

This then, Lord, is the interpretation of the words which Pistis Sophia intoned.

COMMENTARY: CHAPTER 71

"the darknesses, the denser (soul) bodies": usually 'the material darknesses'. Here, as already in Chapter 70, Pistis Sophia is referring to the unpleasant entities in the lower Soul-world (the Chaos realm). This realm is populated by lesser or debased spirits who have coarser, denser soul (astral) bodies.[242]

TEXT: CHAPTER 72   Pistis Sophia intones

It happened, when the First Mystery had heard these words which Matthew had uttered, that he said, "Well said, Matthew; very fine, well-beloved one."

And the First Mystery (from without) continued in his discourse, (*stating that*) Pistis Sophia continued with her intoned words of reverence, saying, "You are the Light which is from on high, for you have saved me and brought me to yourself, and you have not permitted the emanation of the Self-willed One to take away my light. O Light of Lights, I have intoned reverence to you, for you have saved me. You have brought my being out of the Chaos, you have rescued me from those that descend into the darkness."

---

[242] Technically, the Coptic phrase here is ambiguous, as the adopted Grk. noun 'hulikon' here in Coptic remains the same whether singular or plural, and the possessive case of the noun is identical with the plural article.

TEXT: CHAPTER 72 (cont.) **Mariam speaks**
These words Pistis Sophia spoke. Now, therefore, let whoever who has a discerning mind, and who has understood the words uttered by Pistis Sophia, come forward and expound their interpretation. So it then happened, when the First Mystery had finished speaking these words to his disciples, that Mariam came forward and said,

"Lord, my mind is ever comprehending, so I could come forward every time and present the explanation of the words which Pistis Sophia has spoken, but, I am nervous about Peter; [243] for he cautions[244] me because he dislikes our sex.[245] When she had spoken these words, the First Mystery then said to her, "No one shall prevent any person who becomes filled with the spirit of light, from coming forward and expounding the interpretation of what I say. Now, therefore, O Mariam, expound the meaning of the words uttered by Pistis Sophia."

And Mariam responded and said to the First Mystery in the midst of the disciples, "Lord, concerning the meaning of the words uttered by Pistis Sophia, your light-being prophesied of old, through David (*in Psalm 29*)[246], saying, "I will exalt you, O Lord, for you accepted me, and did not permit my enemies to rejoice over me. O Lord, my God, I cried out to you, and you healed me. O Lord, you have drawn my soul forth from Amente, you have saved me from them that descend into the pit (*Sheol*)."

---

[243] "nervous about': usu. 'afraid of', but the Coptic verb here also has the less emphatic meaning of being 'timid', hence nervous.

[244] "cautions me": usu. 'threatens me', that is not consistent with the social reality here; the verb also means 'to warn'; see Commentary.

[245] "dislikes": usu. 'hate', but this appears to be too strong a nuance to use for the Coptic, for Peter was a married man. In addition, the Coptic verb here (ⲙⲟⲥⲧⲉ) is equivalent to the Grk. verb 'miseoe' (μισέω) which means, to dislike, despise or abhor, not only 'to hate'.

[246] Psalm 30 in the Bible.

COMMENTARY: CHAPTER 72
"he cautions me": usu. 'he threatens me". The Coptic text uses a Greek verb 'apeileoe' (ἀπειλεω) which often means 'to threaten', and it also means in Classical Greek 'to intimidate'. But in Hellenistic Greek, as in this codex, it also meant 'to warn' or 'to caution'. That Peter was not actually threatening a fellow disciple, indeed a woman, with verbal or physical aggression, is confirmed by the response of Christ, "No one shall prevent any person....filled with the spirit of light from coming forward...

With this response he is responding to misogynous social tensions, in a culture where women were commonly regarded as inferior to men. His response is not to a disclosure of shocking, unacceptable, abusive bullying by Peter of a woman.

Furthermore, in ancient Palestine no man was permitted to speak, even briefly, to a woman in public (except his wife); so such behaviour as publicly threatening a woman was socially forbidden. And if theoretically it had occurred semi-privately, that is, amongst the followers of Jesus, the other disciples would have intervened.

TEXT: CHAPTER 73
When Mariam had spoken these things, the First Mystery said to her, "Well said; excellent, Mariam you blessed one." He continued in his discourse, and said to his disciples, "Sophia continued with her intonations, and said, "The light has become my Saviour; it has turned my darkness into light for me. It has torn apart the Chaos which surrounded me, and girded me with light."   **Martha speaks**

Then when the First Mystery had finished saying these words, Martha came forward and said, "My Lord, your power has prophesied long ago through David (*Psalm 29*)[247], concerning these words, "The Lord has become a helper to me; he has turned

---

[247] Psalm 30 in the Bible.

TEXT: CHAPTER 73 (cont.) **Pistis Sophia intones** my lamenting into rejoicing. He has torn apart my sackcloth, and girded me with joy."

It then happened, when the First Mystery had finished hearing the words which Martha had uttered, that he said "Well said; excellent, Martha." Then the First Mystery continued in his discourse, and said to his disciples, Pistis Sophia went on further with her intonings,

(Now her reverential words are a soliloquy, i.e., she urges her own innermost nature to offer up reverence to the Christ-light); **Pistis Sophia intones to herself**

"Let words of reverence be intoned, O my being, to the Light, and be mindful of all the light-beings which he has given to you. So all the (*denser*) beings which are within you – let these intone reverence to the name of his holy Mystery. That Mystery which forgives all your transgressions, and who has saved you from all your oppressions by which the Self-willed One had oppressed you. He who had saved your light from the emanations of the Self-willed One, those which are doomed to[248] destruction.

He who had crowned you with light, in his compassion, until he rescued you; he, who enfilled you with purified light. Thus shall your genesis be renewed, (*you will then be*) as an Invisible of the Heights (*once again*)".

With these words Pistis Sophia[249] gave voice to her intonings of reverence, because she was saved, and had considered all the things which I, the First Mystery, had done to her.

COMMENTARY: CHAPTER 73

"your genesis"; or, your origin or beginning. But 'genesis' has the nuance of something actively coming into being from some higher matrix.

"as an Invisible": the Coptic here is too condensed, so

---

[248] "doomed to": lit. 'belong to'.
[249] "Pistis Sophia": the word Sophia is missing in the Coptic; this must be another error by the scribe.

COMMENTARY: CHAPTER 73 (cont.)
additional words were needed. For Pistis Sophia, through the Christ-light, has been in effect re-created, thereby regaining her status as one of the (unexplained) Invisibles. In chapters 29 and 30 she had been identified as an Invisible.

TEXT: CHAPTER 74
It happened then, when the First Mystery had finished speaking these words to his disciples, that he said to them, "Let that person who understands the interpretation of these words come forward and expound it openly." **Mariam speaks**

Then Mariam came forward, and said, "My Lord, concerning the words which Pistis Sophia intoned in her praise, your light-being prophesied long ago, through David, (*Psalm 102*)[250] saying, "Praise the Lord, my soul; let all that is within me praise His holy name and forget not all the recompenses he has given you. He who forgives you all your iniquities, and who heals all your sicknesses. Who saves your life from destruction and puts a crown of loving kindness and compassion on your head. Who satisfies your desires with good things, so that your youth is renewed like that of the eagle."

That is to say, Sophia shall be like the Invisibles who are in the Heights. For he said, "like an eagle", for the dwelling of an eagle is in the heights, and the Invisibles are also in the Heights; this is to say, that Sophia shall become radiant like the Invisibles, just as she was in the beginning."

It then happened, when the First Mystery had heard these words which Mariam spoke, he said, "Well said, Mariam, you blessed one." Then after this, the First Mystery continued in his discourse, and said to his disciples, "I guided Pistis Sophia and led her up into a higher realm (*of the Chaos*), a region which is (*however*) below the 13th Aion, and gave her (there) a new Mystery of the Light, which was not that of her own Aion, the place of the Invisibles.

---

[250] Psalm 103 in the Bible.

TEXT: CHAPTER 74 (cont.)   **Pistis Sophia intones**
And I gave to her also intonings (*i.e., mantric tones*) which came from the Light,[251] so that (*as she resonates with this*) the Rulers of the (debased) Aions would then not prevail against her, as from that hour. And I left her in that region until I should come again to find her, and bring her into her realm, which is in the Heights. It then happened, when I had left her in that region, that she again intoned her words of reverence, saying,

"Through discernment, I intuitively perceived the Light, and so the Light was mindful of me; he heard my reverential intonings. He brought my being out of the Chaos down there, darkened by all its dense (astral-etheric) substance. He has led my being up to a higher, more secure Aion; the Light has set me on the path towards my own realm. And it has given to me a new Mystery, which is not that of my Aion.

It has given to me intonings (*i.e., mantric tones*) which came from the Light. Now, therefore, O Light, all the (debased) Rulers shall see what you have done; they shall fear, and they shall discern truly (*the power of*) the Light."

Therefore Pistis Sophia joyously intoned these reverential words, rejoicing that she had been led out of the Chaos and brought into (higher) realms (but still) below the 13th Aion.

Now, therefore, let that person whose mind is stirred, and who understands the meaning of the triumphal intoning which Pistis Sophia spoke, come forward and expound it."   **Andrew speaks**

Then Andrew came forward and said, "My Lord, this is what your light-being prophesied long ago concerning you, through David, (*Psalm 39; 40 in the Bible*) saying,

"With patience I waited for the Lord, and he has inclined his ear to me, and has heard my prayer. He has brought my soul up out of the pit of misery and out of filthy mire. He has set my feet upon a rock,

---

[251] "came from the Light": usu. 'of the Light' which is confusing, see Commentary.

TEXT: CHAPTER 74 (cont.)

and has guided my steps. He has placed in my mouth a new song: a song of praise for our God. Many shall see and fear, and be afraid, and then will hope in the Lord."

It then happened, as Andrew had presented the thoughts of Pistis Sophia, the First Mystery said to him, "Excellent Andrew, you blessed one."

COMMENTARY: CHAPTER 74

"gave a new Mystery": in these brief words, a very significant esoteric truth is contained. The Christ-light permeating the risen Jesus, imbued Pistis Sophia with a new spiritual capacity and a new significance. That is, she as the archetype in spiritual realms of human intuitive-spiritual discerning or perceptive cognition, has now received a new, empowering element.

This was born out of the trials and eventual triumph, helped by the Christ-light, over the temptations and deceptions of the malignant Rulers (in anthroposophical terms, from the hosts of Ahriman and Lucifer).

"And also I gave to her intonings (*i.e., mantric tones*) *which came from* the Light, so that (in resonating with this) the Rulers of the (debased) Aions would not then prevail against her".

But, in previous translations this is, 'I gave her a song of praise *of* the Light', however this is ambiguous. I conclude that the meaning is not an external praising *of* the Light, but that the transcendent chant or intonings are *within* the light; they were a part of the Light, they came from the Light – and yet were given over to Pistis Sophia for her use, for her to become fully aligned to the Light.

This interpretation means that these intonings are an integral part of the divine Light's being; for this would truly have the power, as Pistis Sophia intones it, to protect her. Whereas a 'song of praise' from Pistis Sophia to the Light, is unlikely to have such unassailable power; compared to a (mantric) intoning which derives from the Light itself.

TEXT: CHAPTER 75

He continued again in his conversation, and said to his disciples, "These are all the things which befell Pistis Sophia. So it happened, when I had brought her to the region which is (*a little*) below the 13th Aion, that I was about to enter into the Light and cease being with her. She said to me,

"O Light of lights, you are about to go to the Light, and cease being with me. But then the empowered One, Adamas, will know that you have withdrawn from me. He will know that the one who can rescue me, is no longer here, and so he will come again to this region. He, and all his Rulers who hate me; and also the Self-willed One shall again give power to his Lion-faced emanation.

Then they shall all come at the same time, and together shall oppress me, to take away all the light which is in me, so that I might become powerless and again without light. Now, therefore, Light of my light, take from them their light, that from this hour on they may no longer be able to oppress me."

It happened, when I had heard these words which Pistis Sophia spoke to me, that I answered her, and said "My Father – he who emanated me into existence – has not yet commanded me to take away their light. But I shall seal up the realm of the Self-willed One and of all the Archons which hate you, because you have perceived truly the Light.

Also I shall seal up the realms of Adamas and his Rulers, so that none of them will be able to wage war against you for the remainder of their allotted time (*as empowered entities*), that is, until the time comes when my Father commands me to take away their light from them.

COMMENTARY: CHAPTER 75
The text of this Chapter is clear.

TEXT: CHAPTER 76
"Then I further said to her, "Listen, so that I can tell you of their time, when that which I have just said to

TEXT: CHAPTER 76 (cont.)

you shall come to pass. It shall happen when the 'Three Times' shall be accomplished." Pistis Sophia responded and said to me, "O Light, how shall I know that the Three Times are accomplished, so that I may rejoice, and be glad that my time shall be near when you are to bring me into my realm? Moreover, I shall also rejoice when you take the light-power from all them that hated me, for I have trusted in your light.

"Then I however responded[252] and said to her, "This will be when you see the portal of the Treasury of the great Light – that portal which has a light-stream reaching down to the 13th Aion, namely The Left[253] – when that portal is opened, then are the Three Times completed." Pistis Sophia continued and said, "O Light, how shall I, in this region, know that (up above) the portal is opened?"

So I responded and said to her, when that portal is opened, then shall all those in the Aions discern this, because of the great light which will stream into all their places.

TEXT NOTE: in Chapter 76

"that portal which has a light-stream reaching down to the 13th Aion": I have added extra words to make the meaning clearer. It is literally, "that portal which opens to the 13th Aion".

TEXT: CHAPTER 76 (cont.)

But moreover, I have arranged them so that none shall attempt any ill against you, until the Three Times are accomplished. But you shall have the power of going into their twelve Aions, whenever you may wish, and also have the ability to return to your (current) realm, in which you now are; this realm which is below the 13th Aion.

---

[252] "then I however answered"; the 'I' is emphatic here in the Coptic, it may also translated as 'But then I, I responded..'

[253] "the Left": As noted earlier this is Aion 13 or Devachan 6.

TEXT: CHAPTER 76 (cont.)

But you shall not have the ability to pass through the portal of the Heights, which is at the 13th Aion, to enter into your (true) realm; the one from which you came forth (*in the beginning*). Moreover, when the Three Times shall be fulfilled, the Self-willed One and all his Rulers will again oppress you, to take away your light.

For he shall be angry, thinking that it is you who have kept his power (down) in the Chaos, and also that it is you who took away the light which was in his power. He will be enraged against you, seeking to take from you your light and cast it down into the Chaos, and give it to his emanation, in order that it may have the strength to come forth from the Chaos and go into its own place.

So, Adamas shall begin (*his renewed opposition*) from these things.[254] But I will remove all those light-beings in him which are from you, and I will return them to you; I will appear in order to take them away from him.

Now, therefore, when they oppress you at that time, utter an intonation to the Light; then I will hasten to your help. I will quickly come to you, (and also) to the realms below you, to take away their light. I will come to this region where I shall have left you, which is below the 13th Aion, (*and remain*) until I can quickly enable you once more to enter into your realm; that realm from which you came forth.

"It happened, therefore, when Pistis Sophia had heard these words which I spoke, that she rejoiced with great rejoicing. And so I placed her in the region below the 13th Aion. I went into the Light, and thus ceased to be near her.

---

[254] "Adamas...begin...from these things": i.e., the dynamics already mentioned shall form the basis for an attack by Adamas. Usu. 'Adamas shall begin these things"; however this bypasses a preposition (ⲉⲣⲟⲟⲩ) and ignores the fact that the Self-willed One has already begun to attack.

COMMENTARY: CHAPTER 76
"the Three Times": the meaning of this is unknown.

TEXT: CHAPTER 77 (cont.)
All these things, therefore, the First Mystery (*Christ*) reported to his disciples, because they happened to Pistis Sophia. He remained for a while (*spiritually*)[255] on the Mount of Olives, narrating all these things among his disciples. He continued in his discourse, and said to them,

"So hence it happened when I was in the world of humanity, that after all these things, I remained for a time (*spiritually*) here by this pathway, on the Mount of Olives. This was after my (spirit) garment had been sent to me, that garment which I had left behind with the 24th Mystery (*reckoning*) from within, which is therefore the First Mystery (*reckoning*) from without. This Mystery is the great Incomprehensible one, within which I became radiant.

This was also after I had entered into the Heights, to receive my two other garments; then I stayed for a time (*spiritually*) with you by this place, which is the Mount of Olives. By then the time of which I had (earlier) spoken to Pistis Sophia was completed: "Adamas with all his Rulers shall oppress you".

TEXT NOTE: in Chapter 77
"after my (spirit) garment had been sent"   and
"after I had entered into the Heights"
These two actions are usually interpreted as yet to happen:
"*before* my (spirit) garment had been sent"
"*before* I had entered into the Heights"

---

[255] "remained for a while (*spiritually*)"; usu. 'he sat (on the ground); but Jesus has no physical body. The Coptic verb here (ϩⲙⲟⲟⲥ) also means 'to remain', or 'to abide' (in Ger. 'sich aufhalten'); so in older Biblical language, 'he tarried (in their presence)'.

TEXT NOTE: in Chapter 77
But this is inconsistent with the entire narrative.[256] The past tense is meant in these two sections; for Jesus had in fact begun by saying, "*after* all these things (had happened)..." not *before*. For the potent battle that Christ undertook to assist Pistis Sophia is in effect based on his acquiring the 'garments' - the sublime spirit-auras - these bestowed the divine status needed for the battle.

So he is now looking back over these events, noting that when he appeared to the disciples on the Mount of Olives, all of the drama had occurred. Back then he had begun to report it all to them. He now takes up his narrative, continuing on with the dramatic events that had then happened.

TEXT: CHAPTER 77 (cont.)
It happened, when this (*predicted*) time was completed - I was about to be in the world of humanity[257], remaining (*spiritually*) near you, on this hill, which is the Mount of Olives - that Adamas gazed downwards from the height of the twelve Aions. There he saw his demonic being, which was in the Chaos, without any light in it at all; for I had taken away its light from it. He saw that it was dark, and it did not have the strength to come to its own realm, which is the 12 Aions.

Then Adamas thought again of Pistis Sophia, and he became extremely furious, thinking in regard to his demonic being in the Chaos, that it was she who had restrained his (emanated) being in the Chaos, and who had taken away its light. So he was very wrathful,

---

[256] In grammatical terms here is another problem with the scribe's work. The preposition used here (ϨΑΘΗ) does mean 'before'; but in Bohairic the similar word ϹΑΘΗ means 'after'; this would confuse the scribe. Prepositions can be vague in other ways in Coptic; e.g., ϨΗ means 'before' in Sahidic but 'after' in Fayumic; whereas ϨΙ means both 'before' **and** 'after' in Sahidic.

[257] "was about to be in the world": usu. 'was in the world...' see Commentary.

TEXT: CHAPTER 77 (cont.)

and added anger upon anger, and hence he emanated out of himself a dark emanation, and also another entity (*of the nature*) of the Chaos, and (yet) another entity, wicked and mighty, in order to oppress Pistis Sophia with these.

Moreover, he created a dark place within his own area, so that he could persecute Pistis Sophia in it. Then he gathered many of his Rulers, and they pursued Pistis Sophia. These two emanations, which Adamas had created, together pursued Pistis Sophia to bring her into the dark place he had created. They oppressed and persecuted Pistis Sophia until they had taken all of her light from her.

Then Adamas took the light from Pistis Sophia, and gave it to his two dark and malignant emanations, that they might carry it into the great lower Chaos which is of darkness and of the Chaos. They then cast it into the being of Adamas which is down there, thinking that her light might come into his own realm, for the Chaos was now very dark, because I (*Christ*) had taken away from the Chaos its light (*thus it resembled the darkness of Adamas*).

It then happened when they pursued her, that Pistis Sophia cried out aloud, she intoned words of reverence to the Light, for I had said to her, "If ever you are oppressed, intone words of reverence to me, and I will come quickly to help you." So it happened, when they oppressed her – I was remaining (*spiritually*) near you, in this place, that is to say, on the Mount of Olives – that she intoned words of reverence to the Light, saying,

Pistis Sophia intones

"O Light of lights, I have trusted in you; save me from all these Rulers who pursue me, and rescue me. Lest they take from me my light, such as the Lion-faced being did. For your light and your out-raying stream of light are not with me. Instead, Adamas was angry with me, saying, "It is you who restrained my being in the Chaos."

Now, O Light, if I have done this, if I have kept it there, if I have done the least violence to that being,

TEXT: CHAPTER 77 (cont.) **Pistis Sophia intones** or if I have oppressed it, as it oppressed me, let all these Rulers which pursue me, take away my light, let them leave me empty. Let Adamas, my enemy, pursue my being, let him seize upon it, let him take from me my light, let him cast it into his dark power, which is in the Chaos, let him put my being into the Chaos.

Now, therefore, O Light, raise me up in your just wrath, exalt your power above my enemies, who have raised themselves up against me to the very end. O hasten, restore[258] me, just as you once said to me, "I will help you."

COMMENTARY: CHAPTER 77
"I was about to be in the world[259]": here Jesus pauses in his narrative of the drama of Pistis Sophia, as it draws towards a close. He re-commences the story, reminding the disciples that the dramatic events had all happened prior to his appearing on the Mt. of Olives, where he stayed perceptible to them for some time, to enable this communicating with him.

The next short final episode did not happen *after* he made his appearance to the disciples, but *before*. So he did not say 'I *was* in the world', but 'I was about to be in...' for he is referring to a past event – but one that was soon to happen, back in the past. This unusual verbal tense is a feature of the Coptic language; but the scribe has incorrectly written down the verb, omitting two letters; so it incorrectly reads 'I was in the..' instead of 'I was about to be...'.[260]

TEXT: CHAPTER 78
It came to pass, therefore, when the First Mystery had finished speaking these words to his disciples, that he said, "Let that person who has understood the

---

[258] "restore me": i.e., vivify me, re-enliven me.
[259] "was about to be in the world": usu. 'was in the world...'; see Commentary.
[260] He wrote, **ⲚⲈⲒϢⲞⲞⲚ** instead of the required **ⲚⲈⲒⲚⲀϢⲞⲞⲚ**, which is the Imperfect of the First Future tense.

TEXT: CHAPTER 78 (cont.)
words which I have spoken, come forward and expound their interpretation."

And James came forward, and said, "Lord, concerning this intonation which Pistis Sophia intoned, your light-being prophesied of old, through David, in Psalm 7, saying, "O Lord, my God, in you I have trusted, save me from those who persecute me; rescue me, lest he seize and carry off my soul, in the manner of a lion, whilst there is no-one who redeems and saves.

O Lord, my God, if I have ever done this, if there has been any injustice in my hands, if I have exacted retribution from them that have done evil to me, then let me fall beneath my enemies, and be empty. Let mine enemy persecute my soul, let him seize it, let him trample down my life into the earth, and lay my honour in the dust. Arise, Lord, in your wrath; exalt your power at the ending of my enemies. Arise within the command which you have decreed."

It then happened, when the First Mystery had heard the words which James had spoken, that he said to him, "Well said, James, beloved one."

COMMENTARY: CHAPTER 78
Psalm 7 in the Septuagint, is also Psalm 7 in the Bible.

TEXT: CHAPTER 79
However, the First Mystery continued, saying, "It happened when Pistis Sophia had finished intoning her words of reverence, that she turned herself around, to see if Adamas, and his Rulers, had turned back, to return to their Aion; but she saw them pursuing her. She turned towards them, and said, "Why are you pursuing me, and declaring that there is no-one to help me; that it (the Light) is not there to save me from you"? But the Light is a judge, true and strong.

Yet he is patient, awaiting the time of which he spoke to me, "I shall come and help you." The Light will not always exert his wrath upon you. But now, this is the time about which he spoke to me. So,

TEXT: CHAPTER 79 (cont.)

therefore, if you do not turn back, if you do not cease pursuing me, the Light will prepare his strength, he will make ready (*for battle*) with all his hosts. He will be ready and empowered to take from you all that is light in you, and you shall become dark. He has brought forth his beings, so as to take your power from you, so that you will perish."

When Pistis Sophia had said these words, she turned her gaze towards the region of Adamas. She saw the darkness area in the Chaos region which he had created; she saw also the two very malevolent emanations of darkness, which Adamas had sent forth to seize upon Pistis Sophia and cast her into the (area of) Chaos which he had created, to oppress her in that region and harass her until they had taken her light from her.

So it happened, when Pistis Sophia had seen these two emanations of darkness and the dark region which Adamas had created, that she was afraid, and cried out loudly to the light, saying, "O Light, behold – Adamas, the violent one, is furious. He has created a dark emanation, and he also emanated out another entity of (*the nature of*) the Chaos.

And also he has created yet another one, dark and of the (*nature of the*) Chaos, and he has prepared this entity (*to attack*). So now, O Light, (behold) the Chaos area which he has created, in order for me to be cast down into it, and to thence remove my light-power from me - so, take away from him his light-power ! And the thought which he has devised, to take away my light-beings - let his light-beings be taken from him ! For such is the iniquity which he has declared - to take away my light-beings - so remove all of his light-beings !"

These are the words which Pistis Sophia spoke in her intonation. So now, whoever is alert of mind, let them come forward and present the meaning of the words which Pistis Sophia has uttered in her song of praise.

COMMENTARY: CHAPTER 79
The text of this Chapter is clear.

TEXT: CHAPTER 80
Then Martha came forward and said, "I am alert in my mind, and I understand the words which you have said. Now, therefore, bid me to present their interpretation openly. The First Mystery answered, and said to Martha, "I bid you Martha, to present the interpretation of the words which Pistis Sophia uttered in her intonings."

So Martha answered and said, "My Lord, these are the words which your light-power prophesied of old through David, in the 7th Psalm, saying, "God is a righteous judge, strong and patient, who does not bring down his judgement every day. If you do not turn around, he shall sharpen his sword; he has bent his bow and made it ready. He has prepared instruments of death for it; he has made arrows for those who will be burnt.

Behold, violence has laboured; it has devised wrongdoings, and has brought forth iniquity. It has dug a pit, it has hollowed it out deeply. Violence shall fall into the pit which itself has dug; its wrong shall fall on its own head, and the injustice on the crown of the head." And when Martha had uttered these words, the First Mystery looking without, said to her, "Well said; excellent, Martha, you blessed one."

COMMENTARY: CHAPTER 80
No comments are needed here.

TEXT: CHAPTER 81
It now happened that Jesus narrated all the things which had occurred to Pistis Sophia when she was in the Chaos, and how she had intoned reverence to the light until it rescued her, leading her out of the Chaos, and brought her into the 12th Aion; and how he had rescued her from all her restrictions through which the Rulers of the Chaos had so oppressed her.

TEXT: CHAPTER 81 (cont.)

Jesus continued in his discourse and said to his disciples, "It happened after these things, that I guided Pistis Sophia, and led her into the 13th Aion. I was exceedingly radiant, there being no measure to the light which was in me. I entered into the realm of the 24 Invisibles, exceedingly radiant. They were agitated in a great commotion; they looked and saw Sophia, who was with me. Her they recognised, but they knew not who I was, they thought that I was some emanation of the Realm of Light.

It happened therefore, when Pistis Sophia saw her fellow Invisibles, that she rejoiced with great joy, and was very glad. She longed to tell them of the wonderful things which I had done for her below in the world of humans, until I had rescued her (from the Chaos). And so she came forward into the midst of the Invisibles, and amongst them she intoned words of reverence to me, saying,

1: "I will give thanks to you, O Light, for you are a Saviour, you are a rescuer at all times.

2: I shall intone these words to the Light, for it has saved me; it has rescued me out of the Rulers, my enemies.

3: And you have rescued me out of all the places: from the higher and the lower regions of the Chaos. And from the Aions of the Rulers of the (planetary) spheres.

4: When I left the Heights, I wandered around in realms in which there was no light, and I was unable to return to the 13th Aion, my dwelling-place.

5: For there was no light in me, nor strength. My being was completely weakened.

6: But the Light saved me from all my afflictions. I intoned words of reverence to the Light, and it listened to me when I was oppressed.

7: It guided me through Creation - (*that is through*) the Aions - in order to lead me up into the 13th Aion, my dwelling place.

8: I shall give thanks to you, O Light, for you have saved me, and (also) for your wondrous deeds

TEXT: CHAPTER 81 (cont.)

amongst humanity[261].

9: When I became deficient in my strength, you gave my strength back to me; and when I became deficient in my light, you filled me with purified light.

10: I have been in the darkness and in the shadow of the Chaos, bound in the mighty bonds of the Chaos, without light in me, for I had provoked the command of the Light;

11: I had transgressed, I had angered the command of the Light, because I had departed from my own realm.

12: And when I descended, I was destitute of my light, and was without light, and there was no-one to rescue me.

13: And in my affliction, I intoned words of reverence to the Light, and it rescued me from all my afflictions.

14: Moreover, he broke apart all my bonds, and brought me forth from darkness and the oppression of the Chaos.

15: I will give thanks to you, O Light, for you have rescued me, and (thereby) your wondrous deeds have taken place in respect of humanity (also).

16: You have shattered the upper gates of darkness and the mighty bars of the Chaos,

17: and you turned me away from the region in which I had transgressed; furthermore, my strength had been taken away because I had transgressed.

18: And I ceased from my Mysteries, and descended to the gates of the Chaos.

19: And when I was oppressed, I intoned words of reverence to the Light and it rescued me from all of my afflictions.

20: You sent to me your out-raying light; this gave me strength and saved me from all of my oppressions.

21: I want to thank you, O light, for you have rescued me, and for your wondrous deeds among humanity."

"These, then, are the words which Pistis Sophia intoned, in the midst of the 24 Invisibles, wanting to tell them of all the wondrous things which I had done

---

[261] "humanity': lit. the genus/species of humans.

TEXT: CHAPTER 81 (cont.)
with her. She wanted them to know that I had descended into the world of humanity, and had given to human beings the Mysteries of the Heights. Now, therefore, let the one who is elevated in their understanding come forward, and give an interpretation of the words of praise and reverence which Pistis Sophia uttered."

COMMENTARY: CHAPTER 81
"guided me through Creation - through the Aions -": usually 'guided me in the creation of the Aions'. My version clarifies that the Christ-Light is guiding Pistis Sophia up through the Aions, not tutoring her as to how to create multiple spirit realms.[262]

"agitated in a great commotion": Here the 24 holy deities are not in a hostile reaction, but rather in amazement. They had not experienced before such a thing as the spiritual-intuitive consciousness of humanity now being empowered through the light rayed forth from the Saviour.

15: "wondrous deeds...thereby...in respect of humanity": Earlier versions are similar, such as 'and your wonders happened in humanity'. But the Coptic text is more emphatic "...*belongs to* humanity" or "...is *associated with* humanity.[263] A more literary form of this is, 'in respect of' humanity.

This sentence is of great importance; its presence confirms the most significant fact of the nature of

---

[262] Here 'Creation' is a noun, not a verbal word: the Sahidic word for Creation ⲥⲱⲛⲧ is closely associated linguistically with the Coptic words for 'fundament'/'basis' in other dialects; Fayumic (ⲥⲏⲛⲧ), Bohairic (ⲥⲉⲛⲧ). And the preposition can be 'through', instead of 'in'; the same peculiarity of the text as in Chapt. 47, which considers ϩⲙ̄ as a variant of ϩⲛ̄.

[263] This word is a letter (ⲁ), here in its secondary "more general" adverbial function, ("die allgemeinere Bedeuting, 'was gehört zu' " - Stern, *Grammatik*. p.345)

COMMENTARY: CHAPTER 81 (cont.)
the Pistis Sophia story.[264] Namely that the second part of the sentence is a direct consequence of the first part; that is to say, what was done for Pistis Sophia by the Christ-light was also inherently, subtly, influencing humanity.

The above words confirm our perspective that Pistis Sophia is the counterpart in spirit realms, of the higher, intuitive cognizing capacity that has been fading from humanity; it is this which spiritually minded souls need, which, when once attained, can be developed into initiatory consciousness. So as she is rescued, and returned to her original unfallen state, it follows that human souls can begin to re-connect to their holistic-intuitive consciousness faculty.

This is the wonder that was achieved amongst humanity which Pistis Sophia is here revering. This is the purpose of the entire drama behind the God-ordained fall of Pistis Sophia into the sphere of malignant Archons (the ahrimanic-luciferic deities), and the involvement of the Christ-reality in the effort to redeem Pistis Sophia, as noted above:

"15: I will give thanks to you then, O Light, for you have rescued me, and thereby your wondrous deeds have taken place in respect of humanity."

"had descended into the world of humanity": Again emphasis is placed on the central fact behind the drama of Pistis Sophia – that the Christ-light has sent its radiant spiritual light into the souls of human beings, **precisely through its act of rescuing Pistis Sophia**.

"given a new Mystery": earlier, in Chapter 74, we are told that Christ gave to Pistis Sophia a new Mystery; i.e., a way of realizing and manifesting sacred spiritual influences. This new situation was suitable for her still not fully redeemed condition; she was in the realms below the 13th Aion, but in a higher part of these lower Aions.

So the soul's capacity for higher intuitive

---

[264] We note that this not the only evidence that the Pistis Sophia entity is an aspect of the human soul.

COMMENTARY: CHAPTER 81 (cont.)
discernment had gained a new aspect to it; born of the struggles to find the way out of the illusions and temptations cast over the soul by malignant deities. So now, by Chapter 81, Pistis Sophia is finally redeemed; and thus the new aspect of the soul's spiritual capacity has been incorporated into the human being's spirit.

TEXT: CHAPTER 82   Philip speaks
It happened then, when Jesus had finished speaking these words, that Philip came forward and said, My Lord, my understanding is now exalted, so I have understood the meaning of the words which Pistis Sophia intoned. For David, the prophet, prophesied concerning it of old, in the 106th Psalm[265] saying, (*there now follows a long quote from this psalm.*)
"Acknowledge the Lord, for he is gracious, his mercy is eternal. May those whom the Lord has saved, declare that he has delivered them out of the hands of his enemies. He has gathered them together out of their lands; from the east and the west and from the north and from the sea.

They have wandered in the desert; in a waterless land. They found not the city of their dwelling-place. Being hungry and thirsty their souls faltered within them. He rescued them from their distresses; they cried out to the Lord, he heard them in their distress. He guided them to a straight pathway, that they might go the place of their dwelling

May they thank the Lord for his mercies and his wondrous works amongst the sons of men. For he has satisfied a hungry soul; he filled a hungering soul with good things. Those who sit in the darkness and in the shadow of death; those who are bound in poverty and iron (chains). They have provoked the word of God and angered the intentions of the Most High (God).

Their hearts were humbled in their suffering, they have become powerless, and there was no one to help

---

[265] Psalm 107 in the Bible.

TEXT: CHAPTER 82 (cont.) Philip speaks
them. They cried out to the Lord when they were in peril, and he has rescued from their constraints; he has brought them forth from darkness and from the shadow of death, and has broken their chains.

Let them acknowledge the Lord in his mercies and his wondrous deeds among the children of men for he has broken the gates of brass, he has burst asunder the bolts of iron. He has received them to himself from out of the path of their iniquity. For they had been brought low because of their iniquities.

Their hearts abhorred all kinds of nourishment, they were near to the gates of death. They cried out to the Lord in their peril, he delivered them from their afflictions. He sent to them his word; he healed them from their troubles. Let them acknowledge the Lord in his mercies, and his wonders among the children of men."

This then, my Lord, is the interpretation of the words which Pistis Sophia spoke. So do listen Lord, that I may now expound it clearly. The word indeed, which David has spoken, "Give thanks to the lord, for he is gracious, for his mercy endures for ever": this is the word which Pistis Sophia spoke, "I will acknowledge you, O light, for you are a Saviour and a deliverer at all times."

And these words which David spoke, "Let them whom the Lord has rescued say, "He has rescued us from the hand of our enemies"; this is the word which Pistis Sophia spoke, "I will intone these words of reverence to the Light, for it has rescued me and freed me from the hand of the Rulers, my enemies." And so on, for the rest of the Psalm.

This then, my Lord, is the meaning of the reverence intoned by Pistis Sophia in the midst of the 24 Invisibles, wanting to tell them of all the wonders which you had done for her, and that they might know that you have given your Mysteries to humanity."

It then happened when Jesus had heard these words which Philip had spoken, that he said, "Well said, Philip, you blessed one; this is the meaning of the words intoned by Pistis Sophia."

COMMENTARY: CHAPTER 82
With this chapter the episode about the fall and redemption of Pistis Sophia comes to an end.

TEXT: CHAPTER 83
It then happened after these things, that Mariam[266] came forward; she worshipped at the feet of Jesus, and spoke, "Lord, be not displeased with me for questioning you, for we question you about everything, seeking to understand everything with precision and certainty. For you have said to us earlier, "Seek that you may find, knock that it may be opened to you; for every one who seeks shall find, and to whomsoever knocks, it shall be opened."

So therefore, Lord, from whom shall we seek, or at whose door shall we knock? Who is able to answer us concerning the sayings about which we question you? Who understands the (spiritual) context[267] of the words concerning which we are questioning you? It is you who have given comprehension of the Light to our intelligence; you have given to us (*the capacity for*) spiritual cognizing and for comprehending very exalted ideas.

Therefore, there is no one in the world of humanity, and there is no one in the heights of the Aions, who can declare to us the answer to the sayings about which we question - except you, who alone knows the cosmos, and who is fully initiated[268] about the cosmos.

For we do not put questions in the way that people of the world do, but we are seeking with knowledge of the Heights, which you have given to

---

[266] This is probably Mariam the Magdalene (or Mariam of Bethany, as these two women may be the same person).
[267] "context": usu. 'power' but the Coptic word also means context or circumstance, or being, etc.
[268] "fully initiated": lit. 'complete/perfected' about the cosmos.

TEXT: CHAPTER 83 (cont.)

us. And we put our questions with the kind of excellent questioning which you have taught us, so that we may frame our questions on this basis. Now, therefore, Lord, be not displeased with me, but unveil to me the subject on which I question you."

It happened when Jesus had heard the words which Mariam the Magdalene had spoken, that he answered and said to her, "Ask what you wish, and I will unveil it to you with precision and certainty. Truly, truly,[269] I say to you, rejoice with great rejoicing, and be very glad. For if you put questions with precision, I shall be very glad that you ask with such care and in the appropriate manner.

It happened when Mariam (the Magdalene) had heard the words which the Saviour spoke, that she rejoiced with great joy, and was exceedingly glad. She said to Jesus, "My Lord and Saviour, concerning then the 24 Invisibles; of what type, of what manner of being are they; or of what quality is their light?

COMMENTARY: CHAPTER 83

The text of this chapter is clear; but there is no information about the 24 Invisibles.

We have now the first identifying of a Mary as 'Mary the Magdalene'. From now on if a 'Mary' is mentioned and is clearly identified as the Magdalene, but the words 'the Magdalene' are not mentioned, these will be added, in brackets.

"Truly, truly": that Jesus here speaks 'Amen, amen,' is the same remarkable feature as found in the Gospel of John. It is very rare for any Biblical text to have 'amen' twice; and it was unheard of in a Hebrew text that this would come first in the sentence; it was always spoken last.

TEXT: CHAPTER 84

Then Jesus answered and said to Mariam the Magdalene, "What is there in this world which

---

[269] "Truly, truly": the text actually has "Amen, amen", as in John's Gospel; see Commentary.

TEXT: TEXT: CHAPTER 84 (cont.)

resembles the 24 Invisibles? Or rather, what *thing* is there in this world which resembles them? Now, therefore, to what shall I liken them; or what shall I say concerning them? For there is nothing in this world with which I can compare them.

Nor is there any form to which I can liken them. Indeed, there is nothing in this world which is of the nature of Heaven. But truly, I say to you that every one of the Invisibles is nine times greater than the Heaven and the sphere above it, and the twelve Aions all together – as I have already told you, on another occasion.

Now, there is no light in this (physical) world which is superior to that of the Sun. But truly, truly, I say to you: the 24 Invisibles are 10,000 times more radiant than the light of the Sun in this world; as I have already told you, on an earlier occasion. For the light of the Sun in its true form is not of this (physical) world, since its light has to pierce through a host of veils and regions.

Whereas the light of the Sun in its true form, which exists in the realm of the Holy Goddess of the Light, is more radiant than the 24 Invisibles, and the great Invisible Primal-father, and also the great Triple-powered God: 10,000 more radiant (than these), as I have already told you on an earlier occasion.

Now, therefore, Mariam (the Magdalene), there is no form in this world, nor any light, nor any shape, similar to the 24 Invisibles, with which I could compare them. Yet after little while I shall bring you and your fellow disciples, your brethren, into the three Realms of the First Mystery, but not as far as the Realms of the place of the Ineffable. In these realms you shall see all their configurations as they really are, and without any resemblances (*being displayed to you*).

TEXT NOTE: in Chapter 84

The initiatory 'journey' will now be briefly described. This is actually a process of an inner expanding of the disciples' consciousness to give them cognition of

TEXT NOTE: in Chapter 84
spiritual realms generally: the spirit realms collectively are called "the Heights". It begins with a more specific journeying: to the realm of the Rulers of the karma-determining cosmic influences, which encompasses the 12 Aions.

TEXT: CHAPTER 84 (cont.)
And when I bring you into the Heights, you shall see the glory of those deities in the Heights; and then you will be in the uttermost wonder and awe.

And when I bring you into the place of the Rulers of the karma-determining cosmic influences[270] you shall see the glory in which they exist. And because of the very great glory in which these deities are enveloped, you will consider this (physical) world as the darkest darkness. And if you (*ye*) gaze down on the world of humanity, it will be as a speck of dust for you, because of the enormous distance by which the realms of the karma-determining cosmic influences are so significantly distant from the physical world, and because of the enormous superiority of the quality of the karma-determining cosmic influences over the physical world.

TEXT NOTE: in Chapter 84
(Now, to the realm of the 12 Aions over-all, not only the defined areas where the holy Rulers of these divine Aions are located.)

TEXT: CHAPTER 84 (cont.)
And when I shall have brought you into the 12 Aions, you shall behold their glory, and because of the intense radiance of *their* greatly superior glory, then the realm of the Rulers of the karma-determining cosmic influences (*Heimarmene*) will appear to you as the darkness of darkness. And it will become as a

---

[270] "karma-determining cosmic influences": as noted in the Introduction. I use these words instead of 'the Heimarmene and the Sphere'.

TEXT: CHAPTER 84 (cont.)
speck of dust for you, because of the enormous distance that it will be distant from you, and because of the enormous superiority of the quality of the Aions over it, as I have already said to you on another occasion.

TEXT NOTE: in Chapter 84
(Now to the realm of the 13th Aion, that is Devachan, level 6; the location of the Invisibles, which includes Pistis Sophia.)

TEXT: CHAPTER 84 (cont.)
And, again, when I shall have brought you to the 13th Aion, you shall see the glory in which this exists. And because of its exceedingly great glory, you will consider the 12 Aions to be as the darkness of darknesses. The place of the Aions will be as a speck of dust for you, because of the enormous distance by which the 13th Aion is so significantly distant from the 12 Aions, and because of the enormous superiority of the quality of the 13th Aion over the 12 Aions.

TEXT NOTE: in Chapter 84
(Now to the Midst, i.e., 14th Aion, Devachan realm, level 7.)

TEXT: CHAPTER 84 (cont.)
And when I take you to the place of The Midst, you shall see the glory in which this exists. Then the 13th Aion shall appear to you to be as the darkness of darknesses. And again, you shall gaze upon the 12 Aions, and the karma-determining cosmic influences together with their associated spiritual realms, with all their qualities and ranks. And all these will be as a speck of dust for you, because of the enormous distance by which the 13th Aion is so significantly distant from them, and because of the enormous superiority of its quality compared with these.

TEXT NOTE: in Chapter 84
(Now to The Right, i.e., 15th Aion, Buddhi level.)

TEXT: CHAPTER 84 (cont.)
And when I guide you into the realm of The Right, you shall see the glory in which it exists. Then shall the place of The Midst be (as dark) for you as the night is, in the world of humanity. And when you gaze (down) to the realm of the Midst, this shall be as a speck of dust for you, because of the enormous distance by which the realm of the Right is distanced from it.

TEXT NOTE: in Chapter 84
(Now to the Treasury of Light, i.e., 16th Aion, Buddhi realm, level 2.)

TEXT: CHAPTER 84 (cont.)
And when I guide you to the kingdom of Light, that is, to the Treasury of Light, and you behold the glory of those there, then shall the place of The Right appear to you as does the Sun at midday in the world of humanity, but when the Sun is clouded over.[271] And when you gaze at the place of The Right, it will become as a speck of dust for you, because of the enormous distance by which the Treasury of Light is so significantly distant from it.

TEXT NOTE: in Chapter 84
(Now to the Inheritance of Light, i.e., 17th Aion, Buddhi realm, level 3.)

And when I take you to the place of those of The Inheritance of Light (those who have inherited the Mysteries of the Light) and you behold the glory in which they exist, then shall the kingdom of the Light (*i.e., The Treasury of Light*) appear to you as similar to the radiance of the Sun in the world of humanity.

And then, if you gaze towards the Treasury of the Light, it will become as a speck of dust for you, because of the enormous distance by which the glory of The Inheritance of Light is so significantly distant from it – and because of the enormous superiority of

---

[271] "clouded over": lit. 'is outside' meaning, that is, not in the field of vision, not visible in the sky.

this, to The Treasury of Light.

COMMENTARY: CHAPTER 84
"Treasury of Light" and "Inheritance of Light": see Diagram 1 in the Introduction, about the structure of this 'initiatory journey'. If this is understood as an event which is soon to actually occur, rather than an indication of what the disciples may one day experience, this is an extraordinary event; a deed of Grace to the disciples.

For they will need to undergo a strengthening of their higher 'I' consciousness in order to experience, and to endure perception of, ever higher, more transcendent spirit realms. To achieve this, they are being promised the vital supportive influences (of the 'I') from the cosmic Christ.

For access to higher Devachan is already rare even for highly developed seers; Plato is one of the few Hellenistic sages to refer to what appears to be Devachan. He refers to it as 'the realm of Ideas'; a realm where sublime deities form the Ideas (the concepts) of what later emerges on the Earth as a reality – such as an animal or plant species. Access beyond Devachan to the first three levels of the exalted Buddhi realm (Aions 15-17), as noted in the Introduction, is only possible to high initiates.

TEXT: CHAPTER 85 Mariam the Magdalene speaks
It came to pass, when Jesus had finished speaking these things to his disciples, that Mariam the Magdalene[272] came forward, and said, 'Lord, be not displeased with me if I question you, for we question concerning every matter with earnestness." And Jesus responded and said to her, "Ask what you will, and I will reveal it to you freely, without parable; and everything which you ask, I will tell you with earnestness and certainty.

---

[272] She is so named in the Coptic, but as noted earlier, if only 'Mary' is there, but the Magdalene is clearly meant, then those words are added in italics.

TEXT: CHAPTER 85 (cont.)

I will initiate you in (*regard to*) all spirit-beings and in the full breadth of all spirit-realities[273], from the innermost divine spirit realities[274], to the most external, cosmic spiritual realities;[275] from the Ineffable One to the darkness of darknesses, that you may be called 'the fully spiritual one',[276] (*i.e., an initiate*), initiated in all wisdom. Now, therefore, Mariam (the Magdalene), ask what you will, and I will reveal the answer to you with great joy and great gladness."

It happened, when she had heard these words which the Saviour had said, that she rejoiced with very great joy, and was deeply glad. Then she said, "Lord, will the people of this world, who have received the Mysteries of the Light, (*in The Inheritance of Light; Aion 17*) be higher in your kingdom than the (*en-souled*) emanations (that are located) in The Treasury of Light (*Aion 16*)?

For I have heard you say, "When I shall have brought you (*ye*) to the realm for receiving the Mysteries of the Light (*i.e., The Inheritance of Light*), then the place of the emanations, that is, the Land of the Light, (*i.e., The Treasury of Light*) will seem to you like a speck of dust, because of the great distance that it will be from you then, and because of the great light which is in it – as compared with The Treasury of Light – that is, the place of the emanations."

So, then, my Lord, shall the people who will have received the Mysteries (*from The Inheritance of Light*), be higher (*in their cosmic location*) than the emanations of Light-world (*The Treasury of Light*); and will they be any higher, (*in their actual level of being*) than those domiciled in this kingdom of light (*The Treasury of Light; Aion 16*)?

---

[273] lit. pleromas.

[274] "the innermost divine spirit realities": lit. 'the interior of the interiors'

[275] "to the most external, cosmic spiritual realities": lit. 'the exterior of the exteriors'

[276] "the fully spiritual one": lit. 'the spiritual fullnesses'; this means an initiate.

COMMENTARY: CHAPTER 85

Mariam the Magdalene is asking from a very high, cosmic perspective here ! She is concerned about, or interested in, just how exalted shall be the consciousness of the new Christian initiates. She asks; shall they rise higher than the second level of the 'Buddhi realm' – yet this second level is, according to Rudolf Steiner, where the great Bodhisattvas are located.

TEXT: CHAPTER 86

Jesus answered and said to Mariam (the Magdalene), "Excellent; indeed, you question concerning every subject with earnestness and precision. But listen, Mariam (the Magdalene), that I may explain to you the completion of the Earth's time-cycles[277], and thus the final end[278] of the (physical) world (*i.e., the universe/cosmos*).

It will not occur now, for I said to you, "If I lead you into the place of those who shall have received the Mystery of Light, from The Inheritance of Light,[279] *then* shall the realm of those emanations (The Treasury of Light) seem to you like a speck of dust, and only like the light of the Sun in the daytime (on Earth).

So, I have said to you, these things shall come about at the completion of the Earth's time-cycles, and thus at the final end of the (physical) world. Then the 12 saviours of the Treasury of Light, and the 12 ranks of each of them, (*these 12 are the seven Voices and the five Trees*); these shall be with me in the place

---

[277] "the Earth's time-cycles": lit. the (Earth's) Aeon, i.e., evolutionary Ages, not Aion nor spirit realm, but 'Aeon' which means long Ages of existence.

[278] "final end": lit. the 'ascending up' (i.e., the dissolving of the cosmos.)

[279] Here I have interpreted the Coptic sequence of ideas differently, otherwise it is illogical: making the Treasury of Light both the place of the Inheritance of Light, with its Mysteries, as well as being the location of the inferior emanations.

TEXT: CHAPTER 86 (cont.)
of The Inheritance of Light. They shall be rulers with me in my kingdom, each being ruler over his emanations, and each being ruler according to his degree of spiritual glory, the great according to his greatness, and the small according to his smallness.

TEXT NOTE about the following part of Chapter 86
The following section is a description of the attainment of spiritual redemption by humanity in a future Age when the physical world has ceased to exist. By then many souls are meant to have received initiation into ever higher divine realities (or 'Mysteries').

But, since this codex is not an introductory text, it assumes that the esoteric Christians have knowledge of the cosmos and its complex structure. As a result, important spirits and spiritual dynamics are named but not explained. I include here a diagram to clarify what is meant, otherwise, the next small section of the codex would remain a confusing riddle.

Firstly, we encounter the words 'Voice' and 'Trees'. Altogether there are 12 of these; and fortunately these have already been explained in the text, at least in part: namely, all 12 are the 'saviours' of The Treasury of Light; they are in effect the leaders of this sublime realm (the second level of the Buddhi realm). Moreover, as just stated in this Chapter, each of these saviours has a host or a grouping of spirits with them.

Now, a 'voice' is perhaps some form of 'intoning' from divine reality. So these 'Voices' may be intonings, emanating from seven of the 12 saviours or leaders of The Treasury of Light. So perhaps seven of these saviours, called Voices, are 'intoning' divine reality. Whereas the other five saviours are described as 'Trees': perhaps these five have the power to bring forth the growth of new spiritual realities down in the astral and etheric levels of the cosmos. This indicates that a zodiac dynamic is operative throughout The Treasury of Light.

What is now to be communicated is actually quite

TEXT NOTE about the following part of Chapter 86 simple, but is very confusing in the telling, so Diagram 2 shows what is meant. The 'saviours' (Leaders or Regents) of these groups are in effect, leaders of the divine influences present in Aion 16: the 2nd level of Buddhi, called The Treasury of Light.

However, these 'saviours' themselves are located in Aion 17, The Inheritance of Light. They ray their influences down into Aion 16, The Treasury of Light. Grouped around each of the saviours are highly spiritualized souls who are located in the Treasury of Light, but these have ascended up to the Inheritance of Light, to some extent, through an initiatory experience.

Diagram 2 shows how in Aion 16 there are influences deriving from either a 'saviour', who is either a 'Voice' (a spiritual resonance) or a 'Tree' (a network of out-raying energies perhaps).

Each one of these twelve spiritual influences will be enveloping a group of redeemed future souls, according to how high these souls have ascended in the twelve possible stages.

Finally, this section then refers to souls receiving the first or second or third, etc, 'Mystery' of the 'First Mystery' (this latter word means God). So, for easier reading, the first word 'Mystery' in all twelve of these repetitive sentences is changed to "mystery-experience", meaning an initiatory experience.

Christ describes the glorious future for redeemed souls, in the Buddhi realms (Aions 26 and 17):

It is now indicated that the successful redemption of humanity will result in souls attaining to the 2nd level of the Buddhi realm, but also having access to the sublime 3rd level of the Buddhi realm, where divine Guides (or 'saviours') will be their guides. This is an awe-inspiring future vista, seeing that in today's world of esoteric-mystical thought, even a small understanding of Devachan is elusive (see Diagram 2).

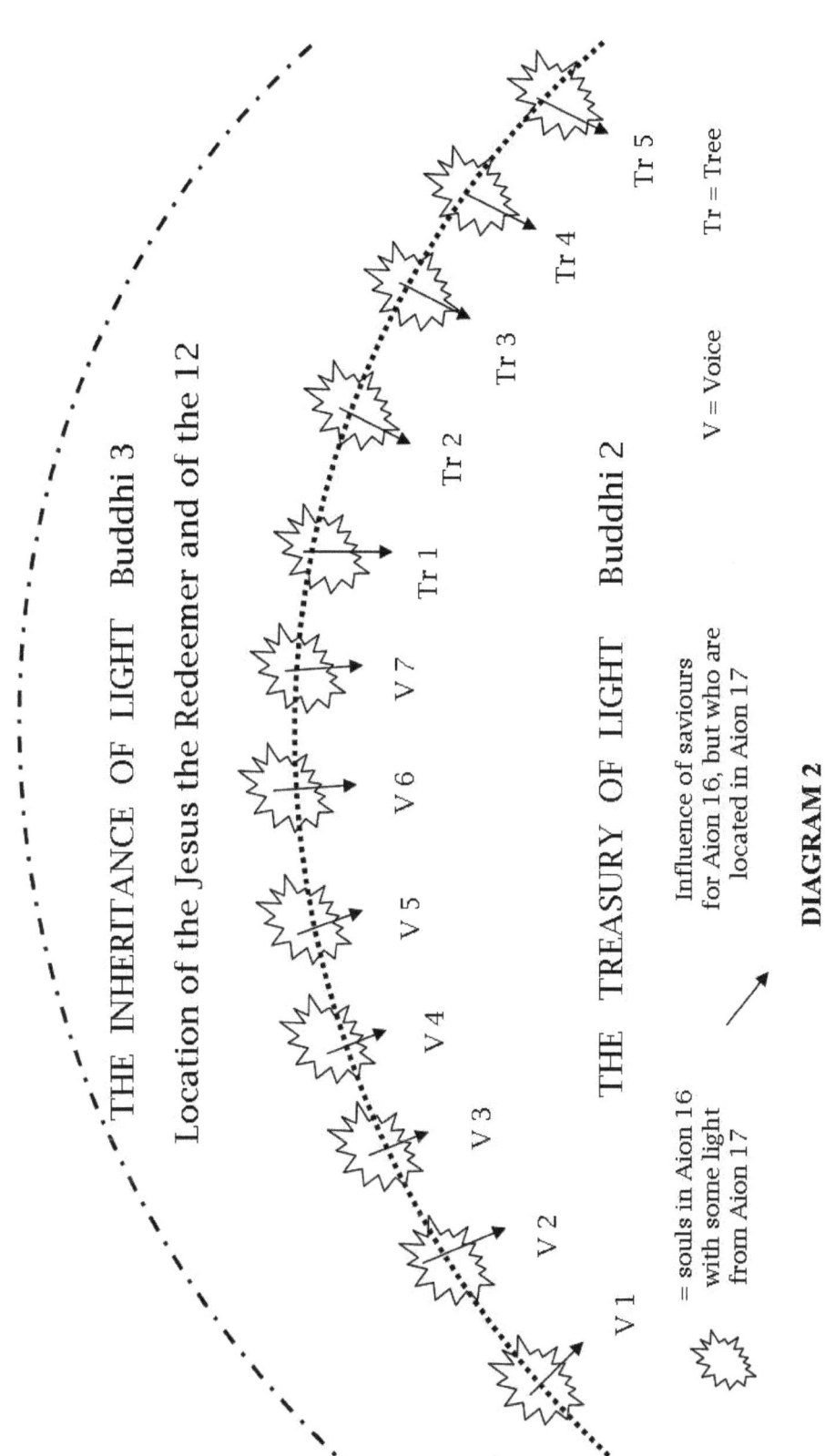

TEXT: CHAPTER 86 (cont.)

And the saviour of the emanations of the first Voice will be in the realm of the souls which shall have received the first mystery-experience of the First Mystery, in my kingdom.

And the saviour of the emanations of the second Voice will be in the realm of the souls which shall have received the second mystery-experience of the First Mystery. And similarly, the Saviour of the emanations of the third Voice will be in the realm of the souls which shall have received the third mystery-experience of the First Mystery.

And the saviour of the emanations of the fourth Voice of The Treasury of Light, will be in the realm of the souls who shall have received the fourth mystery-experience of the First Mystery, in The Inheritance of Light.

And the saviour[280] of the fifth Voice of The Treasury of the Light will be in the realm of the souls who shall have received the fifth mystery-experience of the First Mystery, in The Inheritance of Light.

And the sixth saviour of the emanations of the sixth Voice of The Treasury of Light will be in the realm of the souls which shall have received the sixth mystery-experience of the First Mystery (in The Inheritance of Light.

And the seventh saviour of the emanations of the seventh Voice of The Treasury of the Light will be in the realm of the souls which shall have received the seventh mystery-experience of the First Mystery in The Inheritance of Light.[281]

And the eighth saviour, that is to say, the saviour of the emanations of the first Tree of The Treasury of the Light, will be in the realm of the souls who shall have received the eighth mystery-experience of the First Mystery in The Inheritance of Light.

And the ninth saviour, who is the saviour of the emanations of the second Tree of The Treasury of the Light, will be in the realm of the souls who shall have

---

[280] The text has 'the *fifth* Saviour', but 'fifth' is an error.
[281] Text here has erroneously, The Treasury of Light.

TEXT: CHAPTER 86 (cont.)
received the ninth mystery-experience of the First Mystery in The Inheritance of Light.

And the tenth Saviour, who is the saviour of the emanations of the third Tree of The Treasury of Light, will be in the realm of the souls who shall have received the tenth mystery-experience of the First Mystery in The Inheritance of Light.

In the same manner, again, the eleventh saviour, who is the saviour of the fourth Tree of The Treasury of Light, will be in the realm of the souls which shall have received the eleventh mystery-experience of the First Mystery in The Inheritance of Light.

And the twelfth saviour, who is the saviour of the emanations of the fifth Tree of The Treasury of Light, will be in the realm of the souls of those who shall have received the twelfth mystery-experience of the First Mystery in The Inheritance of Light.

TEXT NOTE: **Arranging of the future Redeemed Souls in the high Aions. This is an obscure section.**

The 12 Disciples may become the vessels of these 12 saviours, in view of a passage in the Book of Revelation about the 12 disciples becoming key parts of the New Jerusalem (Rev. 21:14); and also from comments by Rudolf Steiner to this effect.

The first 7 groups of souls are guided by a saviour of one of the seven Voices; these Voices are in the Treasury of Light, but these saviours are located higher up, in The Inheritance of Light.

The remaining 5 groups of souls are each guided by a saviour in charge of a Tree, from the 1st Tree up to the 5th Tree. Again these Trees are located in The Treasury of Light, whilst these saviours are located higher up, in The Inheritance of Light.

As the diagram makes clear, each of these groups of souls have actually received their initiation (or high, redeemed spirituality), from an initiatory experience undertaken in the next higher level, level 3, of the Buddhi realm, The Inheritance of Light. This is the case even though these souls are located in the

TEXT NOTE: in Chapter 86
lower realm, The Treasury of Light (Buddhi 2).

There now follows details about the levels of authority and glory that various entities will eventually attain; most of these entities are completely unknown to the reader. There is mention of various other spirits, but no further reference of the seven Voices, instead seven Amens are mentioned. (So it remains somewhat obscure.)

TEXT: CHAPTER 86 (cont.)
And the seven Amens[282] and the five Trees and the three Amens will be on my right, because they are rulers in The Inheritance of Light. And the twin saviours, that is, the Child of the Child, and the nine Guardians, shall be at my left, as they are rulers in The Inheritance of Light. And each one of the saviours will rule over the ranks of his emanations in The Inheritance of Light, as they are also rulers in The Treasury of Light.

And the nine Guardians of The Treasury of Light shall be higher than the saviours in The Inheritance of Light.

But the twin saviours shall be higher than the nine Guardians in the kingdom of the Light. And the three Amens shall be higher than the twin saviours in the kingdom of the Light. And the five Trees shall be higher than the three Amens in The Inheritance of Light.

And Jeu,[283] with the Watcher of the veiled threshold[284] of the Great Light, together with the Receiver of the Light (Melchizedek), and the two great Guides and the Great Sabaoth the Good, will be rulers, with the first Saviour of the first Voice of The Treasury of Light.

This is that saviour who will be in the realm of those who have received the first initiatory experience of the First Mystery. For Jeu, and the

---

[282] These may be the same as the 'seven Voices'.
[283] "Jeu": can also be spelt as 'Ieou'.
[284] "Veiled threshold": in the Coptic, simply the word 'veil'.

TEXT: CHAPTER 86 (cont.)
Watcher of the realm of those that are of The Right (*the first level of Buddhi*), and Melchizedek, the great Receiver of the Light, and the two great Guides, have come forth from the purified and ever very pure, light of the first Tree, and as far as the fifth Tree.

TEXT NOTE in Chapter 86:
(Now further details are given about the origin of deities in parts of The Treasury of Light; but of these deities no further knowledge is given; so again a somewhat obscure section.)

TEXT: CHAPTER 86 (cont.)
Jeu is indeed the overseer of the Light, who came forth from the beginning, from the pure light of the first Tree. The Watcher of the threshold of those of The Right, came forth from the second Tree. Whereas the Two Guides came forth from the pure and very purified, light of the third and fourth Trees in The Treasury of Light.

Also, Melchizedek came forth from the fifth Tree; whereas the great Sabaoth the Good, whom I have called my Father, emanated from Jeu, the overseer of the light. Now, the last Helper, by the command of the First Mystery, brought it about that these six (entities), were made to dwell in the realm of (those of) The Right.

TEXT NOTE: chapter 86 (cont.)
Summing this up:
From the 1st Tree: came forth Jeu
From the 2nd Tree: came the Guardian of The Right
From the 3rd & 4th Trees: came the Two Guides
From the 5th Tree: came Melchizedek
And: the great Sabaoth the Good derives from Jeu

TEXT: CHAPTER 86 (cont.)
This was done for the purpose of bringing about the gathering together of the upper Light of the Aions of the Rulers, and of the worlds, and of every life-species which they include. I will tell you of the tasks

TEXT: CHAPTER 86 (cont.)
of each of these; they are tasks which have been allocated to them, throughout the cosmos, as it was expanding forth.

Because of the exalted work in which they are each placed, they shall be co-Regents with the first saviour of the first Voice of The Treasury of the Light. This saviour shall be in the realm of the souls who shall have received the first mystery-experience of the First Mystery.

TEXT NOTE: Here we learn that:
('Sabaoth the Good' is the Father of Jesus, but Jeu is the progenitor or creator of Sabaoth. We also learn that six major deities were to be congregated in The Right, this is Buddhi realm, level 1, and as such, it is the realm above the 7th level of Devachan. The six are: Melchizedek, Sabaoth the Good, the two great Guides, Jeu and the Guardian of The Right.) From this high position these six deities are enabled to gather and harvest whatever there is, lower down, of spirituality (purified light) existing in the devachanic and astral realms.)

TEXT: CHAPTER 86 (cont.)
And the Holy Goddess of the Light, together with the Leader of The Midst (*Devachan 7*) - he whom the Rulers of the Aions call the Little IAO[285], after the name of a great Ruler in their realm - he and the Holy Goddess of Light and his 12 servers, from whom you (ye) have received your form and received your being, will all become rulers with the first saviour of the first Voice in the region of the souls who have received the first initiatory experience of the First Mystery, at the level of The Inheritance of Light.

And the 15 helpers of the seven pure goddesses of the Light, who are in The Midst, shall be distributed among the present places of the 12 saviours, together with the rest of the Heralds (of the Midst), each according to their spiritual glory, that they may be

---

[285] "little IAO": the Coptic has erroneously, the Great IAO

TEXT: CHAPTER 86 (cont.)

rulers with me in The Inheritance of Light. And I shall be ruler over them all in The Inheritance of Light.

All this, however, which I have narrated to you, will not happen now, but will occur at the end of the aeon, that is, at the dissolution of the universe; and when the ascent into the Inheritance of Light of the entire of number of perfected souls shall be accomplished.

So what I have been saying to you will not happen before this ending of the aeon arrives. This end of the aeon will be when each person shall be in their own realm where they have been set since the beginning, until the (*appointed*) number of the gathering together of perfected souls shall be achieved.

Regarding the seven Voices, the five Trees, the three Amens, the Twin Saviours, and the nine Guardians, and the 12 saviours, and those of The Right, and those from the realm of the Midst: all of these deities shall remain in the realm where they have been placed, until the (pre-figured) number of perfected souls have ascended up into The Inheritance of Light.

All the (debased) Rulers who have repented shall also remain in their set place until the (pre-figured) number of perfected souls have ascended. All (these) souls shall arrive at that (*appointed*) time when they are (*able*) to receive the Mystery. Then shall all the Rulers who have repented move on through and arrive at the realm of The Midst.

And then those of the Midst shall baptize them, by the Anointing, and then instil[286] into them the seals (*i.e., the spiritual essence*) of their Mysteries. And they shall be carried through all the realms of The Midst, and they shall be carried through the realm of The Right, and the interior of the realm of the nine Guardians, and the interior of the realm of the Twin saviours, and the interior of the realm of the three Amens, and of the twelve saviours; and the realm of the five Trees and of the seven Voices.

---

[286] "instil into": lit. 'seal them'.

TEXT: CHAPTER 86 (cont.)

Each will give them the seal of its Mystery, and they shall all enter into the realms of The Inheritance of Light. And everyone shall remain in the realm up to which he has received Mysteries in The Inheritance of Light.

In a word, all the human souls who have received the Mysteries of the Light shall lead the way, ahead of all the Rulers who have repented. These souls shall also lead the way, ahead of all those of the realm of The Midst, and of all those of the realm of The Right. And they shall lead the way, ahead of those of the realm of The Treasury of Light. In a word, they shall lead the way, ahead of all those of that realm, thus they shall lead the way ahead of all those in the realm of the first Command.

They shall all enter within their realms; they shall pass into The Inheritance of Light, up to the realm of their Mystery, that each may dwell in the realm of which he shall have received the Mystery. And thus also with those of the realm of The Midst, and those of The Right, and those of the whole realm of the Treasury of the Light: each entity remains at the place of the rank in which he was set from the beginning. This situation shall exist until the universe ascends (*i.e., goes out of existence*)[287].

Each of these spirit-beings is to be accomplishing the appointed task in which he has been placed, in regard to the (*primary goal of*) gathering together the souls which have received the Mystery, because of this task: namely, that they 'seal' all the souls who shall have received the Mystery, and will have passed through their realm, up to the Inheritance of Light.

So now Mariam (the Magdalene), this is the theme about which you questioned me with clarity and precision. As regards the rest of you: 'those who have ears, let them hear'.

---

[287] This phase of non-existence is a Pralaya in Theosophical terms.

COMMENTARY: CHAPTER 86

"received your form and being": the disciples' origin – both form and inner substance – is identified as deriving from the little IAO and the Holy Goddess of the Light and the 12 servers. As stated in Chapter 7, John the Baptist and the Virgin Mary are also said to have in them such influences from the IAO.

"lead the way, ahead": usually 'take precedence over', and the Coptic verb here[288] has both meanings. But the meaning is not that redeemed human souls shall become elevated to a higher rank in the cosmos, and thus take precedence over some of the nine ranks of deities in their exalted realms. Rather, the meaning is that these Christ-permeated human souls shall be advancing their spiritual development through the situation of pioneering a new 'Grace-enveloped' pathway into the future.

TEXT: CHAPTER 87

When Jesus had finished speaking these words, Mariam (the Magdalene) came forward and said, "My Lord, my companion-of-light has ears (*spiritual hearing*) and thus I take up and affirm every word which you have spoken. So now my Lord, concerning these words, "All the souls of human beings which shall receive the Mysteries of the Light in The Inheritance of Light, shall lead the way, ahead of all the Rulers who shall repent, and all those of the realm of those who are of The Right, and the whole realm of The Treasury of Light".

Concerning this statement, my Lord, you have said to us in earlier times, "The first shall be last and the last shall be first"; that is, the 'last' means the entire group of (future redeemed) human souls who shall be the first to enter into the Light-kingdom; and therefore the 'first' means those (spirits) who are in the realm of the Heights.

It was for this reason therefore, Lord that you said to us, "He that has ears to hear, let him hear", that is

---

[288] This verb is: ϣoprr / ϣⲱprr.

TEXT: CHAPTER 87 (cont.)
to say, that you wished to know whether we comprehended all the words which you spoke. This then is what your words mean.

It then happened when Mariam (the Magdalene) had finished saying these words, that the Saviour marveled greatly at the interpretation of his words which she had given, for she had become fully, purely, spirit. And Jesus responded again and said to her, "Well said, spiritual and pure Mariam (the Magdalene); this is the meaning of the word."

COMMENTARY: CHAPTER 87
As from Chapter 83, Mary the Magdalene is specifically named. Before this chapter a 'Mariam' is named 16 times. But it is not clear which woman she is. There are, excluding Mary the mother of Jesus, three other Marys. But we shall call all these other women "Mariam" and not 'Mary'; so that 'Mary' is reserved for Jesus' mother.

There is: Mariam of Clopas   (Jesus' aunt),
         Mariam of Bethany (sister of Lazaros)
         Mariam the Magdalene.

There is also a very brief indicator (in chapter 59) of a further maternal 'Mary' referred to as "another Mary".[289]

In this codex we have encountered so far:
1: Mary, the mother of Jesus
2: the "other Mary" (also a mother?)
3: Mariam #1   (about 16 times)
4: Mariam #2   (called 'the other Mariam'; 3 times)
5: Mariam Magdalene (not until Chapt. 85)

So of the 16 references to a 'Mary' or 'Mariam' in earlier chapters: it is not directly clear to which of the above women these 16 references relate. They need not be to Mariam the Magdalene, although this is a

---

[289] This enigmatic Mary is, I conclude, probably also the mother of a male child.

COMMENTARY: CHAPTER 87 (cont.)
wide-spread academic view. But this view may be wrong, since the text specifically identifies a Mariam as 'the Magdalene' only as from chapter 85. Nor is it clear to whom the three additional references relate ('the other Mariam').

"The first shall be last and the last shall be first": this same topic is discussed in Chapter 57: "The first, they who were created before us, are therefore the Invisibles, for they were created before humans: they and the gods, and the Rulers. And the last are the people who shall receive the Mystery and will be with them in the heavenly realms."

TEXT: CHAPTER 88
It then happened after all these things, that Jesus continued in his conversation, and said to his disciples, "Listen, while I speak to you concerning the glory of those that are in the Heights, how they are just as I have spoken to you concerning them (*in earlier times*) up to this day.

Now, I shall bring you to the realm of the last Helper, whose realm envelops The Inheritance of Light. Now when I have brought you to the realm of this last Helper, in order that you may see the glory in which he exists – then, when I have brought you there, the realm of The Treasury of Light will seem to you simply like a city of this[290] world, because of the magnitude of the last Helper, and because of the mighty radiance in which this deity is enveloped.[291]

Then after this, I shall speak with you about the glory of the Helper who is above the small Helper. But I shall not speak with you about the realm of those (deities) who are above the Helpers, because there exists no type in this world by which to describe them, nor are there any similar things in this world

---

[290] "this world": it appears that the earthly world is meant.
[291] The Coptic here is corrupt, the two place, Inheritance of the Light and the Treasury of the Light, were in the reverse order.

TEXT: CHAPTER 88 (cont.)

like them, with which I could compare them.

There is neither size nor light which resembles them, not only in this world, but also there is no comparison with those of the Heights of Righteousness, from their realm downwards. So for this reason, it is not possible to describe them in this world, because of the great glory of those of the Heights, and because of their vast immeasurable quality. Therefore, there is truly no possibility of speaking about them in this world."

Then it happened, when Jesus had finished speaking these words to his disciples, that Mariam the Magdalene came strongly forward, and said to Jesus, "Lord, be not displeased with me if I question you, because I have questioned you many times. So therefore Lord be not displeased if I question you about everything with earnestness and precision; for my brothers preach this to humankind, that they may hear and repent, and be saved from the harsh judgments of the evil Rulers, that they may enter into the Heights and inherit the Kingdom of Light.

For, my Lord, not only are we compassionate among ourselves, but we are also compassionate to all of humankind, that they may be saved from these harsh chastizements. Now, therefore, Lord, this is why we question on every matter with earnestness and precision, that my brothers may herald it to all of humankind, that they may be delivered from the hands of the mighty Receivers of the outer darkness."

It happened then, when Jesus had heard the word which Mariam (the Magdalene) spoke, that the Saviour answered with great compassion for her, and said to her, "Ask about whatever you will, and I will reveal it to you with precision and certainty, and without any parables.

TEXT: CHAPTER 89

It then happened when Mariam (the Magdalene) had heard these words which the Saviour spoke, that she rejoiced with great rejoicing and was filled with

TEXT: CHAPTER 89 (cont.)

gladness. She said to Jesus, "Lord, by how much, then, is the second Helper greater than the first Helper? By what distance is the former separated from the latter ? Or, again, how many times more radiant is the former than the latter?

Jesus answered and said to Mariam (the Magdalene) in the midst of the disciples, "Truly, truly, the second Helper is distant from the first Helper by a great distance; an immeasurably great distance, both in regard to the height above, and the depth below, with regard to its length and its breadth. There are no means by which it can be measured, whether by Angels or Archangels or by means of the Gods or the Invisibles.

And the second Helper's magnitude is greater than that of the first Helper most exceedingly, by a measure which is not to be reckoned either by Angels, nor Archangels, nor Gods, nor Invisibles. And the former is more radiant than the latter by a measure which is fully impossible to assess. For there is no means of measuring the light which is in him, no possibility of assessing it, either by Angels, or Archangels, or Gods, or Invisibles, as I have already said to you on another occasion.

In like manner, the third, fourth and fifth Helpers are each greater than the preceding one, by an infinite number of times; and their light exceeds the light of the preceding one, and they are removed the one from the other, by an immeasurable distance. A distance not measurable by Angels, and Archangels, by Gods and all Invisibles, as I have already said to you on another occasion. Moreover, I will now tell you of the type of each of them, with regard to their distribution (throughout the cosmos).

COMMENTARY: CHAPTER 89

We learn that there are five Helpers, each one is a great extent higher in the cosmic order, than the one before. And as in several preceding chapters, Mariam the Magdalene is the foremost questioner.

TEXT: CHAPTER 90

It then happened when Jesus had finished speaking that Mariam the Magdalene again came forward, and said to Jesus, "Lord, of what type will they be who have received the Mystery of the Light, in the presence[292] of the last Helper ?

Then Jesus answered and said to Mary in the midst of the disciples, "They who shall have received the Mystery of the Light, when they have come out of the dense (soul) body (*formed from that astral energy which comes*) from the (debased) Rulers, then each one will be placed as regards their rank according to the initiatory experience (*lit. Mystery*) that they have received.

They who shall have received a high Mystery, shall be in a high level; and they who shall have received a lower Mystery, in a lower level. In a word, of whatever regions each shall have received the Mystery, that person shall dwell in its (*corresponding*) level, in The Inheritance of Light.

For this reason I said to you in an earlier time, "In the place where is your heart, there also shall your treasure be."[293] That is to say, in the place of which each shall have received the Mystery, there shall that person remain.   **John speaks**

It then happened, when Jesus had finished speaking these words to his disciples, that John (*i.e., the beloved disciple*) came forward and said, "My Lord and my Saviour, bid me also to speak in your presence, and be not displeased with me if I question you on every matter with earnestness and precision; for Lord, you have promised to me to reveal to us everything about what I may ask you.

So Lord, hide nothing from us all of that about which we question you." And Jesus answered with great compassion, and said to John, "You, also, blessed John, beloved one, I do bid to speak the word which you wish, and I will unveil it to you face to

---

[292] "in the presence of": usu. awkwardly, 'in the midst'; the preposition (ⲙⲏⲧⲉ) here also means 'to be present'.

[293] Similar words are recorded in Matt.6:21 and Lk. 12:34.

TEXT: CHAPTER 90 (cont.)   John speaks

face, without parable, and I will tell you all that you ask me with earnestness and precision."

And then John responded, saying to Jesus, "So then Lord, will everyone (*be required to*) remain in the realm up to which they have received that Mystery? So shall there be no ability to leave that realm for other higher levels (of spirit); and will there be authority to enter lower levels?

COMMENTARY: CHAPTER 90

Here both Miriam the Magdalene and John put questions; and these concern a theme so high that it has all but faded away from the Christian world, except in the awareness of those few souls interested in the initiatory path. The theme is, attaining a conscious awareness in the Buddhi realm, in this case, the third level; the 17th Aion or The Inheritance of Light.

   It is difficult today to be aware of the Soul-world (or astral realm), not to mention Devachan. The Buddhi realm is an even more transcendent realm. To attain awareness of this realm requires developing the higher 'I': and this is precisely what derives from the presence of the cosmic Christ, or Christ-light, in the human being. That is, such initiated souls must actually have brought into blossoming their germinal Spirit-self or 'spirit-body'.[294] (This is indicated in biblical literature by the expression, The Son of God, although this same phrase often refers directly to Jesus himself.)

TEXT: CHAPTER 91

And then Jesus answered and said to John, "Truly, indeed, do you question on every matter with earnestness and precision. So now, John, listen while I speak to you. Whosoever shall have received the Mystery of the Light, will remain in the realm where

---

[294] My book, *The Way to the Sacred* offers a comprehensive guide to this subject.

TEXT: CHAPTER 91 (cont.)
they shall have received the Mystery, and will not have the power of going into the Heights, into the higher spirit levels, above him or her.

Thus they who shall have received the initiation experience (*lit. Mystery*) in the first Command shall have the power to go to the levels (of spirit) *below* them. That is, into all the levels of the third Realm; but that person shall not have the power to enter into the (spirit) levels of the Heights, which are above him or her.

(TEXT COMMENT: this next passage mentions entities or realms which are not explained. It remains unclear.)

TEXT: CHAPTER 91 (cont.)
And, regarding that person (*acolyte*) who shall have received the initiation experiences of the First Mystery, which is the 24th Mystery, reckoning outwards (*i.e., from the central, initial Mystery*); this 24th Mystery is the foremost Mystery of the first Space, which is externalized.

(TEXT COMMENT: 'externalized' here means that the initiate has achieved a comprehension of a Mystery or initiatory process. The initiate has experienced this, so it is no longer veiled within; its essential nature has become 'external' to the initiate's consciousness.)

TEXT: CHAPTER 91 (cont.)
That person then, shall have the power of going into all the levels (*of spirit realms*) which they have comprehended through experiences;[295] but they will not have the power of going into the higher realms (*to which their consciousness has not as yet attained*), or of extending their consciousness[296] into them.

And each person who shall have received the

---

[295] "comprehended through experiences": lit. 'external to themselves' : see Commentary.

[296] "extending their consciousness": lit. 'moving in them'.

TEXT: CHAPTER 91 (cont.)
initiation experience in the sequences of those 24 Mysteries, will go as far as that realm where they have received the Mystery, and each person will have the power of exploring all the levels and places which they have comprehended through experiences.[297] But they do not have authority to access the levels above them, or to traverse these levels (*in their consciousness*).

And they who shall have received the initiation experience in the levels of the First Mystery, which is in the third Space, shall have the power of going into all the lower levels, and of exploring them all, but they will not have the power to enter the higher realms, or of exploring them.

TEXT NOTE: in Chapter 91
(Now three higher deities are introduced, each a kind of trinity within themselves, but about which little is said.)

TEXT: CHAPTER 91 (cont.)
Now, regarding that person who shall have received the Mystery of the First Thrice-spiritual One, i.e., that deity who is empowered over all the 24 Mysteries and who is regent over the realm of the First Mystery. I shall speak to you (*later*) about the realm this deity received at the spreading-forth of the cosmos (*at the beginning of creation*).

That person who shall receive the Mystery of the first Thrice-spiritual One: that person will have the power of descending into all the lower realms. But they will not have the power of ascending up into the Heights, that is, to the higher levels, which are all the sequences in the realm of the Ineffable One (*i.e., God*).

And that person who shall have received the Mystery of the second Thrice-spiritual One, shall have the power of going into all the levels of the First Thrice-spiritual One, and of exploring them all, and

---

[297] comprehended through experiences": lit. 'are external to them'.

TEXT: CHAPTER 91 (cont.)
all the sequences that are therein; but they will not have the power of going into the levels of the Heights of the third Thrice-spiritual One.

And whoever who shall have received the Mystery of the third Thrice-spiritual One, who rules the three Thrice-spiritual Ones and the three Realms of the First Mystery all together, (he or she has authority to enter all the levels below them); but they will not have the power of going into the Heights, to the higher levels, which are the levels of the realm of the Ineffable One.

TEXT NOTE: in Chapter 91
('The Ineffable One' is elsewhere identified as God; but meaning the sublime deity who is higher than, and more veiled than, the 'First Mystery'; the deity who is also identified as 'God' and who is called "The First Mystery who gazes within". Whilst the cosmic Christ – who is often speaking through Jesus, in the Gospels, and in this text also – is called "The First Mystery who gazes without".)

TEXT: CHAPTER 91 (cont.)
But whoever shall have received the absolutely empowered initiatory process of the First Mystery, (that is) of the Ineffable One – namely the 12 initiatory processes of the First Mystery, which hold sway over all the areas of the First Mystery – this person (*i.e., the initiate*) who shall receive *that* initiatory process shall have the power of exploring all the levels of the areas of the three Thrice-spiritual Ones, and also of the three Realms of the First Mystery, including all their levels.

And they shall have the power of exploring all the levels of The Inheritance of Light, of exploring this from without within, and from within without, from above below, and from below above, from the height to the depth, and from the depth to the height, from the length to the breadth, and from the breadth to the length.

In a word, they shall have authority to experience

TEXT: CHAPTER 91 (cont.)
(*lit. move abou*t) in all the levels of the Inheritance of Light. And this person shall have the authority to remain in whatever level they choose in the Inheritance of the kingdom of Light.

Truly, I say to you that this person, when the cosmos is dissolved, shall be empowered over all the levels of The Inheritance of Light (*i.e., Buddhi 3*).

And whoever shall have received the Mystery-experience of the Ineffable One - **which experience is myself** - that Mystery knows why there is darkness, and why there is light.

TEXT NOTE: in Chapter 91
So here we learn that the initiate whose path is created and sustained by the cosmic Christ, if they thereby attain to a comprehension of the highest divine reality - through an initiatory process of the highest level, called "the absolutely empowered" mystery - achieves enlightenment which gives empowerment within the sublime 3rd level of the Buddhi realm. Moreover, we also learn that this same degree of initiation is defined as bestowing enlightenment or cosmic consciousness, from God; i.e., the Ineffable One.

"when the cosmos is dissolved": this means when the current evolutionary Age, is completed. This appears to mean in terms of Rudolf Steiner's teachings on the evolutionary cycles of our planet, when the 'Earth aeon' ends and before the new aeon, the 'Jupiter aeon', commences, as the cosmos re-emerges from its cosmic sleep.

"Mystery-experience...which is myself": a very significant declaration: God can be understood as united with the cosmic Christ and its human vessel, Jesus. This is also as the Gospel of John teaches.

TEXT NOTE: in Chapter 91
Note now that a new section of this chapter begins, about the vast, all-encompassing nature of the highest initiation consciousness - that which brings

TEXT NOTE: in Chapter 91
an inner communion with God.[298] The wisdom which this 'Mystery' confers on the person is now described by giving many short examples of what this wisdom is. The word Mystery, which is repeated on every line, I am translating as 'mystery-experience'. Otherwise all these repetitive sentences would be, "the Mystery of the First Mystery knows why..."

TEXT: CHAPTER 91 (cont.)
And that mystery-experience (*of the Ineffable or First Mystery*) knows why the darkness of darknesses came into existence, and why the Light of Lights came into existence.
And that mystery-experience knows why the Chaos came into existence, and why The Treasury of Light.
And why the Light-world has been created, together with the realm of The Inheritance of Light.
That mystery-experience knows why all the chastizements of sinners came into existence, and why the peace of the kingdom of Light.
That mystery-experience knows why sinners came into existence, and why inheritances of light.
That mystery-experience knows why the unrighteous came into existence, and why the good.
That mystery-experience knows why the chastisements came into existence, and why all the (*joy-giving*) emanations of light came into existence.
That mystery-experience knows why sin came into existence, and why baptisms and mysteries of light came into existence.

That mystery-experience knows why the fire of chastizement came into existence, and why seals of light came into existence, so that the fire would not harm them.
That mystery-experience knows why blasphemy came into existence, and why words of reverence to the

---

[298] This may be the equivalent of the "the 7th degree" of antiquity, as referred to in the work of Steiner.

TEXT: CHAPTER 91 (cont.)

Light.

That mystery-experience knows why prayers to the Light came into existence.

That mystery-experience knows why cursing came into existence, and why blessing.

That mystery-experience knows why wickedness came into existence and why deceit.

That mystery-experience knows why slaying came into existence, and why the enlivening of souls.

That mystery-experience knows why adultery and fornication came into existence, and why there is purity.

That mystery-experience knows why intercourse came into existence, and why continence.

That mystery-experience knows why pride and boasting, came into existence and why humility and gentleness.

That mystery-experience knows why tears came into existence, and why laughter.

That mystery-experience knows why slander came into existence, and why an affirming conversation.

That mystery-experience knows why readiness to hear came into existence, and why the disregard of others.

That mystery-experience knows why complaining came into existence, and why innocence and holiness.

That mystery-experience knows why sin came into existence, and why purity.

That mystery-experience knows why strength came into existence, and why weakness.

That mystery-experience knows why movement of the body's limbs[299] came into existence, and why they are so used.

That mystery-experience knows why poverty came into existence, and why riches.

That mystery-experience knows why (carefree) wealth came into existence in the world, and why enslaving poverty exists.

---

[299] "body's limbs": the text only has 'body'.

That mystery-experience knows why death came into existence, and why life has arisen.

COMMENTARY: CHAPTER 91
This last section of the chapter is clear.

TEXT: CHAPTER 92
It then happened when Jesus had finished saying these words to his disciples, that they rejoiced with great joy, and were deeply gladdened on hearing his words. And Jesus continued, saying to them, "So listen my disciples while I tell you about all the initiatory-experience of the Ineffable One (*God*).

TEXT NOTE: in Chapter 92
(The word Mystery, which is repeated on every line, I am again translating as 'mystery-experience'.)

TEXT: CHAPTER 92 (cont.)
Because that mystery-experience knows why there is mercilessness and why there is mercy.
That mystery-experience knows why there is destruction, and why everlasting eternity.
That mystery-experience knows why there are reptiles, and why they shall be destroyed.
That mystery-experience knows why there are wild beasts, and why they will perish.
That mystery-experience knows why there are beasts of burden, and why birds.

That mystery-experience knows why there are mountains, and why there are precious stones therein.
That mystery-experience knows why there is the dense matter of gold, and why the dense matter of silver.
That mystery-experience knows why there is the dense matter of copper, and why that of iron and of stone.

That mystery-experience knows why there is the

TEXT: CHAPTER 92 (cont.)

dense matter of lead.

That mystery-experience knows why there is the dense matter of glass,[300] and why the dense matter of wax.

That mystery-experience knows why there are herbs and plants, and why all material substances exist.

That mystery-experience knows why the waters of the Earth came into existence, and all things within in; and why the Earth also came into existence.

That mystery-experience knows why the seas exist and why the waters have arisen and why the wild beasts of the seas exist.

And that mystery-experience knows why the dense world-material has arisen, and why it shall be utterly destroyed.

COMMENTARY: CHAPTER 92

The teachings in Chapter 92 are clear.

TEXT: CHAPTER 93

Yet again my disciples and companions and brothers, let everyone be vigilant[301] as to the spirit which is in them. May you listen and receive and understand every word which I speak to you. For, from this hour hence, I shall begin to speak with you concerning all the initiatory knowledge of the Ineffable One.

That mystery-experience knows why there is a west, and why an east.

That mystery-experience knows why there is a south, and why a north.

Yet again, my disciples, hearken and continue to be attentive, that you may hear the entire initiatory knowledge of the Mystery of the Inexpressible.

That mystery-experience knows why there are demons, and why humans.

---

[300] Glass was invented about 4,000 years ago.
[301] The word here, 'naephalios' (νήφαλιος) although often used for 'sober' also means to be vigilant, attentive.

TEXT: CHAPTER 93 (cont.)

That mystery-experience knows why there is heat, and why the pleasant breeze.
That mystery-experience knows why there are stars, and why clouds.
That mystery-experience knows why the Earth gained its depths, and why the waters came over it.
That mystery-experience knows why the earth dried and why the rain came upon it.
That mystery-experience knows why there is famine, and why abundance.

That mystery-experience knows why there is white frost, and why beneficial dew.
That mystery-experience knows why there is dust, and why delightful freshness.
That mystery-experience knows why there is hail, and why pleasant snow.
That mystery-experience knows why the west wind came into existence and why the east wind.
That mystery-experience knows why the fire of the heights came into existence and why the waters.

That mystery-experience knows why the east wind came into existence.
That mystery-experience knows why there is a south wind, and why a north wind.
That mystery-experience knows why there are the stars of heaven, and the disks of the planets, and why there is the firmament with all its veils.
That mystery-experience knows why the Rulers of the spheres came into existence, and why the spheres with all their places.

That mystery-experience knows why the tyrannical Rulers of the (debased) Aions came into existence and why their spheres with all their places; and why those Rulers who have repented, came into existence.
That mystery-experience knows why there are serving-spirits, and why there are decans.
That mystery-experience knows why there are Angels, and why Archangels.

TEXT: CHAPTER 93 (cont.)

That mystery-experience knows why there are lords, and why gods.

That mystery-experience knows why there has been jealousy in the Heights, and why there has been lack of jealousy.

That mystery-experience knows why there is hate, and why love exists.

That mystery-experience knows why there is discord, and why reconciliation.

That mystery-experience knows why there is avarice, and why renunciation of all things; and why the love of money.

That mystery-experience knows why there is selfish grasping and why there is being satiated.

That mystery-experience knows why partners came into existence, and why unpaired ones.

That mystery-experience knows why godlessness came into existence and why the love of God.

That mystery-experience knows why the planets came into existence, and why the fixed stars.

That mystery-experience knows why the Thrice-powered Ones came into existence, and why the Invisible Ones.

That mystery-experience knows why the Primal-Fathers came into existence and why the Pure Ones.

And that mystery-experience knows why the powerful Self-willed One came into existence and why his hosts.

That mystery-experience knows why the Thrice-spiritual One came into existence and the great Invisible Forefather.

That mystery-experience knows why the 13th Aion came into existence, and why the place of those of The Midst.

That mystery-experience knows why there are the Receivers of The Midst, and why the holy goddesses of Light.

That mystery-experience knows why there are the

289

TEXT: CHAPTER 93 (cont.)
Servitors of The Midst, and why the Angels of The Midst.
That mystery-experience knows why there is the Light-world, and why the great Receivers of the Light.
That mystery-experience knows why there are the Guardians of the realm of those of The Right, and why the leaders of these (Guardians) exist.

That mystery-experience knows why the Portal of Life came into existence, and why Sabaoth the Good came into existence.
That mystery-experience knows why the place of those of The Right exist, and why the Land of Light, that is, The Treasury of Light, came into existence.
That mystery-experience knows why there are the emanations of light, and why the twelve saviours.
That mystery-experience knows why there are the three Portals of the Treasury of Light, and why the nine Watchers.
That mystery-experience knows why there are the Twin saviours[302], and why the three Amens.
That initiatory-experience knows why there are the five Trees, and why the seven Amens.
That mystery-experience knows why there is the Mixture which (once) did not exist, and why it has been purified.

COMMENTARY: CHAPTER 93
"the Mixture which (once) did not exist": usually, "does not exist'. But this makes no sense. As in earlier passages (chapters 10 and 59) the present tense should be the past tense. The word "once" is not in the Coptic, but it reinforces the past tense. Otherwise the text, left in the present tense, is illogical.[303]

---

[302] Nothing is known of these Twin Saviours.
[303] Technically; the situation is: Normally the past tense is ⲚⲈϤϢⲞⲞⲚ; so there are two possible reasons for this confusion.
One: there is a variant of this word, as the past tense, with the first 2 letters reversed (Stern, *Grammatik*, p.214). Two:

COMMENTARY: CHAPTER 93 (cont.)

The sentence is powerfully emphasizing the primary concept of the initiatory wisdom underlying Christian Gnosticism: that the Mixture, or the inferior, 'densified' level of the cosmos, did not always exist; and the aim of the Christ or cosmic Light-being is to help humanity rise above this level. This is a core point already in Chapter 8; and is the final truth in this list which the initiation wisdom of God, or the First Mystery, reveals.

TEXT: CHAPTER 94

And Jesus continued further in his conversation and said, to his disciples, "Continue to be attentive, my disciples, and let each of you bring forward in yourself, the capacity to perceive the Light, so that you may hear with certainty. For from this time on, I will describe for you the entire true realm of the Ineffable One,[304] and what kind of realm it is. But when the disciples heard these words from Jesus, they withdrew and were very discouraged.

Mary the Magdalene came forward, she bowed down at the feet of Jesus, worshipping him; she cried aloud and wept, saying: "Have mercy upon me, Lord; for have not my brethren heard and lost all courage because of the words which you have spoken? Now, therefore, Lord, concerning the spiritual knowledge of all the things which you have said are in the Mystery of that Ineffable One, I heard you say, "From this time on, I shall begin to tell you the entire initiatory wisdom of the Mystery of the Ineffable One."

But now, regarding these words, you have not proceeded to give an entire presentation of this. Therefore, my brethren, (though) they have been hearing, they have lost courage; they have ceased to perceive how you are discoursing, because of the

---

the non-Copt scribe has mistakenly transposed these two letters since normally: ɛnqϣooN is a *present* tense prefix and NɛqϣooN is a *past* tense prefix.

[304] "Ineffable": i.e., that which cannot be expressed in words.

TEXT: CHAPTER 94 (cont.)

words you have been using. Now, therefore, Lord, if the initiatory wisdom of all these things is in that (First) Mystery, who is the person in this world who shall be able to understand that Mystery and all its initiatory wisdom, and the special words[305] which you have used, when speaking about it?

COMMENTARY: CHAPTER 94

This chapter is quite clear.

TEXT: CHAPTER 95

When Jesus heard the words which Mariam (the Magdalene) said, knowing that the disciples had heard, but that they were beginning to lose courage, he encouraged them, saying; do not be in grief concerning the Mystery of the Ineffable One, thinking that you will not understand it. Truly, I say to you that this Mystery is for you, and for everyone who shall give ear to you and who shall relinquish the whole world, thus all the dense matter therein, and who shall relinquish all the evil thoughts that are therein, and shall relinquish all the concerns of this world.[306]

Therefore, I now say to you, that for everyone who shall (*inwardly*) relinquish the entire world and everything in it, and shall submit themselves to that which is divine, this Mystery is easier than all the Mysteries of the kingdom of Light. It is simpler to understand than all the rest, and it is clearer than them all. They who shall arrive at knowledge of that Mystery, will be inclined to give up the whole of this world and all its concerns.

For this reason I said to you earlier, "Come to me all you that are oppressed with cares, and labour under their weight, and I will give you rest, for my burden is light and my yoke is gentle."[307] Now,

---

[305] "special words": lit. 'type of words used'.
[306] "this world": the text has aeon/aion (αἰών) which can also include the physical world.
[307] Similar words were placed in Gospel of Matthew (11:30).

TEXT: CHAPTER 95 (cont.)

therefore, whoever shall receive that Mystery, has relinquished the whole world, thus all the material concerns that are therein. Therefore, my disciples, do not grieve, thinking that you will never understand that Mystery.

Truly, I say to you, that Mystery is easier to understand than all Mysteries of the kingdom of Light. And truly, I say to you, that Mystery is yours and also those who shall relinquish the whole world, thus all the matter that is therein.

Now, therefore, hearken, my disciples, my friends and my brethren, that I may impel you to the understanding of that Mystery of the Ineffable One. These things I say to you, because I have already taught you the knowledge of all the structure of the cosmos; for indeed, knowledge of the structure of the cosmos *is* the Mystery of the Ineffable One (*i.e., the cosmic initiatory wisdom imparted by communion with God*). So now I may speak with you, to advance your understanding of this Mystery.

This Mystery knows why the five Helpers were bestirred, and why they came forth from the Fatherless Ones. And it knows why the great Light of Lights was bestirred and why it came forth from the Fatherless Ones.

TEXT NOTE in Chapter 95:

"thus all the dense matter therein": this is a substantial statement; those who wish to become initiated need to be inwardly free of the influence of 'hyle' or matter on their consciousness, for this inherently blinds the soul to the spiritual aspects of life.

The gods begin their work in the cosmos:

"were bestirred": throughout the next section of the chapter, various ranks of deities are stirred into activity.[308] In the next section, the Christ refers to further, more detailed knowledge that the high

---

[308] The Coptic word here is directly from Greek (σκύλω), which means 'to tear' or 'to be troubled', 'to go to the effort' or to 'be astir'; this latter meaning is meant here.

Gnosis initiatory wisdom from the 'First Mystery' can provide. These deities have long descriptive names, but nothing is known about them. (This is an obscure section.)

TEXT: CHAPTER 95 (cont.)

That Mystery knows why the First Command was bestirred, and why it was separated into the seven Mysteries, and why it is called the First Command, and why it emanated from the Fatherless Ones.

That Mystery knows why the Great Light of the Light-dividing One was bestirred, and why it remained without emanation, and why it came forth from the Fatherless Ones.

That Mystery knows why the First Mystery was bestirred, that is to say, why the 24th Mystery, reckoning outwards, was bestirred; and why it replicated within itself the 12 Mysteries, in accordance with the numbering of the Unbounded-Ones[309]; and why it came forth from the Fatherless Ones.

And that Mystery knows why the 12 Immoveable Ones were bestirred and why they were established with all their ranks, and why they came forth from the Fatherless Ones.

And that Mystery knows why the Unshakeable Ones were bestirred, and why they set themselves up in 12 ranks, and why they came forth from the Fatherless Ones, who belong to the sectors established in the realm of the Ineffable One.

And that Mystery knows why the Unthinkable Ones, who belong to the second Space of the Ineffable, were bestirred, and why they came forth from the Fatherless Ones.

That Mystery knows why the 12 Un-designated Ones were bestirred, and why they were established behind all ranks of the Unrevealables, despite themselves being incomprehensible and infinite; and why they came forth from the Fatherless Ones.

---

[309] Or the "Incomprehensible Ones"; the Grk. term is ambiguous; see Commentary.

TEXT: CHAPTER 95 (cont.)

That Mystery knows why these Unrevealables were bestirred: they who did not disclose themselves, nor bring themselves into manifestation, according to the regulation of the Only-one, the Ineffable, and why they came forth from the Fatherless Ones.

And that Mystery knows why the Even-deeper Ones were bestirred and why they were arranged into one rank only; and why they came forth from the Fatherless Ones.

And that Mystery knows why the 12 ranks of the Ineffable Ones were bestirred and why they have divided themselves into three parts; and why they came forth from the Fatherless Ones.

And that Mystery knows why the Imperishable Ones, consisting of 12 ranks, were bestirred, and why they have distributed themselves, one behind the other, (*despite*) being of one rank. But also why they have then divided themselves and thus formed various ranks, even though they are incomprehensible and infinite.

And that Mystery knows why the Ineffable Ones were bestirred, and divided into three parts, and why they came forth from the Fatherless Ones.

And that Mystery knows why the Perpetually-existent Ones, in their twelve ranks, were bestirred, and why they were then set in a single rank, one behind the other; and why they were (then) divided, and formed various separated ranks, even though they are unbounded and infinite, and why they came forth from the Fatherless Ones.

And that Mystery also knows why the Endless Ones were bestirred, and why they established themselves into 12 endless realms, and why they were placed in three levels of these realms, according to the arrangements of the Only One, the Ineffable: and why they came forth from the Fatherless Ones.

TEXT NOTE:

("realms": usually translated as 'space', but this as

TEXT NOTE: in Chapter 95
such does not exist in spirit realms.[310] So I have chosen 'realms' to suggest specific non-spatial 'areas' wherein the influence of these deities prevails.

It is quite intriguing now to read of how a high deity is associated with the 'first' or 'second' realms in God, i.e., in the First Mystery. Fortunately, this theme of several 'realms' will become clearer in later chapters.)

TEXT: CHAPTER 95 (cont.)
And that Mystery knows why the Unbounded Ones –
who belong to the ranks of the Only One, the Ineffable One – were bestirred, and why they came forth from the Fatherless Ones, until they reached the location of the First Mystery, which is the second Realm.

That Mystery knows why the 24 myriads of the Praise-singers were bestirred, and why they separated beyond the threshold[311] of the First Mystery, which is the Twin Mystery, looking within and without, of the Only One, the Ineffable One; and why they came forth from the Fatherless Ones.

That Mystery knows why all the Unbounded Ones which I have just enumerated – those who are in the regions of the second Realm of the Ineffable One, that is to say, in the location of the First Mystery – why they were bestirred, and why these Unbounded Ones and Endless Ones came forth from the Fatherless Ones.

TEXT NOTE: in Chapter 95
"in the location of the First Mystery": it is unexpected that the Ineffable One (or God who is veiled) is within the area of the 'First Mystery who gazes within', (or less veiled God).

TEXT: CHAPTER 95 (cont.)
And that Mystery knows why the 24 Mysteries of the

---

[310] "location": The Grk. term here means: territory, area, position, location, whereabouts, site or space.
[311] "threshold": lit. 'curtain'.

TEXT: CHAPTER 95 (cont.)
first Triune Ones were bestirred, and why they are called the 24 'locations' of the first Triune-spirit, and why they came forth from the second Triune-spirit.

And that Mystery knows why the 24 Mysteries of the second Triune-spirit were bestirred, and why they came forth from the third Triune-spirit.

And that Mystery knows why the 24 Mysteries of the third Triune-spirit were bestirred – and they are the realms of the third Triune-spirit – and why they came forth from the Fatherless Ones.

TEXT NOTE: ('realms' here can be understood as portals through which this Triune-spirit manifests its core nature.)

TEXT: CHAPTER 95 (cont.)
And that Mystery knows why the five Trees of the first Triune-spirit were bestirred, and why they were arranged in sequence behind each other, and yet also bonded to each other – they and all their ranks; and why they emanated from the Fatherless Ones.

TEXT NOTE:
(Now 'Trees' are mentioned: these are presumably referring to multi-branched emanations of spiritual influences that are sent forth into its realm, by the deity mentioned.)

TEXT: CHAPTER 95 (cont.)
That Mystery knows why the five Trees of the second Triune-spirit were bestirred, and why they came forth from the Fatherless Ones.

That Mystery knows why the five Trees of the third Triune-spirit were bestirred, and why they came forth from the Fatherless Ones.
And that Mystery knows why the Particularly Unbounded Ones, of the first Triune-spirit, were bestirred, and why they came forth from the Fatherless Ones.

And that Mystery knows why the Particularly Unbounded Ones, of the second Triune-spirit, were

TEXT: CHAPTER 95 (cont.)
bestirred, and why they emanated from the Fatherless Ones.

And that Mystery knows why the Particularly Unbounded Ones, of the third Triune-spirit, were bestirred, and why they emanated from the Fatherless Ones.

That Mystery knows why the first Triune-spirit (*reckoning*) from below – which belongs to the ranks of the Only One, the Ineffable – was bestirred, and why it emanated from the second Triune-spirit.

That Mystery knows why the third Triune-spirit (*from below*), which is the first Triune-spirit (*reckoning*) from above, was bestirred; and why it came forth from the 12th Primary Triune-spirit[312], which is in the last area of the Fatherless Ones.

TEXT NOTE: in chapter 95
(The Triune-spirits are not explained; however, from this sentence it appears that above them there are 12 higher ranking deities, from whom the Triune-spirits derive. This suggests a triune zodiacal dynamic. These higher ranking beings exist in a realm which is close to the enigmatic 'Fatherless Ones'.)

TEXT : CHAPTER 95 (cont.)
That Mystery knows why all the 'locations' which are in the realm of the Ineffable One were spread out, together with all those (entities) which are within them, and why they emanated from the last sector[313] of the Ineffable One.

That Mystery knows why of itself, it became bestirred also, in order to emanate forth from the Ineffable – from He who rules over them all. It is He who caused them all to be distributed according to their ranks.

---

[312] "Primary Triune-spirit": lit. 'pro-Triune-spirit; 'pro' here meaning primary or 'higher in existence and rank'.
[313] "last sector": lit. 'last member/part'.

COMMENTARY: CHAPTER 95

Here the Light of Lights (the cosmic Christ), through Jesus, is declaring that the *highest* initiatory knowledge, or Gnosis – that which derives from God (the First Mystery or the Ineffable One) – provides answers to the deepest, most cosmic questions which the soul on the initiatory Christian path could formulate. Also some brief details of how these deities are arranged in the cosmos are given.

One also learns of three Triune deities; and that there are three types of 'Particularly Unbounded' deities, and that each of these emanated from one of the Triune-spirits.

It is also stated that the third Triune-spirit itself derives from 'the 12th Primary Triune-spirit': this latter deity is not explained. But it is clear that there are 12 of these 'primary' Triune deities, and there are also three Triune spirits which are *not* primary.

"Unbounded Ones": an obscure Greek term, which is left untranslated by Schmidt and McDermot. It may well be 'Incomprehensible Ones', or possibly 'Non-location Ones'.[314]

TEXT: CHAPTER 96

All this I will explain to you, when I am speaking[315] of the unfolding of the cosmos (*as it entered into existence*). In a word, I shall speak (further) with you about all that I have (so far) explained to you. Those things which shall happen, and those which are to come about; those which emanate, and those which come forth. Those which are outside, above the others, and those which are implanted within them.

Those which shall occupy the realm of the First Mystery; and those which are in the realm of the Ineffable One. I will speak to you of these, because I shall be revealing them to you (*in the future*). These I

---

[314] If the text is corrupt here, the name of these beings might be, "Non-separated Ones" (if the Grk. χωρις was meant, not χωρης).

[315] "when I am speaking": this phrase is not in the Coptic, but is needed to make sense of the paragraph.

TEXT: CHAPTER 96 (cont.)
will explain to you, by location and by rank, when discussing the unfolding of the cosmos; and I will reveal to you all the Mysteries which are empowered over them; together with their 'Above Triune-spirits' and 'Beyond Triune-spirits' which command their Mysteries and their ranks.

So, consequently, it is the central spiritual reality (*lit. 'Mystery'*) of the Ineffable One which knows why all these have come into existence, and through which deity they arose. Hence this, the central spiritual reality (*lit. Mystery*) is (present) within all these (*deities*); and it this same central spiritual reality which *is* the arising into being of all these, and *is also* the (*spiritual influence*) establishing them (in the cosmos)

This central spiritual reality of the Ineffable One is in all these (*spiritual realities*) of which I have spoken, and of which I shall speak when discussing the unfolding of the cosmos. This spiritual reality (*lit. Mystery*) is in them all, and this is the unique spiritual reality of the Ineffable.

Hence the spiritual knowledge which I have declared to you, and that which I have not yet spoken to you, but all of which I shall speak, when discussing the unfolding of the cosmos, and the entire knowledge about each of them, and hence why they exist: all of this is (*the expression of*) the unique Word of the Ineffable One.

And I will explain to you the distribution (*in the cosmos*) of the Mysteries of all these spiritual realities: the types of each of these, and the manner of initiation through all their sigils.

TEXT NOTE in Chapter 96:
("the manner of initiation through all their sigils": a deeply esoteric statement. Usually,
'the manner of their completion in all their patterns (or figures/forms)'.

TEXT NOTE in Chapter 96:
But this has little meaning, as it misses the point.[316] This sentence is referring to a core secret of esoteric Christianity concerning how such an initiate could know the essence of each of the various leading beings in the spirit realms and become empowered regarding them.
This was to be done by means of drawing or visualizing an occult symbol known as a sigil. This is the core theme of the associated *Books of Jeu*.

TEXT NOTE in Chapter 96:
Initiation in the early Christian groups
As noted in the Introduction, the very idea that the early church had a secret inner section in which initiation was conducted, was totally left out of all Christian theology, as from the fourth century.

Yet the discovery of the letter from Clement of Alexandria which directly refers to Christians being initiated – in the ancient esoteric sense of the word – provides more evidence that this was the case. That is, early Christians sought and achieved an 'above-the-body' consciousness; that is, an expanded cognitional capacity beyond the body's sensory capacities, (becoming clairvoyant). They thereby encountered various deities and lesser spirits in spiritual realms.

Such initiation experiences now form the underlying basis of the rest of the text. But this is normally described as attaining to a 'mystery'; the word 'initiation' is rarely used, but this is what is meant.

Also, there is no information given as to just what these initiatory experiences were; the age-old requirement of secrecy in the Mysteries also applied here. One concludes, that those who were granted access to this codex already knew what happened in

---

[316] For here the Coptic verb (ϫⲱⲕ) normally translated as 'completing', is the equivalent of the Greek verb teleisthai (τελεῖσθαι) used for both 'completing' and for 'being initiated'.

these initiatory experiences or 'Mysteries'. It is confusing that the word 'Mystery' was also used to mean the core spirit qualities and dynamics of a deity.

TEXT: CHAPTER 96 (cont.)
And I will tell you of the Mystery of the Unique One, the Ineffable One: all its types, all its sigils and its over-all[317] arrangement. And also why it emanated from the final tone[318] of the Ineffable One, for this Mystery is that which has established all these (*types and sigils of the Ineffable One, mentioned above*).

And this Mystery of the Ineffable One (*i.e., its core spiritual reality*) is also the unique 'Word', which exists within the intonations[319] of the Ineffable One.

TEXT NOTE in Chapter 96:
"ineffable": this means 'cannot be expressed in words', it does not mean 'unknowable'.
"unique Word": a phrase of immense depth ! The spiritual core of God's being is the Word or Logos: that unique (uniquely-created) god, whose being is at one with God.
"final tone": 'final' here means the end phase of the Ineffable One (God) raying forth its creative intentions into Creation, into externalized reality. Only in the final phase, as the cosmos took shape, could this be arranged in specific configurations, and only then could this be condensed into sigils by initiates.
"Word....intonations": This is what later would be called the 'Logos', in the Prologue to the Gospel of John. These communications were probably experienced by John some decades before he set out to write his Gospel. As noted in the Introduction, this

---

[317] "over-all": lit. 'entire'.
[318] "tone"; usu. 'member' or 'limb'; the Coptic word here is taken from the Grk. 'melos' (μέλος) which means 'limb' or 'tone'.
[319] "intonations": lit. 'speech'. Deities may not always speak; they can ray forth creative intentions and cosmic wisdom in what I refer to as 'intonings'.

TEXT NOTE in Chapter 96: (cont.)
codex has been specifically crafted into a literary form, but the above phrase does appear to pre-date the Gospel.

The seed-thought of the Prologue in John's Gospel
It is especially significant to consider that, according to the codex, John was present in these sessions in which the disciples are experiencing the risen Jesus.[320] So, he was hearing this communication, proclaiming "the unique 'Word' is existing within the intonations of the Ineffable One".[321] These words are obviously closely associated with what became known as the Logos or Word in the Gospel of John. "In the Beginning was the Logos, and the Logos was inwardly with God, and the Logos was a divine being (a god)". Jn. 1:1

This Logos is the great primal Logos, who was, according to Rudolf Steiner, the creator of the zodiacal system; that is of the influences of the zodiac upon the Earth. My *Gospel of John, an Initiatory Quest Translation and Commentary*, has extensive comments on the primal Logos as distinct from the solar Logos (or 'cosmic Christ'). Included in that book is a corrected translation of a passage from Origenes about these two deities.

The next sentence is an immensely deep statement about the presence of God, or the Ineffable One, as being the primary influence subtly active in the initiate when he or she attains to a high degree of initiatory consciousness.

TEXT: CHAPTER 96 (cont.)
The spiritual being (*lit. Mystery*) of the Ineffable One has stewardship over the unveiling of the meaning of all the words which I have spoken to you (*experienced*

---

[320] As mentioned in the Introduction, I regard this John as Lazaros-John.

[321] Of course, to those scholars who view this context as pious fantasy, these words in the codex were composed many years after the Gospel of John was written, in imitation of this.

through an initiatory process).

TEXT NOTE: in Chapter 96 (cont.)
"it has stewardship over the unveiling of the meaning of all the words…"
This points to a truth affirmed by Rudolf Steiner – and other spiritual sages – which is in effect indicating that, as the human being begins to develop its (germinal) spiritual nature so that the Spiritual-self comes into existence, this is due to the Divine (God) permeating and guiding the soul, as if awakening from a slumber within a person.

This especially esoteric teaching was not seen by earlier translators, and consequently there is no agreement by them as to its meaning, and the role of the Ineffable here; hence these differing translations;
"it is the economy of the solution of the meaning of all the words" (Mead)
"it is the arrangement of the resolving of all the words (ist die Einrichtung der Auflösung aller Worte: Schmidt)
"it is the organisation of the release of all the words" (Horner)
"it is the arrangement of the explanation of every word" (McDermot)

"unveiling": the direct meaning of the Coptic verb used, (πβω) is 'resolving', 'solution' or 'release'. But here this 'resolving' is in effect, an unveiling of meaning to the initiate.

"Stewardship": the Greek word used here is 'oikonomia' (οἰκονομια) which means 'economy' in the archaic sense of the structuring and organizing of something. But today it is translated as 'administration', 'managing', etc. However, it was used by New Testament writers to mean 'stewardship', i.e., having the responsibility to care for something or someone. Hence my translation: "the Ineffable One has stewardship over the unveiling of the meaning of all the words…" (*experienced through an initiatory process).*

The next section is about existence after death
TEXT: CHAPTER 96 (cont.)
And whoever is to receive the unique Word of that Mystery, which I shall declare to you with all its types, and all its configurations, and the manner of being initiated in its Mystery – listen to me now. For you are all initiated; (*i.e., you are*) quite fully initiated[322] persons, thus you shall (now) bring to completion knowledge of all this Mystery, with its entire configuration, because to you all Mysteries are entrusted.

So now listen, while I declare to you *that* Mystery, namely: whoever shall receive the unique Word of that Mystery which I have told you, whenever that person shall come forth from the dense body (*which is produced by the influences*) of the Rulers, then receivers for the Erinyes appear, and release that person from their dense body. It is these receivers for the Erinyes who release the soul which is departing from the dense body.

But when these receivers for the Erinyes release a soul who has received the unique Mystery of the Ineffable – that Mystery which I have declared to you – it will become like a great radiant stream of light, in the midst of those Receivers.

TEXT NOTE: in Chapter 96
"Erinyes": a striking feature of this chapter, where a Greek term for spirits who take charge of normal souls after death; a Hebrew equivalent is unknown, probably non-existent. [323] The Erinyes (pronounced 'eh-rin-ee-ez') occur in Greek literature from Homer onwards, and became widely known. They appear in

---

[322] "quite fully initiated": usu. 'all-perfect" or 'all-perfection'. But the disciples are not "fully perfect' people, as this same codex shows. The Grk. term used here can mean 'completely, fully', or less absolutely, 'quite fully', as in 3 Macc. 7:16 "received (*quite*) full enjoyment of their deliverance" (παντελῆ σωτηρίας ἀπόλαυσιν...) εἰληφοτές).

[323] "Erinyes": Technically, the codex has 'Erinaioi', an unusual spelling; this may be an alternative form, in the plural dative case; it should be Erinues (Ἐρινυες).

TEXT NOTE: in Chapter 96
later Greek and Roman texts, as spirits whose task is to maintain the natural and moral order of the cosmos.[324]

So this codex is teaching that these spirits exist, and in effect, they determine the partially unpleasant context of departed souls as they journey through the Soul-world. Their task is to ensure that the after-death journey is correlated to the ethical/unethical nature of the soul; that the right corrective chastizement for unethical behaviour is encountered; that is, they act educationally, as a kind of externalized conscience upon the human soul.

This phenomenon is thus separate from the 'inherent' conscience that people know today, which was first presented, according to Rudolf Steiner, in the Hellenistic Age; in Euripides' play "Orestes" (about 400 BCE). The codex presents these spirits as the 'other side' of the personal, inherent conscience; as realities in the astral realm. (This is similar to how Pistis Sophia is the 'other side' of the incarnate persons potential for intuitive consciousness.)

The Erinyes ensure that the unethical soul qualities in the deceased person result in that soul being subject to the power of the debased Rulers (Archons); this is in short, the requirements of karma, and is determined in Heimarmene.

TEXT: CHAPTER 96 (cont.)
Then those receivers shall be very afraid of the light of that (initiated) soul; those receivers shall become disempowered and sink down, and desist (from their actions) altogether, from fear of the intense light they have seen.

And the soul which has received the Mystery of the Ineffable One, shall soar up into the Heights, becoming (as it were) a great radiant stream of light. And the receivers shall not be able to take hold of it, nor will they know of the path which it takes, for it has become a radiant light-stream, and is soaring into

---

[324] Liddell and Scott, *Greek-English Lexicon*, entry, "Ερινός".

TEXT: CHAPTER 96 (cont.)

the Heights. No entity shall be able to restrain it at all in any way, nor be able to come near to it.

Instead, this soul shall pass through all the realms of the (holy) Rulers and all the realms of the emanations of the Light. It shall give no explanation in any realm, nor make any defence, nor any secret sigils; neither indeed shall any entity of the (holy) Rulers be able to approach that soul.

Nor shall any entity from the emanations of the Light be able to approach that soul; instead all the realms of the Rulers and all the realms of the emanations of the Light shall intone praise, each in their (respective) places[325], from reverence[326] of the radiant light-stream which envelops that soul.

(This shall happen) whilst the soul passes through all of these, until it enters into the inheritance of the Mystery which it has received. That is, into the Mystery of the Only One, the Ineffable One – and has united with its intonings.[327] Truly, I say to you that it shall be in all the realms, in the time a man needs to shoot an arrow.

TEXT NOTE: within Chapter 96

("united with its intonings": that is, the intonings of God or the First Mystery. Usually the Greek word here (melos – μέλος) is understood to mean 'limbs' or 'members'; but this is very unlikely here. For 'melos' also means 'tone'; and thus is pointing to the tones or 'intonings' pervading the cosmos, which, together, *are* in effect, God.

In the next section, the intention of the Saviour is to show that an acolyte in the esoteric schooling who achieves a high degree of initiation, although a human person in the world, and therefore belongs to a quite different rank of being than the various ranks of deities, will nevertheless be affirmed by all these

---

[325] "places": lit. 'realms' which is inconsistent; a scribal error.
[326] "from reverence': usu. 'from fear' which is not consistent.
[327] "intonings": usu. 'limbs' or 'members'; see Text Note.

deities.)

TEXT: CHAPTER 96 (cont.)
So now, truly, I say to you that every person (*i.e., acolyte*) who shall attain that Mystery of the Ineffable, and accomplish all of its types and sigils, is a person in the world. That person is certainly different[328] to the Angels; and yet that initiate[329] shall be greatly praised by them. That initiate is a person in the world; certainly different to the Archangels, and yet that initiate shall be greatly praised by them.

TEXT NOTE:
(Each sentence now starts with "He is a man in the world", but, by this is meant an initiated acolyte, whether man or woman. So it is better understood as, "That initiate is a person in the world...")

TEXT: CHAPTER 96 (cont.)
That initiate is a person in the world; certainly different to all the empowered Ones[330], and yet that initiate shall be praised by them.
That initiate is a person in the world; certainly different to all the Lords, and yet that initiate shall be praised by them.
That initiate is a person in the world; certainly different to all the Gods, and yet that initiate shall be praised by them.
That initiate is a person in the world; certainly different to all the Luminaries[331], and yet that initiate shall be praised by them.
That initiate is a person in the world; certainly

---

[328] "certainly different:" usu. "but is superior to ..." see Commentary for more about this.
[329] The second part of each of these sentences simply has 'he': it does not have the word 'initiate'; but I have replaced 'he' with 'initiate' to avoid an unintended apparent sexism and to make clear that an initiated acolyte is actually meant.
[330] "empowered Ones": lit. in Greek, 'Tyrants'.
[331] "Luminaries': i.e., 'Light-givers' or the deities of the stars and planets.

TEXT: CHAPTER 96 (cont.)

different to all the Pure Ones, and yet that initiate shall be praised by them.

That initiate is a person in the world; certainly different to all the Triune-spirits, and yet that initiate shall be praised by them.

That initiate is a person in the world; certainly different to all the Primal Father-spirits, and yet that initiate shall be praised by them.

That initiate is a person in the world; certainly different to all the Invisible Ones, and yet that initiate shall be praised by them.

That initiate is a person in the world; certainly different to the great Invisible Primal-father, and yet that initiate shall be praised by him.

That initiate is a person in the world; certainly different to all those of the Midst, and yet that initiate shall be praised by them.

That initiate is a person in the world; certainly different to all the emanations of the Treasury of Light, and yet that initiate shall be praised by them.

That initiate is a person in the world; certainly different to the Mixture, and thus that initiate shall be entirely elevated over it.

That initiate is a person in the world; certainly different to the entire realm of the Treasury of Light, and yet that initiate shall be praised by it.

TEXT NOTE in Chapter 96

"that initiate is *certainly different* to ... and yet that initiate shall *be praised by*....".

Here my translation varies greatly from all previous ones as regards these repeated phrases. These are usually,

"he is *superior* to...and will be *exalted over* them..".

But firstly, although the Coptic word (ⲟⲩⲟⲧ) does mean 'superior', a very similar word (ⲟⲩⲱⲧ) means 'to be different, to vary'.[332] I conclude that again some

---

[332] Technically, ⲟⲩⲱⲧ does in fact mean 'different' in the related Bohairic Coptic dialect, especially when it is followed by a preposition, as in these sentences, as ⲟⲩⲟⲧ is

TEXT NOTE in Chapter 96

confusion has occurred with the scribe; this is quite likely, because although ⲟⲩⲟⲧ ('superior') seems quite unlike ⲟⲩⲱⲧ ('different'), it isn't. For the 'ⲱ' is simply 'ⲟ' in a more intense form; it is the same vowel. And it is this latter word (ⲟⲩⲱⲧ – 'different') which is meant (except in one or two instances). For 'superior' (ⲟⲩⲱⲧ) cannot be correct here, because a highly spiritual person remains a human being. A human being cannot be raised up many cosmic levels to become higher than an Archangel or a Principality or a Seraphim, etc.

That the scribe has used a word which is slightly different to the correct word is the same kind of mistake he made earlier, with 'power' and 'soul'. As noted in the Introduction, the Coptic word ϭⲟⲙ means 'power', or 'strength', but not 'being', that word is ϭⲓⲛ. But 'ϭⲓⲛ' can also be spelt ϭⲓⲙ. Whereas ϭⲟⲙ can also be spelt ϭⲉⲙ.

This fluid situation would have confused the scribe, who apparently identified ϭⲓⲙ ('being') with ϭⲉⲙ ('power'). In that case, he used one of these two very similar words for *both* meanings; although the second, less intended meaning ('power) is only meant a couple of times.

Likewise, here in Chapter 96, he wrongly uses one word for two meanings, although the second, less intended, meaning ('superior') is also only meant a couple of times. (We note that there are about 250 errors in the Coptic text.)

But the initiate, although approaching now the spirituality of an Angel, is still not an Angel; for these spirits are a cosmic evolutionary level above us. So it is even less thinkable for an initiate to become a much higher deity.

"and that initiate will be praised by them": usually 'will be elevated over them'. The Coptic word here

---

(by ⲉ). This would have further confused the scribe about the two words.

(ⲭⲓⲥⲉ) means either 'to elevate/exalt' or 'to honour/praise'.[333]

TEXT: CHAPTER 96 (cont.)
That initiate is a person in the world; but that person shall become a ruler with me in my kingdom.
That initiate is a person in the world; but that person is a ruler in the Light.
That initiate is a person in the world; but that person is not of this world.
And, truly, I say to you:
    that initiate is I – and I am that initiate.

TEXT NOTE: in Chapter 96
An immensely significant and sacred declaration. These words from the cosmic Christ are also discernible in the Gospel of John, when read from an initiatory perspective. The following three samples from this Gospel are teaching the same truths as in Chapter 96 of the Pistis Sophia codex. The first extract is from the episode of the 'walking on water'; that is, disciples entering into the Soul-world, and trying to experience the Christ within.
All three extracts are taken from my translation,[334] this extract is from my second version of these verses, in which some commentary has been placed;

6:19 However, having moved deep into this realm, they perceive the spirit of Jesus is there, away in the distance, and yet as if near to the soul boat, and so they were afraid.
6:20 But he declares, "I am the I (in you); do not have fear."
6:21 They were thus willing to receive him into their soul boat, and their soul immediately reached that

---

[333] Technically, the preposition, "praised *by* them' (ⲉⲣⲟⲟⲩ) has many uses, including a dative nuance, as in chapt.59 "these which were seen *by* the emanations of the Self-willed One; and chapt. 107, 'no Mystery can hear *from* them", etc.

[334] *The Gospel of John, an Initiatory Quest translation and Commentary*, Threshold Publishing, 2022.

TEXT NOTE: in Chapter 96
secure sense of 'I' towards which they were striving.

This next extract from chapter 8 is deeply esoteric and concerns the after-life;
8:23 So then he said to them, "You are from below, but I am from above; you are of this world, but not of this world am I.
8:24 "For this reason I said to you, that you will die away in your sins, for if you do not inwardly discern that *I am the 'I am'* – then you will die away in your sins."
Then, in v. 8:28 the Christ, through Jesus, says,

"Whenever you have exalted the Son of Man, then you will know that **I am the 'I'** {in you}; and so {you will know} "from myself I do nothing, but only as the Father taught me".[335]

TEXT: CHAPTER 96 (cont.)
And so, at the dissolution of the world, which is when the All ascends, and thus when the (full) number of perfected souls will ascend together, I shall become ruler. I shall be ruler in the midst of the last Helper, and thus ruler over all the Light-emanations, ruler over the seven Amens, the five Trees, the three Amens, and the nine Guardians, ruler over the Child of the Child, that is, the Twin Saviours.

And ruler over the 12 saviours and the entire number of perfected souls who shall have received the Mystery in the Light. Then, all those souls who have received the mystery-experience of the Ineffable One, shall become fellow-rulers with me; they shall be seated on my right hand, and on my left, in my kingdom.

Truly, I say to you, those souls are I, and I am those souls.

---

[335] The substantial differences here from the usual versions are based on a close reading of Papyrus #75, and is explained in an Appendix in that book.

TEXT NOTE: Chapter 96
(Most of the spirit entities mentioned above remain an enigma, for very little, if anything, is said about them.)

TEXT: CHAPTER 96 (cont.)
This is why I said to you in earlier times, "You shall be seated on your thrones, on my right hand and on my left in my kingdom, and you shall reign with me." So for this reason I have not hesitated, nor have I been ashamed, to call you brethren and friends, for you shall be fellow rulers with me in my kingdom. These things, then, I said to you, knowing that I would give to you the Mystery of that Ineffable One: namely,

that this Mystery *is* myself, and I am that Mystery.

Now, therefore, not only shall you reign with me in that kingdom, but all souls who receive that Mystery shall be fellow rulers with me in my kingdom. And I am they, and they are myself; but my throne (*i.e., my empowerment*) shall be exalted above theirs. And because you shall suffer afflictions in this world beyond all people, until you have preached all the words which I shall speak to you, in my kingdom, your thrones (*empowerment*) shall be joined to mine.

Therefore I said to you earlier, "In the place where I shall be, there will be also with me my twelve helpers"; but Mariam the Magdalene and John the virgin,[336] shall be higher than all the disciples, and all those people who shall receive the Mystery of that Ineffable. These two shall be on my left hand and on my right, and I am they: and they are myself.

They shall be your equals in all things, except (*since you are my disciples*) your thrones (*empowerment*) shall be more excellent than those others. My throne (*empowerment*) shall be of a higher nature than yours and of those (other) souls who shall find the Word of the Ineffable One.

---

[336] "the virgin": as noted earlier, this means he has attained to his Spiritual-self, whose origins are not of the Earth.

TEXT: CHAPTER 96 (cont.)

Truly, I say to you, the person who shall know this Word, shall understand the spiritual wisdom within all these words which I have spoken to you. (This they shall acquire) both with regard to depths and height, with regard to length and breadth. In short, they shall possess the spiritual wisdom within all the words which I have said to you. And the spiritual wisdom also of those which I have not spoken to you; but these I will declare to you, according to their realm and their rank, as set out when the cosmos came into existence.

Truly, I say to you, they shall know how the cosmos was established, and they shall know what type (of spirits) are all those of the Heights; and they shall know why the cosmos came into existence.

COMMENTARY: CHAPTER 96

"seated on your thrones": The word 'throne' is a symbol of spiritual authority in Biblical literature; hence it is also sometimes used as a metaphor directly for spiritual sovereignty or empowerment; this occurs in passages where a throne is not meant, even as a symbol.

"Mariam the Magdalene and John the virgin": we learn that John and Mariam Magdalene are two highest-ranking initiated disciples of Christ.

A woman called quite specifically, "Mariam *the Magdalene*" is first mentioned in Luke's Gospel. In my *The Gospel of John*, I have endeavoured to demonstrate that this title is very significant, because it is an initiatory epithet; it is not referring to a possible home-town of this woman.

It is discreetly alluding to this Mariam as having the task of developing a consciousness which towers up beyond the physical, into the realm of the Dead. In the above book, I note that some scholars have concluded that 'Mariam the Magdalene' is the same woman as Mariam of Bethany – she who is the sister of John. This would mean that references to Mariam the Magdalene are to Mariam of Bethany. This is possible, but what is the reality here, remains unclear.

COMMENTARY: CHAPTER 96
One venue for these sacred spiritual 'communications' was possibly the house in the village of Bethany, belonging to John, Martha and Mariam. For this reason, as noted earlier, I conclude that the 'Mariam' who put questions to Jesus, (in chapters 43-63), was Mariam of Bethany, rather than Mariam the Magdalene (assuming they are two persons). In chapter 61, Christ says of this woman, "Mariam, you blessed one, who shall inhabit every kingdom of light", these words can certainly be applied to Mariam of Bethany.

TEXT: CHAPTER 97
And when the Saviour had said these things, Mariam the Magdalene came forward and said, "Lord, be not displeased with me, if I question on all things with precision and certainty. Now, my Lord, is the word of the Mystery of the Ineffable one thing, and the word of the knowledge of the entire cosmos another thing?"

The Saviour answered and said, "Yes, the Word of the Mystery of the Ineffable is one thing, and the Word of the knowledge of the entire cosmos is another thing." Then Mariam (*the Magdalene*) responded again and said to the Saviour, "Lord, be patient with me if I question you, and be not displeased with me. Now, Lord, unless we live and attain knowledge of the spiritual wisdom of the entire word of the Ineffable One, we will not be able to inherit the light-kingdom ?"

The Saviour responded and said to Mariam (*the Magdalene*), "That is so, for everyone who receives a Mystery of the light-kingdom will go forth and inherit (spiritual light), up to the realm in which they have received Mysteries (whilst incarnate).

But that person will not know the spiritual wisdom concerning the All, the entire cosmos. That is, such person will not know why all of this came into existence, unless they have (already) come to know the unique 'Word' of the Ineffable One: this unique

TEXT: CHAPTER 97 (cont.)
Word, which is the spiritual wisdom of the entire cosmos; (and exists within the intonations of the Ineffable One.[337])

Again (I declare) clearly:

I am the spiritual wisdom of the entire cosmos.

Moreover, it is impossible to experience[338] this unique Word of spiritual wisdom (*of God, the Ineffable One*), unless one receives the primal Mystery of that Ineffable One.[339]

TEXT NOTE in Chapter 97:
(The initiate has to receive the primal Mystery, i.e., the core spiritual wisdom, of God (the Ineffable One) to be able to experience the unique Word of spiritual wisdom. The two things are practically the same reality: the Word being the perceptible manifestation of God. In experiential terms, until the initiate has been granted some understanding of the core spiritual-being (*the Mystery*) of God, that initiate can not experience the great cosmic intonations of God.

This is indicated in Chapter 96, "this Mystery of the Ineffable One (*i.e., its core spiritual reality*) is also the unique 'Word', which exists within the intonations of this Ineffable One.")

TEXT: CHAPTER 97 (cont.)
But (even so) every person who shall receive Mysteries in the Light, will go forth and inherit (the Light) up to the realm in which they have received mystery-experiences[340] of the Light (*whilst incarnate*).
Therefore I said to you earlier, 'He that believes in a prophet, shall receive a prophet's reward, and he that

---

[337] As this was described earlier, in Chapter 96.
[338] "experience": lit. 'know'.
[339] The Coptic is ambiguous here; it may be "unless one first receives the Mystery of the Ineffable One".
[340] lit. 'Mysteries'.

TEXT: CHAPTER 97 (cont.)

believes in a just man, shall receive a just man's reward.' That person shall enter into the realm of which they have received its Mystery. Whoever receives a lesser Mystery, shall inherit a lower realm; and whoever receives a higher Mystery, shall inherit the realm of the Heights.

And each shall dwell in their place in the light of my kingdom; each shall have power over the lower ranks (of beings), but he or she will not have power to enter into the higher ranks.

That person shall remain in that realm to inherit the Light of my kingdom; in sublime light for which there is no measure, among the gods and the Invisibles. That person shall be in great joy and great gladness.

TEXT NOTE: This next section:

is about those who are initiated to various high levels, by having a mystery-experience of God – the First Mystery that gazes within. There are 12 levels of such divine mystery-experiences; and these give access to the sublime Buddhi realms (Aions 15 to 17).

TEXT: CHAPTER 97 (cont.)

Now listen, for I wish to speak with you concerning the glory of those who receive the mystery-experience (*lit. Mystery*) of the First Mystery. So regarding that person who receives the mystery-experience of the First Mystery, when the time comes for them to leave their body of matter, which is derived from the Archons, then the receivers for the Erinyes appear, and bring the soul of that person out of their body.

But *that* (*initiated*) person shall become as a great stream of light among the Erinyes, and so they shall have fear in the presence of that soul. Thus, that soul shall ascend (*unhindered*), passing through all the realms of the Rulers, and all the places of the

TEXT: CHAPTER 97 (cont.)
emanations of the light (*of those realms*).[341]

This soul shall not give an answer, nor a defence, nor a secret sign, in any place of the light nor in any place of the Rulers. Instead it shall journey across
and pass through all the realms, thus it shall proceed; and have mastery over[342] all the realms of the first Saviour.

TEXT NOTE in Chapter 97
("no answer, defence or secret sign": an especially veiled esoteric theme; that the soul on its after-life journey needs awareness of certain dynamics and spirit realities in each of the astral and devachanic realms. These it acquires through becoming ever more purified; also there are 'Guardians' of each realm who require one of more of the above three responses. But the holy, initiated soul is fortunate, it already has acquired these before death.)

TEXT: CHAPTER 97 (cont.)
But when the time comes to leave the body of matter, derived from the Rulers, for any person who receives the second mystery-experience of the First Mystery, together with the third and the fourth, until they reach the 12th mystery-experience, the receivers for the Erinyes appear, and they bring this soul out of their body of matter derived from the Rulers.

Then those souls shall become a great light-stream amongst the receivers for the Erinyes, who will thus be afraid of the light and shrink away (*lit. fall down on their faces*). And those souls shall straightway enter into the Heights, that they may be carried above all the places of the Rulers and all the places of the light-emanations (*of their realms*); they shall give

---

[341] "the light: the astral light of the debased Rulers in those realms, who enforce the punitive results of unethical actions upon the soul.

[342] "have mastery": usu. 'rule over', which seems unlikely; for the verb here also means to have authority or be empowered.

TEXT: CHAPTER 97 (cont.)
neither answer, nor defence, in any place whatever, nor any secret sign, instead they shall pass through all the realms. And they shall be empowered in all the places of the 12 saviours.

And thus those who have received the second mystery-experience of the first Mystery (*together with the third and the fourth, up to the 12th mystery-experience*), shall be empowered in all the realms of the second saviour in The Inheritance of the Light.

TEXT NOTE: in Chapter 97
(Each of the 12 mystery-experiences of the First Mystery has its own leading spirit (or saviour). So when attaining to the 3rd mystery-experience, for example, the initiate is guided by the saviour of that experience.)

TEXT: CHAPTER 97 (cont.)
In similar manner also, those who have received the third mystery-experience of the First Mystery, and also the fourth, the fifth, the sixth, up to the twelfth, these shall be empowered in all the places of the saviour, as far as that person has received that initiatory experience (*lit. Mystery*).

And that person who shall have received in sequence (*after the previous eleven initiatory experiences*) the twelfth mystery-experience of the First Mystery – that is to say, the most empowering mystery-experience, (of the First Mystery) concerning which I will speak with you – that person then, who will have received those 12 initiatory experiences which pertain to the First Mystery, when they depart from the world, they shall pass as a mighty light-stream through all the realms of the Rulers and all the places of the light (*of their places*). That person shall also be empowered in all the realms of the 12 saviours.

But these souls even so, will not be equal to that soul who receives the unique (*peerless*) Mystery of the Ineffable. Yet the person who receives that unique mystery-experience shall remain in those ranks

TEXT: CHAPTER 97 (cont.)
(*mentioned above*), because they are (*in fact*) exalted ranks; thus such a person will remain within the ranks of the 12 saviours (*in the Inheritance of the Light*).

COMMENTARY: CHAPTER 97
There is regrettably, no information given to the reader about the 12 initiatory experiences. But later the 12 saviours are identified as important deities in The Inheritance of the Light.

TEXT: CHAPTER 98   Mariam speaks
It then happened, when Jesus had finished speaking these words to his disciples, that Mariam the Magdalene came forward, and made obeisance at the feet of Jesus, "Lord, tolerate me and be not displeased with me, if I question you; but have mercy upon us, Lord, and unveil to us the matter on which we shall question you. So now, Lord, how is it that the First Mystery has twelve mystery-experiences, whereas that Ineffable One has but one Mystery? Jesus answered and said to her, "Indeed, the Ineffable One has but one Mystery, however it encompasses three Mysteries; and each of these three is of a different type.

But furthermore, that one Mystery (*of the Ineffable One*), encompasses five mystery-experiences, while still remaining one. And the type of each of these five is different, but these five Mysteries are equal to one another in the Mystery of the kingdom of The Inheritance of Light.

Yet the type of each of these five is different, and their realm is higher and more elevated than the entire realm of the 12 mystery-experiences of the First Mystery. Thus, in the kingdom of Light they are not similar to the First Mystery.

In like manner, also, the three Mysteries (*of the Ineffable One*) are not similar in the kingdom of Light, for the type of each of them is different. And in the kingdom of Light they also are not similar to the First

TEXT: CHAPTER 98 (cont.)

Mystery[343]. Furthermore, the type of each one of these three, and the type of the configuration of each one, is different from one another.

If you fully accomplish the mystery-experience of the First Mystery – i.e., persist[344] and accomplish it very well in all of its sigils – then, (*at your death*), you will come out of your body immediately, and become (*as*) a great ray of light, and pass through all the realms of the Rulers and all the (*associated*) places of the light, whilst all the Rulers are in fear of that soul, until it reaches the place of its empowerment.[345]

A section about the initiated helping the Dying
TEXT: CHAPTER 98 (cont.)

(Now regarding) the second mystery-experience of the First Mystery – if you complete this very well in all of its sigils: a person who does so complete this initiatory experience, may speak *that* over the head of anyone who is departing from their body, that is, he may declare it into both ears.

Then the deceased person who is on the point of departure (*and who was also initiated earlier*) has thereby received the mystery-experience for a second time; thus he becomes a partaker in the word of truth. Truly, I say to you, when that person departs from the body of matter, their soul shall become a great ray of light; it shall pass through every realm until it has come into the realm of that Mystery.

However, if a (dying) person has not received mysteries (earlier) – and thereby was not a partaker in the word of truth – but if someone who is initiated[346] speaks *that* mystery-experience[347] above the head of a person who is departing from the body – someone

---

[343] "to the First Mystery": codex has an erroneous repeat "of the First Mystery, of the First Mystery…"

[344] "endure": usu. 'stand' which is irrelevant; the verb here (ⲁϩⲉⲣⲁⲧ) also means 'to persist', or to endure.

[345] "empowerment": lit. 'kingdom'.

[346] "in initiated": lit. 'has completed the Mystery'.

[347] That is, the "second mystery-experience of the First Mystery".

TEXT: CHAPTER 98 (cont.)

who in life received no Mystery, thus is not sharing in the word of truth – then truly, I say to you, that person, when they depart from that body, will not be judged in any realm of the Rulers.

Nor shall that person be chastised in any realm at all, nor shall the fire touch them, because of the great Mystery of the Ineffable which is in him. Truly, I say to you, that this person shall become as a great ray of light.

So I say to you regarding that person who has not received a Mystery, and is not a partaker of the word of life – when someone who completes *that* mystery-experience, speaks that over the head of the person who is departing from the body and who has not received a Mystery, and is not sharing in the word of truth (*there will be a blessed outcome.*)

Truly I say to you, when that person comes forth from the body, they shall not be judged in any place of the Rulers, nor will they be chastised in any place, nor shall the fire touch them, as the result of the great Mystery of the Ineffable One which is with them.

It shall be speedily brought about that the spirits shall quickly hasten, and conduct him along (from place to place) and from rank to rank (of beings) until he is brought into the presence of[348] the Holy Goddess of the Light. Meanwhile, all (the spirits in the) realms are in fear of the Mystery and the sign of the kingdom of the Ineffable One which is with him.

So when he is brought before the Holy Goddess of the Light, this Holy Goddess of Light shall perceive the Mystery and the sign of the kingdom of the Ineffable One which is with him. The Holy Goddess of the Light shall marvel at this, and she shall then assess him. But she shall not allow the spirits to bring him to the Light until he has harmonized his soul's nature with the light of that Mystery. That is (*the soul-state achieved by*) the purifications associated with renunciation of the world, and also of all the matter

---

[348] "into the presence of": the text simply has, 'before'.

TEXT: CHAPTER 98 (cont.)

which is in it.

Then the Holy Goddess of the Light seals him with a higher seal, (the result of) which is this: in whatever month he came out of his material body at death, she allows him to be cast back down (*i.e., be reincarnated*) into a (material) body in that same month[349] (*in his next life*); and into a body which will be undefiled.[350]

Thus he may find (*with his consciousness unhindered by a sluggish body*) the true Godhead and the higher Mysteries, so that he may inherit these and the Light eternal. This is the gift of the second mystery-experience of the Mystery of the Ineffable One.

Furthermore, regarding the third mystery-experience of the First Mystery:[351] that person who does complete that mystery-experience, shall not only inherit the realm of that Mystery when they come forth from their body. But also, when they perform the Mystery and accomplishes it with all of its sigils - that is, when that person carries out that initiatory experience, and very finely accomplishes it - they can help a person who is dying.

This person can invoke that Mystery over a person who is coming out of their body, someone who has not known that (*or any*) mystery-experience[352] - whether because that person has delayed entering, or has just never entered[353] (*the initiatory quest*). Then I say to you, regarding this person who has come out of his body - someone who (is then placed) in the severe chastizements of the Rulers, that is, in their harsh judgments and in their fires. I say that if the name of this mystery is pronounced on his behalf,

---

[349] "same month": hence one is reborn in the same zodiac sign, see Commentary.

[350] "undefiled": or 'righteous' or 'good (morally)'.

[351] "First Mystery": Coptic erroneously has 'the Ineffable One'.

[352] "has *not* known that mystery-experience": usu. '*has* known'; but this is illogical, the Coptic has omitted 'not'.

[353] "just never entered" : lit. 'he has not delayed' i.e., not bothered to be involved.

TEXT: CHAPTER 98 (cont.)
they (*i.e., the spirits who supervise the after-death journey of the soul*) will hasten quickly to remove him, handing him over to one another, until he is brought before the Holy Goddess of the Light.

(End of section about helping the Dying)

COMMENTARY in Chapter 98:
We learn that an initiated Christian can assist the dying in their after-life journey by invoking that mystery over them.
A: an initiate of the **second mystery-experience** of the First Mystery can do this:
   1: for **an initiated soul**
Their soul becomes as a great ray of light; it shall pass through every realm until it has come into the realm of that Mystery (in upper Devachan)

2: for **a non-initiated but spiritual soul**
We learn that this person, when they depart from that body, will not be judged[354] in any realm of the Rulers. Nor shall that person be chastised in any realm at all, nor shall the fire touch them.....They will not be chastized in any place, nor shall the fire touch them, as the result of the great Mystery of the Ineffable One which is with them. But the Holy Goddess of Light shall still not allow that soul to have access to the upper Devachanic realms of light.

We then learn that an initiate of the **third mystery-experience** of the First Mystery can do this for: another person who has **not** attained to any mystery-experience – and who is in the harsh judgments and in the fires of the Rulers…if the name of this mystery is pronounced on his behalf, the spirits who supervise the after-death journey of the soul will hasten quickly to remove him, handing him over to one another, until he is brought before the Holy Goddess of the Light.

---

[354] "judged": that is, spiritually assessed to determine the next part of the journey.

TEXT: CHAPTER 98 (cont.)

So now, everyone who shall receive one of the five Mysteries of the Ineffable One, when that person comes forth from the body, they shall inherit (*a spirituality*) up to the realm of the (*associated*) mystery-experience. Now, the realm of those five mystery-experiences (of the Ineffable One) is higher than the realm of the 12 mystery-experiences of the First Mystery, and is superior to all the Mysteries below them.

Yet the mystery-experiences of the (group of) five Mysteries of the Ineffable One are equal to one another in their own realm, but they are not as high as the (group of) the three Mysteries of that Ineffable One.

And whoever receives one of the mystery-experiences in the (group of) three Mysteries of that Ineffable One: that person, on departing from the body, shall inherit up to the realm of that (*associated*) mystery-experience. And these three Mysteries are equal to one another in the kingdom, and are higher than the (group of) five Mysteries of the Ineffable One in the kingdom. So, (although) more exalted than the five Mysteries, they are not as high as the unique (peerless) Mystery of that Ineffable One.

TEXT NOTE: in Chapter 98
Clarifying the Ineffable One and the First Mystery

1: at the highest level in the Divine order is:
 The Ineffable One, who is higher than the First Mystery
 It has **one** peerless (i.e., unequalled) Mystery – but this can also be viewed as consisting of three 'mystery-experiences'   and yet also as five 'mystery-experiences'

The 3 are of a higher nature than the group of 5.

TEXT NOTE: in Chapter 98
And yet although these groups of 3 or 5 make up the One peerless Mystery, each of these eight are somehow less exalted than the unique Mystery.

TEXT NOTE: in Chapter 98
 So, the complete, unified and inherently integrated Mystery, is greater in spiritual power and glory than the separated-out sum of its eight parts.
 Then just below the Ineffable One is:
The First Mystery (usually understood to be God)
  It has 12 mystery-experiences
  It also has 12 saviours; one for each of the 12 mystery-experiences)

TEXT: CHAPTER 98 (cont.)
Whoever receives also the one (*peerless*) Mystery of that Ineffable One, shall inherit the place of the whole kingdom according to its glory, of which I have already spoken unto you on another occasion.

A person may also receive the Mystery which pervades[355] the entire Realm of that Ineffable One, and also all the other Mysteries which are united within the intonings of that Ineffable one. Of these I have not yet spoken to you, concerning both their distribution (when the cosmos came into existence), and the manner in which they were arranged, and the type of each of them.

I have not told you why it is called the Ineffable One, nor why it is extending out with all its parts, or how many parts there are therein, or its over-all structuring. I shall not speak of this now, but when I am speaking about the extent and structuring of the cosmos, I shall tell you of these, one by one. That is, of its extent and a description of how it is, and the integration of all its parts which belong to the stewardship of the Only One, the true unapproachable God.

Therefore within the realm of that Ineffable One, each shall receive his or her mystery-experience, as far as that realm in which they did receive this (whilst on the Earth). So, they shall inherit this, there in the realm of that Ineffable One. And those souls in the entire realm of that Ineffable One, do not give

---

[355] "pervades the": the text simply has lit. 'is *in* the entire space'.

TEXT: CHAPTER 98 (cont.)

answers nor defence, nor sigils; for such (*initiated*) souls are without sigils and have no receivers (*spirits who take charge of them*). Instead they shall pass through all the realms until they arrive at the region of the realm of the Mystery which they have received.

In like manner also, they who shall receive the mystery-experience of the second place, they need have neither answers, nor defence. Thus they have no sigils in that world; it is the place of the first mystery-experience of the First Mystery.

But those of the third Realm, of the exterior, that is to say, the third Realm (reckoning) from without: in that place it is so that every realm has its receivers, and its answers, its apologies, and its sigils.

I shall tell you of these in the future, when I tell you about that Mystery; when I have told you about how the cosmos came into existence.[356] However, at the dissolution of the cosmos, which shall happen when the number of perfected souls is complete and the spiritual intention (*lit. Mystery*) through which the cosmos came into existence, has been fulfilled, I will spend a thousand years, according to the years of the Light, as ruler of the emanations of the Light, and over the entire number of the perfected souls – those who have received all of the Mysteries.

COMMENTARY: CHAPTER 98

"harmonized his soul's nature with.." a difficult Coptic text, which is lit. 'until he has completed all the duties (or way of life/conduct) of the Light'.[357]

"undefiled": this is not meant in an absolute sense; the Greek word used here dikaios (δίκαιος) means:

---

[356] "the cosmos": this is not the modern scientific multi-galaxy universe, but just what it encompassed is not stated.

[357] Other versions: "completed the total citizenship of the Light" Mead)/ "has completed the way of life of the Light"(Schmidt) / "completes the whole life-course of the Light"(MacDermot) / "completes all the duties of the Light" (Horner).

COMMENTARY: CHAPTER 98 (cont.)

good, righteous, or just. An identical view is found in The Apocrypha (*the Wisdom of Solomon* (8:20); the writer speaks of himself as a soul who had been pre-existing. He is thereby implying a past life which produced a good karma for this life with regards to his physical body,

"As a child I was born to excellence, and (so) a noble soul fell to my lot; or rather, I myself was noble and therefore I entered (*again*) into an undefiled[358] body..."

The concept of reincarnation had been accepted amongst mainstream Hebrew sages for a long time, but kept discreetly in the background; however in Josephus it comes to the fore. In his treatise of about CE 94, *Against Apion*, (2.218), Josephus writes about the fate of souls after death, because of the wars and civil commotion causing many causalities at the time. He states that if a person dies through noble actions then,

"...the soul comes into earthly being again (*reincarnates*), at the completed (*cosmic*) cycle, to then receive a better earthly life.[359]

"in that same month": this means that the person shall very probably, but not always, have the same zodiac sign in their next incarnation. Or it could mean that a very similar grouping generally, of cosmic influences will be operative at the next birth. Either of these options was obviously viewed as helpful to the person's journey towards ever more insight into the significance of such cosmic influences.

In this next section: that is Chapter 99, the final outcomes for souls, in the divine realms, when the Earth is no more, are presented.

---

[358] "undefiled": in Grk. 'amianton' (ἀμίαντον) which means undefiled or righteous.

[359] The Greek ...γενέσθαι τε πάλιν καὶ βίον ἀμείνω λαβεῖν ἐκ περιτροπῆς. "at the completed cycle": literally, 'out of the turning-point', (or turning around, or circuit). Translated by Whiston as, "at a 'certain revolution of things'..."

TEXT NOTE: for Chapter 99   (cont.)
This next section involves realms and areas of realms, depending upon the level of initiation (i.e., 'receiving of a mystery') which a soul has attained. It is an obscure section, because we have no information about these various realms and their Mysteries.

TEXT: CHAPTER 99
It then happened when Jesus had finished speaking these words to his disciples, that Mariam the Magdalene came forward and said, "Lord, how many years is a year of the Light, in years of the (physical) world?

Jesus answered and said to Mary "A day of the Light is a thousand years in the world, so 365,000 years of the world make one single year of Light. So I shall be reigning for 1,000 years of the Light amidst the last Helpers, and over all the emanations of the Light, and over the total number of perfected souls[360] who have received the Mysteries of the Light.

And you, my disciples, and all those who have received the Mystery of the Ineffable One, shall remain with me, on my right hand, and on my left; ruling with me in my kingdom.

And they also who shall receive the three mystery-experiences[361] of the Ineffable One, shall be fellow rulers with you, in the kingdom of Light. But they shall not be equal with you, nor with those who have received the one (*peerless*) Mystery of the Ineffable One; instead they shall remain behind you, and yet shall be rulers.

And those who shall receive the five mystery-experiences of that Ineffable One, shall abide behind those of the three mystery-experiences, and yet shall be rulers. Whereas they who shall receive the twelve[362]

---

[360] "perfected souls": i.e., souls who have conquered their unspiritual qualities.
[361] The codex erroneously includes here "of the five Mysteries".
[362] "twelve": the codex has 'the twelfth'; it is unclear which is meant.

TEXT: CHAPTER 99 (cont.)

mystery-experiences of the First Mystery, shall also abide behind those of the five Mysteries of the Ineffable One, and they shall be rulers also, according to the rank of each one of them.

And they who have received the Mystery in all the places of the realm of the Ineffable One, shall also be rulers, but they shall abide ahead[363] of those who have received the mystery-experience of the First Mystery, distributed according to the glory of each of them.

Thus they who have received a higher mystery-experience, shall be in the higher realms, and they who have received a lesser mystery-experience shall be in lower realms – these both shall be as rulers in my kingdom of Light. It is these alone to whom is assigned the kingdom of the first Realm of the Ineffable One.

Those also who have received all the mystery-experiences of the second Realm, which is the realm of the First Mystery, shall also remain in the Light of my kingdom, distributed according to the glory of each of them. Each of these shall be in the area of that Mystery which they had received (*whilst alive*).

Thus they who shall have received a higher mystery, will be in the higher realms, and they who shall have received a lower mystery, will be in the lower realms in my kingdom of Light. This is the inheritance of the kingdom of the second Realm of the Ineffable One.

In addition, those who receive all the mystery-experiences of the third[364] Realm, that is of the first Realm (reckoning) from without, those again will abide behind the third ruler, distributed throughout the Light of my kingdom, according to the glory of

---

[363] "ahead of"; most versions have 'remain behind', but this is illogical, Mead has seen this and has 'abide with'. An error in the Coptic here: the incorrect use of the preposition (ⲛⲥⲁ) which means 'behind', perhaps because it can mean 'ahead' with the verb (ⲥⲱⲕ).

[364] "third Realm": codex has 'second Realm; but logically the third Realm is meant, as Mead also concluded.

TEXT: CHAPTER 99 (cont.)
each of them.

Each shall be in that realm of which they have received the mystery-experience, thus they who have received higher mystery-experiences, shall be in higher realms, and they who have received lower mystery-experiences, shall be in lower realms. These are the three allotted areas of the kingdom of Light.

Now the Mysteries of these three inheritable sectors[365] of Light are very numerous. You shall find them in the two great Books of Jeu. But I will give you and tell you the great Mysteries of each inheritable sector: which are more exalted than all their realms, that is to say, are superior to all their realms and ranks. It is these (Mysteries) which can bring all of humanity into the higher realms, according to the relevant inheritable portions (of the Light).

But as for the rest of the lower Mysteries, you have no need of these. However, you will find them in the two Books of Jeu, which Enoch wrote, as I spoke with him from out of the Tree of Knowledge and from out of the Tree of Life, in the Paradise of Adam.

Now, when I have finished explaining to you the entire distribution of the cosmos, I shall give to you, and I shall declare to you, the great Mysteries of the three assignable sectors of my kingdom. These are the pinnacles[366] of the Mysteries which I am giving to you, and which I shall declare to you, in all their patterns and all their types and all their ciphers and seals of the last Realm (*reckoning from inside*); that is, the first Realm, (reckoning) from outside. And I shall declare to you the answers, defences and secret symbols of that area.

As regards the second Realm, reckoning from within, there are no answers, defences and secret symbols or seals; only types and patterns.

---

[365] "inheritable": lit. 'allotable' or 'assignable' sectors from the Grk. word klaeros (κλῆρος) which means what is allotted to, or falls to, a person via the dice or decisions of others or gods.

[366] "pinnacles": lit. 'heads'.

COMMENTARY: CHAPTER 99
"great Books of Jeu": 'Jeu': the actual Coptic word is spelt Ieou (ιεογ), and is so presented by Mead and Horner; but this name has become simplified, through Schmidt and MacDermot, as 'Jeu'. An ancient document, the Bruce codex, was found about the same time as the Pistis Sophia codex; and contains what is assumed to be these Books of Jeu. These are however of limited interest in today's world, being mainly occult sigils and rows of letters, most of which are not words as such.

"which Enoch wrote": that Enoch is the author of, or perhaps scribe for, the Books of Jeu, indicates the degree of reverence which these early esoteric Christians (with strong Essene associations) felt for these books and for Enoch. The majority of the Book of Enoch itself, was I conclude, derived from the Essenes' leader, The Teacher of Righteousness, with perhaps sections added later by his students.

TEXT: CHAPTER 100   Andrew speaks
When the Redeemer had finished saying these things to his disciples, Andrew came forward and spoke, "Lord, be not displeased with me, but have compassion for me, and reveal to me the mystery of the discourse concerning which I shall question you, for it has been hard for me, so I have not understood it."
The Saviour answered and said to him, "Ask concerning that which you desire to query, and I will reveal it to you face to face without parable." So Andrew responded and said, "I am astonished and marvel greatly concerning how people in the world, and (thus) in bodies formed of this (earthly) matter, depart from the world.

That is, how they can (then) make their entrance into the kingdom of Light and obtain their inheritance in it - yet first they must pass through all the firmaments, filled with all these Rulers, and Lords and Gods, and all the great Invisible Ones, and all those of the realm of The Midst, and those of the

TEXT: CHAPTER 100 Andrew speaks

entire realm of The Right, and all the great Ones of the emanations of the Light."

Now when Andrew had said these things, the spirit of the Saviour was stirred within him. He cried out, and said, "For how long am I to endure you (*Andrew*)? For how long am I to suffer you?"[367] (*Then speaking to all the disciples*) have you (ye) still not understood, and are ignorant?" Do you (ye) not know and understand, that you yourselves, with each other, and all the Angels, all the Archangels, Gods, and Lords, all Rulers, all the great Invisibles, all those of The Midst, and those of every realm of The Right, all the Great Ones of the emanations of the Light, with all their glory, were created from the same malleable substance[368] and same (spirit) material,[369] and same essence[370]; so you are all from the same mixture (*of these realities*).

And by the command of the First Mystery, the mixture is restricted and constrained until all the great Ones of the light-emanations with all their glory are purified, until they are cleansed from the mixture; until they are purified. They were purified not of themselves, but of necessity, in accordance with the stewardship of that unique One, the Ineffable One.

---

[367] The rebuke is directed at Andrew, not all the disciples, as the end of the chapter makes clear; revealing that the Coptic is defective here, as it has a plural pronoun, when it should be singular.

[368] "malleable substance": the Coptic here (ⲟⲩⲱϣⲙ) is equivalent to the Grk. noun phurama (φύρᾱμα) which means either 'dough' or as in this text, 'that which is malleable'; i.e., spiritual 'substance' (consciousness) which the gods can refine.

[369] (spirit) 'material': the Grk. term here, 'hyle' can mean physical matter or 'what anything consists of'; whether an object in the physical world or a being or an energy-form in spirit realms.

[370] "essence": the Grk. here 'ousia' (οὐσία) means either substance or essence or sub-stratum; and can refer to a physical object or a spiritual reality.

TEXT: CHAPTER 100 (cont.) **Andrew speaks**
These great deities indeed did not at all undergo suffering, nor changes of realms, nor have they at all been troubled, nor poured themselves into different bodies, nor have they been in any affliction.

Whereas you (humans) in particular, you are the residue of The Treasury (of the Light), of the place of the realm of the Right, of all the Invisibles, and of all the Rulers. In short, you are the residue of all these.

And you have been in great sufferings and great tribulations, from being cast[371] into different bodies of the cosmos (*in its various levels*). And after all these afflictions which came from yourselves, you then have struggled and fought, from within yourselves, so that you have renounced the whole world with all the matter that is in it. And you have not ceased to seek, until you found all the Mysteries of the kingdom of Light. These have purified you, and transformed you into refined light most pure, indeed you have become pure light itself.

For this reason I said to you previously, "Seek, that you may find."[372] I have now said to you, 'You are to seek out the Mysteries of the Light which purify the body of matter, and make it into pure, very purified, light.'

Truly I say to you, that for the sake of humanity, because it is in a material condition[373] I have placed myself in tribulation;[374] (thus) I have brought all the Mysteries of the Light (to humanity), so that I may purify them. For humanity is the residue[375] of all the

---

[371] "Cast into": the Grk. term here (metangismoi - μεταγγισμοι), is literally, '*decanted* into various bodies'.

[372] These words were later recorded in Mt.7:7 & Lk. 11:9.

[373] "in a material state": lit. 'is of matter'.

[374] "in tribulation": lit. 'exerted or troubled myself'.

[375] "residue": it is that not yet refined soul-substance which is left over after the divine beings have developed and ascended. The Coptic word (cорм) also means 'garbage' (or 'refuse' in 19th-20th century English), but that definition of human beings is obviously not intended here.

TEXT: CHAPTER 100 (cont.) **Andrew speaks**
denser soul-'substances'[376] of the denser soul-substance of the Rulers.[377] Otherwise, no soul in the whole of humanity would have been saved; nor could souls have inherited the kingdom of Light, unless I had brought to them the purifying Mysteries.

Now the emanations of the Light have no need of any Mystery, for they are pure; but it is the human race who needs this, because it is all denser soul (*astral*) residues (*i.e., astral-substance residues*). For this reason, I once said to you, "The healthy have no need of a physician, but those who are sick."

TEXT NOTE:
"all denser soul (*astral*) residues": this definition confines itself to the soul-body; the human being also has finer qualities from which the Spiritual-self is gradually emerging.

TEXT: CHAPTER 100 (cont.)
Those of the Light have no need of Mysteries, for they are purified lights; rather, it is human beings who have need of these, for they are denser soul residues. For this reason then, preach to all of humanity this, 'Do not cease to seek both day and night, until you find the purifying Mysteries'. And say to them, 'Relinquish the whole world, with all the matter therein', for those who buy and sell in this world, those who eat and drink of its dense matter, and whoever lives in its anxieties and in all its associated 'interlinkings', (*without maintaining a spiritual awareness*) gather ever fresh dense substance to his or her own substance (*already accreted*), because the whole world and all that is therein, and all its associated interlinkings, are dense residues.

And so every soul shall be questioned as to their

---

[376] "soul-'substances'": lit. this is 'hyle' or denser substance; but in this case, of the soul (soul-body), or 'astrality', not of the physical material body.

[377] "of the Rulers": I have added this needed clarifying phrase, base on the passage above, "In short, you are the residue of all these Rulers."

TEXT: CHAPTER 100 (cont.)
cleansing. For which reason, then, I said to you earlier, 'Relinquish the whole world with all the dense substance therein', that you may not add other coarse substance to the coarse substance which is already in you.

TEXT NOTE: in Chapter 100
"gather ever fresh dense substance": this perspective has an alienating or confusing effect on the soul in today's world. I conclude that it is not about 'fleeing' from the material world, which for incarnate people is unhealthy, but rather it is about guarding one's soul against a 'matter-bound' or materialistic consciousness.
"*without maintaining a spiritual awareness*": these words I have added because just before this, the Saviour has urged that this be done, i.e., "find the purifying Mysteries".

TEXT: CHAPTER 100 (cont.)
Therefore, preach this to the whole of humanity, saying, 'Relinquish the whole world and all its associated interlinkings, that you may not add further dense substance to the dense substance which is already in you.' And say to them, 'Cease not to seek day and night, and do not re-affirm your self,[378] until you have found the purifying mysteries which shall cleanse you, and will transform you into purified light, that you may enter into the Heights and inherit the Light of my (*Christ's*) kingdom.'

Now therefore you, Andrew, and all your brethren and fellow disciples, because of your renunciations and all your sufferings, which you have endured in every realm, that is, with your transformations in each realm; namely, having been cast[379] into various

---

[378] "re-affirm your self": that is, 're-establish inwardly' your self by building upon a new foundation, one of higher purity.
[379] "Cast into": the Grk. term here (metangismoi - μεταγγισμοι), is literally, '*decanted* into various bodies'.

TEXT: CHAPTER 100 (cont.)

(kinds of) bodies – because of all these afflictions, and also because you have received the purifying Mysteries, you have become pure, very pure, light. For this reason you all shall ascend on high, and enter into all the places of the emanations of the Light, and become rulers eternally in the kingdom of Light.

But when you come forth from the body and go to the Heights and reach the place of the (debased) Rulers, then all these Rulers shall be put to shame before you, because you derive from the residue of their coarse soul-substance and yet you have become purer light than they themselves.

And when you have come into the realm of the great Invisibles, and into the realm of those of The Midst, of those of The Right, and into the realms of all those great emanations of the Light, you shall receive praise among them all, for you are the residue of their dense soul-substance – but you have become a light more purified than them all. And all the realms shall intone praise to you, until you have entered into the realm of the kingdom.

When the Saviour said this, Andrew knew clearly, and not only he, but also all the disciples, knew with certainty that they shall attain to the kingdom of Light. They all threw themselves down together at the feet of Jesus and cried aloud, wept and implored the Saviour, saying, "Lord, forgive our brother for sinning." The Saviour responded saying, "I forgive and will forgive; it is for this reason that the First Mystery has dispatched me (to the Earth): that I may cancel the sins of everyone."

COMMENTARY: CHAPTER 100

"your sufferings, which you have endured in every realm, *that is, with* your transformations in each realm; *namely*, having been cast into various (kinds of) bodies."

This is usually,

'your sufferings, which you have endured in every realm, *and* your transformations in each realm; *and*

COMMENTARY: CHAPTER 100 (cont.)
having been cast into various (kinds of) bodies'.[380]

These few brief phrases have a potent esoteric meaning. For the sufferings referred to, are *caused* by (not *in addition* to) cosmic processes that the disciples have undergone in different levels of the cosmos. These words appear to allude to the disciples' many incarnations and consequent many tribulations in their journey after death through the spirit realms, as part of their determination to succeed in the initiatory quest.

But the previous versions leave the references to 'transformations' and being 'cast into various (kinds of) bodies' as additional experiences, thus hanging in the air, with no cause nor context.

"become purer light than": i.e., than the debased Rulers.

"a light more purified than": i.e., than the light belonging to divine beings in high spirit realms. This suggests that the future redeemed human beings will have gone through a more extensive purification process, in life after life, and in the spirit realms after death, than the deities in these divine realms.

This reflects the large cosmic view, that these gods would not have undergone such an arduous interaction with matter; the dense material world not being a place where their primordial history played out.[381]

"may cancel the sins": usually, 'forgive'; but I conclude the original Greek verb had a different meaning here to its meaning in the preceding sentence "I forgive and will forgive". For the Greek verb was most likely 'aphiaemi' (ἄφιημι) which commonly means 'to forgive' or pardon; but it also

---

[380] Technically, the usu. versions treat (ⲁⲩⲙ) as meaning 'and', instead of 'namely' and 'that is'; but the Coptic is derived from the Grk. (καί) which has these meanings, and others as well.

[381] Rudolf Steiner concluded that the evolutionary development of deities occurred in such remote aeons wherein matter as such had not yet come into such a dense, hardened, mineralized state as we have today.

338

COMMENTARY: CHAPTER 100 (cont.)
can occasionally mean 'to cancel'.

Understanding 'forgiveness' esoterically
In the first instance, Jesus is forgiving or pardoning of Andrew's non-understanding, and says that he will be like this in other future occasions. And this is also what Jesus taught people to do regarding each other; i.e., to pardon or dismiss any antipathy in one's soul regarding anti-social actions against oneself or others.

But my contemplation of the theme of forgiveness in the Gospels has yielded some surprising results. There is another reason for Christ coming to the Earth, and this is what the second sentence is referring to, "First Mystery has dispatched me (to the Earth): that I may *cancel* everyone their sins".

This is about an action which only a deity can do[382], and which reaches into the realms of spirit (such as those of the after-life). This action cancels, or brings release from, the 'sinfulness' of the soul; not just a specific deed, but from the lower soul qualities overall.

This second sentence cannot mean that the primary reason for Jesus being dispatched to the Earth was to forgive everyone their ignorance or misunderstanding of general spiritual truths; for there is no end to that. Rather he was sent to the Earth to make possible a vital new upwards impetus in humanity's evolving, and therefore their soul state. That is, the canceling of 'sins' – this means, enabling release from, or gradual cancelling of, the lower self.[383]

---

[382] It is this kind of deliverance which people have sought from their priests in various religions, since remote ages. In esoteric Christian understanding, the cosmic Christ has this power to a degree unequalled in prior Ages.

[383] There is also the third action from Christ regarding 'sins'; this has the Greek verb 'airoe' (αἴρω) and this means to 'take up and away'. This occurs in John1:29 and concerns, as Steiner explains, the removal from the subtle

COMMENTARY: CHAPTER 100 (cont.)

It is this other meaning of the verb, 'to cancel sins', which is central to the majestic words recorded in Matt. 26:28 about his impending death on Golgotha, "This is my blood of the (new) covenant, which is poured-out for the cancelling of sins."

That is, it shall be through the sacrificial actions of Jesus, and the consequent on-going presence of the Christ-light in the Earth, that the impetus in human souls from the 'lower-self', which brings about 'sinning', can weaken and eventually disappear.

In this second sentence, there was, I conclude, a different Greek word, which is quite rare in the New Testament, and is translated (incorrectly) as 'forgiving'. It has a very different meaning; it is 'aphesis' (ἄφεσις) which means 'release from' or 'cancelling of'; this is quite different to pardoning/forgiving.

Translating these two different verbs with the same English word "forgive' has brought about confusion. And, regrettably the Coptic language uses the same Coptic verb (ⲕⲱ) for both these processes, for both Greek words.[384]

We need to note the striking fact – but here is not the place to consider this theme in detail – that the esoteric Christians who were using such texts as this codex, were accepting of reincarnation and karma, and yet they also accepted 'cancelling of sin' as a gift of Christ. So we conclude that they certainly would not view such 'forgiveness' i.e., cancelling of sin, as obliterating the dictates of karma.

It was deliverance from the power of the 'lower-self' which Christ offers, not an over-riding of destiny (i.e., of one's karma, which derives from a previous earth life) as later chapters in the codex reveal. For in

---

energies of the planet itself of damaging influences engendered by 'sins'.

[384] The Coptic language uses the Greek verb 'aphesis'; but it is used to mean 'to ransom' or 'to redeem'; in Coptic is ⲥⲱⲧⲉ.

COMMENTARY: CHAPTER 100 (cont.)

these chapters the karmic consequences of any unethical actions are viewed as remaining, and having their consequence for a future life.

There now follows a page in Coptic which has been inserted here; but it comes from the end of some other, unknown book of initiatory Christianity wisdom.
So this does not follow on from the preceding chapter. But this is counted as "**Chapter 101**"; it is somewhat obscure.

TEXT 'CHAPTER 101'

....And those who are worthy of the Mysteries of the Ineffable One, which are those Mysteries that have not gone forth - these exist in the presence of[385] the First Mystery. And, to describe them through a likeness and a similitude, to help you understand them, these Mysteries are as 'members' of the Ineffable One. And each of these exist (in a state) appropriate to its glory.

The head according to the worth of the head, the eye according to the worth of the eye and the ear according to the worth of the ear; and in like manner with the rest of the members. So that the situation becomes clear: there exist many members, but one body.

This I say as an example, and similitude, and a likeness, but not as a true form; nor have I revealed the Word in truth, rather, the Mystery of the Ineffable One. And the members which are within it - according to the Word to which I have compared it - that is, those who dwell with the Mystery of the Ineffable, and those who dwell within it, and also the three Realms which follow after them, according to the Mysteries: to all these, I am their treasure, in truth and truthfulness; and apart from me, there is (for them) no treasure which does not have its like in this world. But still, there are words and Mysteries and

---

[385] "in the presence of": lit. 'before'.

TEXT CHAPTER 101 (cont.)

other realms.

Therefore blessed is that person who has found the words of the Mysteries (of the first Realm): that Mystery which is from without. And a god is that entity who has found these words of the Mysteries of the second Realm – which is in The Midst (7th level of Devachan). And a Redeemer and an Uncontainable is that one who has found the words of the Mysteries of the third Realm, which is within. Hence such an entity is more excellent than the universe (*as described above: the three Realms*). So he is equal to[386] those who are in the third Realm, because he has received the Mystery in which they exist, and upon which they have their foundations[387]; therefore he is similar to them.

Moreover, that person who has found the words of the Mysteries which I have described to you, through a comparison, saying that they are 'members' of the Ineffable: truly, I say to you that such a person has found the words of the Mysteries in divine truth, and is the foremost[388] in truth, and is like the Ineffable One.

For through those words and Mysteries -- (gap in the page) -- and the cosmos itself has the First as its foundation. Hence that person who found the words of those Mysteries is like the First. For it is the gnosis of the knowledge of the Ineffable about which I have spoken with you today.

DOCUMENT THREE

"A part of the Books of the Saviour"

This next document is not a direct continuation of documents 2 and 3, but it is compatible with them.

---

[386] "equal to": or 'acceptable to'.
[387] "have foundations": lit. 'stand', but in a non-literal sense.
[388] "foremost": lit. 'first in truth'.

TEXT: CHAPTER 102

Jesus continued with his discourse, saying to his disciples, "When I have gone into the Light, then preach to the entire world; 'Do not cease from seeking day and night, and thus do not re-affirm[389] yourselves until you find the Mysteries of the Light, which will purify you and make you into pure light and lead you into the kingdom of Light.'

Say to them, 'Relinquish all this world and all the matter within it; that is, all its troubles and sins, so that you may be worthy of the Mysteries of the Light, and be saved from all the chastizements within the judgments.

Say to them, 'Renounce complaining that you may be worthy of the Mysteries of the Light, and be saved from the fire of the dog-faced One.

Say to them, 'Renounce listening (*to untruths?*) that you may be worthy of the Mysteries of the Light, and be saved from the judgments of the dog-faced One.

Say to them, 'Renounce quarrelsome-ness[390] that you may be worthy of the Mysteries of the Light, and be saved from the punishments of Ariel.

TEXT NOTE: in Chapter 102

(**Ariel**: That this spirit entity is named, is significant. Much uncertainty has existed regarding the meaning of Ariel; but scholars have shown convincing evidence that Ariel is a word borrowed from the ancient Akkadian language, and means The Underworld; the realm of the Dead. So Ariel is either a primary spirit in the realm of the Dead, or is that realm itself – in the negative sense of the lower Soul-world, where disempowered and 'sinners' have to exist.[391] (Ariel can be both the realm and its ruling spirit.)

---

[389] "re-affirm"; or 're-instate'.
[390] "quarrelsome-ness": the Coptic word here is obscure.
[391] Parson, W. C. *On the Unified Authorship of the Oracle to Ariel Isaiah* 29: 1-8) (Studia Antiqua, June 1916 Vol 15. No.1_ & Feigin, S. *The Meaning of Ariel* Journ. Bib. Lit. 1920; (https://www.jstor.org.stable/3260202

TEXT: CHAPTER 102 (cont.)

Say to them, 'Renounce false libel that you may be worthy of the Mysteries of the Light, and be saved from the streams of fire of the dog-faced One.

Say to them, 'Renounce false testimony that you may be worthy of the Mysteries of the Light, and be saved from the streams of fire of the dog-faced One.

Say to them, 'Renounce pride and boasting that you may be worthy of the Mysteries of the Light, and be saved from the fire-pits of Ariel.

Say to them, 'Renounce gluttony that you may be worthy of the Mysteries of the Light, and be saved from the judgments of Amente (*the Egyptian name for Purgatory*).

Say to them, 'Renounce gossip, that you may be worthy of the mysteries of the Light, and be saved from the fires of Amente.'

Say to them, 'Renounce malice, that you may be worthy of the Mysteries of the Light, and be saved from the torments which are in Amente.'

Say to them, 'Renounce avarice, that you may be worthy of the Mysteries of the Light, and escape from the rivers of fire of that dog-faced One.'

Say to them, 'Renounce love of the world, that you may be worthy of the Mysteries of the Light, and be saved from the coats of pitch and fire of that dog-faced One.'

Say to them, 'Renounce usurping of property, that you may be worthy of the Mysteries of the Light, and be saved from the rivers of fire of Ariel.'

Say to them, 'Renounce evil speech, that you may be worthy of the Mysteries of the Light, and be saved from the punishments of the rivers of flame.

Say to them, 'Renounce wickedness, that you may be worthy of the Mysteries of the Light, and be saved from the seas of fire of Ariel.'

Say to them, 'Renounce lack of compassion, that you may be worthy of the Mysteries of the Light, and be saved from the judgments of the rivers of fire of the dragon-faced Ones.'

Say to them, 'Renounce wrath, that you may be worthy of the Mysteries of the Light, and be saved

TEXT: CHAPTER 102 (cont.)

from the judgments of the rivers of fire of the dragon-faced Ones.'

Say to them, 'Renounce cursing, that you may be worthy of the Mysteries of the Light, and be saved from the seas of fire of the dragon-faced Ones.'

Say to them, 'Renounce thieving, that you may be worthy of the Mysteries of the Light, and be saved from the boiling[392] seas of the dragon-faced Ones.'

Say to them, 'Renounce violent robbery[393] that you may be worthy of the Mysteries of the Light, and be saved from Yaldabaoth.'

Say to them, 'Renounce slandering, that you may be worthy of the Mysteries of the Light, and be saved from the fire-rivers of the Lion-faced One.'

Say to them, 'Renounce fighting and strife, that you may be worthy of the Mysteries of the Light, and be saved from the boiling rivers of Ialdabaoth.'

Say to them, 'Renounce ignorance (*of the spirit?*) that you may be worthy of the Mysteries of the Light, and be saved from the servitors of Ialdabaoth and the seas of fire.'

Say to them, 'Renounce evil-doing, that you may be worthy of the Mysteries of the Light, and saved from all the demons of Ialdabaoth and all his punishments.'

Say to them, 'Renounce frenzy,[394] that you may be worthy of the Mysteries of the Light, and saved from the seething seas of pitch, of Ialdabaoth.'

Say to them, 'Renounce adultery, that you may be worthy of the Mysteries of the kingdom of the Light, and saved from the seas of sulphur and pitch of the Lion-faced One.'

Say to them, 'Renounce murder, that you may be worthy of the Mysteries of the kingdom of the Light, and be saved from the crocodile-faced Ruler – the one

---

[392] "boiling": lit. 'bubbling.

[393] Coptic obscure: it seems that not simply robbery but violent seizing of goods is meant (ϥⲱϭϥ = a 'seizer-robber').

[394] "frenzy": this probably refers to occult practises wherein a spirit entity manifests through its ensnared human soul.

TEXT: CHAPTER 102 (cont.)

who is in the first chamber of the outer darkness.'

Say to them, 'Renounce lack of compassion due to impiety, that you may be worthy of the Mysteries of the kingdom of the Light, and be saved from the Rulers of the outer darkness.'

Say to them, 'Renounce godlessness, that you may be worthy of the Mysteries of the kingdom of the Light, and be saved from weeping and gnashing of teeth.'

Say to them, 'Renounce sorceries, that you may be worthy of the Mysteries of the kingdom of the Light, and be saved from the great cold and hail, of the outer darkness.'

Say to them, 'Renounce blasphemy, that you may be worthy of the Mysteries of the Light, and saved from the great dragon of the outer darkness.'

Say to them, 'Renounce erroneous teachings, that you may be worthy of the Mysteries of the Light, and saved from all the punishments of the great dragon of the outer darkness.'

Say to those who teach erroneous teachings, 'Woe to you, for if you do not repent, and don't abandon your errors, you shall come into the punishments of the great dragon in the outer darkness, which is very terrible; and they (*the receivers*) shall not cast you (*ye*) back into the world for an Age; instead, you will be outside (*of this world*); that is, non-existent (*for an Age*).

TEXT-NOTE in Chapter 102

"the dissolution of the cosmos": this is when a large time-cycle finishes and creation is 'breathed back in' by the Creator, until its next cycle begins.

"outside of this world you will be non-existent"; usually the translation is, "you will be non-existent to the end". However, this would mean the soul is destroyed, is eternally dead; but this is then the same punishment as announced for the next 'sinning' – so this cannot be correct, because the next punishment is said to be 'more severe'. So 'non-existent to the end', i.e., forever, appears incorrect here,[395] where 'non-existent' means not incarnate; and perhaps not even tangibly present in the Soul-world.

TEXT: CHAPTER 102 (cont.)
Say to those who abandon the true teachings of the First Mystery, 'Woe to you, for your punishment is more severe than that of all other souls, for you shall remain in the great cold, with ice and hail amidst the dragon of the outer darkness. From this hour they shall not cast you (back) into the world, during the Aeon. Then, at the dissolution of the cosmos, your soul shall waste away[396] and become existence-less, throughout the Aeon.

TEXT-NOTE in Chapter 102
"Then, at the dissolution of the cosmos, your soul shall be corroded and become existence-less, during the Aeon":
Usually this is "at the dissolution of the cosmos your soul shall be *consumed* and become existence-less, *forever* (eternally).
The cause of the different interpretations is that the key Coptic word here (eneh - ⲈⲚⲈϨ) means either 'eternally', or an Age/Aeon or Aion.[397] So either this soul will be eternally extinguished, or it will unable to continue its incarnations during this entire aeon; and thus it shall lag behind the rest of humanity, but it shall still exist, to re-enter the world, in a later Age/aeon.

The ambiguity here, connected with the Coptic

---

[395] The cause of the different interpretations is that the Coptic here (ϢⲀⲂⲞⲖ) is ambiguous; it means either 'forever' or 'the end (of)' or 'to the outside of'.

[396] The Grk. verb here ἀναλισκεσθαι means to be consumed or wasted: that is, in effect subject to attrition.

[397] "until the Age": the word 'the' could be left out in parallel Greek phrases; e.g. in *Epist. Ignat. to Ephesians* τῇ ἠποωρισμένῃ πρὸ αἰώνων : "she, predestined before (the) Ages".

TEXT-NOTE in Chapter 102
word meaning either 'eternally' or 'an Age', recalls famous words of Christ in Matthew's Gospel on a similar theme. Words which have been seriously mistranslated for nearly 2,000 years. In Matt 25:46, as in the NIV,
"They (sinners) shall go away to eternal punishment, but the righteous to eternal life."
So here is a similar theme of the future of humanity in connection with reward and punishment. But generally unacknowledged in the theological world, the word 'aioenion' (αἰώνιον) here means a spirit realm, an Aion; it does not mean 'eternal'.

Furthermore, as regards 'punishment', the Greek word here, 'kolasin' (κόλασιν) meant a somewhat painful *corrective treatment*, as when a farmer pruned an unhealthy olive tree; it did not mean a punishment inflicted to cause suffering. There is no statement in the Gospels about 'sinners', declaring that they enter into an eternal punishment. Instead, Jesus is saying here, "They (sinners) shall go away (*after the dissolution of the current cosmos*) to an Aion where painful corrective action is experienced, but the righteous shall go to an Aion where they enjoy divine (aionic) existence."

TEXT: CHAPTER 102 (cont.)
Say rather to the people of the world, 'Be tranquil[398], that you may receive the Mysteries of the Light and go to the Heights – to the kingdom of the Light.
Say to them, 'Be loving to people, that you may be worthy of the Mysteries of the Light, and enter into the Heights, into the kingdom of the Light.'
Say to them, 'Be of a gentle nature, that you may receive the Mysteries of the Light, and enter into the Heights; into the kingdom of the Light.'
Say to them, 'Be peaceful, that you may receive the Mysteries of the Light, and enter into the Heights; into the kingdom of the Light.'
Say to them, 'Be merciful, that you may receive the

---

[398] "Tranquil": lit. 'be calm/silent/quiet'.

TEXT: CHAPTER 102 (cont.)
Mysteries of the Light, and enter into the Heights; into the kingdom of the Light.'

Say to them, 'Be charitable to the poor and the sick and distressed, that you may receive the Mysteries of the Light, and enter into the Heights; into the kingdom of the Light.'

Say to them, 'Be God-loving, that you may receive the Mysteries of the Light, and enter into the Heights; into the kingdom of the Light.'

Say to them, 'Be righteous, that you may receive the Mysteries of the Light, and enter into the Heights; into the kingdom of the Light.'

Say to them, 'Be ethical, that you may receive the Mysteries of the Light, and enter into the Heights; into the kingdom of the Light.'

Say to them, 'Relinquish everything, that you may receive the Mysteries of the Light, and enter into the Heights; into the kingdom of the Light.'

These are the (ethical) boundaries of the pathways for those who are worthy of the Mysteries of the Light. Therefore, to such souls as have made this kind of renunciation, give the Mysteries of the Light, and hide nothing from them at all, even if they are sinners, and have been in all of the sins and all the iniquities of the world: those which I have just recounted to you. Do this so that they may turn around and repent, and be in submission (*to the ethical course of action*).

COMMENTARY: Chapter 102
No especial commentary is needed here.

TEXT: CHAPTER 103
This I say to you now: give them the Mysteries of the kingdom of Light, and do not conceal these from them at all. For it is because of sinfulness that I brought the Mysteries into the world; so that I may cancel all their sins; sins which they have committed since the Beginning. For this reason have I said to you "I did not come to call the righteous."

Therefore, I have brought (*access to*) the Mysteries,

TEXT: CHAPTER 103 (cont.)
so that the (*future*) sins of all people may be cancelled, and (thus) people can be brought into the kingdom of the Light. For these Mysteries are the gift of the First Mystery to erase the sins and iniquities of all sinners.

The next section is about:
Guidance for existence after death   Mariam speaks
It came to pass, when Jesus had finished saying these things to his disciple, that Mariam came forward, and said to the Saviour, "My Lord, regarding a righteous person, who is perfected in righteousness - a person who has no sin[399] at all - yet a person who has not ever received Mysteries of the Light. When the time comes for that person to come forth from the body, will it be tormented in the chastisements and judgments, or not?

TEXT NOTE: in Chapter 103
"perfected in righteousness": this is a traditional religious phrase meaning that the person has not sinned against the requirements in esoteric Judaism/early Christianity regarding morality. If taken in its ultimate sense, then only Jesus himself would qualify for this description.

TEXT: CHAPTER 103 (cont.)
The Saviour then answered, and said to Mariam, "Regarding a righteous person, who is perfected in righteousness, and who has never committed any sin at all, but who has never received Mysteries of the Light. When the time has arrived for this person to come forth from the body, then immediately the receivers of one of the three great Triple-powers - among whom is a great deity - snatch the soul of that person away from the receivers of the Erinyes.

They shall circle around with it for three days, among all the creatures of the world, and after the three days they shall lead it down into the Chaos, to

---

[399] "sin": as noted earlier 'sin' is unethical behaviour.

pass it through the chastisements of the judgments, so they send it (thereby) to all the judgments.

TEXT NOTE: in Chapter 103
"circle around among all the creatures of the world": a statement which derives from deep esoteric knowledge. These helpful, guiding spirits accompany the newly-deceased (probably unknown to it), as it undergoes the three-day separating from the physical body, in a dreamy state. A solution to this striking phrase is found in the work of Rudolf Steiner.

He taught that that over three days, the etheric and soul (astral) energies of the soul, are released from the physical body and these spread out ever further, partially merging into the enveloping, circling cosmos (the planetary spheres).[400]

There the soul is amongst the 'group-souls' of the many and varied creatures with which we share life on the Earth. (But not necessarily conscious of this.) Rudolf Steiner taught that our etheric body also undergoes a similar experience, as it has some energies drawn from the same source as that of the various animal species.

TEXT: CHAPTER 103 (cont.)
The fires of the Chaoses, however, will not trouble it greatly, but they shall trouble the soul somewhat, for a short time (only). Because the receivers will take pity on it and quickly hasten to bring it forth from the Chaoses, and lead it into the pathway of the Midst, among all the (debased) Rulers.

But these Rulers do not punish this soul with their harsh punishments; however, the fire of their realms do trouble the soul, partly. But if the receivers take the soul to the realm of Jachthanabas the Merciless, he will certainly *not* be able to punish it in his evil judgments, but he can restrain it for a short while, during which time the fire of his punishments do

---

[400] This process causes people in a near-death experience to feel that they are expanding, becoming a vast being.

TEXT: CHAPTER 103 (cont.)
trouble it, partly.

Again they (*the receivers of one of the three great Triple-powers*) quickly have mercy upon it, and speedily bring it up from those places there. But they do not bring it into the (debased) Aions, so that the Rulers of these Aions are unable take it away into the firmament[401] (*the planetary spheres*).

Instead they bring it into the pathway of the light of the (spiritual) Sun, and (thereby) bring this soul to the Holy Goddess of the Light. She scrutinizes it and finds that it is free of sins. But she does not allow them to take it to the Light, because a signifier of the power[402] of the Mystery is not within it.[403]

Instead, she imprints upon it a higher 'seal', and lets it be cast into the (soul-)body[404] among the Aions of holiness.[405] This soul shall be virtuous, and (hence) shall find (*in their next incarnation*) the sign of the Mysteries of the Light; and thus shall inherit the kingdom of the Light eternally (*when their incarnations cease.*)

If a person has committed sin once or twice, or three times, then they shall cast it forth into the world, according to the kind of sin it has committed. I shall tell you of their types when I have finished speaking to you about the structure and extent of the cosmos.

---

[401] "into the firmament": usu. 'by theft'; but I conclude that the Grk. word (steresimoes) in the codex should have been 'stereoema' which means 'firmament'; for of these two, this latter word fits the context much more meaningfully.

[402] "power": usu. 'kingdom', which can't apply here. The Coptic (ερο-ρρο) means kingdom, or power, reign, authority.

[403] "signifier": the Coptic term (мαειν) means: sign, feature, mark.

[404] "(soul-) body": usu. 'body" i.e., physical body, but this can not apply in spirit realms; e.g., Pistis Sophia also (in Chpt. 65) has a 'body', but of course, a 'soul body', not a physical body.

[405] "holiness": lit. 'righteousness'.

TEXT: CHAPTER 103 (cont.)
But truly, truly,[406] I say to you that even if a righteous person has committed no sins at all, it is not possible for that person to be taken to the kingdom of Light, because they do not have the sign of the realm of the Mysteries. In short, it is impossible to bring souls to the Light without the Mysteries of the kingdom of the Light.

COMMENTARY: CHAPTER 103
"the Holy Goddess of the Light": as noted in earlier chapters, this is usually 'the Virgin of the Light'; very little is said about this deity's location or rank.

"shall inherit the kingdom of the Light eternally": one can ask, how does this correlate to a core declaration in the Gospel of John, "No person comes to the Father except through me" (14:6). The spiritual nurturing and ennobling of a soul, given by the Holy Goddess of the Light can be viewed as deriving from 'The First Mystery', or God; and this deity could be viewed as 'the Father'.

TEXT: CHAPTER 104   John speaks
It then happened, when Jesus had finished speaking these words to his disciples, that John came forward and said, "Lord, if a man is a sinner, a transgressor, accustomed to every iniquity, but has ceased all this for the sake of the kingdom of the Heavens, and he has relinquished the world with all the matter which is within it.

  And we then give to him the beginning of the Mysteries of the Light - these which are in the first Realm from without. But when he has received these Mysteries, after a short while he reverts and again transgresses; then again he changes and ceases from all sin.

  So he has changed and ceases from all sin, and turns and relinquishes the world with all the matter which is within it. Then he comes to us and is deeply repentant, and if we really know that he is in the

---

[406] "Truly, truly": lit. 'Amen, amen'.

TEXT: CHAPTER 104   John speaks

truth, that he yearns for God – so that we then give to him the second Mystery of the first Realm from without.

But should he, as before, after a short while, revert and again transgress, so he is again in the sins of the world; and yet once more he again repents and ceases from the sins of the world, and again relinquishes the world with all the matter which is within it, and be in great contrition. Now, if we know with certainty that he is not a hypocrite, and so that we change our attitude, and again give him the beginning of the Mysteries – these which are in the first Realm from without.

But now should he, in a similar manner, again change and commit sin; thus he is (*immersed*) in every kind of sin – do you wish that we should forgive him seven times? That is, do you wish that we should give to him the beginning of the Mysteries which are in the first Realm from without, seven times or not?

The Saviour answered again and said to John, "Forgive his sin not only seven times, but truly, I say to you, forgive him such sin, many times seven times, and each time give to him the beginning of the Mysteries which are in the first Realm from without. For perhaps you shall win the soul of that person, and they shall inherit the kingdom of Light.

Concerning this you (*ye*) asked me once, saying, 'Whenever our brother should sin against us, do you wish for us to forgive him as many as seven times?' I answered, and said to you in a parable, 'Not only as many as seven times, but as many as seven times seventy.' Now therefore forgive him a multitude of times, and give to him every time the Mysteries which are from without, these which are in the first Realm. Perhaps you shall gain indeed the soul of that brother, and he will inherit the kingdom of Light.

Truly, truly, I say to you, whoever will maintain one soul in life, and thus save it, besides the glory which they have in the kingdom of Light, will receive much further glory on account of the soul which they

TEXT: CHAPTER 104
John speaks

saved. Hence whoever does deliver a multitude of souls, beside the glory which that person has in (the kingdom of the Light) will receive still more glory on account of the souls which they have saved.

COMMENTARY: CHAPTER 104

A mystery-experience was probably an influx of a divine light, whilst sacred mantric words are intoned, deepening one's consciousness and empowering one's spirit.

Next Chapter: initiating those who then become unworthy. This section refers to initiating some Christians, as if it were a well-established process.

TEXT: CHAPTER 105
John speaks

Then when the Saviour had said this to them, John started forward, and said, My Lord, bear with me, if I question you. For now I am about to ask you concerning everything, concerning the manner in which we are to preach to humanity. If therefore I should give to that person a Mystery among the Mysteries of the beginning, these which are in the first Realm from without: if I should give to him many Mysteries, and he later does that which is not worthy of the kingdom of the Heavens, do you wish for us to let him pass through to the Mysteries of the second Realm or not?

The Saviour answered and said to John, "If that person is not hypocritical, but in truth longs for God, and you have given him many times the Mysteries of the beginning, but because of compulsion from the elementary-spirits within the karma-determining cosmic influences (*i.e., lower Devachan*)[407], this person has not done that which is worthy of the Mysteries of Light, allow them to proceed, and give to that person the first Mystery of the second Realm. Perhaps you shall gain the soul of that person.

---

[407] That is Heimarmene.

TEXT NOTE: in Chapter 105
"elementary-spirits": here an occult Greek term is used, 'Stoicheia'; this word refers to spirits of lesser rank than the gods, who act as servitors, carrying out the actual details of spirit processes. Their rank cannot be definitely identified as the various Greek sources are not in agreement. They allude to different types of minor spirits.

TEXT: CHAPTER 105 (cont.)   **John speaks**
And even then if he is not worthy of the Mysteries of Light, but he commits transgression again and any kind of sin, yet then again repents and is in deep repentance, and relinquishes (*inwardly*) the whole world, and ceases from all the sins of the world, and you know with certainty that he is not a hypocrite, then turn to him again, and forgive his sin, let him proceed: give to him the second Mystery of the second Realm of the First Mystery. Perhaps, indeed, you shall win the soul of that brother, that he may inherit the kingdom of the Heavens.

In the next section:
What to do when an initiated person becomes unworthy
TEXT: CHAPTER 105 (cont.)   **John speaks**
However, if again this person does not do what is worthy of the Mysteries, but he again commits transgression and any kind of sin; and yet again after this, again he repents and is in deep repentance, and relinquishes (*inwardly*) the whole world, and ceases from all the sins of the world, and longs truly for God, then you turn to him again, and forgive him, accept the repentance from him, because the First Mystery is compassionate and merciful.

Let that person pass through (*into the esoteric group*), and give them the three Mysteries, one after the other - those which are in the second realm of the First Mystery. But if that person *again* transgresses and is in all kinds of sin, then from that moment onwards, do not forgive him, nor accept his repentance; instead let that person be a disgrace and

TEXT: CHAPTER 105 (cont.) John speaks
a transgressor among you.

For truly, I say to you, those three Mysteries shall become as a witness to his last repentance (*to be accepted*), and so from this hour on, that person shall not have any repentance (acknowledged). For truly, I say to you, the soul of that person shall not be brought back[408] into the higher world[409] from this time onwards (*after his death*), but shall instead be in the abodes of the dragon of the outer darkness.

For about the souls of people such as this, I have once spoken a parable to you, saying, 'If your brother sins against you, admonish him between yourself and he, alone. If he listens to you, you shall win your brother. If he does not listen to you, then bring another person with you. If he does not listen to you and the other, bring him before the congregation. If he does not listen to these others, then let him be as a disgrace and a transgressor among you.'[410]

For concerning the souls of people of this kind, I also once said to you, 'Every word shall stand by means of two or three witnesses.' This means that those three Mysteries shall bear witness to his last repentance. Truly, I say to you, even if that man were to repent, there is no Mystery which can forgive his sins and accept his repentance. There is no Mystery at all hearing him, except only the first mystery-experience of the First Mystery and the Mysteries of the Ineffable One. They alone will accept the repentance of that man and will forgive his sins, for those Mysteries are compassionate and merciful-minded, and grant forgiveness at any time.

COMMENTARY: CHAPTER 105
No especial commentary is needed here; except we note that these 'mystery' procedures are indirectly shown to be a very real feature, and not uncommon,

---

[408] "brought back": usu. 'cast back (down)'; I agree with Till that the verb (**TCTO**) here means 'make to return'.
[409] "higher world": lit. 'world on high'.
[410] These words were later recorded in Matt. 18:15-17.

in the life of these 'initiatory' Christian groups.

TEXT: CHAPTER 106 John speaks

When the Saviour had said these words, John continued his questioning, and said to the Saviour, "Lord, if a brother, who is a very great sinner, has relinquished the whole world with all the matter therein, all its sins and all its interests, and we test him, and know that he is not a deceiver and a hypocrite, but that he has a real desire to be in the truth.

And we know that he is worthy of the Mysteries of the second Realm or the third Realm: do you wish that we give to him from the Mysteries of the second or the third Realm, even though that person has not received any Mystery at all from the kingdom[411] of the Light?

The Saviour answered and said to John, in the midst of the disciples, "If you know with certainty that this person has relinquished the whole world with all its cares, all its associated interests and all its sins, and that he is not in (a state of) cunning, nor in hypocrisy.

Nor is he simply curious about your Mysteries – what kind of realities these are – but that he is longing for God in truth, then do not conceal the Mysteries from such a person, but give to them from the second Realm and from the third.

But you yourselves should ascertain as to which Mystery that person is worthy; and regarding that for which he is worthy, give to him. So do not conceal such from him, lest when you conceal from him, you become guilty of a great offence.

If, after you have given him once of the Mysteries from the second Realm or of the third, and he does turn again to his transgressions, nevertheless you shall again give them to him a second time, and also until a third time. But if he then still transgress, you shall no longer give him them; thus those three Mysteries shall bear witness to his last repentance

---

[411] "kingdom": the codex has erroneously, 'Inheritance".

TEXT: CHAPTER 106 (cont.) John speaks
(*which was accepted*).

Truly, I say to you, he who shall give the Mysteries again to such a person in the second or in the third Space, is subject to a great judgment. So let that person be for you as a transgressor and a stumbling-block. Truly, I say to you, the soul of that man will not be cast back into the world, as from that hour; his dwelling shall be in the midst of the jaws of the dragon of outer darkness, the place of weeping and gnashing of teeth. And at the dissolution of the world, his soul shall be eaten into by the cruel coldness and the very intense fire.

Then at the dissolution of the cosmos, this soul shall become corroded, and become existence-less, throughout the Aeon.

However, should that person *again* repent and relinquish the whole world, all its cares, and all its sins, and is in a severe (penitential) way of life and great repentance, nevertheless, no Mystery shall accept their repentance; none shall give ear to them, to accept the repentance, and grant them the forgiveness of their sins; with the exception of the mystery-experience of the First Mystery and the mystery-experience of that Ineffable One.

These (two) alone will accept repentance from such a person, and grant that soul forgiveness of sins, for these Mysteries are compassionate and merciful, and forgiving of sins at all times.

COMMENTARY: Chapter 106

"these Mysteries are compassionate...": the meaning here is that the actual nature of the two deities involved, God and the even higher, more veiled *primal* God is such that anyone who gains an inner alignment to these very high holy deities will be enveloped by, and blessed by, a compassionate and forgiving love.

Next section: What to do with initiated persons who were being deceitful, and betrayed the Mysteries

TEXT: CHAPTER 107   John speaks

Then, after the Saviour had said these things, John continued his questioning, saying, "Lord, allow me to put questions to you, and be not displeased with me, for I am questioning with clarity and exactitude, concerning the way in which we are to preach to people of the world.

So the Saviour responded and said to John, "Question me about all things which you are querying, and I shall reveal it to you directly, openly, without parables, that is, exactly.

Then John answered and said, "Lord, when we go forth to preach, and enter into a city or a town, and the people of that city come to meet us, but they are not known to us. Now, if they are very cunning and hypocrites, and do receive us and take us into their houses, but they only want to (superficially) experiment with the Mysteries of the Light.

So they are being deceitful to us with their submissive manner, however we (mistakenly) think that they love God, and that we should give them the Mysteries of the kingdom of Light. But afterwards we discover that they have acted in a manner unworthy of the Mysteries.

For we then find out that they have been hypocritical with us, and have deceived us. Furthermore, we discover that in many places they have (*set up*) a mockery of these Mysteries: they are parodying us and our Mysteries (in such places). So what is it that should then befall such people?

The Saviour answered and said to John, "When you have entered a city or a town and if you go into a house and they receive you, then give to them a Mystery. If they are worthy, you shall win their souls, and they shall inherit the kingdom of Light. But if they should be unworthy, and are being deceitful to you, and if they also make a mockery of the Mysteries, parodying you and the Mysteries – then invoke the first mystery-experience of the First Mystery, which shows mercy to everyone.

Say: "Thou, O Mystery, which we have given to these impious and wicked souls: they have not done

TEXT: CHAPTER 107 (cont.)

what is worthy of thy Mystery, but have made a parody of us – return the Mystery to us and make them strangers to thy kingdom forever."

Then shake off the dust of your feet as a witness against them, saying, 'May your souls be as the dust of your house.'[412] And truly, I say to you, all the words and all the Mysteries of the realm up to which they have received sigils, will be taken away from them.

Concerning such people I have spoken to you, at an earlier time in a parable, saying, "When you enter a house and are received, say to them, 'Peace be with you'. And if they are worthy, allow your peace to come upon them. But if they are not worthy, let your peace return to you,"[413] if these people act in a manner unworthy of the Mysteries of the kingdom of Light.

But if they behave hypocritically and with guile towards you, without your being aware of this, and you give them the Mysteries of the kingdom of Light, but afterwards they make a mockery of the Mysteries, and parody you and my Mysteries, then you shall perform the first mystery-experience of the First Mystery, and it will give back to you every mystery-experience that you have given to them; and it will make them strangers to the Mysteries of Light forever.

For truly, I say to you, such persons shall not be led back[414] into the higher world[415] from this time onwards, but instead (*after death*), their dwelling shall be amidst the jaws of the dragon of outer darkness.

And even if they do again have a time of repentance, and relinquish the whole world, with all

---

[412] These words were (later) recorded in Matt.10:14, Mk.6:11, Lk.9:5 & 10:11.

[413] These words were (later) recorded in Matt. 10:12-13, Mk.6:10, Lk.9:4-5 & 10:5-6.

[414] "brought back": usu. 'cast back (down)'; but the verb (**TCTO**) here means 'make to return'.

[415] "higher world": 'higher' is omitted in error by the scribe.

TEXT: CHAPTER 107 (cont.)

the matter therein, and all the sins of the world, and are then entirely submissive to the Mysteries of the Light - no Mystery can hear them, nor forgive their sins: except that unique (peerless) Mystery of the Ineffable One, who has mercy upon everyone and forgives every person their sins.

COMMENTARY: CHAPTER 107

"such persons shall not be led back into the higher world from this time onwards": the Coptic here needs correcting; it states, as in previous translations, "such persons shall not be led back down (*i.e., reincarnate*) into the (physical) world again." But this text is inconsistent with the next paragraph where a future life on the Earth for that person is alluded to.

So there is here actually a repeat of what was said in Chapter 105 where we are told of a person who is initiated but who reneges: they will not again be allowed up into the realms of Light from that hour.

"will be taken away from them": there is a suggestion here that the secret words and mystical sigils will be removed from these scheming people by the use of magical powers: that all memory of the secret words will removed from them, and the graphic aspects (the sigils) will be magically transported out of their reach.

TEXT: CHAPTER 108   Mariam speaks

It then happened when Jesus had finished speaking these words to his disciples, that Mariam made obeisance at the feet of Jesus; she prostrated herself at them.[416] Mariam then said, "Lord, allow me to question you; be not displeased." The Saviour answered and said to Mariam, "Ask what you wish, and I will reveal it to you with freedom."

(Next section: Interceding for the souls of the Dead)

---

[416] "feet of Jesus": this is a set phrase, not a literal fact; as the risen Saviour has no physical body.

TEXT: CHAPTER 108 (cont.)   **Mariam speaks**

And Mariam said, "Lord, then, supposing that a brother is good and righteous, and we have perfected him with all the Mysteries of Light, and that this brother has a brother or relative; or in other words, he has a connection to another man, and this latter is a sinner and impious – or even if he be not a sinner – but on this person's passing from the body, the heart of the good brother is troubled and mourns over him, because the deceased has entered the judgments and punishments (*in the Soul-world*). Now, Lord, what is it that we should do, so as to release him from the punishments and powerful judgments?

The Saviour answered and said to Mariam, I have already spoken to you about this subject, on another occasion, but listen while I reply to you, so that you may be fulfilled in all Mysteries; that you may be called 'Those who are perfected in the fullness of all spirit realities.'

So, regarding everyone who commits sin, and those who do not commit sin: if you wish that they be removed (*more quickly*) from all chastizements and all severe judgments, and also that they be transferred into a righteous body (*when the time for reincarnating draws near*) – such as will (*help the soul*) find the Mysteries of the Godhead, and thence enter into the Heights, and inherit the kingdom of Light.

Then perform the third Mystery of the Ineffable One, saying, "Set free the soul of the person whom we are thinking of in our hearts; set this soul free from all the torments of the Rulers; hasten speedily to bring this soul up to the Holy Goddess of the Light. In this same[417] month let the Holy Goddess of the Light seal that soul with an excellent seal; and in this same month let the Holy Goddess of the Light cast that person into a body that shall be righteous and good (*when the time for reincarnating draws near*), so that

---

[417] "same month": here an unclear Coptic idiom is used, (ϩⲣⲁⲓ ϩⲙ̄ ⲛⲉⲓⲉⲃⲟⲧ ⲛⲉⲓⲉⲃⲟⲧ) other possibilities are: 'in this very month', 'in every month'.

TEXT: CHAPTER 108 (cont.)   Mariam speaks
this person may enter into the Heights, and inherit the kingdom of Light."

And if you say these words, then truly, I say to you, all those (entities) that serve in all the ranks of the judgments of the Rulers, will set to work to (*speedily*) pass that soul on to one another, until they bring it up to the Holy Goddess of the Light. And the Holy Goddess of Light shall seal it with the sign of the kingdom of that Ineffable One.

And she shall give it to her receivers, and the receivers will cast it into a body which shall become righteous, and (*help the soul*) find the Mysteries of the Light, and become good, and arise to the Heights and inherit the kingdom of Light. Behold, this is what you ask of me.

COMMENTARY: CHAPTER 108
Here we encounter a remarkable testimony to the existence of an esoteric ritual procedure for the Dead amongst initiatory Christian circles. Rituals and prayers for the Dead had been a major part of the religious activity of humanity across the world for millennia. In Christian churches this would evolve into a very substantial obligation, and highly valued contribution. Namely, rituals and masses would be developed to help souls with their after-death journey, which was understood by grieving loved ones to be at times painful.

Since this codex has its origin amongst initiatory groups in early Christianity, the process described here requires the capacity to perform an unidentified Mystery activity (the third mystery-experience). Empowered by this, and gifted with clairvoyance, these esoteric Christians were to then entreat a divine entity (the Holy Goddess of Light) to intervene and alleviate the suffering of a departed friend.

These initiated persons also implored that a better, that is, a less dense, body would be created for this soul, for its next incarnation. This would enable the person to maintain and nurture a consciousness of the spiritual aspect of life.

Next section: avoiding the agony caused by death from torture

TEXT: CHAPTER 109

Mariam then responded, "So then, Lord did you not bring Mysteries into the world so that a person need not die by the death which has been allocated to them by the (debased) Rulers of the karma-determining cosmic influences (and their associated spiritual realms)[418]? Whether it is determined that one is to die by the sword, or to die by the waters, or through tortures, or with violent torments that are within the law, or by some other evil death.

Have you not brought Mysteries into the world, so that by means of these, a person should not die by the Rulers of the karma-determining cosmic influences, but rather that a person should die by a sudden death: that a person should not suffer torments from deaths such as these?

For they who persecute us for your sake, are of very great number; so multitudes pursue us because of your name. But, when they torment us, we can utter the Mystery, and immediately depart from the body without suffering any pain.

The Saviour answered and said to all of his disciples, "Concerning the matter on which you question me, I have spoken to you on an earlier occasion, but listen again so that I may tell you once more. (This concerns) not only you, but every person who accomplishes the first mystery-experience of the First Mystery;[419] whosoever now will perform that Mystery and accomplish it in all of its sigils, types and stations.

This person does not come out of the body when he or she[420] is carrying out the Mystery, but instead after

---

[418] Lit. "Heimarmene'.

[419] "The First Mystery": usu. 'the Ineffable One' as the Coptic states; but this is an error; in chapter 102 of these Mysteries it is said, "For these Mysteries are the gift of the First Mystery".

[420] "he or she": lit. 'he' but as noted earlier, both genders are meant.

TEXT: CHAPTER 109 (cont.)

the person has *completed* this Mystery, by carrying out all its sigils, types and stations (then they will then come out of the body).

Accordingly[421], every time when such a (persecuted) person[422] invokes that Mystery, that person shall (indeed) rescue themselves from everything which the Rulers had pre-determined to befall them. And in that hour this person comes forth from the body of matter, formed by the Rulers; and their soul shall become as if a great light-stream, and shall soar up into the Heights, passing (unharmed) through every realm of the Rulers and every realm of the Light, until it reaches the place of its (own) realm.

Nor does it give answers, nor defences, in any realm at all, for it has no (*need of*) secret symbols (*to pass through a realm.*)

COMMENTARY: CHAPTER 109

Those who conclude that this codex originated two centuries after the time of Jesus, may view this section as 'retrospectively' included as part of a third century fictitious document, to give comfort to their groups, or to impress them. But the Book of Acts testifies to ferocious persecutions of Christians occurring even before the Resurrection, so I conclude that this section, like the majority of the codex, originated in communications of a clairvoyant nature, with the Saviour, about a very real danger.

TEXT: CHAPTER 110   Miriam speaks

And when Jesus had spoken these words, Mariam again hastened to cast herself before Jesus,[423] and made obeisance before him, saying, "Lord, I will

---

[421] "accordingly"; this makes clearer the implication of the literal meaning: 'thereafter' or 'afterwards therefore'.

[422] "such a person invokes": lit. 'he shall invoke'; this refers to initiated Christians as referenced above.

[423] "cast herself before Jesus": lit. 'cast herself at Jesus' feet'; but this is a figure of speech, as Jesus has no physical feet.

TEXT: CHAPTER 110 (cont.)   **Miriam speaks**
question you yet again; reveal (the answer) to us and hide nothing from us." Jesus replied and said to Mariam, "Ask about whatever matter you wish, and I will reveal it to you openly, without parable."

Mariam answered and said, "Well then, Lord, have you not also brought the Mysteries to the world concerning poverty and wealth, and concerning weakness and strength, and concerning diseases and healthy bodies; in a word, because of all things like this?

In order that, when we go to places in the region, and the people do not believe us, and do not heed our words, that we may perform a Mystery of this kind in those regions, so then the people may truly know, in truth, that we are preaching the words of the God of the All.

TEXT NOTE: in Chapter 110
"may truly know": the Mystery involved here, is the exercise of a spiritual power of healing; it is not the kind mentioned earlier wherein the soul perceives, and is thus communing with, divine spirits, through a clairvoyant or higher consciousness being bestowed.

TEXT: CHAPTER 110 (cont.)   **Miriam speaks**
The Saviour answered and said to Mariam, Concerning this Mystery about which you are questioning me, I explained this to you at an earlier time, but I shall repeat it, and now declare the word to you. So now, Mariam, (this concerns) not only you, but every person who shall accomplish the Mystery of "raising the dead": this Mystery makes wholesome[424] (*the influences of*) lesser spirits, and cures all pains and all sicknesses and the blind and the lame and the maimed and the dumb and the deaf.

TEXT NOTE: in Chapter 110
"lesser spirits": not evil 'demons', but 'daemons': the implication here is that these are spirits who have an

---

[424] "makes wholesome": lit. 'cures'.

TEXT NOTE: in Chapter 110
influence upon the various organs of the human body.

"Raising 'the dead': *that is*, curing the lame and the blind and the deaf and the mute; indeed all sicknesses": for here 'raising the dead' is a phrase which is not to be taken literally; it is a figure of speech. It is a term for healing the sick, or for ennobling the soul of those who were not inclined towards godliness.

"The dead" was an Aramaic idiom which referred to people who were not in a positive situation, and is so used often in the New Testament. Thus in the Gospels of Matthew and Luke, when a man declines to follow Jesus immediately, because his father is soon to die, and thus says, 'Let me go and bury my father', Jesus replies, "You follow me, and let the dead bury the dead."

Here, as various scholars report, 'bury my father' is an Aramaic idiom, still in use in a 20th century Aramaic-speaking village. It means to take care of someone until that person dies.[425]

When Jesus says 'the dead' he is talking to a close follower, and for that reason he describes those who are not able to, or are not interested in, joining with him, as 'the dead'. This stark way of speaking is not what Jesus would normally use. But the man in question is a follower of Jesus, hence a more abrupt way of speaking was used.

So Jesus is saying, "Let those who are not reaching out for the new life which I am offering, take care of those who are soon to die." It was a custom amongst the Hebrew religious teachers, and Christian writers, when contrasting any 'sinful' people with a consciously religious or spiritual person, to refer to them as 'dead'; for example,

"As for you, when you were dead in your transgression and sins..." (Eph.2:1), "But the widow who lives for pleasure, is dead, even whilst she

---

[425] For example, Lamsa, G. *Holy Bible from the Ancient Eastern Text*, p.959.

TEXT NOTE: in Chapter 110
lives…" (1 Tim. 5:6) and "you have a reputation (*lit. a name*) for being alive, but you are dead…" (Rev.3:1) Likewise, Jesus once sent out his disciples, commanding them to, "Heal the sick, raise the dead, cleanse those with leprosy, drive out demons".

Here again, 'raise the dead' means to restore persons to health or to a spiritually right soul-state. The phrase 'raise the dead' is not to be understood in a literal way, for the power to bring a deceased person back into earthly life is immense, and only demonstrated twice by Jesus himself. And Steiner taught that those events occurred for exceptional initiatory purposes.

It would almost always be unethical to bring a deceased person back to life, as this would be a huge intervention in the destiny of that person, their society, and in the reality of earthly life.

But in earlier translations, this passage is understood differently, and translated as "Raising the dead; *and* curing the lame and the blind and the deaf and the mute; indeed all sicknesses", but it is in fact, "Raising the dead, *that is*, curing the lame and the blind and the deaf and the mute; indeed all sicknesses":

The Greek word translated as 'and' means not only 'and', but also 'that is', etc. This is the meaning here; only one mystery is involved. Moreover, this 'mystery' is said to be accessible to whoever reaches that Mystery; not only the disciples. So it is very unlikely that such a potent power would be made available to people other than the disciples; and even with the disciples it would be very rare. Finally if the disciples, and others, had such powers *The Book of Acts* and various non-Biblical accounts of the early church would have certainly mentioned such spectacular events.

(The next paragraph was incomplete, and required some additional words to clarify its meaning.)

TEXT: CHAPTER 110 (cont.)   **Miriam speaks**

If that person who receives this[426] Mystery and completes it, and afterwards seeks to understand anything – poverty and riches, weakness and strength, disease or healthy body, and all cures for the body, he shall attain that understanding. In a word, he who completes that Mystery and asks about anything which I have mentioned above, he shall attain that. And if such a person seeks for the power of "raising the dead", that is, curing the lame and the blind and the deaf and the mute, indeed all sicknesses and pains, it will happen to that person with careful attentiveness.[427]

As the Saviour said this, the disciples came forward and cried out together saying, " O Saviour, you have made us very distracted because of the great things which you have said to us. You have borne us aloft; our souls felt impelled to surge forth up to you, because they are from you.

Now, at this time, because of the great things which you have said to us, our souls have become very distracted. They were greatly stirred in this distracted state, pushing us to go forth from ourselves[428] and to arise into the Heights, to the realm of your kingdom."

COMMENTARY: Chapter 110

"our souls are from you": this is a profound truth, referring to the cosmic Christ (enveloping Jesus), as the origin of the human soul. This same truth that was later placed in the Prologue of the Gospel of John,
1:3 All things through it were created, and without the Logos was created not even one thing that has

---

[426] "this Mystery": the text erroneously has '*a* Mystery'.
[427] "careful attentiveness": usu. 'with speed', the Grk. word here (spoudae - σπουδή) also means, diligent, attentive careful.
[428] "to go out of ourselves": but usu. 'come out of us'; which is illogical; whereas 'out of ourselves' means in effect, to go into a state of transcending one's normal soul-boundaries.

COMMENTARY: Chapter 110 (cont.)
been created.[429]
1:4 In the Logos was life, and then the life was the light of human beings.

The great third century sage, Origenes, was clear about this. Origenes writes in his *Commentary on the Gospel of John*, that the Christ, that is, the Logos, is individuated, by existing within human beings.

This is a revolutionary statement; for now the Logos is no longer just an individual entity from long ago in the Beginning, with God. It is also now an individuated entity, because, through the deed of Christ, it is slumbering within the human being.[430]

TEXT: CHAPTER 111
When the disciples had said this, the Saviour continued his discourse, saying to his disciples, "When you go into cities or kingdoms or countries, preach to them at first, saying 'Seek always, and do not cease, until you find the Mysteries of the Light, which will take you into the kingdom of the Light.'

Say to them, beware of false teachings. For many will appear in my name and say:
'It is I (your Messiah)'!
But it will not be I; and thus they (the false messiahs) shall lead many astray.

TEXT NOTE: in Chapter 111
"It is 'I' – (your Messiah)" !
This sentence occurs in the Gospel of Mark (13:5-6) in the context of the future re-appearing of the Messiah. "Jesus said, Take heed, that no person deceives you, for many shall come in my name, saying, 'It is I'...take heed and watch".

But here in the Pistis Sophia codex, as in the

---

[429] Logos is called the neuter 'it' as we don't think of deities as gender-based, and the Light (a neutral word in Greek) is now the form of the Logos.
[430] See my *The Gospel of John, an Initiatory Quest Translation*.

TEXT NOTE: in Chapter 111 (cont.)
Gospel, the Greek has the profound esoteric expression, "ego eimi". This meant in daily life simply, " It's me ! ", or " It is I ! "

But this Greek term has a second meaning; it points to the words of God to Moses (in the Book of Exodus) when God is revealing to Moses what His name is. Both the Hebrew and the Greek on this level mean:

A: "I am the 'I':

That is, I (God) am your 'I am'.

In Biblical terms, only 'God' can say that – which is in effect, the Jahve-Christ reality. Here in the codex, it appears to have only the more straightforward historical meaning : 'It is I – your Messiah". However, the deeper, second meaning may also be meant:
"I am the 'I' (or, I am your 'I am')
If so, then this is a profoundly meaningful initiatory truth, indicating that the higher 'I', as it develops in the human being, derives from the Divine.

TEXT: CHAPTER 111 (cont.)
Now, therefore, to all who draw near to you, and are spiritually discerning of you, and thus are attentive to your words, give to them the Mysteries of the Light; and do not hide anything from them. To those for whom it is appropriate, give them the higher Mysteries; and to those for whom it is appropriate, give the lesser Mysteries; so conceal nothing from anyone (for whom it is appropriate).

But the Mystery-act of "raising of the dead" – that is, of healing the sick, give to no one. Nor give instruction in it, for this Mystery belongs to the (divine) Rulers; it and all its invocations. For this reason, do not give it to anyone, nor teach it, until you establish belief throughout the entire region; in order that, when you enter into cities or the countryside, and they do not receive you, nor believe in you, nor pay attention to your words, you may

TEXT: CHAPTER 111 (cont.)

then "raise the dead" in those places; that is, heal the lame, the blind, and all kinds of diseases in those places. Then, by all such means they will believe in you, that you preach the God of all creation[431] and they will have belief in all your words. When the Saviour had said this, he continued with his discourse. He said to Mariam, "So now Mariam, listen concerning the theme[432] about which you questioned[433] me: 'What exerts pressure on a person's soul until they sin?'

(In this next section:
The earthly soul, its spiritual part and its Double)

So now, hear. When the babe comes into the world, the spiritual-being is feeble in it, the soul also is feeble in it, and the counterfeit spirit (*the Double*) is also feeble in it; in a word, all three of them are feeble.

None of them has any perception of anything, whether good or evil, because of the burden of forgetfulness; which is very heavy. Moreover, the body too, is feeble. But the (growing) child absorbs the pleasurable sensory world of the (debased) Rulers.

During this process, the person's spiritual-being absorbs into itself a portion of the spirit which is mixed in with the pleasurable sensory world.

And also the soul draws into itself a portion of the soul-substance which is within the pleasurable sensory world.

And its 'counterfeit spirit' draws into itself some evil together with its lusts: a portion of evil which is

---

[431] "all creation": lit. 'of the All'.
[432] "theme": lit. 'word'.
[433] the theme of what causes sin was a major topic for people interested in spirituality and salvation; obviously Mariam had earlier asked about this. In previous chapters, Jesus refers to various earlier queries coming from his disciples or instruction sessions.

TEXT: CHAPTER 111 (cont.)

within the pleasurable sensory world.

Whereas the body (*of matter*) draws into itself the physical matter (*i.e., nutrition*) present in the pleasurable sensory world; this material substance has no capacity to perceive and thus to interact,[434] (*as it is devoid of sentiency*).

In contrast to this, the Destiny of the person (*their karmic dynamics*) absorbs nothing of the pleasurable sensory world, because it is not interwoven[435] in this. Instead, the mode of being[436] in which this Destiny comes into the world, remains just as it was.

And gradually, the spiritual-being, and the soul, and the Double (*lit. 'the counterfeit spirit'*), all become stronger; and each of these then perceives and responds, according to their nature. The spiritual-being perceives and interacts, in order to seek out the Light of the Heights. By contrast, the soul perceives and responds, in order to seek out the place of righteousness; but this place (*the astral level around the earthly world*) is a mixture, for it is the place of the Mixture (*of noble and debased astral qualities*).

However, the Double (*the counterfeit spirit*) seeks out all evil and lusts and sins. And immediately, these three (*our germinal spiritual-being, our soul and Double*) each begin perceiving and thus responding, according to their own nature. Whereas the body can sense nothing, unless it draws in spiritual being-ness from the pleasurable sensory world (*which would bestow some sentiency on it*).

Hence the receivers of the Erinyes instruct their servitors to accompany them, to become witnesses to all the sins which are committed, with regard to the manner in which these souls are to be chastized in

---

[434] "and thus to interact": I have added this phrase, because as the next paragraph shows, this interaction of the human being through what it perceives, is the core message of these words of Christ.

[435] "interwoven": lit. 'not mixed in'.

[436] Coptic here is (ϭοτ) and means: condition, mode of being, type of, etc.

TEXT: CHAPTER 111 (cont.) **Miriam speaks** the judgments.
And consequently after this, the Double observes all the sins and evil which the Rulers of the great karma-determining cosmic sphere[437] have commanded for the soul; and the Double conveys this to the soul. Whereas the spiritual-nature within it, impels the soul to seek after the place of the Light, and of the entire Godhead.

TEXT NOTE: in Chapter 111
"the *spiritual-being* is feeble in it": usu. 'the power'. But the word here (ϬΟΜ) is the same word (which does mean 'power') that the scribe mistakenly used, early in the codex, for 'soul' or 'entity' or 'being', which correctly is ϬΙΝ or ϬΙΜ. But since in this section of the chapter the 'entity' or 'being' is given a higher place than the soul, here it has to mean the somewhat germinal 'spirit-being' or 'spiritual-nature' of the person.

"the pleasurable sensory world:" usually 'food' (Schmidt), or 'the foods' (MacDermot); Mead is much nearer with 'the delights'. What is meant is that the now incarnate soul, enjoying the pleasures of existing in the world of matter, begins to absorb, through mental perceiving, that which constitutes the earthly reality. So not only sense impressions, but also ethereal and astral energies are interacted with, as we are also immersed in these.

We interact with these, both those of a debased matter-focused type, and of the higher spiritual 'light'. This latter pervades the world, behind or above the material-sensory level. Also included in terms of absorption, are material substances which simply build up the body.

So here is where the crucial inner battle – spiritually observed – begins. Does the person absorb and delight in, purely material sensations and thoughts – which weigh down the soul, even degrade it – or has it some awareness of higher ideas and

---

[437] lit. 'the Heimarmene'.

TEXT NOTE: in Chapter 111 (cont.)
higher realities? The Coptic word here (ⲧⲣⲩϥⲟⲟⲏⲅⲉ) is derived from the Greek noun, 'truphai' (τρυφή) which does not mean 'food', but "an object in which one has pleasure".[438]

There are several Greek words for food; however these include the very similar word, trophae (τροφή). Unfortunately 'truphai' was incorrectly used for 'food' instead of 'trophae' on one occasion in this codex; but on the other five occasions a correct word is used for food. This error has blurred the meaning of truphai, causing the uncertainty in some earlier translations.

This general perception, that whatever is subtly, deceptively malignant in our physical world, is experienced and absorbed by human beings as pleasurable, is a truth, widely known in ancient spiritual traditions. It is not denouncing innocent and wholesome earthly delights.

TEXT: CHAPTER 111 (cont.)
And the Double (*i.e., the counterfeit spirit*) leads the soul astray, and constantly impels it to commit all its unethical deeds and all of its lusts and all of its sins, and it is continuously allocated to the soul, and is hostile to the soul; making it do all this evil, with all its sins. Also the Double incites the servitors of the Erinyes, so that they do become witnesses to all the sins which it shall cause the soul to do.

TEXT NOTE: in Chapter 111
The Erinyes are spirits whose task is to bring about corrective chastizement of unethical behaviour; that is, they act educationally upon the human being; as a kind of externalized conscience for the human soul. They are not malignant spirits. The word for 'chastize' is taken from the Greek (kolasis - κόλασις) and although it could mean to punish, including retribution decreed by gods, it also meant to undertake a (possibly severe) pruning of a diseased or

---

[438] Scott & Liddell, *English-Greek Dictionary*. This word can also mean daintiness or delicateness.

ailing tree; so it meant a corrective measure. It is this second meaning that applies to those who have died, in their journey through the After-life realms.

TEXT: CHAPTER 111 (cont.)
Furthermore, when the soul rests at night, or during the daytime, the Double influences it in dreams, and in fact with earthly desires. The Double causes the soul to desire everything worldly. In short, it incites the soul towards everything which the (debased) Rulers have (generally) decreed for it.

Thus it becomes the enemy of the soul, impelling it to do that which the soul does not want to do. So now, Mariam, *this* is the enemy of the soul, and it is this which incites the soul to carry out all its sins.

TEXT NOTE: In this section is:
The after-death experience of a non-initiated soul

Now when the life of a person is completed, then firstly there comes forward the Destiny of that person (*a spiritual figure signifying its karmic obligations*), and this leads the person to their death, through the agency of the (debased) Rulers with their (ensnaring) bonds – bonds by which the soul is bound, through (the dictates of) the karma-determining cosmic influences.[439]

Thereafter the receivers of the Erinyes appear and take that person out of their body. Then these receivers spend three days circling around with that soul in all the realms; sending it into all the Aions of the cosmos.

Then the Double (*counterfeit spirit*) and its Destiny-spirit[440] follow that soul; whilst the person's spiritual-being withdraws, up to the Holy Goddess of the Light.

---

[439] lit. 'Heimarmene' (the lower section of Devachan).
[440] "Destiny-spirit": a spirit representing its karmic obligations.

TEXT NOTE: in Chapter 111

The Erinyes: as noted earlier, their task is to ensure that the after-death journey is correlated to the ethical or unethical deeds of the soul; including that the right corrective chastizement for unethical behaviour is encountered.

"three days circling around in all the realms": as noted earlier, this is about the sensation the soul experiences as it is released from the body. This separating from the body occurs during the first three days after death. There is a preliminary sensation of expanding out into the planetary spheres.

TEXT: CHAPTER 111 (cont.)

Then after three days the receivers of the Erinyes lead the soul to the Amente (*the Soul-world*) of the Chaos (*i.e., the lower Soul-world*). And they bring it down to the Amente, where they hand it over to those spirits who chastise. Then these receivers withdraw to their own realms, in accordance with the administering of the deeds of the (debased) Rulers in relation to the coming-forth (from the body) of human souls.

And the Double (*counterfeit spirit*) becomes the receiver of the soul, because it is assigned to it; transporting it according to the sins which this Double had caused the soul to commit; it is very hostile to the soul.

And when the soul completes the chastizements in the Chaoses according to the sins which it had committed, the Double brings it up from these Chaoses; for it was assigned to the soul, transporting it to every realm because of the sins which it has committed (*in those realms*). Then it leads the soul forth, on to the pathway of the Rulers of The Midst.[441]

And when the soul reaches this realm, its Rulers question it about the spiritual dynamics (*lit.*

---

[441] The Midst: this is the 7th level of Devachan.

TEXT: CHAPTER 111 (cont.)

Mysteries) of its Destiny (*karma*).[442] But if the soul has not discovered[443] the spiritual dynamics of its Destiny (karma), then the Rulers (themselves) enquire into the Destiny of these influences. Then those Rulers chastize[444] that soul according to the sins for which it is right to be chastized. I shall explain to you the types of chastizements in the over-all configuration of the cosmos.

Now when it happens that the chastisements of that soul in the judgments of the Rulers of the Midst are completed, the Double (*the counterfeit spirit*) brings the soul up, out of all the realms of the Rulers of the Midst. The soul is brought into the presence of the Light of the Sun, in accordance with command of the first human, Jeu. And it brings the soul before the judge, the Holy Goddess of the Light. She assesses the soul and finds that it is a sinning soul.

She then casts her light-being into it, for the sake of establishing (*over centuries*) the soul (*i.e., its new soul-body*), together with its (future physical) body, and together with the commonality of (its) perceiving. I shall explain to you the nature of all this in the over-all configuration of the cosmos.

COMMENTARY: in Chapter 111

"Jeu: as noted earlier, this is actually 'Ieou'. Very little is said about this entity: it is a very high spiritual being who established the various roles and places of the debased Archons; and is described as the Overseer of the divine Light.[445]

"the commonality of (its) perceiving": This unusual, and very unexpected, Coptic phrase has been

---

[442] "karma": lit. Fate.
[443] "discovered": lit. 'found'.
[444] "chastize": as noted earlier, this chastising is a corrective action, aiming to educate the soul about its ethics.
[445] The inferior documents, texts 4 & 5, contain fantastical statements about Jeu.

COMMENTARY: in Chapter 111 (cont.)
difficult[446] for earlier translators; it is used with no explanation as to what it is about. Firstly, I note that in any serious text about spiritual beings and realms, the faculty of perception is an underlying theme.

It is clear that perceiving refers to a fundamental, but subtle, aspect of human consciousness. The divide between clairvoyant perceiving and physical perceiving is usually noted and the former validated, in spiritual texts.

In this codex, clairvoyant perceiving is emphasized in key sections; e.g., in Chapter 83,
> It is you who have given comprehension of the Light to our intelligence; you have given to us (the capacity for) perception (of the Light) and for grasping very exalted ideas.

But here in Chapter 111, the emphasis is different; namely, that a divine being, an exalted Goddess, needs to equip each soul, as it prepares to reincarnate, with the ability to perceive the sensory physical world in a manner which is accurate, and therefore results in a mental image, or other sensory impressions, such as tones, odours, etc, *which will be common to all humankind.*

This raises the question, why would our sensory perceptions not be common, i.e., the same, to all people? Is that not a given fact? The implication here is that without this Goddess who is located somewhere within the realm of the Christ, each person would perceive a tree, or a perfume, or a sound, quite differently to other people.

There appears to be no text from antiquity which refers to this chaotic scenario. There is however a direct reference to this possible scenario, and how it was overcome, in the work of Rudolf Steiner. He taught that in remote times, as primordial humanity was beginning its long journey across the Ages, in life after life, the sense-organs were threatened with a

---

[446] 'the sharing of perception' (Schmidt & Horner) / 'the communion of perception' (McDermot)/ 'the community of sense' (Mead).

COMMENTARY: in Chapter 111 (cont.)
serious problem; they were about to be pervaded, and thus distorted, by the soul's own vehement, primitive passions, deriving from the debased, malignant spirits.

This would prevent an objective relaying of the factual sensory object via the sensory organs, across to one's consciousness; instead a distorted, subjective impression would be received. Steiner saw that the compassion of the pre-incarnate Jesus (in spirit realms) was intensely stirred in regard to this impending psychological 'imprisonment' of the human soul's consciousness in the physical world. Jesus entreated the cosmic Christ to assist humanity.

As a result, the cosmic Christ rayed-forth divine healing light into the Earth's aura, enabling a clear, objective faculty of perception to occur. This task of the cosmic Christ involved directly overcoming the influences of malignant spirits (the ahrimanic-luciferic hosts).

This scenario corresponds well with the above reference to a 'commonality of perception' constituting a priority for the divine spirits, as they prepare a soul for its new life. But whether this is what the words of Christ are referring to here, is unclear.

TEXT: CHAPTER 111 (cont.)
Then the Holy Goddess of the Light seals that soul and gives it to one of her receivers, and ensures it is carried into a body which is appropriate to the sins which it has committed. Truly, I say to you, she will not release that soul from the transformations of the body, before it has given its last cycle, according to what is appropriate.

And concerning all this I will tell you all the types (*i.e., variations*) of these things, and also the types of bodies into which souls shall be cast according to their sins; all this I shall tell you when I finish telling you of the over-all configuration of the cosmos.

COMMENTARY: CHAPTER 111
"transformations of the body": another reference to reincarnation. Christ revealed this to be a truth to his inner circle, but this conflicts very much with the exoteric doctrines of the church. However, the disciples would not have been at all surprised, given that this truth was known to the inner circle of Jewish leaders, the Pharisees, as we noted in the Introduction.

TEXT: CHAPTER 112
(The After-Death Experience of an initiated soul)
And Jesus continued further in his conversation, "Furthermore, if there is a soul which has not listened to the Double (*counterfeit spirit*) in all of its deeds, and thus has become morally good, and receives the Mysteries in the second Space, or those of the third Space which are within, then, when the time arrives for the coming forth from the body of that soul, the Double follows after that soul.

This, together with the soul's Destiny (*a spiritual figure signifying its karmic obligations*) follow along after the soul, on the pathway by which it is go up to the Heights. Yet, whilst it is still far from the Heights, this soul speaks forth the Mystery of the releasing of the seals and all the bonds of the Double; bonds by which the (debased) Rulers bound it (*this Double*) to the soul.

And when these Mysteries are thus spoken, the bonds of the Double are released, and these cease coming into the soul. The Double then releases that soul, in accordance with the injunctions issued to it by the Rulers of the great karma-determining cosmic influences (Heimarmene); in that these declare, "Release not this soul unless it speaks the Mystery of the breaking of all the seals with which we have bound it."

It shall then happen, when a soul has spoken forth the Mystery of the breaking of the seals and of all the bonds of the Double (counterfeit spirit), that the latter shall cease to burden that soul, and shall cease

TEXT: CHAPTER 112 (cont.)

to be bound to it.

At that moment the soul then speaks forth a Mystery, and (*thereby*) dismisses 'the Destiny-spirit' to its own place amongst the Rulers who are in the pathway of The Midst. And then the soul speaks forth a Mystery, and (*thereby*) sends the Double (*counterfeit spirit*) to the Rulers of the karma-determining cosmic influences (*the lower levels of Devachan*); to the place in which the Double became bound to the soul (*originally*).

TEXT NOTE in Chapter 112

"in the pathway of The Midst": an especially deep revelation, showing again that deep initiatory wisdom is at core of this document. The Midst is the seventh, the highest level, of Devachan. Karmic influences, binding the soul to the Earth, encompass all of Devachan; but have no presence in the realms beyond (such as the Buddhi realm; i.e., Aions 15 to 17).

TEXT: CHAPTER 112 (cont.)

And in that moment, the soul becomes (like) a great out-raying stream of Light. Then the receivers of the Erinyes, who had brought the soul out of its body, are afraid of the Light and make obeisance before it.[447] So in that moment, the soul becomes like a great out-raying stream of Light – becoming a great wing of Light, and penetrates every place of the Rulers and every level of the Light, until it reaches the place of her realm; the realm wherein the soul had received Mysteries.

But now, if another soul has received Mysteries in the first Realm from without, (whilst on the Earth), and after receiving Mysteries and completing them, should turn and sin again, even after completing the Mysteries: but then the time for the coming-forth (from the body) of that soul is due, so the receiver of the Erinyes arrive, to lead that soul out of its body.

---

[447] Lit. 'fell on their faces' before it.

TEXT: CHAPTER 112 (cont.)
And then the Destiny and the Double[448] follow that soul. Because the Double is bound to it with the seals and bonds of the (debased) Rulers.

So the Double follows that soul which travels on the pathways of the Double. It speaks forth the Mystery of the undoing of all the bonds and all the seals with which the (debased) Rulers bind that soul to the Double.

TEXT NOTE: in Chapter 112
"pathways of the Double": that is, the soul's nature has a strong resonance with the spirit-dynamics of the Double, and is thus linked to its path.

TEXT: CHAPTER 112 (cont.)
And when the soul speaks forth the Mystery of the undoing of all the seals, the bonds of the seals which bind the Double into the soul, are released immediately.

And in the moment the soul speaks forth the Mystery of the releasing of the seals, the bonds of the seals which bind the Double to the soul are immediately released, and it ceases to be allotted to that soul.

And in the moment the soul speaks forth a Mystery, it restrains the Double and the Destiny and dismisses them; so these now follow (*along behind*) it. So neither of them have authority, however, the soul has authority over them. And in that moment the receivers of the soul appear and snatch that soul, with the Mysteries it has attained, from the receivers of the Erinyes. These Erinyes withdraw to the works of the Rulers with regard to the arranging of the coming forth of (other) souls (*from their bodies*).

Whilst the receivers of the soul, who belong to the Light become wings of light for that soul; they become garments of light for that soul. But they do not lead it into the Chaoses, because it is not lawful

---

[448] lit. the 'counterfeit soul'.

TEXT: CHAPTER 112 (cont.)

to lead into the Chaoses a soul who is initiated (*lit.* '*has received Mysteries*'). Instead they guide it into the pathway of the Rulers of (the debased) Midst. And when it reaches these Rulers of The Midst, they come forth to encounter it, full of fear, and (enveloped) in fierce heat, and of dreadful appearances.

In short, they are in great, immeasurable fear. Then, in this moment the soul speaks forth the Mystery of defence from them[449]. They then become exceedingly afraid and yield[450] from fear of the Mystery which the soul has uttered, namely from the defence which it has intoned.

Then this (*initiated*) soul dismisses the destiny-enforcing[451] role of these spirits saying, "Receive back to yourselves your destiny-enforcing ! From this moment I shall not come again into your realms; I have become a stranger to you forever. I shall go to the place of my inheritance."

And when the soul has said this, the receivers of the Light soar aloft with it, up to the Heights, and guide it out of the Aions of the karma-determining cosmic influences (*Heimarmene*), thus leading it up through all the Aions whilst the soul intones the defence for each of these Aions, together with the seals. I shall (later) explain to you the nature of all this, in the over-all configuration of the cosmos.[452]

And the soul gives back the Double (counterfeit spirit) to the Rulers, and it speaks forth to them the Mystery of the bonds with which the Double was bound to her. And the soul says to them, "Receive back your Double ! From this moment I am not entering your realms again. I have become a stranger to you forever."

Then the soul hands over to them the seals, together with the (*mantric*) defence. Having declared

---

[449] "defence from them": lit. 'from their defence'.
[450] "yield": lit. 'fall on their faces'
[451] "karma-enforcing": lit. just the one word 'Fate' (i.e., karma).
[452] "of the cosmos": usu. 'of the mysteries': but the Coptic is in error here; it cannot be 'Mysteries'.

TEXT: CHAPTER 112 (cont.)
this, the receivers of the Light soar aloft with the soul, taking it out of all the Aions of the karma-determining cosmic influences (*Heimarmene*). So they take it out of all the Aions. The soul gives back to every realm, the defence against each realm; (thus she returns) the defence against every realm, together with the seals of the empowered Ones: of the Ruler, Adamas.

The (*initiated*) soul presents the defences of all the Rulers of all the realms of the (debased) Left – of whom I will tell you all the defences and seals, when I explain the over-all configuration of the cosmos. So then the receivers will bring that soul to the Holy Goddess of the Light, and then that soul presents to this Holy Goddess of the Light, her seals and the holy spiritual radiance[453] of her reverential intonings.

TEXT NOTE in Chapter 112
("her seals": these are the seals which the soul has been absorbing from this Goddess's light. A seal is the spiritual essence of something, a kind of portal into that deity or realm.)
"the Left": this is Aion 13, (Devachan 6), but here it refers to the debased aspect of this realm.

TEXT: CHAPTER 112 (cont.)
The Holy Goddess of the Light and also the seven goddesses of the Light, all examine that soul, so that they may all find their signs within it: namely, their seals, their baptisms and spiritual 'anointing oil'. And the Holy Goddess of the Light seals that soul, and the receivers of the Light baptize that soul, and give it the spiritual 'anointing oil'. And each of the goddesses of the Light seals the soul with her seal.

And also, the receivers of the Light give it over to the great Sabaoth the Good, who is at the portal of The Life, in the realms of those of The Right; he who

---

[453] "holy spiritual radiance": lit. 'glory'; which means here the inherent holiness of its spiritual nature.

TEXT: CHAPTER 112 (cont.)

is called The Father. And this soul offers up to him the radiant splendour[454] of her reverential intonings[455], and her seals and her[456] defences. Then Sabaoth the Good seals this with his seals (*i.e., affirms her by imbuing it*).

Then the soul offers up[457] its spiritual (*initiatory*) understanding, and the radiant splendour of its reverential intonings, and the seals of the entire realm of those of The Right.

TEXT NOTE in Chapter 112

The above paragraph is briefly noting a sublime event, wherein the initiated person has attained to the first level of the Buddhi realm (Aion 15); which is called The Right. Usually the above interaction is translated differently, where 'his' is preferred over 'hers':

"And this soul offers up to *him* the holy spirituality of *his* songs of praise and *his* seals and *his* defences. Then Sabaoth the Good seals this (*i.e., affirms it by imbuing it*) with his seals."[458]

But this means that the initiated soul is offering to the deity its own inner nature, and whilst this is possible, it is very unlikely, because in this dynamic the soul is presenting its spiritual attainments to the Deity. It is also unlikely that 'the Father' would have *reverential* intonings, since all the lesser beings are to revere him. It is even less possible that the Father has 'songs of praise'.

TEXT NOTE: A sublime communion

So here the 'perfected' (initiated) soul undergoes a communion through its high initiatory consciousness with that of a divine spirit called 'the Father'; and

---

[454] lit. 'Glory'.

[455] usu. the more prosaic phrase, 'songs of praise'.

[456] "her": usu. 'his' as in the Coptic text; but I conclude that this is an error.

[457] "offers up": lit. 'gives (over)'.

[458] "Sabaoth the Good": as noted in the Foreword, nothing is known of this deity.

TEXT NOTE: A sublime communion
with other high deities in that realm. (How this 'Father' is related to 'the Father' referred to in the Gospels, is not clear.)

"spiritual (*initiatory*) understanding": usually translated as 'knowledge' or even 'science'. The Greek word here is 'epistaemae' (ἐπιστήμη), which does have the above meanings also. But what is meant with this word here is a cosmic initiatory understanding or gnosis; the word 'knowledge' is insufficient to convey this. As the initiatory Hermetica text teaches, "Gnosis is the goal of spiritual understanding ('epistaemae'); and spiritual understanding is the gift of God."[459]

TEXT: CHAPTER 112 (cont.)
They all seal it (*the soul*) with their seals; and Melchizedek, the great receiver of the Light, who is in the realm of those of The Right (*Buddhi 1, Aion 15*), seals that soul. Then all the receivers of Melchizedek also seal that soul, and lead it up into The Treasury of Light (*Aion 16*).

And the soul offers up her radiant splendour, and the reverence and praise of her reverential intonings, together with all the seals of the realms of the Light. Then all those of The Treasury of Light seal it with their seals, and then it goes up to the Inheritance of Light.

COMMENTARY: CHAPTER 112
No further comments are needed here.

TEXT: CHAPTER 113
Now after the Saviour had said these things to his disciples, he then said to them: "Do you understand in what manner I am speaking with you?" Mariam started forward again and said, "Yes, my Lord, I understand in what manner you are speaking, and I will comprehend all of the words. Now at this time,

---

[459] In the Grk. (*Libellus* 10) Γνῶσις δὲ ἐστιν ἐπιστήμης τὸ τέλος, ἐπιστήμη δὲ δῶρον τοῦ θεοῦ.

TEXT: CHAPTER 113 (cont)

concerning these words which you have spoken, my mind has brought forth four thoughts within me.

And my companion-of-light has guided (me), and has rejoiced, and has welled up within me, wishing to come forth from me, and to go into you. So now my Lord, listen to me and I will say to you the four thoughts which have come into existence within me. The first thought which has arisen within me, concerning the word which you have spoken: "So the soul gives the defence and the seal (*i.e., the core spiritual signifier*) against all the Rulers which are in the places of the Ruler, Adamas. And it offers[460] the reverence and the radiant splendour of all their seals and the reverential intonings, to the places of the Light."

Concerning these words now, you once said to us, when a coin was brought to you, and you saw that it was of silver and copper, you asked, "Whose image is this?" They said, "That of the Caesar." But when you saw that it was a mixture of silver and copper, you said, "Give therefore what is Caesar's to Caesar, and what is God's to God". That is to say, when the soul receives Mysteries, it gives the defence against all the Rulers of the realm of the Ruler, Adamas. And the soul offers the reverence and the radiant splendour to all those of the Light.

And the word, "Being made up of silver and copper, it glistened as you beheld it" – that is a signifier[461] of this: that in the soul is the presence of the Light, which is the refined silver, but (also) in it is the Double (*counterfeit spirit*), namely the denser copper. This, my Lord, is the first thought.

TEXT NOTE: in Chapter 113

"It glistened as you...": the origin of these words, revealing a different version of the famous incident, is unknown. This incident is mentioned in all three

---

[460] The text includes "the defence and": this is a repetition made in error by the scribe.
[461] Lit. 'a type'.

TEXT NOTE: in Chapter 113
synoptic Gospels, and in the Gospel of Thomas and also in a papyrus fragment (P. Egerton 2).[462] But only the Pistis Sophia codex has the above version. I have altered the incorrect sequence of the sentence; as given in previous versions "It shone, when you saw it was made of silver and copper."

TEXT: CHAPTER 113 (cont.)
Now the second thought you have just finished saying to us, about the soul who receives Mysteries:
'And when it reaches the Rulers of the (debased) Midst (Devachan 7), these come forth full of fear. Then, in this moment the soul speaks forth the Mystery of defence from them. They then become exceedingly afraid and yield, from fear of the Mystery which the soul has uttered. Then this soul dismisses their destiny-enforcing saying, "Receive back to yourselves your destiny-enforcing ! And it dismisses the Double (counterfeit spirit) to it place.

And the soul intones the defence for each of these Aions, together with the seals of each of the Rulers who are on the pathway to the Midst. And the soul offers up her radiant splendour, and the reverence and praise of her reverential intonings, together with all the seals of the realms of the Light.'

Now concerning this thought my Lord, you once spoke, through the mouth of our brother Paul, saying, "Give taxes to whom taxes are due, give revenue to whom revenue is due, give respect to whom respect is due, and give honour to whom honour is due; and do not owe anything to anyone."

That is to say, my Lord, the soul which receives Mysteries gives the defence against all places (*of the debased Rulers*). This, my Lord, is the second thought.

TEXT NOTE: in Chapter 113
The above words of St. Paul are also to be found in his epistle to the Romans (13:7), that was written

---

[462] As noted by Davies and Allison in *Matthew 19-28*, in the Internat. Crit. Commentary, T & T Clark, 1997.

TEXT NOTE: in Chapter 113
about CE 55, which is ten years or so after the dates implied in the Pistis Sophia codex (approx. CE 33-44), for these communications from the risen Jesus. So what does this mean? I conclude that it is entirely possible that these words were spoken by Paul in the late 30's, after his escape from Damascus and return to Jerusalem, or in the early 40's, and heard by some disciples elsewhere; and then written down later. For Paul was already founding churches in the late 30's of the first century.

TEXT: CHAPTER 113 (cont.)
Regarding the third thought, this concerns the word which you spoke to us earlier, "...the Double is hostile to the soul; making it do all this evil, with all its sins. It incites the servitors of the Erinyes, so that the soul is (*definitely*) chastized for all the sins which the Double shall cause the soul to do."

So the soul after death goes through chastisements for whatever sins it commits; and it is impelled (*but not compelled*) to be like this, because of its own Double. Moreover, the Double ensures that the servitors of the Erinyes, who act as 'karma note-takers' definitely are made aware of these sins. So the Double has a twofold way of attacking each person.

Now, about these words, you said to us earlier, "The foes of the man are the dwellers in his house"; that is, the dwellers in the house are the Double (counterfeit spirit) and its Destiny-spirit. These are always hostile to the soul, making it commit all sins and all iniquities. This then, my Lord, is my third thought.

TEXT NOTE: in Chapter 113
"and its Destiny-spirit": this is the only place where the Destiny-spirit is presented as an enemy of the soul; usually it is the Double which is like this. The reason for this is that Mariam has gained a deep initiatory knowledge from Jesus. Rudolf Steiner's work brings some clarity here, namely that the karma-impelling influences (the Destiny Spirit) are

TEXT NOTE: in Chapter 113
wisely determining one's future. But there is another aspect to this; it is the spiritual dynamics behind one's karma which bind one to the Earth. The ethical debts incurred from past lives need to be balanced out, or neutralized. When there are no more karmic debts, then the human being is free to ascend up into a higher state of being.

However, spiritual powers demand that karmic requirements are met; in that sense the Destiny-spirit can be viewed as an enemy of the soul. But this perspective is not emphasized in the work of Rudolf Steiner, because in the modern age, we are much more focused on the duties and opportunities offered by life on Earth, than were people of 2,000 years ago.

TEXT: CHAPTER 113 (cont.)
The fourth thought also concerns words which you earlier said, "The soul, when it comes forth from the body and proceeds on the way with the Double (counterfeit spirit), may not have found the Mystery of the releasing of all the bonds and the seals which bind it to the Double, so that it ceases to be allotted to the soul."

Now if it does not find this Mystery, the Double takes the soul into the presence of the Holy Goddess of the Light, who is the judge. And the judge, the Holy Goddess of the Light, examines the soul and finds that it has sinned, and since the soul also has not found the Mysteries of the Light, she hands it over to one of her receivers. Her receiver leads it further, and casts it into a body (*after a long time*). And the soul does not come out of the transformations of the body (*i.e., reincarnating*) until it has done (*i.e., completed*) its last cycle.

TEXT NOTE: in Chapter 113
There is a deep message here; that an initiated soul can cease being in the 'transformations of the body'. That is, the soul can bring its potential future reincarnations to an end earlier than the last possible

TEXT NOTE: in Chapter 113 (cont.)
Age for any incarnation to happen on this planet.

"*after a long time*": there is no mention in the text of the time between one incarnation and the next, but Rudolf Steiner's research suggest that it is often around 600 – 1,000 years.

Bringing reincarnation to an early end

We experience yet again the much more cosmically focused nature of esoteric Christianity, compared to normal Christian thought. For in that other highly esoteric Christian text, *The Book of Revelation*, there is a veiled statement from the risen Jesus which affirms the above words.

A substantial commentary written on this initiatory text from an initiatory perspective is very rare, but from my research, a brief text in chapter 3 (v.12) is shown to allude to this desirable outcome for spiritually advanced (initiated) Christians; namely that of shortening the number of future incarnations; "The one who is triumphant (in initiatory striving)[463] I shall make into a pillar in the temple of my God; and he never need to depart from it…"

TEXT: CHAPTER 113 (cont.)

Now, regarding these words, you did say in an earlier time, "Settle matters quickly with your adversary, while you are with him on the road, or your accuser may hand you over to the judge, and the judge may hand you over to the officer, and you may be thrown into jail, and you do not get out of there until you have paid the last penny."

TEXT NOTE: in Chapter 113

The above words are very similar to the account given in Matthew's Gospel (5:25). But I note that this is a Gospel passage which in recent times has been incorrectly translated; an extra phrase has been

---

[463] "triumphant in initiatory striving": the word here 'nikoen' (νικῶν) was used for sports and other daily challenges, but also for initiatory striving (e.g., *Hermetica*: Stobaei, excerpt 2B.)

TEXT NOTE: in Chapter 113 (cont.)
added. For example, in the NIV and NRSV: "Settle matters quickly with your adversary, *who is taking you to court / on the way to court.*"

The phrase about 'taking you to court' is not in the Greek, it has been added to try to make sense of the passage. For this extra phrase places the scene in the earthly world of disputes. But as Mariam is about to discuss, it is entirely about working to improve one's soul; getting rid of unethical traits whilst incarnate, thereby avoiding difficult times in the Soul-world after death.

TEXT: CHAPTER 113 (cont.)
Now, these words are clearly about every person who comes forth from their body and travels on their path with the Double, and who does not find the Mystery for releasing of all the seals and all the bonds, so that it can release itself from the Double, which is bound to it.

That soul who has not found the Mysteries of the Light and the Mysteries of the releasing of the Double to which she is bound – well, if the soul has not found this, then the Double leads that soul to the Holy Goddess of the Light. Then the Holy Goddess of the Light, the judge, hands that soul over to one of her receivers, and her receiver casts this soul into the sphere of the Aions. (*That is, into the karma-determining cosmic influences and their associated spiritual spheres, or Heimarmene.*)

This soul does not come out of the transformations of the body (*i.e., reincarnating*) until it has done (*i.e., completed*) the last cycle allotted to it. This then, my Lord, is the fourth thought.

COMMENTARY: CHAPTER 113
The words are similar to Matthew's Gospel (5:25), "agree with your adversary..." but I do not see this as evidence of the codex originating long after the Gospels were written. The codex itself indicates that these dialogues occurred about CE 33-44. So, when

COMMENTARY: CHAPTER 113

Jesus spoke the above words (between CE 30-33) the disciples would have heard them, as Mariam says here. Statements from Clement of Alexandria (AD 150-210) concerning the early years of the church suggest that the Gospel of Matthew was composed by CE 42.[464] Also the work of Thiede and D'Ancona (*The Jesus Papyrus*) has revealed substantial evidence for an early date. Such early dating is widely rejected, but it is not disproven. It may be confirmed in the future that the Gospel of Matthew, or a proto-type of it, was composed very early.[465]

TEXT: CHAPTER 114   Mariam speaks

It then happened, when Jesus heard these words of Mariam, that he said, "Excellent, you all-blessed Mariam: spiritual one ! This is the meaning of the words which I have spoken. Mariam responded, saying, "Yet my Lord, I will further question you, for as from now I want to question you on all things with exactness. For this reason, my Lord, be patient with us and reveal to us all things about which we question you, for the sake of the manner in which my brothers will herald it to the all of humanity.

And when she had said this to the Saviour, the Saviour answered, saying to her with great compassion, "Truly, truly, I say to you that not only will I reveal to you all things about which you shall question me, but from now on I shall reveal to you other things about which you have not thought to ask about; things which have not entered into the hearts of human beings. Things which also those gods who are among human beings, do not know. So therefore,

---

[464] In his *Stromata* (6:5), where he concludes on the basis of a non-canonical text, *The Preaching of Peter,* that the apostles did not leave Jerusalem for 12 years after the Resurrection, during which time Matthew wrote his Gospel.

[465] This is not the place to discuss dating principles of a Gospel, but the pivotal event of the destruction of the temple and the apparent dependency upon Mark, are not without problems.

TEXT: CHAPTER 114 (cont.)   **Mariam speaks**
Mariam, question me on what you wish to enquire, and I shall reveal it to you directly, without parables.

COMMENTARY: CHAPTER 114
"gods among human beings": this probably means the Angels and Archangels; two classes of deities who are closer to humans and more involved with people.

TEXT: CHAPTER 115 (cont.)   **Mariam speaks**
So Mariam responded and asked, "Of what type are the baptisms which cancel sins"? For I have heard you say that the servitors of the Erinyes follow the soul, and bear witness regarding it, for all the sins which it has committed, so that they can establish the guilt of the soul, in the judgments. So now, my Lord, do the Mysteries of the Baptisms wipe out the sins which are in the hands of the servitors of the Erinyes, so that they forget them? My Lord, tell us as to the type (of baptism); how they cancel sins. For indeed we wish to know this exactly.

Then the Saviour answered, saying to Mariam, "You have spoken very well. The servitors (of the Erinyes) are indeed those who bear witness to all sins. So they remain in the judgments because they take hold of the soul, and establish the guilt of all the souls of sinners who have not received Mysteries. And they restrain them in the Chaoses (*i.e., lower Soul-world*), chastizing them.

But these servitors are not able to come forth out of those realms to reach up to the levels which are above the Chaoses, to thereby establish the guilt of the souls which emerged in[466] those higher levels (*after death*). For it is not lawful (*for any entity*) to overpower the souls who have received Mysteries and

---

[466] "emerged in": usu. 'came forth in', which has little meaning. When the soul leaves its body, it emerges in the appropriate level of the Soul-world, i.e., finds its place there, or appears; and this can be above the lower darker 'Chaos' levels.

TEXT: CHAPTER 115 (cont.)
to then lead them into the Chaoses, to enable the servitors of the Erinyes to establish their guilt.

But the servitors of the Erinyes establish the guilt of the souls of sinners, detaining these who have not received Mysteries which may guide them out of the Chaoses. Whereas those souls who have received Mysteries, these servitors have no power with which to establish their guilt, because these souls do not come forth from their realms.

But also if these (*initiated*) souls did come (*into the realms of the Chaoses*), the servitors would not able to prevail against them. Moreover, they cannot lead such souls into the Chaoses.

But listen further, that I may tell you the word in truth, as to what type is the Mystery which cancels sins. So now, if the soul sins whilst in the world, the servitors of the Erinyes appear (*after death*) and become witnesses of all the sins which that soul has committed. They do this so that in case the soul departs from the realms of the Chaoses, these servitors may still establish their guilt within the judgments which are *outside* of the Chaoses.

And also the Double becomes a witness to all the sins which the soul commits, so that it too may establish the soul's guilt within the judgments which occur *outside* of the Chaoses. And not only so that it (the Double) bears witness to these, but – as regards all the sins of the soul – it seals these sins and binds them to the soul, so that all the Rulers of the judgments of the sinners may recognize it as a sinning soul.

TEXT NOTE: in Chapter 115
("recognize it as a sinning soul": again the hostility of the lower-self or Double is emphasized.)
"baptism": the idea of a water immersion to cleanse and purify the soul had long existed in Judaism, and was known as a mikvah.

TEXT: CHAPTER 115 (cont.)
Thus they may know the number of sins it has

TEXT: CHAPTER 115 (cont.)
committed by the seals which the Double has bound to it. So they may chastize the soul in a way appropriate to the number of sins it has committed. In this way, are all sinning souls dealt with.

But now, as regards that person who receives the Mysteries: the Mystery of those things resembles a great fire, very powerful and wise; and it 'burns up' all the sins. It permeates the soul in a hidden manner, and it dissipates all the sins which the Double had bound to it.

And when it has finished purifying all the sins which the Double had bound to the soul, it permeates the body in a hidden manner, and subtly pursues all the persecutors, and separates these off towards the side of the bodily part of the person.

TEXT NOTE: in Chapter 115
"the body": probably included here is the 'etheric body', that is, the life-forces with all of their elemental energies, because as Hellenistic esotericism was aware, these energies are essential for the functioning and health of the physical body.
"persecutors": these are minor spirits (perhaps 'elemental entities') who constitute the debased qualities.

TEXT: CHAPTER 115 (cont.)
For it pursues the Double and the Destiny-spirit, separating them from the Spirit-being and the soul, by putting them on the side of the bodily nature. Thus on the one side, there is the Double and the Destiny-spirit and the body (of matter); and separated from these, are the Spirit-being and the soul.

In contrast to this, the Mystery-experience of the Baptism remains in the middle place of these two parts; in that it continually separates one from the other. So that it makes them (*the Spirit-being and the soul*) clean and purifies them, so that they do not become stained by matter. This, Mariam, is the way in which the Mystery-experiences of the Baptisms cancel sins and all iniquities.

COMMENTARY: CHAPTER 115
So the 'Mystery' is not about 'pardoning' sins; instead it brings about the cancelling of the fallen or sinful soul qualities. That is, it helps to vanquish the debased soul qualities or energies. But as throughout this codex, the actual nature of a 'Mystery-experience' is not revealed; just how such divine influences are invoked, and how the power of these influences is made effective, is kept secret.

Secondly, this Mystery is not about the same kind of 'baptism' as that which became traditional in Christianity. In ancient Greece the word 'baptism' did not always mean to be immersed in water as a sacred ritual. It also meant to dip some food into wine or another liquid, or dyeing a piece of cloth, or to be drenched by something, or to go into a deep sleep.

So here both Jesus and Mariam are referring to a 'baptism' which cancels sinfulness, as the result of enveloping or 'immersing' the Earth in holy 'fire'; that is, permeating the Earth with divine energies which extinguish the energies that underlie unethical soul qualities.

TEXT: CHAPTER 116   Mariam speaks
Now, when the Saviour had said this, he said to the disciples, "Do you understand in what way I am speaking with you?" The Mariam started forward and said, "Yes, my Lord, I fully enquire into all the words which you speak. So, concerning the word about the cancelling of sin (*i.e., sinfulness*) which you explained to us in a parable, in an earlier time saying, "I came to cast fire upon the Earth" and again, "What do I wish, except that it be kindled". You have clearly shown the difference between (*and yet connection of*) the two activities), saying, "I have a baptism, to be baptized in (it)." and "How shall I endure, until this is accomplished?

"Do you think that I have come to cast peace upon

TEXT: CHAPTER 116 (cont.) **Mariam speaks** the Earth? No; instead, division I have come to cast. So as from this time, five shall be in one house; three will be divided against two, and two against three."

This, my Lord, is the word which you have spoken clearly. Further, concerning the word which said, "I have come to cast fire upon the Earth", and "What do I wish, except that it be kindled?" This means, my Lord, that you have brought the Mysteries of the baptisms into the world, and what else pleases you except that it (the baptism) should consume all the sins of the soul, and purify them?

And afterwards you explained clearly the difference between, (a*nd also the connection of*) the two activities, saying, "I have a baptism to be baptized in", and "how shall I endure until it is accomplished?" This means, that you shall not remain in the world until the baptisms are completed, and the initiated[467] souls are cleansed.

And, furthermore, the word which you earlier said to us, "Do you think that I have come to cast peace upon the Earth? No; instead, division I have come to cast. So as from this time, five shall be in one house; three will be divided against two, and two against three." So, this is the Mystery of the baptisms which you have brought into the world.

These have made a division in the bodies of (the human being) of the physical world, because it has separated the Double, the Destiny-spirit and the body (of matter) into one portion, and the Spirit-being and the soul into another portion. That is, there will be three against two, and two against three." Then as Mariam had said this, the Saviour responded, "Excellent, you spiritual and light-pure Mariam. This is the meaning of the words."

COMMENTARY: Chapter 116
"cast fire upon the Earth": this is an intriguing esoteric interpretation of this saying, later included in the Gospel of Luke (12:49).

---

[467] "initiated souls": or 'the perfected souls'.

TEXT: CHAPTER 117   Mariam speaks

"to cast peace upon the Earth": again an intriguing esoteric interpretation of this saying, later included in the Gospel of Luke (12:51).'

Mariam responded again, and said, "My Lord, I shall continue to question you. So, Lord permit me to question you. See, we now know clearly the kind of baptism which cancels sin. But now, as regards the Mystery of the three Realms, and the Mystery of the First Mystery, and the Mystery of the Ineffable: in which way do they cancel sin? Do they cancel this **in the same way** as that of the baptisms (*spoken of earlier*), or not?

The Saviour replied and said, "No; rather all the Mysteries of the three Realms cancel (*the impact of*) the sins of the soul in all the realms of the Rulers; all the sins which the soul has committed from the beginning. They cancel this for them, and furthermore, they cancel the (*impact of*) sins which it will commit, for the length of time during which each of the mystery-experiences will remain effective. The time up to when each one of the Mysteries shall remain effective, I shall explain to you when I tell you about the over-all configuration of the cosmos.

So this is the situation (*regarding a soul on the initiatory path*); the mystery-experience of the First Mystery (God) and the mystery-experiences of the Ineffable One (*the veiled God*) cancel out the (*impact of*) the sins of that soul on all the realms of the (debased) Rulers; all the sins and all the iniquities which the soul has committed (in the past).

And not only do they cancel the (*impact of*) all these, but also they do not allow (*the impact of*) sin to be written into (*the substance of*) these realms, from this hour forward until eternity, because of the gift of that great Mystery and its immensely great glory.

COMMENTARY: CHAPTER 117

"**a mystery-experience**": the reader encounters here a profoundly sacred revelation of esoteric Christianity in this remarkable codex. Its deeply cosmic, yet straightforward nature, indicates its

COMMENTARY: CHAPTER 117

origin from the risen Jesus. We can conclude that a mystery-experience involves becoming the recipient of an influx of a divine light, whilst sacred mantric words are intoned, radically expanding one's consciousness and empowering one's spirit.

To review what has been said here about help with sins, from divine beings: the first modality revealed is the enveloping (or 'baptizing') of the soul with a divine 'fire' from the cosmic Christ.

This eradicates the elemental energies which form the matrix of unethical, unspiritual soul qualities inside the human soul. It also partitions the human being; separating the lower aspect, especially the Double, from the soul.

The second modality is entirely different; this cancels or removes the sin from the cosmos; from whatever cosmic realm it is placed in. The divine influences involved here are twofold: from 'God', as the First Mystery, but also from the even higher, more veiled, aspect of 'God', who is referred to as the Ineffable One.

In the esoteric Christology of Rudolf Steiner, I found an explanation of this second aspect of assisting human beings with their sin. This second aspect views sin as having an objective impact on the cosmos. That is, the impact of unethical behaviour on the actual fabric of the Earth's life-forces and its astral aura. Such behaviour can manifest in a future Age as a tainted, damaged, part of the Earth.

Rudolf Steiner taught that if the spiritually aware soul prays sincerely to the Saviour, entreating that such damage may be prevented from becoming a future reality, then the Christ-power will ensure that this 'pre-emptive healing' is brought about, as an act of Grace.

TEXT: CHAPTER 118

As the Saviour said this to the disciples, he asked, "Do you understand the manner in which I am speaking to you?"

Mariam responded again, and said, "Yes, my Lord, I

TEXT: CHAPTER 118 (cont.)

have already grasped every word that you have said. So therefore my Lord, concerning the word which you spoke, "All the Mysteries of the three Realms cancel sins and cover over the sins' iniquities." David, the prophet, has prophesied long ago concerning this word, saying, "Blessed are they whose sins have been taken away[468], and whose iniquities have been covered." So, then, he prophesied long ago concerning this same word.

And the word which you have spoken, "As to the mystery-experience of that First Mystery and the Mystery of the Ineffable One, for those receive these sins, they cancel out the (*impact of*) the sins of that soul which the soul has committed in the past, and they also they do not reckon them from this hour forward until eternity."

Concerning this word, David once prophesied about this, saying, "Blessed are those to whom the Lord God does not impute iniquity..." (*Psalm 32*) That is to say, sins will not be imputed from this hour, to those who have received the mystery-experiences of the First Mystery, and who have received the Mystery of the Ineffable One.

He said, "Excellent, you spiritual and light-pure Mariam. This is the meaning of the words." And Mariam continued further, and said, "My Lord, if a person receives some mystery-experiences from the mystery-experiences of the First Mystery, but that person turns again and sins and transgresses, yet again he turns, and now repents and prays in each of his mysteries, will he be pardoned or not?

The Saviour replied and said, "Truly, truly, I say to you that everyone who receives the mystery-experiences of the First Mystery, if he turns and

---

[468] "taken away": usu. 'forgiven', but as explained earlier there is the cosmic meaning, beyond 'forgive'; to take away, or remove. And this is meant here, the Hebrew verb used here is 'nasa' (נָשָׂא) which can mean 'forgive', but its much more commonly used for 'take away', lift up, bear along or bear away.

TEXT: CHAPTER 118 (cont.)
transgresses twelve times, but then repents twelve times, and prays in the mystery-experience of the First Mystery, he will be forgiven.

But if after twelve times he should transgress again, turning back and transgressing, he shall not ever be pardoned; even if he should turn again to his Mystery, whichever it may be. For him, there is no means of (real) repentance – unless he has received the mysteries of the Ineffable One, who has compassion at all times and pardons sins always.

COMMENTARY: CHAPTER 118
This chapter continued to discuss sacred Christian initiatory wisdom on a vital subject; the nullifying by the Saviour of the effect on the Earth's soul and life-forces of unethical acts of human beings.

TEXT: CHAPTER 119   Mariam speaks
Mary continued further and said: "If even they who have received the mystery-experiences of the First Mystery turn back and commit sin, and if they pass out of the body without repenting, will they inherit the kingdom of Light or not, since they have received the gift of the First Mystery?

The Saviour answered, and said to Mariam, "Truly, truly, I say to you, every person who has received mystery-experiences in the First Mystery, yet having transgressed for the first, and the second and the third time, if he passes out of the body without repentance, his judgment is more severe than every other.

For his dwelling is in the midst of the jaws of the dragon[469] of the outer darkness, and at the end of all this, he shall become corroded in the torments and

---

[469] "jaws of the dragon": this appears to be a partially realistic, partially metaphorical description of a leading malignant deity whose identity is not revealed.

TEXT: CHAPTER 119 (cont.) Mariam speaks shall be existence-less during the Aeon,[470] because he has received the gift of the First Mystery, yet has not continued therein.

Mariam responded and said, "My Lord, all people who shall receive the mystery-experience of the Mystery of the Ineffable One, but have transgressed and ceased in their faith, but again, later, whilst they are still in life, have turned and repented, how many times will this be forgiven to them?

The Saviour answered and said, "Truly, truly, I say to you, every one who shall receive the Mysteries of the Ineffable One, not only shall his sin be pardoned if he transgress once and turn again and repent, but also if he transgresses any number of times, and then, while still in life, turn again and repent – and should he not be a hypocrite – but turn again and repent and offer prayers in each of his mysteries, it shall be forgiven him every time. Because he has received the gift of the Mysteries of the Ineffable One, for those Mysteries are compassionate and forgiving at all times."

And Mariam answered again and said to Jesus, "So then, Lord, as to those that receive the Mysteries of the Ineffable One, and again turn back and commit sin, and fall away in their faith, and who also pass from the body without repentance, what will happen to people of that kind?

The Saviour responded and said to Mariam, "Truly, truly, I say to you, all people who shall receive the Mysteries of the Ineffable One: these souls who receive from those Mysteries are certainly blessed. But if they turn and sin, and leave their body before repenting, the judgment of those persons is much worse than all (other) judgments; it is exceedingly severe. Even if those souls were new, so it would be

---

[470] As in chapt. 102, the regressive soul is either existence-less throughout an Aeon and thus slides back in evolutionary progress an entire Aeon, (or possibly, but less likely, dies forever.)

TEXT: CHAPTER 119 (cont.) Mariam speaks their first incarnation[471] they shall not return into the (*sequence of*) transformations of the body (*i.e., to further incarnations*) from this hour onwards, and will not be able to do anything (*to correct their plight*), but shall be cast outwards, into the outer darkness, and shall be corroded in the torments, and shall become existence-less throughout the Aeon.

COMMENTARY: Chapter 119
"souls are new": This striking statement is not explained, as this document is not an introductory text. But we can conclude that in this esoteric Christian world-view, souls may have been reincarnating since remote Ages, whilst others, who have an inherent high spirituality may be having their first incarnation, and have retained the presence in their soul of those divine influences in which they were immersed in spirit realms.

"judgment…is much worse": the implication here is that an initiated person has allowed their soul to reject the peerless, sublime holy influences by which they were being ennobled and guided. For the topic here is about being initiated into the Mysteries of the Ineffable One: the highest God.

So it is vitally important for that person to repent and clamber out of the malignant state they have sunk into, before their death. Otherwise malignant spirits, active opponents of the spirit, can make more use of them, than of an unethical person whose higher awareness was not for a time empowered.

"existence-less": that is, such a soul enters a kind of 'limbo' or non-active state in which their ongoing evolving and interaction with the cosmos pauses.

TEXT: CHAPTER 120
When the Saviour had said these things, however, he said to his disciple, "Do you understand the manner

---

[471] "first incarnation": lit. 'first time that they come into the world'.

TEXT: CHAPTER 120 (cont.)

in which I am speaking with you?"

Mariam answered and said, "Yes, Lord, I have understood the words which you have spoken, "Those who will receive the mysteries of the Ineffable One: blessed indeed are those souls. But if they turn back and sin, and if they fall away in their faith, and then come forth from the body without repentance, it is not possible from that moment, to return into the transformations of the body, nor for anything else, but they shall be cast forth into the outer darkness, and in that place they shall become corroded in the torments, and shall be existence-less throughout the Aeon."

Concerning this word, you have spoken to us earlier, saying, "Salt is good; but if the salt becomes insipid, with what shall it be salted? It is of no use for the refuse heap, nor for the soil." That is, blessed are all the souls who receive the Mysteries of the Ineffable One. But if they once transgress, they are not fit to return to the body from this hour forth; nor are they fit for anything, but they are to be cast into the outer darkness, and they shall become corroded in that place.

Then as she said this to the Saviour, he replied, "Excellent, you spiritual and light-pure Mariam. This is the meaning of the words." Mariam spoke further, saying, "My Lord, regarding all the people who have received the mystery-experiences of the First Mystery, and the Mysteries of the Ineffable One.

That is, of those who have not transgressed, and whose faith in the Mysteries was sincere, not hypocritical, but who by the compulsion of the karma-determining cosmic influences, shall sin again, but then again turn and make repentance, and offer prayer anew in each of their Mysteries, how often shall it be forgiven them?

The Saviour answered and said to Mariam, amidst his disciples, "Truly, truly[472], I say to you, all those who shall receive the Mysteries of the Ineffable One,

---

[472] Lit. here is, 'Amen, amen'.

TEXT: CHAPTER 120 (cont.)

and also the mystery-experiences of the First Mystery, but who then sin, and each time through the karma-determining cosmic influences, whilst they are still living, turn and repent, and remain in any of their Mysteries: they shall be forgiven each time, because those Mysteries are compassionate and forgiving, always.

Now, it was because of this that I once said to you, "These Mysteries will not only cancel those sins which these souls have committed from the beginning, but in addition, from this time onwards, no sins will be imputed to them. Concerning this, I have said to you, "They receive repentance at all times and the Mysteries shall also cancel the sins which have been committed anew."

If on the other hand, those who receive the mystery-experiences of the Mystery of the Ineffable One, and the mystery-experiences of the First Mystery, then turn and sin and (later) come forth from their body without having repented – then they shall be similar to those who have transgressed and have not repented. For their location shall also be in the midst of the jaws of the dragon of the outer darkness. They shall become corroded, and shall be existence-less, throughout the Aeon.

For this reason, I have said to you, "All people who shall receive the Mysteries, if they knew the time of their coming forth from their body, would guard themselves (ethically) and not sin, so that they may inherit the kingdom of Light for ever.

COMMENTARY: CHAPTER 120

No especial comments are needed for this Chapter.

TEXT: CHAPTER 121

When the Saviour said this to the disciples, he asked, "Do you understand the manner in which I am speaking to you?" Mariam replied and said, "Yes, my Lord, I have correctly understood all the words which you have said. Now, concerning this word which you spoke to us earlier, "If the house-holder knew at what

TEXT: CHAPTER 121 (cont.)

hour of the night the thief would come, to break in and ransack the house, he would stay awake, and not allow the man to break into his house."

Now after Mariam had said this, the Saviour responded, "Excellent, you spiritual Mariam ! This is (the meaning of) the word. The Saviour continued again and said to his disciples, "Proclaim to all people who shall receive the Mysteries in the Light, saying, 'Take heed that you do not sin, lest you add evil to evil, and then come forth from the body, without having repented; becoming strangers to the kingdom of Light for an aeon." When the Saviour had said this, Mariam responded and said, "My Lord, so great then is the compassion of those Mysteries which pardon sins every time."

The Saviour answered and said to Mariam in the midst of the disciples, "Today, any king, who is a man of the world, may give a gift to people who are similar to himself, but also he may pardon murderers and pederasts, and the rest of the very grievous sins, which are deserving of death (*under the Law*).

If it is appropriate for a man who is of the world to have extended this mercy, then how much more is it appropriate for the Ineffable One and the First Mystery, who are the Lords of the Cosmos, to act with authority in the manner which to them is valid; so that they pardon those who receive Mysteries (*but then become unethica*l).

COMMENTARY: CHAPTER 121
No comments are needed for this chapter.

TEXT: CHAPTER 122
After this Jesus spiritually sees a woman having (previously) come to him to repent. He had already baptized her three times, but (thereafter) she had not done what was worthy of the baptisms.

TEXT NOTE: in Chapter 122
"Jesus sees spiritually a woman": regrettably a primary verb in Coptic for 'see' (ⲛⲁⲩ) is used for a

TEXT NOTE: in Chapter 122
variety of Greek verbs that mean to see, whether clairvoyantly or physically.[473] Here Jesus is no longer in a flesh body, he is in a spiritual continuum, and is therefore perceptible to those disciples who have some seership. So it is unlikely that he is pointing to a physical person who is in proximity to the group. It is more likely that he specifically invoked a spiritual image of this woman, and ensured that Peter is also able to behold this image.

"He had already baptized her": here 'baptism' refers to this mysterious secret, mystery-experience. That is, to being enveloped as it were, in a divine influence; not being immersed in a pool of water. So we can conclude that this woman was a member of the esoteric Christian groups, and that Jesus did initiate such people during his three-year ministry.

TEXT: CHAPTER 122 (cont.)
Now the Saviour wished to test Peter, to see if he were compassionate and forgiving, as he had commanded the disciples to be. So he spoke to Peter saying, "Look, I have baptized this woman three times, but by the third time, she did not do that which is worthy of the baptisms of the Light.

Now Peter, why does she make even her body useless? So therefore, Peter, perform the Mystery of the Light, which severs souls from The Inheritance of the Light. Perform that Mystery so that it may cut off the soul of this woman from The Inheritance of the Light.

But as the Saviour said this, he was testing Peter, to see if he was compassionate and forgiving. Now when the Saviour said these things, Peter said, " Lord, allow her this (moral error) one time, so that we may (later) give her the higher Mysteries; and if she is suitable (for the Mystery) then you have allowed her to inherit The Inheritance of the Light. But if she is not suitable, then you have cut off this woman from The

---

[473] Those used for clairvoyance were theaomai (Θεάομαι), theoepeoe (θεωρεω) and especially horaoe (ὁράω).

TEXT: CHAPTER 122 (cont.)

Inheritance of the Light.

Thus, after Peter had said this, the Saviour knew that he was compassionate and forgiving. Now when all this had happened, the Saviour said to his disciples, "Have you understood all these words, and the soul dynamics[474] of this woman?" Mariam answered and said, "My Lord, I have understood the mystery-experiences involved in the events that have befallen this woman. Now, you have spoken to us at an earlier time in a parable, concerning the things which have happened to her, saying, "There was a man who had a fig-tree in his vineyard, and he came to look for some fruit, but he found not a single one on it.

He said to the gardener, "Look, for three years I have come here to look for fruit on this fig-tree, but I have not found any produce on it at all. So, cut it down; why is it making the soil useless? But the gardener responded, saying to him, "My Lord, have patience with it this year also, and I shall dig around it and give it compost. And if it bears fruit in another year's time, then you have thereby allowed it (to thrive). However, if you do not find any fruit at all, then you have cut it down. The Saviour responded and said to Mariam, "Well said, you spiritual one. This is the meaning of the word."

COMMENTARY: Chapter 122

"make even her body useless": this forms a parallel to 'make the soil useless'. It may be alluding to the woman's physical, incarnate existence as being of little value, if she does not seek to progress spiritually.

The fig-tree story is mentioned here because the incident with the woman is pointing to the intention of the initiatory (Mystery) experience to develop in her a higher consciousness (or failing to). For the fig-tree is a metaphor for clairvoyance amongst esoteric

---

[474] "dynamics": lit. a pattern, model or archetype.

groups of antiquity.[475]

TEXT: CHAPTER 123 (cont.)   **Mariam speaks**
Mariam continued again, and said to the Saviour, "My Lord, a person who has received the Mysteries, but has not done what is appropriate to them, instead has turned and has sinned, but thereafter has repented, has been deeply repentant – is it permitted for my brothers to once again give him the Mystery which he received, or otherwise, to give him a mystery-experience from among the lower Mysteries – is that permitted, or not?

The Saviour then responded and said, "Truly, truly, I say to you that neither the mystery-experience which he has received, nor any lower mystery-experiences, will give ear to him, to pardon his sins. But it is the Mysteries which are *higher* than those which he has received, which shall make a response to him[476] and pardon his sins.

Now, therefore, Mariam, let your brothers give him a higher Mystery than that which he has received, and his repentance shall be heard and his sins be cancelled. The mystery-experience which he may receive a second time or any number of times, will not grant him the cancelling of his sin, but only a higher Mystery than the one he has previously received will grant him such cancelling of sin.

But if he has already received the three Mysteries in the second Realm, or in the third Realm from within, and then turns back and transgresses – then no Mystery can give ear to him to help him in his repentance, neither Mysteries higher nor lower than the one he has received; except for the mystery-experience of the First Mystery and the Mystery of that Ineffable One. It is these that shall give ear to him and receive his repentance".

And Mariam responded and said, "My Lord, a human being who has received Mysteries, as many as

---

[475] See my *The Gospel of John* where this theme is discussed in relation to Nathanael being brought to meet Jesus (1:48).
[476] lit. 'listen to him'.

TEXT: CHAPTER 123 (cont.)   **Mariam speaks**
two or three, in the second or third Realm and has not transgressed, and is still in his faith, having uprightness, without hypocrisy; what shall happen to him?

Then the Saviour answered and said to Mariam, "For every person who has received Mysteries in the second Realm and in the third Realm and has not transgressed, and is without hypocrisy – for souls of this kind, it is permitted to receive Mysteries in the Realm which they wish; from the first as far as the last, because they have not transgressed.

COMMENTARY: CHAPTER 123
Again it becomes evident just how central to their life was the initiatory path with the these early Christians. To undergo an initiatory mystery-experience was not uncommon. In the Gospels there are a number of hints as to the reality of initiatory experiences and the consequent acquisition of occult powers of those in the 'Jesus movement'. Perhaps the most potent of these is the revelation that two of the disciples (at least) possessed the occult power of invoking destructive fire-spirits. (Lk.9:54)

TEXT: CHAPTER 124
And Mariam continued and said, "Again, Lord, concerning the person who has known the Divine and has received one of the Mysteries of light, and (then) has turned back and transgressed and committed iniquity, and has not turned again and repented, and also as to the person who has not found the Divine, and has not known it, and who is a sinner, and still an impious person. Both of these persons eventually come forth from the body: which of the two, will suffer most in the judgments?"

The Saviour answered and said to Mariam, "Truly, truly, I say to you, the person who has known the Divine, (that is) who has received the Mysteries of the Light, but who has then sinned, and has not turned to repent. This person shall experience suffering in the

TEXT: CHAPTER 124 (cont)
.chastizements of the judgments; a suffering many times more severe in comparison with the ungodly and lawless man, who has not known the Divine. Now therefore, whoever has ears to hear, let them hear.

Then as the Saviour had said, Mariam started forward, and said, "My Lord, my companion-of-light-has ears, thus I have understood all that which you have spoken. Concerning this word then, which you had spoken to us in a parable saying, "The servant who knows the will of his master, and yet has not prepared, nor done, the will of his master, shall receive many blows, but he who has not known and has not done (the will of his master), shall receive but few blows. For to whom more has been entrusted, of him more shall be asked, and to whom many things have been committed, of him many shall be required."

That is to say, Lord, he who knows the Divine and has found all the Mysteries of the Light, and (then) has transgressed – he shall be chastized with greater chastisements than he who has not known the Divine. This, Lord, is the interpretation of the word.

COMMENTARY: Chapter 124
No comments are needed here.

TEXT: CHAPTER 125   Mariam speaks
And Mariam continued further and said to the Saviour, "My Lord, since the teachings[477] and the Mysteries have (now) become revealed (to people) – then, as souls incarnate (*lit. 'come into the world'*) in many cycles (*of re-birth*), but are neglectful of receiving the Mysteries, hoping that, when they come into the world (*reincarnate*) at another later cycle, they shall then receive the Mysteries: will these souls not be in danger of never attaining to the receiving of

---

[477] "the teachings": the Coptic has lit. 'the faith' which appears to mean here the teachings of Jesus and his disciples.

TEXT: CHAPTER 125 (cont.)   Mariam speaks
the Mysteries?

The Saviour answered and said, "Proclaim to the whole world, saying to people, 'Strive, so that you receive the Mysteries of the Light in this Age which has a set time-span,[478] so that you enter into the kingdom of the Light.

Do not pass day after day, nor cycle (*life-time*) after cycle (*life-time*), hoping that you may attain to the receiving of the Mysteries when you come into the world in yet another later cycle (*of re-birth*).

For indeed these souls do not know when the number of perfected souls will be reached; because when the number of perfected souls is reached, I shall close the portals of the Light. Then from that hour, no one shall enter in, nor thereafter shall anyone go out. For the number of perfected souls will then be completed. And thereby the (*manifesting of the*) mystery-process of the First Mystery (God) will also be completed; it was for the sake of this (manifesting of God) that the cosmos was created: concerning this –

I am that mystery-process.

(or   **the 'I' I am is that mystery-process**)

And from that hour no one will go into the Light, and no one will come forth. For at the completion of the time of the number of the perfected souls, before I lay fire to the world in order to purify the Aions and the veils and the firmaments and the whole Earth, and (thus) all the matter which is upon it, whilst humanity is still in existence.

TEXT NOTE: in Chapter 125
"close the portals of the Light": this emphasis on a specific cosmic time-frame in which humanity has to achieve spiritual goals is very similar to a passage in Matt. 25:10 where after the wedding guests have entered the room, the door is shut, and no-one else

---

[478] See Commentary about this phrase.

TEXT NOTE: in Chapter 125 (cont.)
can enter.

"I am that mystery": another profound expression of esoteric Christianity; that the 'cosmic Christ' (or Light of Lights) *is* the Cosmos. Meaning that this deity, who also manifests through the risen Saviour, is the spiritual being underlying our cosmos: this is in effect, the Logos. That is a deity whose nature encompasses the planetary spheres and its associated zodiacal elements.

But there is a second, equally profound, implication here. The original Greek sentence certainly included 'ego eimi' which often simply means "I" in an emphatic sense. But it also means, as we noted earlier, " the 'I' I am "; that is the person's sense of self, or their 'I', which has been spiritualized and has the Christ within it. This especial Greek term is obscured in Coptic, but these two possibilities are still implied in the Coptic version of the Greek phrase, 'I am'[479]

"...for which the cosmos was created –
                                    concerning this,[480]
    I am that mystery.
or the 'I' I am *is* that mystery

These extraordinary words are declaring that when the core nature of God becomes manifest in human souls, then this process is brought about by the influence of the Christ-light in these spiritualizing souls. And this can only happen because the First Mystery is inherently within Christ.

This cosmic Christianity concept is in fact in the Gospel of John (8:28), although most translations do not see it, as the Greek text in this verse is complex, because it has the initiatory 'ego eimi' phrase in it.

In v. 8:28 Jesus, or rather, the Christ through Jesus, says:

---

[479] In Coptic, ⲁⲛⲟⲕ.

[480] The text appears in error here; it has the relative pronoun here (ⲉⲧⲉ) "*that is/which it*, but it should be (ⲉⲧⲃⲉ) 'concerning this', 'about this'.

TEXT NOTE: in Chapter 125 (cont.)
"Whenever you have exalted the Son of Man, then you will know **I am the 'I'** {in you}; also {you will know} 'from myself I do nothing, but only as the Father taught me'." (These things I {Jesus} speak...)

The expression 'the Son of Man' refers to the Spiritual-self or that spiritual reality which is born in the soul through the mystery-experience of God – 'the First Mystery'. Both the Pistis Sophia text and this verse in the Gospel are teaching that this process only occurs when the cosmic Christ is present in the soul, creating a higher 'I' or sense of self, which is sustained by the Christ-light. It also can only happen because of the interconnectedness of the First Mystery or God and Christ.

But usually this verse is translated differently,
"So Jesus said, "When you have lifted up the Son of Man, then you will know *that* I am the one *I claim to be*, and that I do nothing on my own, *but speak* just what the Father has taught me."

The words shown in italics were added to make sense of the verse, or other words were included from what is actually the next verse. This has been done because the initiatory message is not perceived. My translation is supported by Papyrus 75, dated as of about CE 175. This early papyrus has outstanding punctuation marks, the result of thoughtful contemplation of the sentences.

It uses a particular dot for the full stop, and a different kind of dot for a pause; whereas some early papyrus texts have only scanty and ambiguous punctuation. An examination of the papyrus shows that in verse 28, the scribe placed a full stop after 'taught me'; this is clearly visible in the papyrus.[481]

---

[481] Papyrus Viewable at https://digi.vatlib.it/view/MSS_Pap. Hanna.1 (mater verbi) This verse is on page 2b7r.

TEXT: CHAPTER 125 (cont.) **Mariam speaks**

Now in that time, in those days, the faith and the Mysteries will be the more revealed. And many souls will come (*i.e., incarnate*) by means of the cycles of the transformations of the body. And as they come into the world, some of them of this current time, who have heard me teaching, about the completing of the number of the perfected souls, shall find the Mysteries of the Light; and they shall receive these Mysteries. They shall arrive at the portals of the Light, but then discover that the number of perfected souls is complete: this is the completion of the First Mystery and comprehension of the All.

And they find the portals of the Light are closed, and that it is impossible for anyone to go within, or for anyone to go out, from this time. Now those souls will knock at the portals of the Light, saying, "O Lord, open to us." I will answer and say to them, I do not know you, where you come from. And they will say to me, "We have received from your Mysteries, and we have fulfilled all your teachings, and you have taught us on the streets."

And I will respond and say to them, 'I do not know you; who you are, you who do deeds of iniquity and evil up until now. Because of this, go to the outer darkness."

And in that hour they will go to the outer darkness, that place where is weeping and gnashing of teeth. So, because of this, preach to the whole world. Say to them: 'strive that you relinquish the whole world and all the matter in it, that you may receive the Mysteries of the Light, before the number of the perfected souls is completed, that you may not be left before the door of the portal of the Light, and be taken to the outer darkness.'

Now when the Saviour had said these things, Mariam started forward again, and said: "My Lord, not only does my companion-of-light have ears, but my soul has heard and has understood every word which you say. Now at this time, my Lord, concerning the words which you have spoken, "Preach to the people of the world, say to them, 'strive to receive the Mysteries of the Light in this Age, which has a set time-span, so that you may inherit the Kingdom of the Light'.........

COMMENTARY: CHAPTER 125

"Age with a set time-span": lit. 'limited time', usu. 'troubled time' or 'restricted time'. The Coptic word here for 'time' also means a specific period of time,[482] and thus an Age. Also, another Coptic word here[483] can mean 'troubled', but also 'restricted', or 'under pressure', as well as limited/defined, rather than endless or expansive.

(Here a large gap in the codex brings this third document to an end prematurely.)

END NOTE:

In the codex, two more documents were bound in with documents 1, 2 and 3; these are documents 4 (of 50 pages) and document 5 (of 12 pages). I am not including them in this book, as explained in the Introduction. They are written in a manner that has similarities to document 3, and they deal with some of the themes encountered in the first three documents. But they present narrow and fantastical religious views, which are incompatible with the profound contents of the first three texts.

---

[482] in Coptic, ογοειν·

[483] In Coptic, ϩοχχ/ϩηοε·

APPENDIX 1: The connection of the Light of Lights (Christ) to God (First Mystery) and to the human 'I'.

The key statements about the inner connection of the Light of Lights (the cosmic Christ) to God (the First Mystery) and about the presence of this deity in the higher human 'I'.

CHAPTER

96   p. 309
    And, truly, I say to you:
    that initiate is I – and I am that initiate.

96   p. 312
    Truly, I say to you, those souls are I,
    and I am those souls.

96   p. 313
    this Mystery *is* myself, and I am that
    Mystery.

96   p. 313
    ...and I am they, and they are myself.

97   p. 316
    I am the spiritual wisdom of the entire cosmos.

125   p. 415
    It was for the sake of this mystery-process of
    manifesting God, that the cosmos was created:
    and concerning this,
    I am that mystery-process.

The origin of Pistis Sophia in the Light of Lights
Chapter 68   p. 219
  I am a purified radiance of your out-raying light.

APPENDIX 2: Pistis Sophia as humanity's higher soul

Most of the statements which demonstrate that Pistis Sophia is the spirit counterpart of the human soul's higher capacity for cognizing are in Chapter 81.

CHAPTER 81

Pistis Sophia longed to tell them (her fellow Invisibles) of the wonderful things which I had done for her below, in the world of humans.

p.248

#8: I shall give thanks to you, O Light: for you have saved me, and for your wondrous deeds amongst humanity.

p.248

#15: I will give thanks to you, O Light, for you have rescued me, and thereby your wondrous deeds have taken place in respect of humanity (also).

p.249

#21: I want to thank you, O light, for you have rescued me, and for your wondrous deeds among humanity."

p.249

GLOSSARY

Ahriman: a demonic entity inciting hatred and coldness of heart

Aion: a spirit realm

Aeon: an Age or long period of time

Astrality: the realm or state of sentiency

Astral body: the soul or soul-body

Cosmic Christ: the leader of the deities in the Sun-sphere, i.e., the Powers or the Elohim

Buddhi realm: a divine realm from where Buddhi, the eternal Monad derives

Devachan: above the astral realm, below Buddhi

the Double: our lower-self or 'counterfeit spirit'

Elemental spirits: a term used for various lesser spirits, especially those active in the four ethers

the Ethers: four subtle energies which bring about the four states of matter

Etheric body: the life-force organism of humans and animals

Lucifer: a fallen deity inciting enthusiasm but also sensuality and naïve selfishness

Spiritual-self: when purified emotions, thinking and will are achieved, this emerges as the eternal spirit, composed of devachanic 'substance'

INDEX

(Key occurrences only of words are noted)

12 Light-powers, 158
12 thrones, 158
13th Aion, 161, 177, 216
24 emanations, 103
24 Invisibles, 255
a new Mystery, 237, 251
above the coats of skin, 222, 225
Abraham, 25
Adam, 29
Adamas, 72, 93, 209, 210, 215, 217, 226, 238, 240, 242, 243, 245, 246
Ahriman, 21, 107
air-sprite, 174
Amen, 86
Amen, amen, 86, 255
Amente, 141, 143, 232, 344, 378
an Invisible, 235
ancient initiates, 37
Andrew, 145, 146, 175, 236, 332, 337
Angels, 47, 66, 130, 288, 308
Apocalypse of Adam, 19
Archangels, 47, 288, 308
Ariel, 343, 344
arrow, 215
astrologers, 74
baptism, 399
Baptism, 398
Barbelo, 21, 57, 112, 183, 193, 199, 200
basilisk, 209, 211, 212, 214, 226, 229
Basilisk-headed, 209
blessed, 184
Book of Enoch, 19
Book of Job, 107
Books of Jeu, 28, 331
Buddhi plane, 15
cancel sin, 401
cancel sins, 340
cancel the sins, 337
cast into Mary, 59
changed the pathways, 93
Clement of Alexandria, 395
coin, 389
commonality of (its) perceiving, 379
Compassionate love, 190
conscience, 306
Consort, 102, 114, 131, 138, 156
corrective treatment, 348
counterfeit human beings, 97
counterfeit human soul, 86
counterfeit souls, 88
counterfeit spirit, 373
crown, 182, 211
crown of light, 181, 210
crucified me, 51
daemons, 367
darkness area, 246
debased counterpart, 71
decan, 130, 131
decans, 56, 57, 81, 146

423

deliverers, 136
dense (astral) substance, 223
dense astral matter, 130
dense entities, 169
denser (soul) bodies, 231
denser entities, 149
depart from that body, 322
Destiny, 377, 379
devachanic, 22
dictates of karma, 340
direct her gaze, 105
dismisses the Destiny-spirit, 383
dismisses the Double, 390
Double, 373, 376, 377
dove, 12, 200
dragon, 209, 357
Dragon, 212
dragon-faced, 345
dream-vision, 194
dross, 94
dwellers in his house, 391
eagle, 235
elect, 95
Elias, 54
Elijah, 53
Elisabeth, 53, 196
Elohim (*plural*), 148
Enoch, 331, 332
Epistle of the Hebrews, 20, 26
Erinyes, 305, 306, 317, 318, 350, 374, 376, 377, 378, 383, 384, 391, 396, 397
Essenes, 28

etheric bodies, 54
Fate-predictors, 80
fig-tree, 411
Fire of Wisdom, 146, 147
First Command, 105
freedom, 106
Gabriel, 53, 56, 197, 202, 203, 210, 211
garment, 61
garment of light, 12, 93, 99, 200
gnoses, 149
had been in former times, 208
Harrowing of Hades, 13
Hastener, 88
Heimarmene, 18, 68
Hermetica, 19, 22
Holy Goddess of the Light, 55, 184, 270, 322, 352, 381
hostile, 378
hostility of Peter, 126
hulikos, 77
humanity is the residue, 334
hyle, 22
I am a purified radiance, 221, 225, 420
I am that Mystery, 313, 420
I am that mystery-process 415, 420
Iabraoth, 200
Ialdabaoth, 108, 111, 345
Ieou, 332
in respect of humanity (also), 249, 421
Ineffable, 51

Ineffable One, 293, 300, 302, 303, 320
intonings, 307
intuitively perceived, 160
intuitively perceptive wisdom, 9
Isaiah, 75, 76
Isis, 23
James, 161, 213, 244
jealous, 151
Jesus Christ, 27
Jeu, 72, 81, 87, 159, 161, 268, 269, 379
John, 133, 278
John the Baptist, 54, 195, 196
karma, 328
Kingdom of the Heavens, 76
Light of Lights, 167
Light-Aions, 108
light-beings of (Pistis) Sophia, 204
light-garment, 65, 99, 101
Light-purifier, 27
Lion-faced, 108, 130, 154, 155, 159, 160, 166, 169, 171, 178, 209, 211, 238, 345
Lion-faced being, 104
lion-faced Ruler, 108, 111
Little IAO, 53, 270
Little Sabaoth, 199
Logos, 302, 371
long delay, 92
Lower Devachan, 15
Lucifer, 21
magic rites, 79
Mariam, 78, 235
Mariam of Bethany, 314
Mariam the Magdalene, 254
Mariam the Magdalene and John, 313
Martha, 128, 178, 233, 247
Mary the mother of Jesus, 182
Matthew, 140, 227
Melchizedek, 24, 88, 89, 91, 268, 269
Michael, 202, 203, 210, 211
Mixture, 291
mother of Jesus, 191
my brother, 156
my denser entities, 227
my Father, 202, 211
My Father, 238
my mother, 56
Mystery experience, 355
nervous about Peter, 232
Ode 1, 183
Ode 33, 187
Ode 6, 204
Ode 22, 213
Ode 5, 180, 181
Ode 25, 222, 223
Ode 22, 227
commonality of (its) perceiving, 379
Order of Melchizedek, 27
Origenes, 371
other Mariam, 195
other Mary, 185
Paradise of Adam, 331
parodying us, 360

Paul, 390
personification, 33
Peshitta Bible, 26
Peter, 168, 204
Philip, 139, 140, 141, 144, 252
Pistis Sophia, 9, 24, 101
Praise-singers, 296
priestly Messiah, 194
Proverbs, 165
Psalm 68, 119
Psalm 70, 125
Psalm 69, 129
Psalm 101, 134
Psalm 87, 141
Psalm 129, 145
Psalm 81, 147
Psalm 24, 151
Psalm 30, 156
Psalm 34, 162
Psalm 119, 168
Psalm 51, 170
Psalm 108, 175
Psalm 50, 178
Psalm 44, 190
Psalm 90, 213
Psalm 29, 233
Psalm 102, 235
Psalm 39, 236
Psalm 7, 245
Psalm 106, 252
Psalm 32, 403
raise the dead, 369
raising the dead, 367
Receive back your Double, 385
reincarnation, 328
righteousness, 190
royal Messiah, 194
rushing water, 138

Sabaoth, 28, 76, 196, 197, 199, 202, 269, 386
Sabaoth the Good, 76
sacred wisdom, 190
Salome, 170, 180
salvation, 83, 149
second garment, 62
Self-willed One, 104, 171, 172
Septuagint, 143, 148
serpent, 209, 228
serpent-headed, 211
serving-spirits, 90
sevenfold Double, 212
Shades, 142
Sheol, 141
Solar plexus, 77
soliloquy, 234
some Light-Aions created, 108
soul-body, 23
souls are new, 406
St. Paul, 145
test Peter, 410
that initiate is I, 311, 420
that same month, 323
The (debased) Left, 386
The Book of Revelation, 393
The Book of the Dead, 143
The Left, 201
The Midst, 54, 56, 270, 271, 383
the mother of Jesus, 196
The Right, 57, 76, 259, 269, 387
The Testimony of Truth, 185

they are myself, 313
Thomas, 140, 150, 152, 221
those souls are I, 312, 420
three days, 350, 378
Three Times, 239, 240
transgressing angels, 72
Trimorphic Protennoia, 21
Triple-powered Self-willed One, 108
true unapproachable God, 326
two Messiahs, 185
unpaired Ones, 99
Upper Devachan, 15
vindictive, 177
virgin, 135
virginal purity, 183
Vision about the Egyptians, 76
visionary dream, 189
Voice and Trees, 263
Watchers, 105
Wisdom, 165
Wisdom of Solomon, 328
without suffering any pain, 365
wondrous deeds among humanity, 249, 421
Yaldabaoth, 345
zodiacal, 56

Select Bibliography

Apocrypha and Pseudepigrapha of the Old Testament, edit. Charles, R.H. Oxford, OUP, 1978.
Apocrypha – New Testament, edit. W. Schneemelcher, trans. R. Wilson, Philadelphia, Westminster Press, 1964.
Apocryphal New Testament, edit. James. M. Oxford, UP, 1975.
Anderson, A. *The Gospel of John: an Initiatory Quest Translation and Commentary*, Threshold Publishing, 2022
Bernard, J.H. *The Odes of Solomon*, Wipf & Stock, Oregon, 2004.
Bruce, F.F. *The Epistle to the Hebrews, The new International Commentary*, Grand Rapids, Eerdmans, 1990.
Crum, W.E. *A Coptic Dictionary*, OUP, 1939.
Charles, R.H. ed. *Apocalypsis Henochi Graece*, Leiden, Brill, 1970.
Charlesworth J. & Crabbe, L. edit. *Critical Reflections on the Odes of Solomon*, Sheffield Academic Press, 1998.
The Complete Text of the Earliest NT Manuscripts, edit. Comfort & Barrett, Baker Books, Grand Rapids, 1999.
Davies and Allison, *Matthew 19-28*, in the International Critical Commentary, T & T Clark, 1997.
Farrar, F.W. *The Epistle of Paul the Apostle to the Hebrews*, Cambridge UP, 1894.
Daniélou, J. *Theology of early Christianity*, London, Westminster, no date.
Daniélou, J. *Theology of Jewish Christianity*, London, Westminster, 1964.
Fürst, J. *Hebräisches und Chaldäisches Handwörterbuch über das Alte Testament*, Leipzig, Vlg. von Bernhard Tauchnitz, 1863.
Thomas, Gospel of, trans. Guillaumont/Puech /Quispel /Till/ Yassah/ Masih, E.J. Brill, Leiden, 1959.
Gesenius: Hebrew and Chaldee Lexicon to the Old Testament, trans. S. P. Tregelles, London, S. Bagster & and Sons, 1857.

Greek-English Lexicon of the New Testament, W. Bauer; trans. W. Arndt & W. Gingrich, 2nd edit, Univ. Chicago, Chicago, 1979.
Greek-English Lexicon, comp. H.G. Liddell & R. Scott, Oxford, Clarendon Press, 1996.
Evans, E. *The Books of Jeu and the Pistis Sophia as Handbooks to Eternity*, Brill, 2005.
Grimme, H. *Oden Salomos*, C. Winters Vlg., Heidelberg, 1911.
Hermetica: Greek/Latin with English translation, edit. W.Scott, Shambhala, Boston, 1995.
Horner, G. *Pistis Sophia*, SPCK, 1924.
Lamsa, G. *Holy Bible from the Ancient Eastern Text.*
Lünemann, Gottlieb. *Handbook to the Epistle to the Hebrews*, Edinburgh, Clark, 1882.
Mead, G.R.S. *Pistis Sophia*, Watkins, London, 1921.
MacDermot, V. *Pistis Sophia*, Brill, 1978.
Moffat, J. *The Epistle to the Hebrews, The Internat. Critical Commentary*, Edinburgh, Clark, 1968.
Nag Hammadi Library, edit. Robinson, J., Leiden, E.J. Brill 1977.
Novum Testamentum Graece: 28th rev. edit. Aland
The Greek New Testament 4th rev. edit. Aland
ΟΙΓΕΝΟΥΣ, ΤΩΝ ΕΙΣ ΤΟ ΚΑΤΑ ΙΩΑΝΝΗΝ ΕΥΑΓΓΕΛΙΟΝ ΕΞΗΓΤΙΚΩΝ (Origenes, *Commentary on the Gospel of John*) Cecile Blanc, edit. Editions Du Cerf, Paris, 1996.
Parson, W. C. *On the Unified Authorship of the Oracle to Ariel Isaiah* 29: 1-8); Studia Antiqua, Vol 15, June 1916.
Stern, L. *Koptisches Grammatik*, T.O.Wiegel Vlg., Leipzig, 1880.
Schmidt, C. / Till, W. *Koptische-Gnostische Schriften*: Erster Band, *Die Pistis Sophia*, Berlin, Akademie Vlg, 1959.
Smith, M. *Clement of Alexandria and a Secret Gospel of St. Mark*, Harvard UP,1973.
Schwartze, M.G. *Pistis Sophia Opus Gnosticum Valentino Adiudicatum* edit. J.H. Petermann, Ferdinand Dümmler's Buchhandlung, Berlin, 1851.
Septuagint: Septuaginta id est Vetus Testamentus Graece iuxta LXX interpretes; edidit, Alfred Rahlfs,

Stuttgart, Privilegierte Würtembergische Bibelanstalt, (no date, ca. 1932).
Septuagint: Η ΠΑΛΑΙΑ ΔΙΑΘΗΚΗ ΚΑΤΑ ΤΟΥΣ ῾ΕΒΔΟΜΗΚΟΝΤΑ   sixti qvinti pontificus maximi Lipsiae, 1824.
Steiner, R. GA 89, Rudolf Steiner Nachlassverwaltung, Dornach, 2001
Steiner, R. GA 95, Rudolf Steiner Nachlassverwaltung, Dornach, 1978
Steiner, R. GA 123, Rudolf Steiner Nachlassverwaltung, Dornach, 1978
Theologisches Wörterbuch zum Neuen Testament, edit. Kittel, G., Vlg. Kohlhammer, Stuttgart, Vol. 3, 1965.
Wallis-Budge, E.A. *The Gods of the Egyptians*, New York, Dover Press, 1969.
Wallis-Budge, E.A. trans. The *Egyptian Book of the Dead*, London, RKP, 1969.
Wallis-Budge, E.A. *The Egyptian Heaven and Hell*, La Salle, USA, Open Court Publishing, 1989.
Wallis-Budge, E.A. *The Gods of the Egyptians*, Vol. 2
Westendorf, W. *Koptisches Handwörterbuch*, Vlg. Carl Winter, Heidelberg Univ., 1965.
Zinner & Mattison, the *Nuhra Version,* 2020, www.academia.edu
Zohar, 5 vols. trans. Sperling H. & Simon, M., London, Soncino, 1970.
Der Sohar, Das Heilige Buch der Kabbala, trans. Ernst Müller, Vienna, Vlg. Dr. H. Glanz, 1932.

Books by this Author

Living a Spiritual Year: seasonal festivals in both hemispheres (new, expanded edition)	1992
	2016
The Way to the Sacred	2003
The Foundation Stone Meditation: a new commentary	2005
Dramatic Anthroposophy: Identification and contextualization of primary features of Rudolf Steiner's anthroposophy. (PhD thesis)	2005
Two Gems from Rudolf Steiner	2014
The Hellenistic Mysteries & Christianity	2014
Rudolf Steiner Handbook	2014
Horoscope Handbook – a Rudolf Steiner Approach	2015
The Meaning of the Goetheanum Windows	2016
The Lost Zodiac of Rudolf Steiner	2016
Rudolf Steiner's Esoteric Christianity in the Grail painting by Anna May	2017
The Vidar Flame Column – its meaning from Rudolf Steiner	2017
Rudolf Steiner on Leonardo's *Last Supper*	2017
Rudolf Steiner's First Class Verses	2018
Blessed - Rudolf Steiner on the Beatitudes	2018
The Soul's Calendar - annotated with Commentary	2019
The Soul's Calendar - pocket edition	2019
The Apocalyptic Seals from Rudolf Steiner	2020
The Mysteries of Ephesos	2021
The Gospel of John; an Initiatory Pathway Translation & Commentary	2022

Also, under the pen-name Damien Pryor:

The nature & origin of the Tropical Zodiac	2011
Stonehenge	2011
Lalibela	2011
The Externsteine	2011
The Great Pyramid & the Sphinx	2011

WEBSITE: listing all of the Author's books

www.rudolfsteinerstudies.com

www.ingramcontent.com/pod-product-compliance
Lightning Source LLC
Chambersburg PA
CBHW050924240426
43668CB00020B/2422